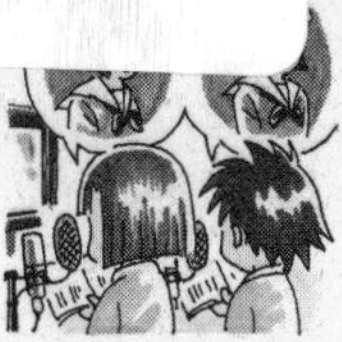

Yumi Hotta

There's a dialogue in the [original Japanese] anime episode 73 between two girls at Haze Junior High:

Girl A: Argh... my midterm ranking dropped.
Girl B: You got the rankings list? Our class hasn't gotten it yet. I bet our teacher forgot!!
Girl A: Bye, Akari.

The voice actors playing these parts are actually Sanae Kobayashi, who is the voice for Akira, and Reiko Takagi, who voices Waya.

—Yumi Hotta

It all began when Yumi Hotta played a pick-up game of go with her father-in-law. As she was learning how to play, Ms. Hotta thought it might be fun to create a story around the traditional board game. More confident in her storytelling abilities than her drawing skills, she submitted the beginnings of **Hikaru no Go** to **Weekly Shonen Jump**'s Story King Award. The Story King Award is an award that picks the best story, manga, character design and youth (under 15) manga submissions every year in Japan. As fate would have it, Ms. Hotta's story (originally named "***Kokonotsu no Hoshi***"), was a runner-up in the "Story" category of the Story King Award. Many years earlier, Takeshi Obata was a runner-up for the Tezuka Award, another Japanese manga contest sponsored by **Weekly Shonen Jump** and **Monthly Shonen Jump**. An editor assigned to Mr. Obata's artwork came upon Ms. Hotta's story and paired the two for a full-fledged manga about go. The rest is modern go history.

HIKARU NO GO VOL. 21
SHONEN JUMP Manga Edition

STORY BY YUMI HOTTA
ART BY TAKESHI OBATA
Supervised by YUKARI UMEZAWA (5 Dan)

Translation & English Adaptation/Naoko Amemiya
English Script Consultant/Janice Kim (3 Dan)
Touch-up Art & Lettering/Inori Fukuda Trant
Design/Julie Behn
Editor/Gary Leach

Printed in Canada

Published by VIZ Media, LLC
P.O. Box 77010
San Francisco, CA 94107

10 9 8 7 6 5 4 3 2 1
First printing, November 2010

www.viz.com

THE WORLD'S
MOST POPULAR MANGA
www.shonenjump.com

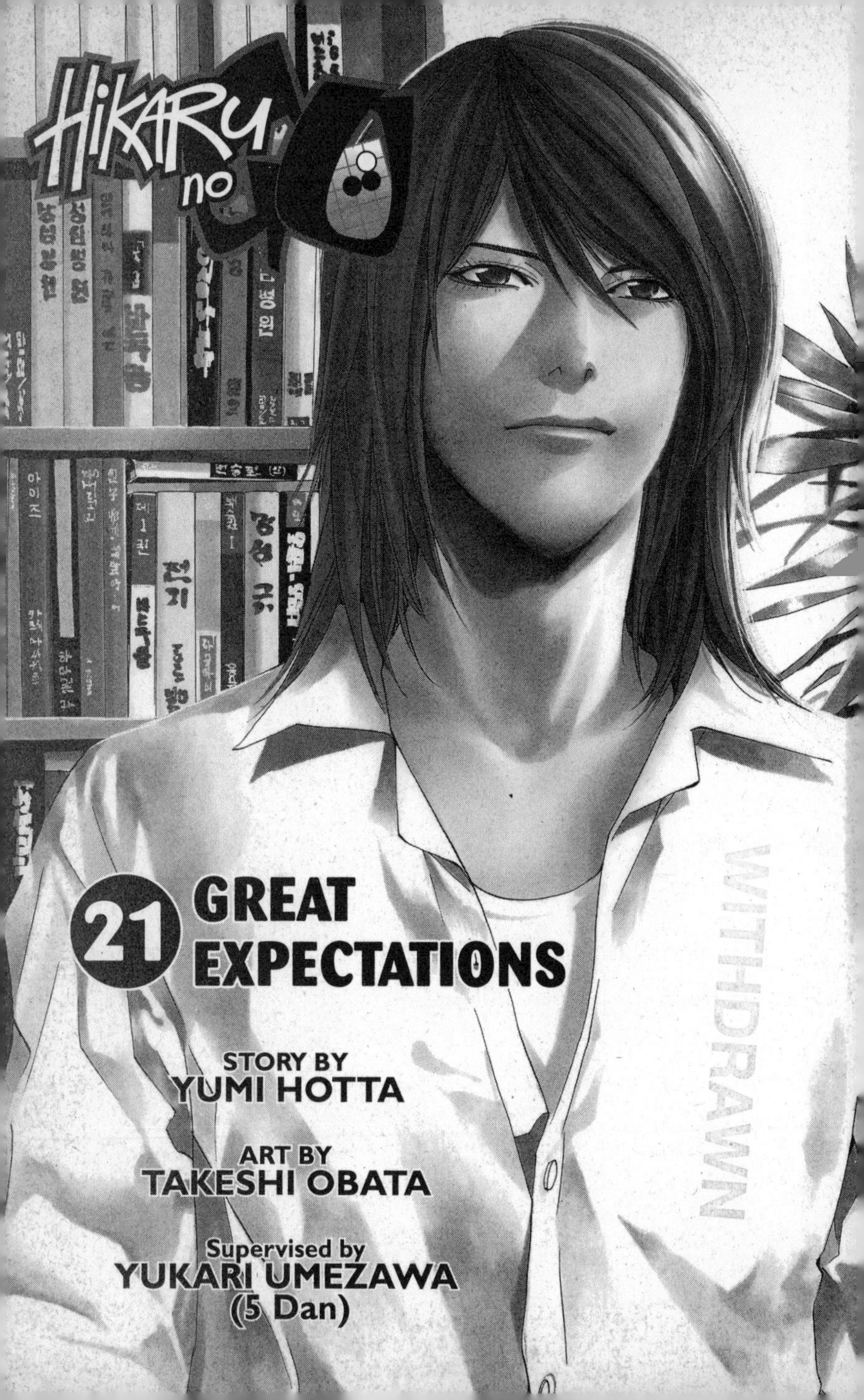

Hikaru no Go

21 Great Expectations

STORY BY
YUMI HOTTA

ART BY
TAKESHI OBATA

Supervised by
YUKARI UMEZAWA
(5 Dan)

CHARACTERS VOL.21

● Kiyoharu Yashiro ●

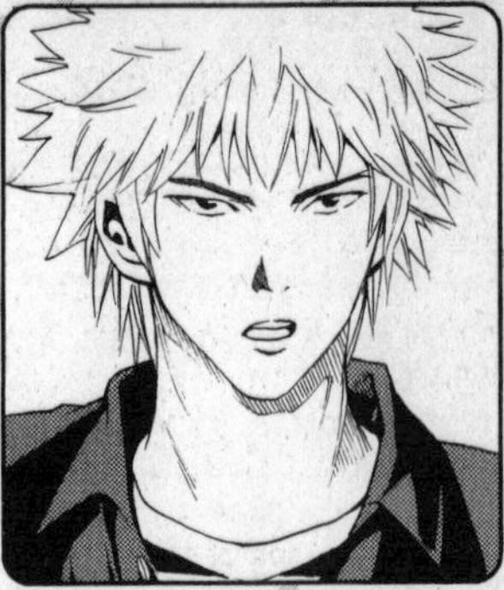

● Hikaru Shindo ●

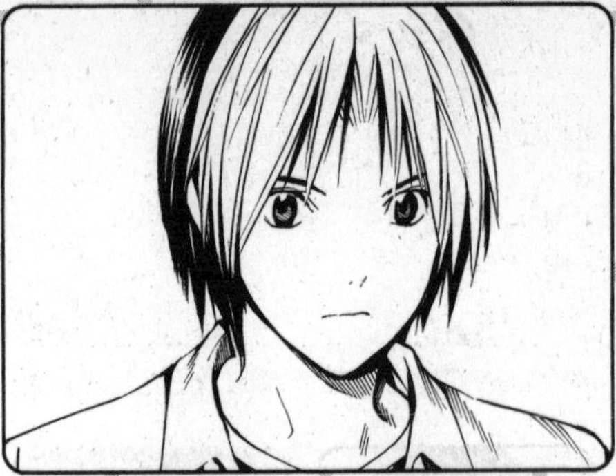

Meet the Characters

● Yoshitaka Waya ●

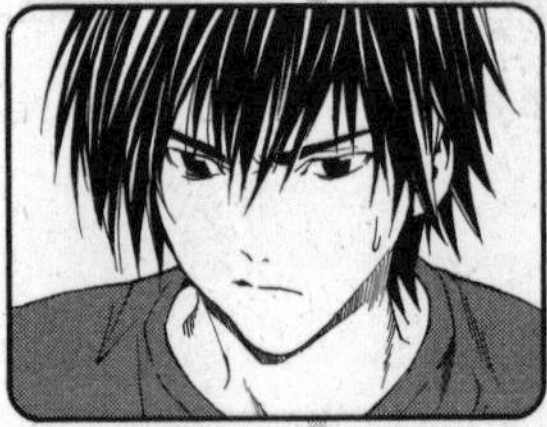

● Atsushi Kurata ●

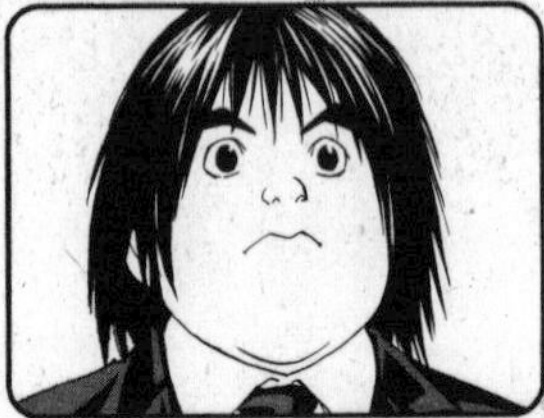

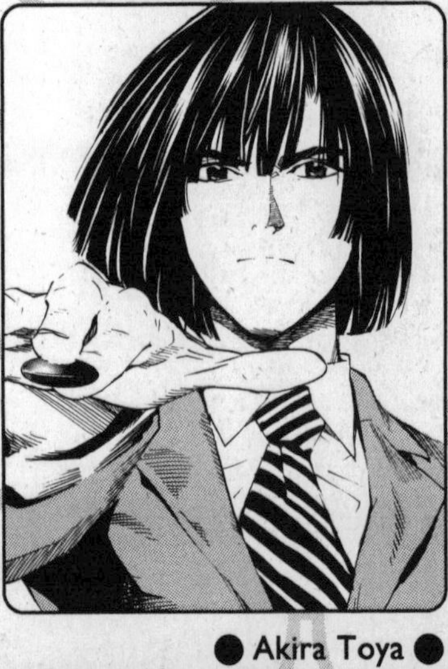

● Akira Toya ●

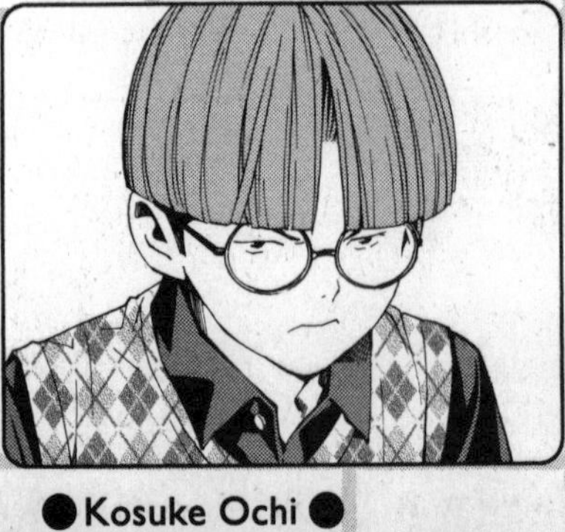

● Kosuke Ochi ●

Story Thus Far

Hikaru Shindo discovers an old go board one day up in his grandfather's attic. The moment Hikaru touches the board, the spirit of Fujiwara-no-Sai, a genius go player from Japan's Heian Era, enters his consciousness. Sai's love of the game inspires Hikaru, as does a meeting with the child prodigy Akira Toya – son of go master Toya Meijin.

Hikaru turns pro and finally stands on the same playing field as Akira, slowly but surely improving his skills. He hears of an international team tournament for Japanese, Chinese and Korean go players age 18 and under called the Hokuto Cup. Of the three spots on the Japanese team, one is already awarded to Akira. Qualifying matches to determine the remaining two members have begun. The eight contenders are split into two groups of four. The two who win two matches snag spots on the team. Clearing the first round are Hikaru, Waya, Ochi and Yashiro, the new rising star of the Kansai Go Association. The second round is Hikaru vs. Yashiro and Waya vs. Ochi. Yashiro makes the game a wild one, and Hikaru fights back with the same bold spirit. It develops into a ferocious and unpredictable battle that astonishes those watching. Meanwhile, Waya seems to have the advantage in his game against Ochi, but Ochi's plays are solid and strong. Which players will end up winning places on the Japanese team?!

●Koyo Toya●

●Ogata Judan●

●Suyong Hong●

●Ko Yong Ha●

●Zhao Shi●

●Yang Hai●

●Kosemura●

●Kuwabara Hon'inbo●

CONTENTS

21

GAME 166
Yashiro Loses!   7

GAME 167
The Boys   27

GAME 168
One Month Before the Hokuto Cup   49

GAME 169
Great Expectations!!   69

GAME 170
The Korean Go Association   89

GAME 171
Evidence of Existence   109

GAME 172
The Toya Residence   129

GAME 173
Toya Will Be First   149

GAME 174
Heading to the Hokuto Cup   169

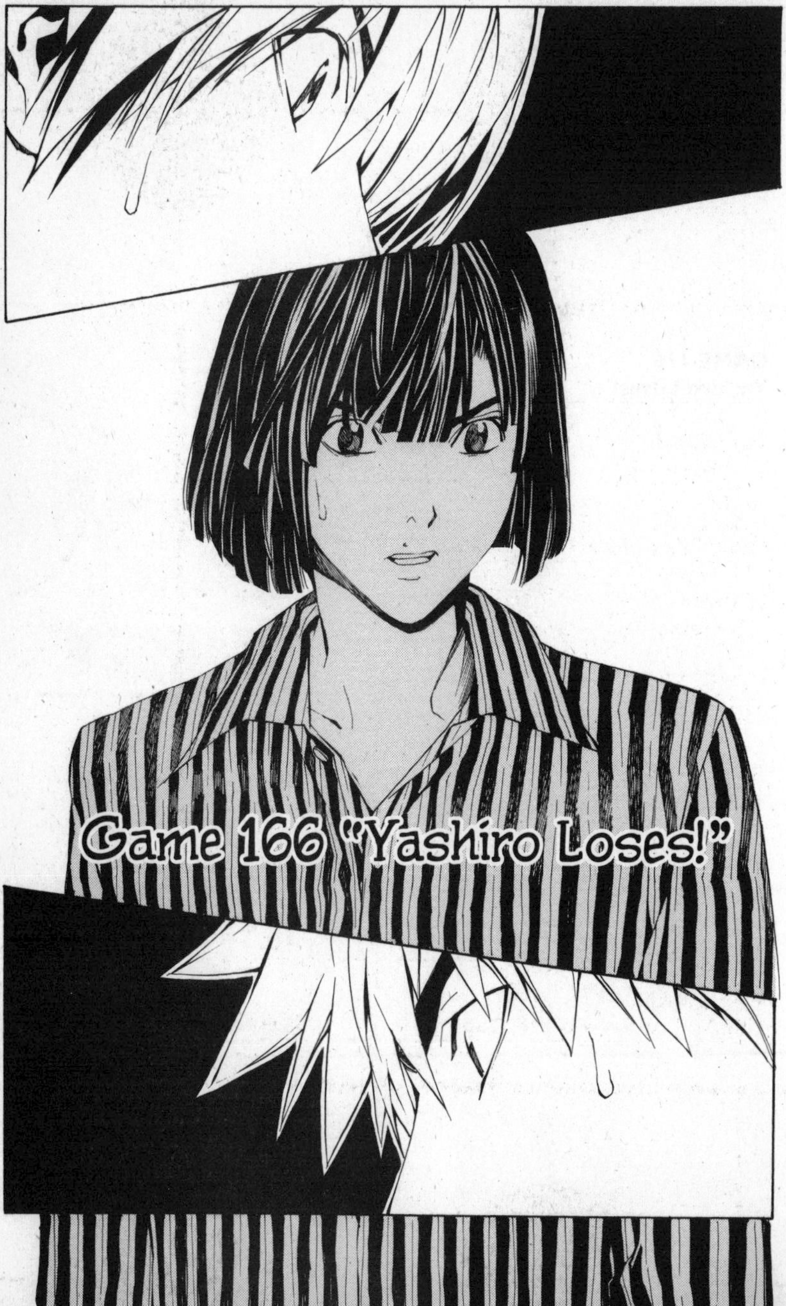
Game 166 "Yashiro Loses!"

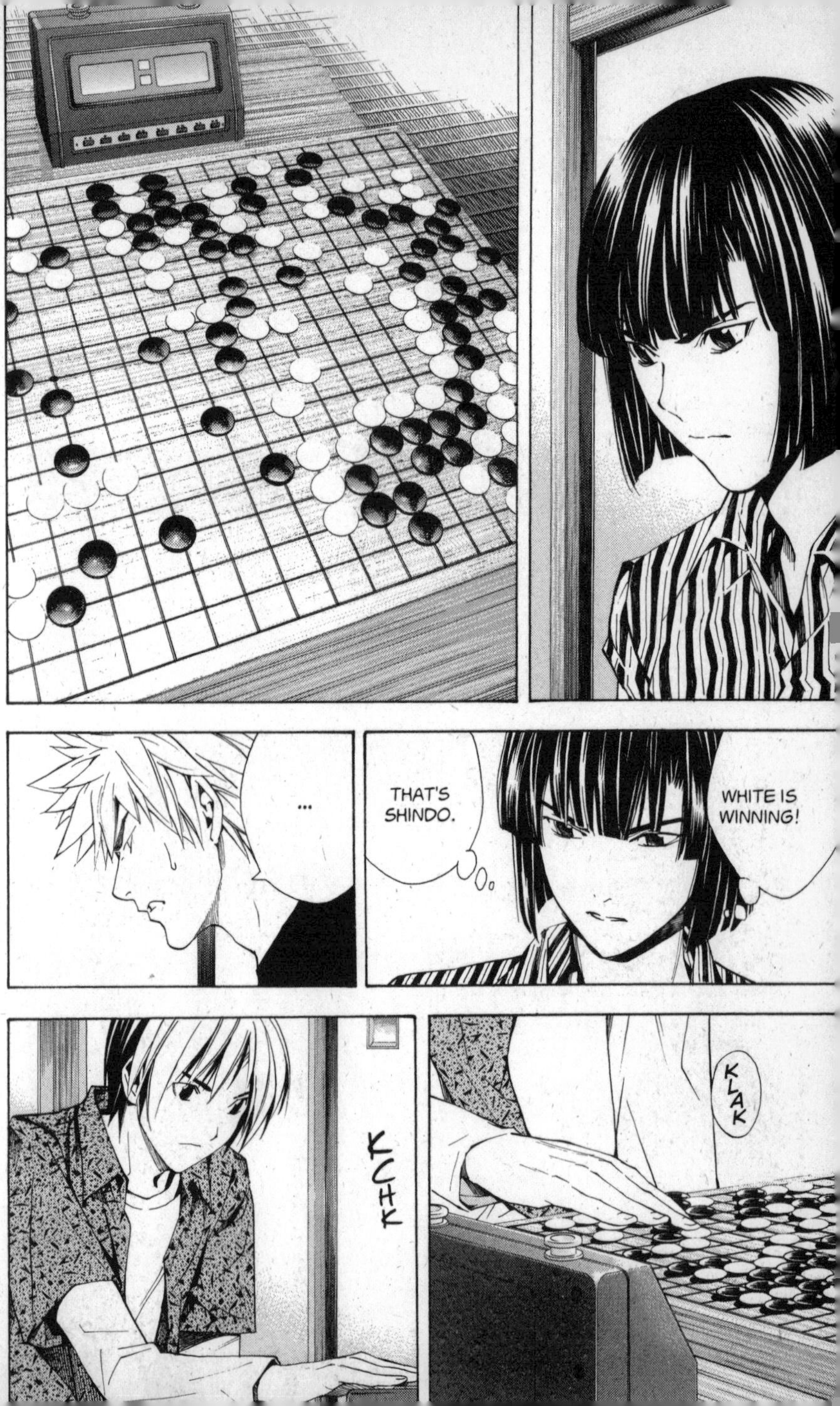
WHITE IS WINNING!
THAT'S SHINDO.
...
KLAK
KCHK

READ THIS WAY

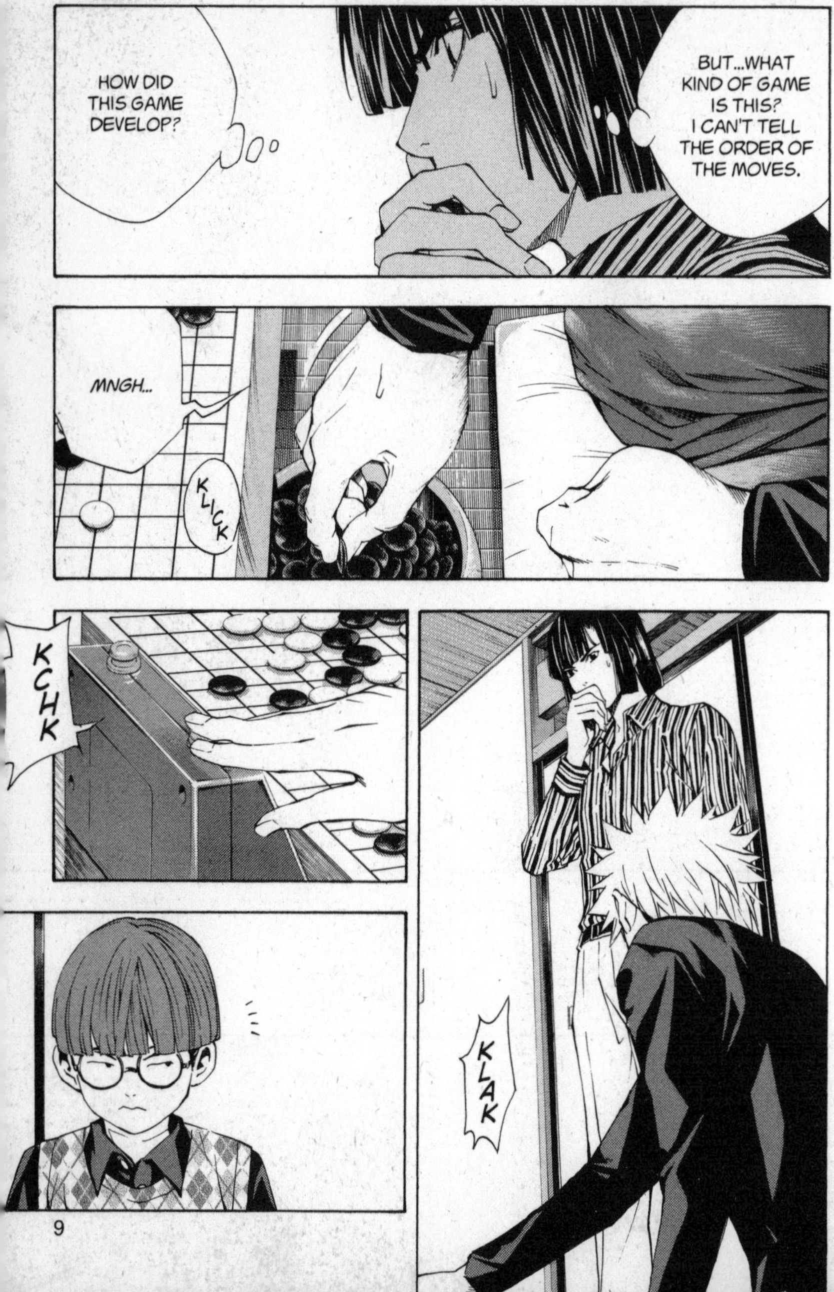
BUT...WHAT KIND OF GAME IS THIS? I CAN'T TELL THE ORDER OF THE MOVES.
HOW DID THIS GAME DEVELOP?
KLICK
MNGH...
KLAK
KCHK

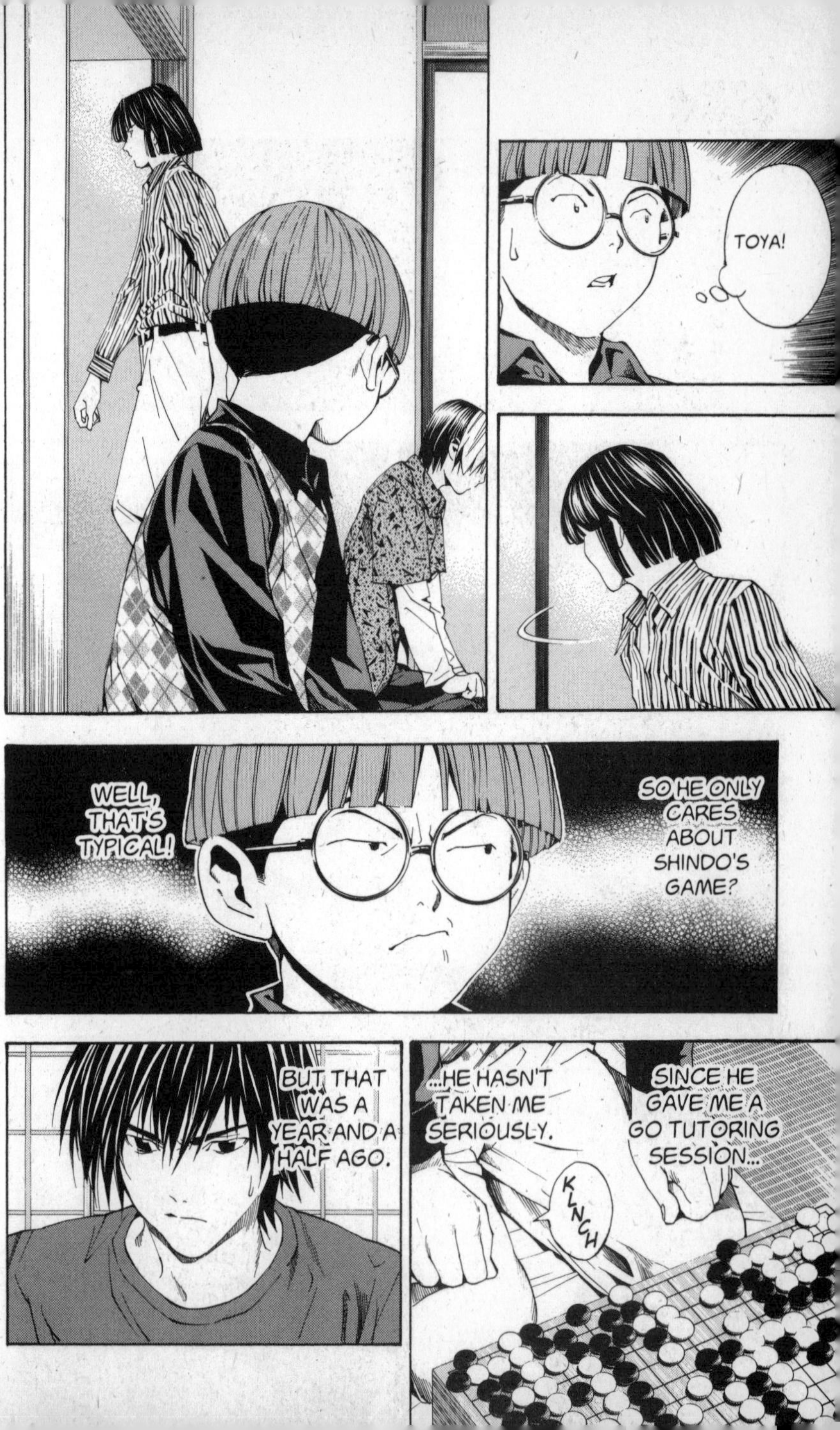
TOYA!
SO HE ONLY CARES ABOUT SHINDO'S GAME?
WELL, THAT'S TYPICAL!
SINCE HE GAVE ME A GO TUTORING SESSION...
KLNCH
...HE HASN'T TAKEN ME SERIOUSLY.
BUT THAT WAS A YEAR AND A HALF AGO.

READ THIS WAY

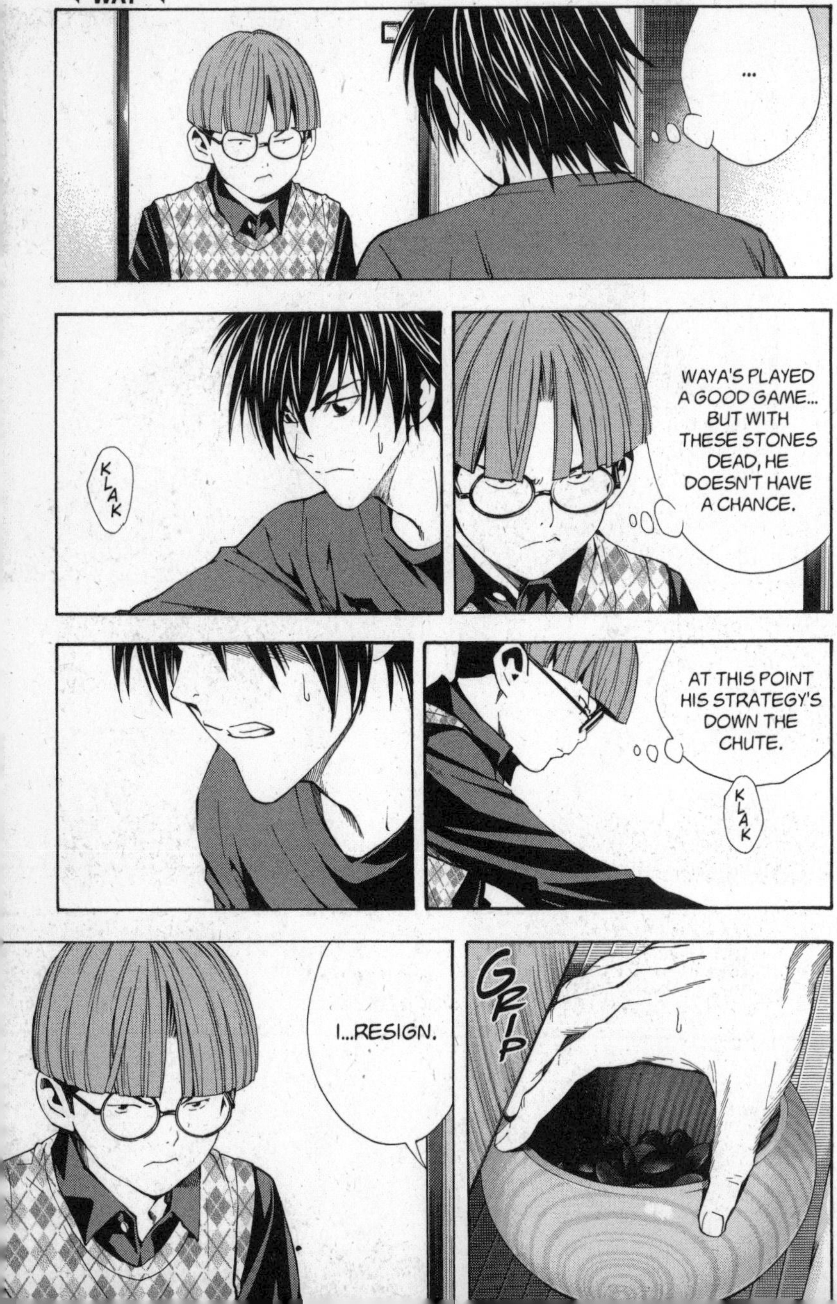
...
WAYA'S PLAYED A GOOD GAME... BUT WITH THESE STONES DEAD, HE DOESN'T HAVE A CHANCE.
KLAK
AT THIS POINT HIS STRATEGY'S DOWN THE CHUTE.
KLAK
GRIP
I...RESIGN.

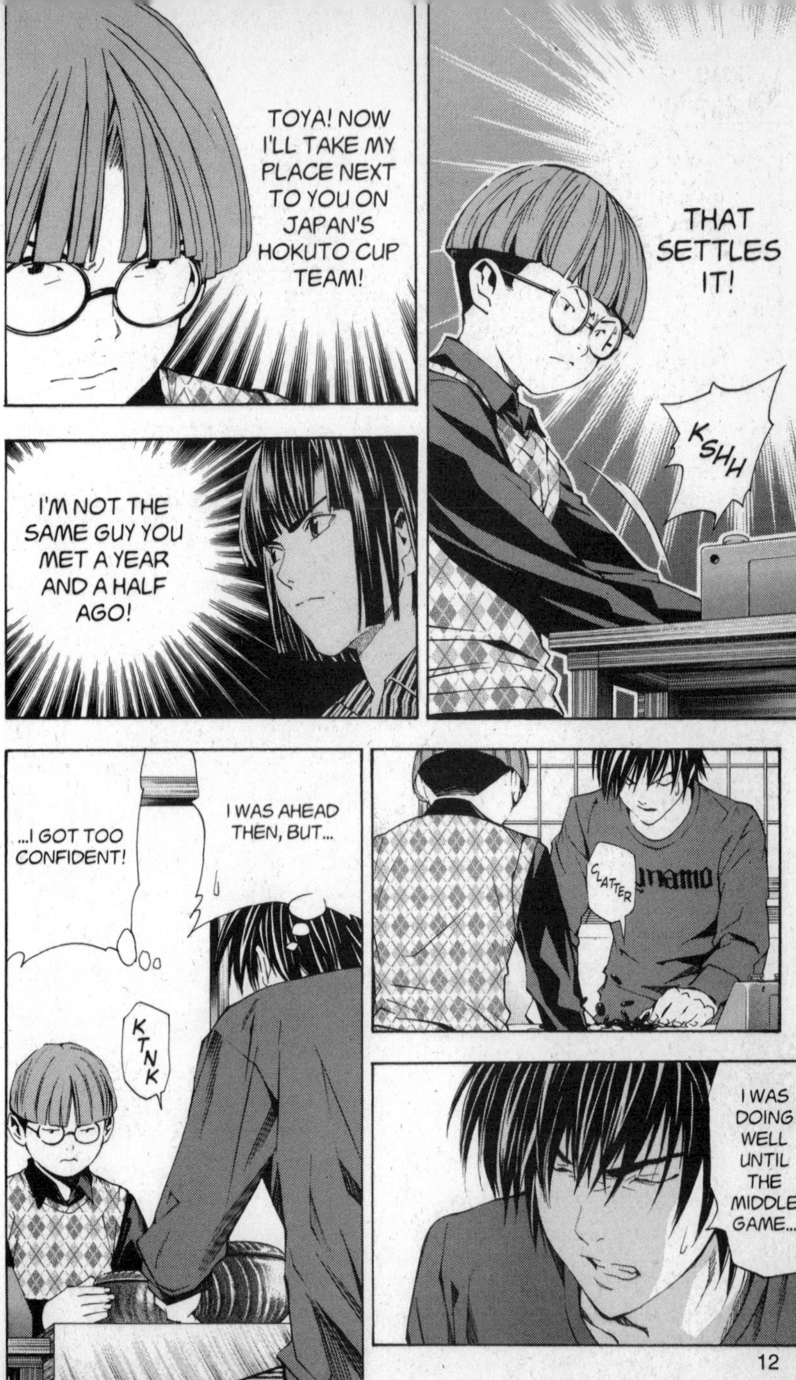
THAT SETTLES IT!
KSHH
TOYA! NOW I'LL TAKE MY PLACE NEXT TO YOU ON JAPAN'S HOKUTO CUP TEAM!
I'M NOT THE SAME GUY YOU MET A YEAR AND A HALF AGO!
CLATTER
I WAS DOING WELL UNTIL THE MIDDLE GAME...
I WAS AHEAD THEN, BUT...
...I GOT TOO CONFIDENT!
KTNK

READ THIS WAY

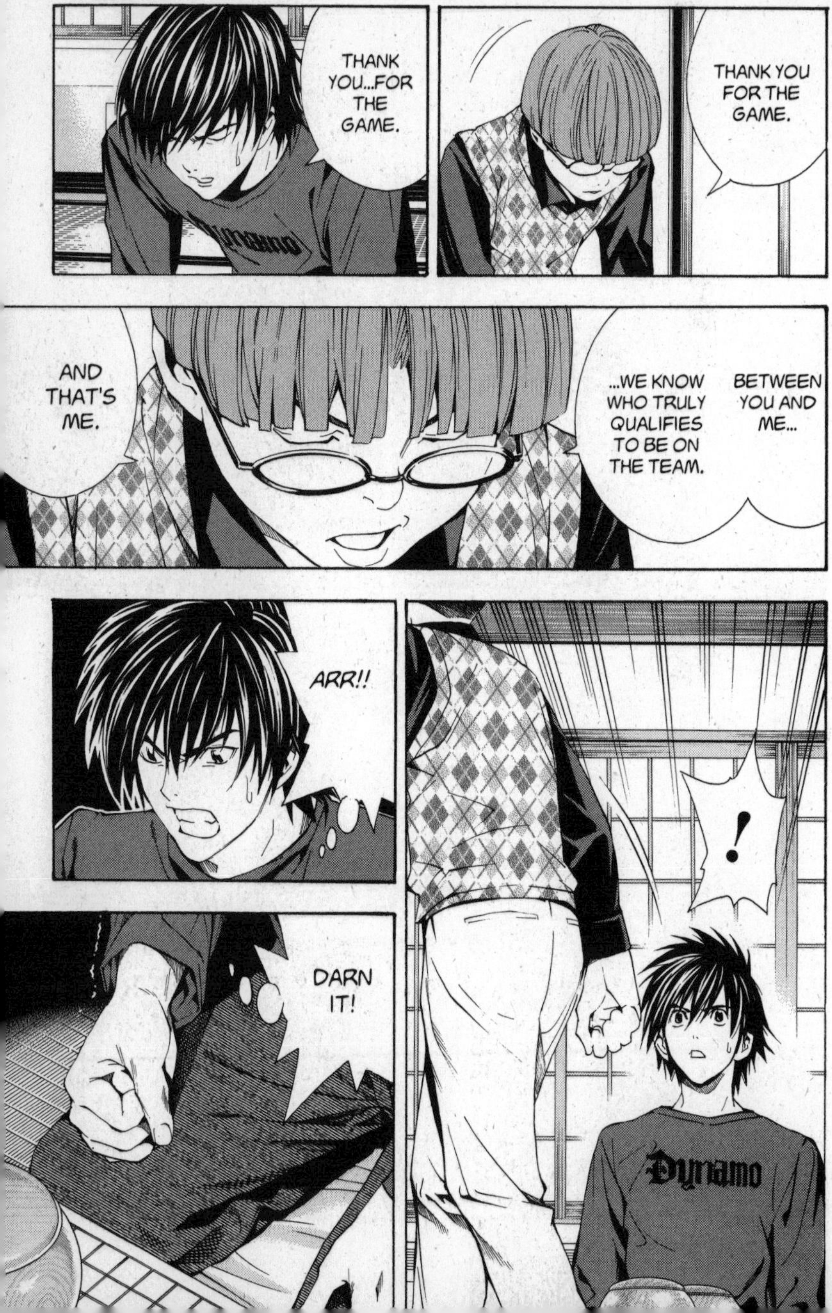
THANK YOU FOR THE GAME.
THANK YOU...FOR THE GAME.
BETWEEN YOU AND ME...
...WE KNOW WHO TRULY QUALIFIES TO BE ON THE TEAM.
AND THAT'S ME.
!
ARR!!
DARN IT!
Dynamo

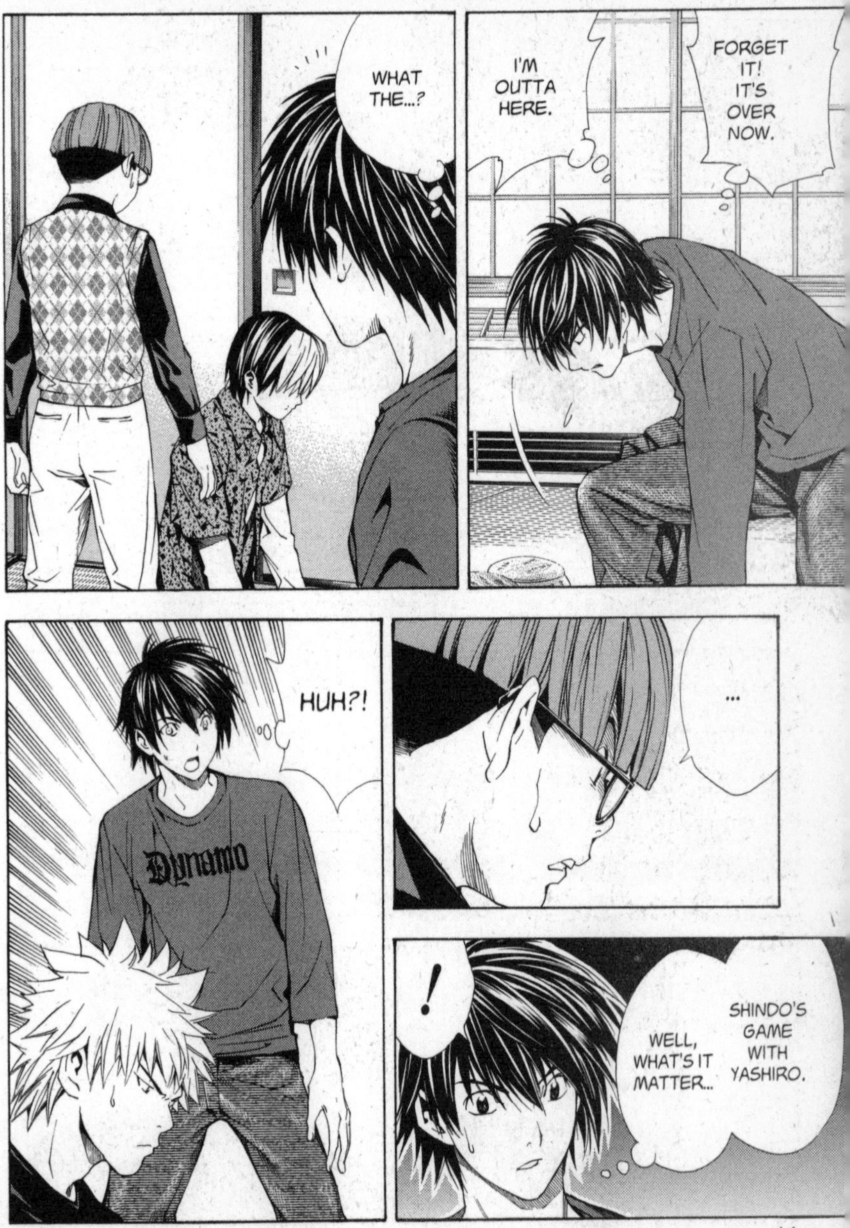
FORGET IT! IT'S OVER NOW.
I'M OUTTA HERE.
WHAT THE...?
...
!
SHINDO'S GAME WITH YASHIRO.
WELL, WHAT'S IT MATTER...
HUH?!
Dynamo

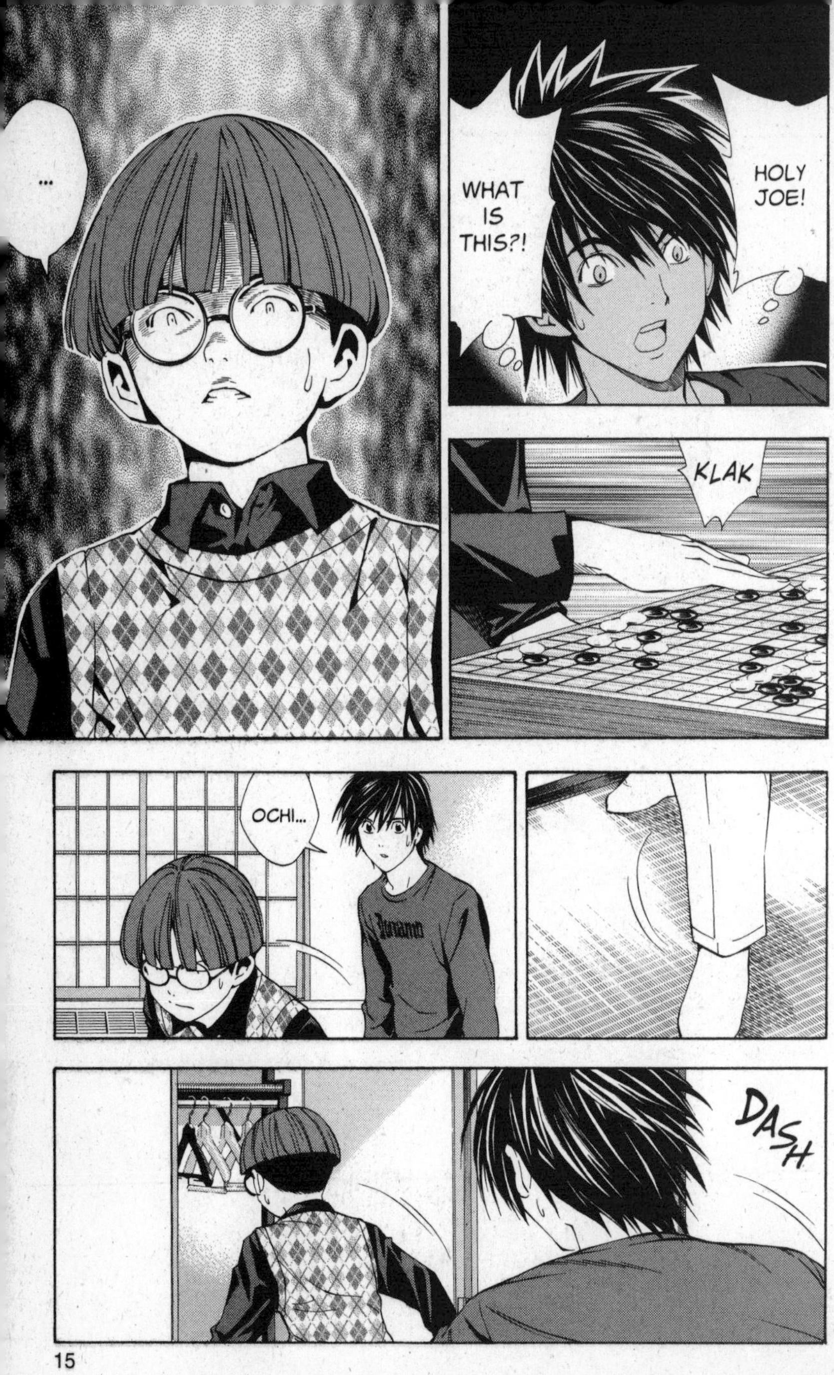
HOLY JOE!
WHAT IS THIS?!
KLAK
...
OCHI...
DASH

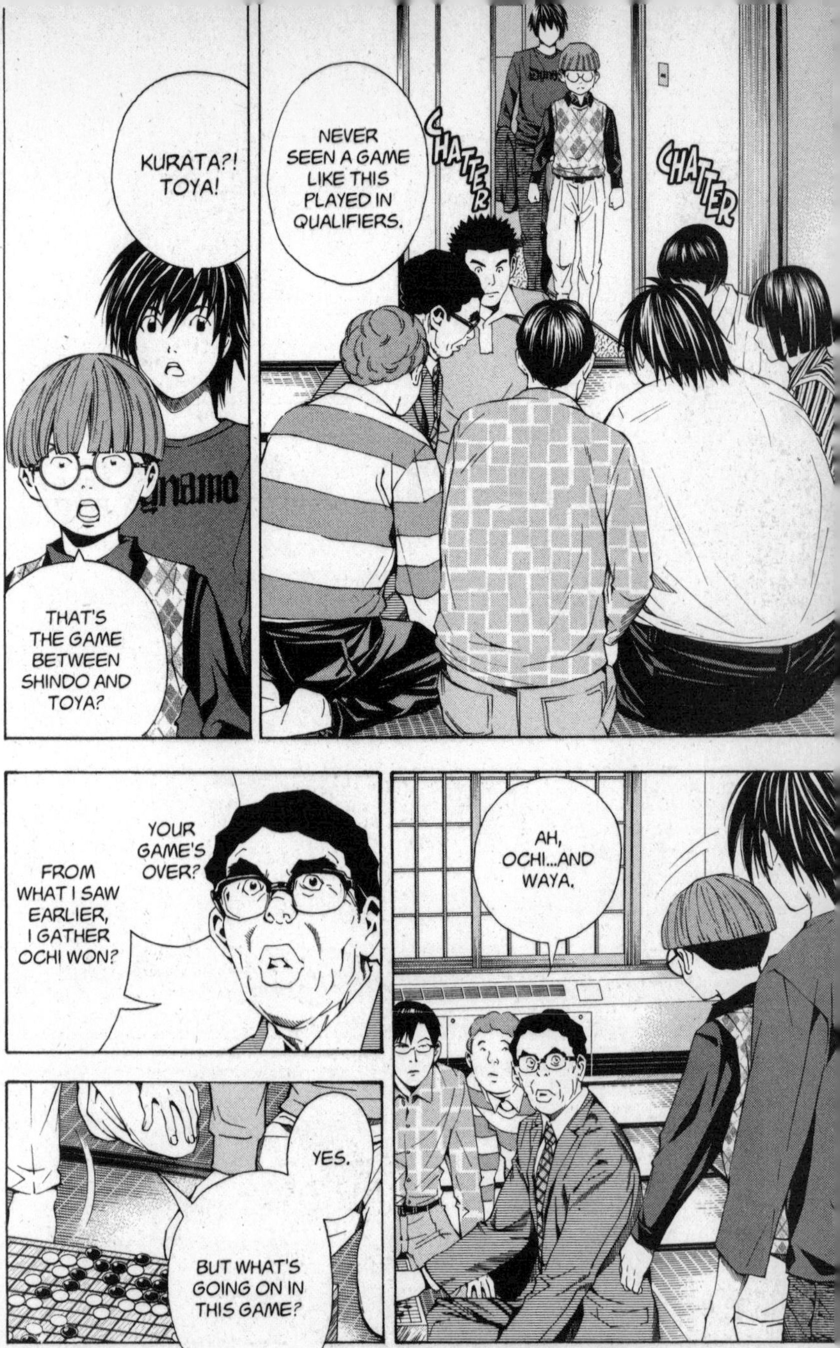
NEVER SEEN A GAME LIKE THIS PLAYED IN QUALIFIERS.
CHATTER
CHATTER
KURATA?! TOYA!
THAT'S THE GAME BETWEEN SHINDO AND TOYA?
AH, OCHI...AND WAYA.
YOUR GAME'S OVER?
FROM WHAT I SAW EARLIER, I GATHER OCHI WON?
YES.
BUT WHAT'S GOING ON IN THIS GAME?

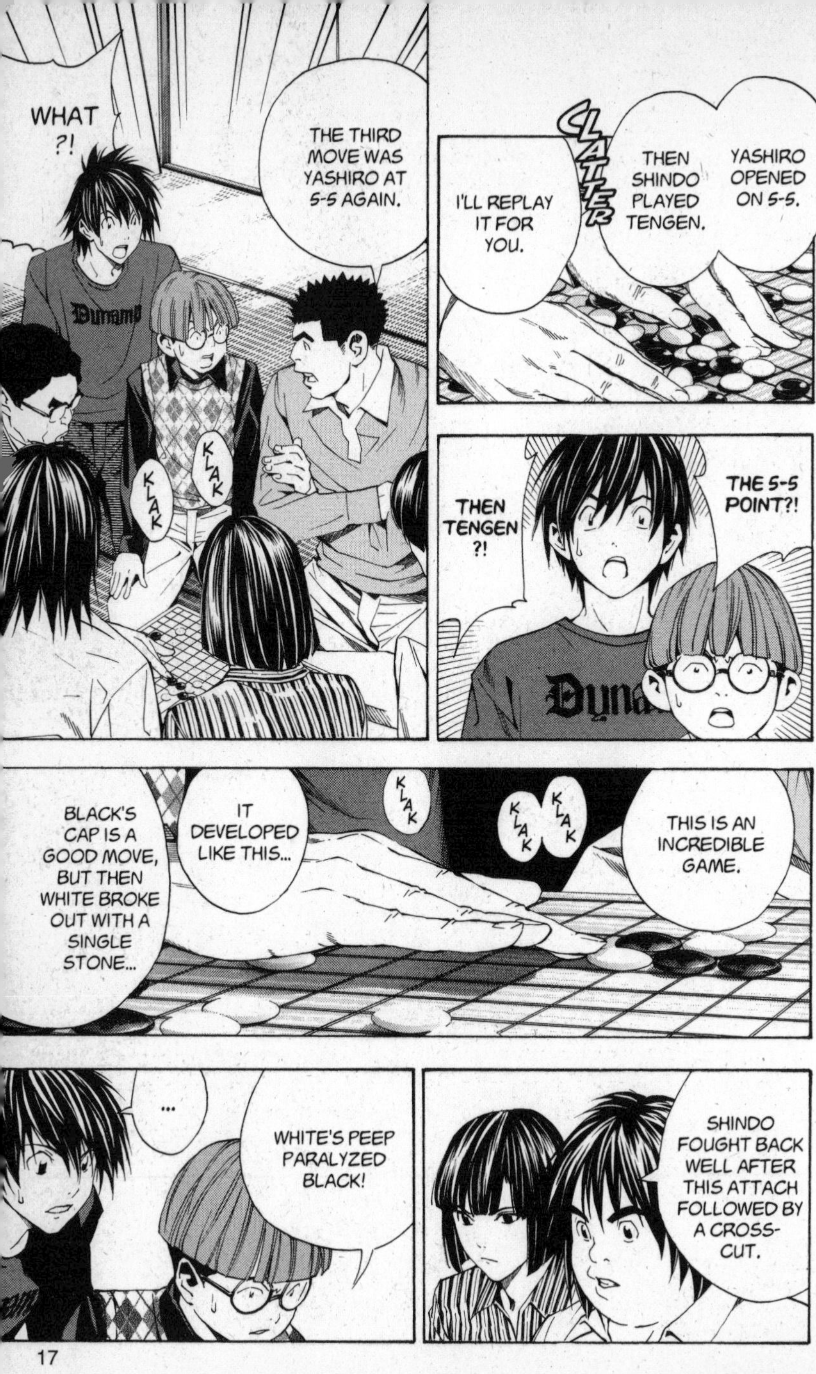
YASHIRO OPENED ON 5-5.
THEN SHINDO PLAYED TENGEN.
CLATTER
I'LL REPLAY IT FOR YOU.
THE 5-5 POINT?!
THEN TENGEN ?!
THE THIRD MOVE WAS YASHIRO AT 5-5 AGAIN.
WHAT ?!
KLAK
KLAK
THIS IS AN INCREDIBLE GAME.
KLAK
KLAK
KLAK
IT DEVELOPED LIKE THIS...
BLACK'S CAP IS A GOOD MOVE, BUT THEN WHITE BROKE OUT WITH A SINGLE STONE...
SHINDO FOUGHT BACK WELL AFTER THIS ATTACH FOLLOWED BY A CROSS-CUT.
WHITE'S PEEP PARALYZED BLACK!
...

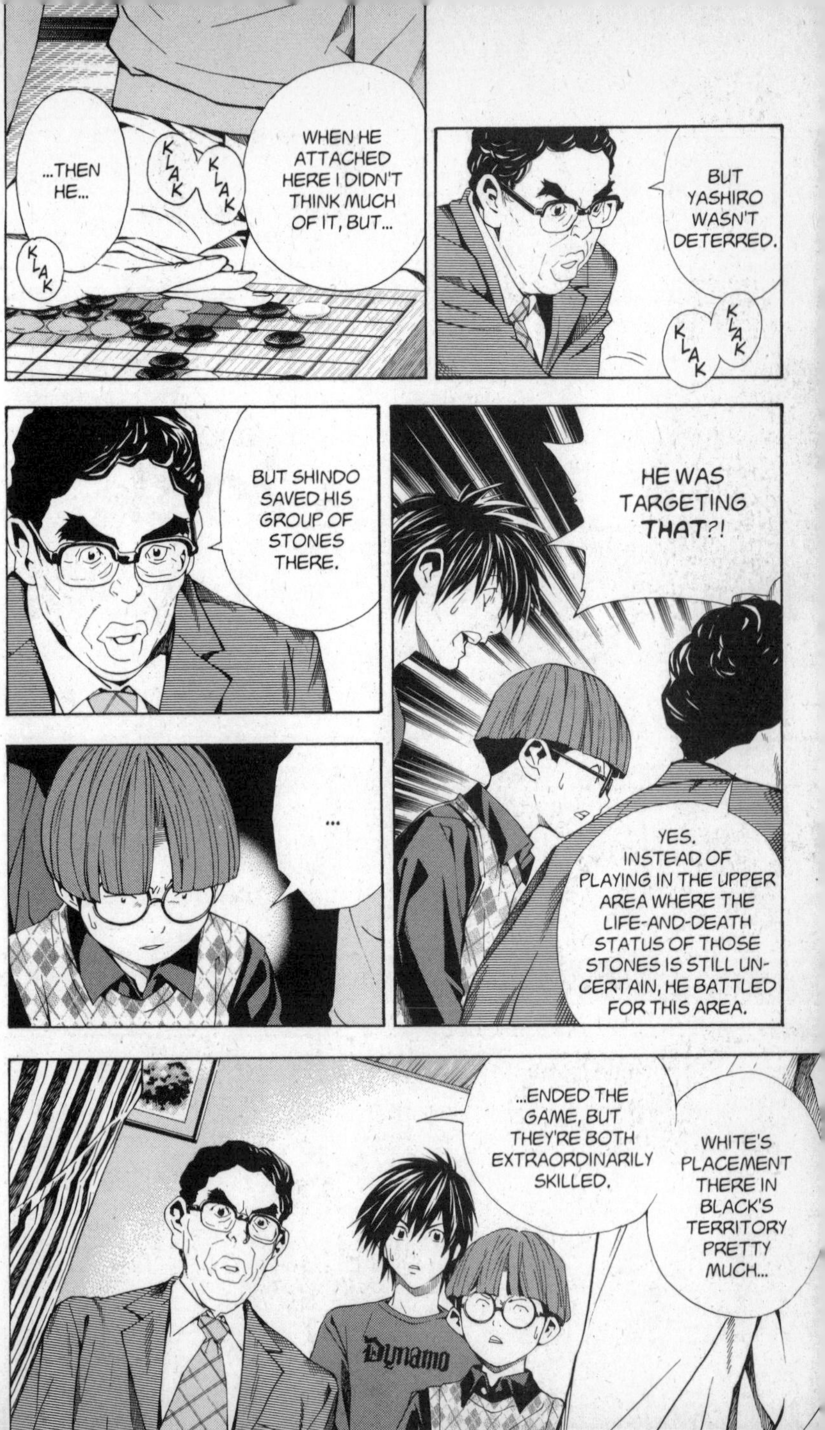
BUT YASHIRO WASN'T DETERRED.
KLAK
KLAK
WHEN HE ATTACHED HERE I DIDN'T THINK MUCH OF IT, BUT...
KLAK
KLAK
...THEN HE...
KLAK
HE WAS TARGETING THAT?!
YES. INSTEAD OF PLAYING IN THE UPPER AREA WHERE THE LIFE-AND-DEATH STATUS OF THOSE STONES IS STILL UNCERTAIN, HE BATTLED FOR THIS AREA.
BUT SHINDO SAVED HIS GROUP OF STONES THERE.
...
WHITE'S PLACEMENT THERE IN BLACK'S TERRITORY PRETTY MUCH...
...ENDED THE GAME, BUT THEY'RE BOTH EXTRAORDINARILY SKILLED.
Dynamo

READ THIS WAY

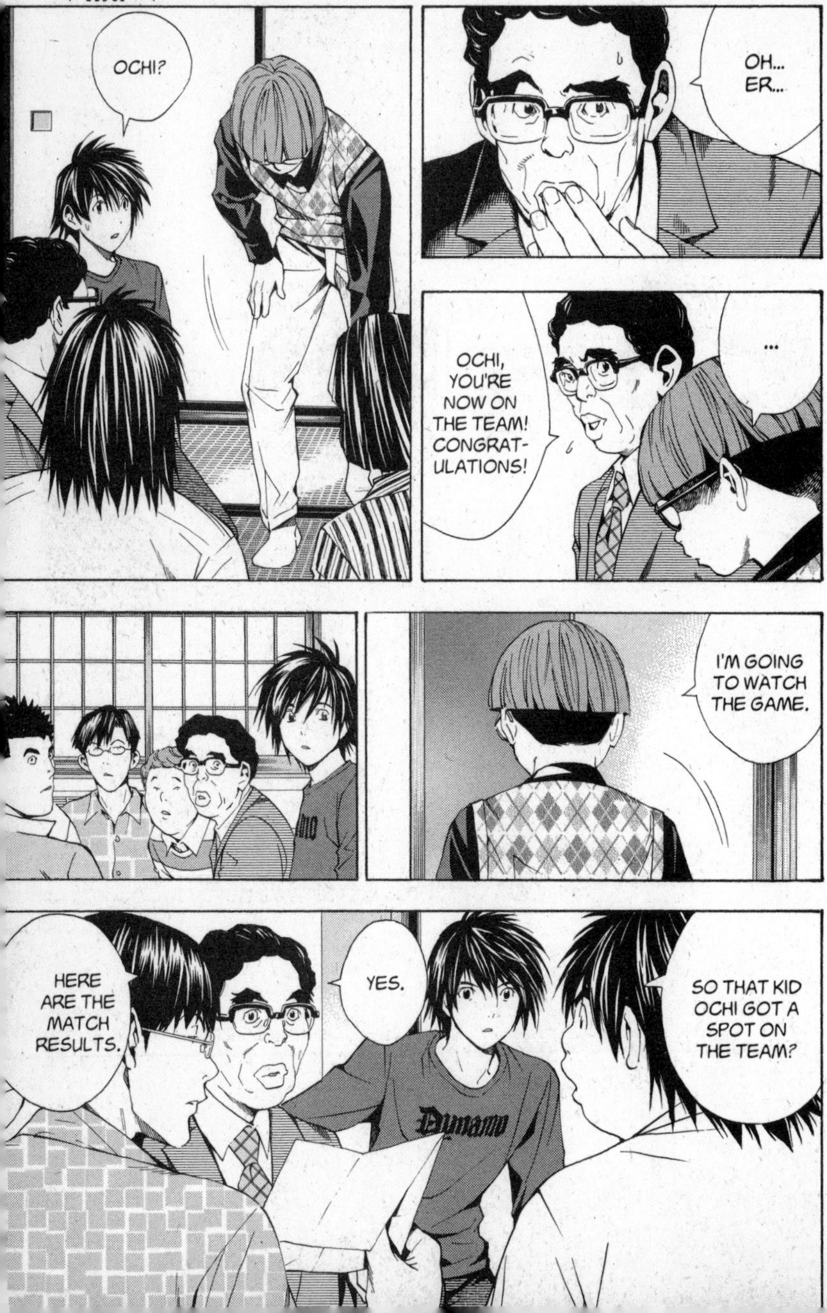
OH... ER...
...
OCHI, YOU'RE NOW ON THE TEAM! CONGRAT-ULATIONS!
OCHI?
I'M GOING TO WATCH THE GAME.
SO THAT KID OCHI GOT A SPOT ON THE TEAM?
YES.
Dynamo
HERE ARE THE MATCH RESULTS.

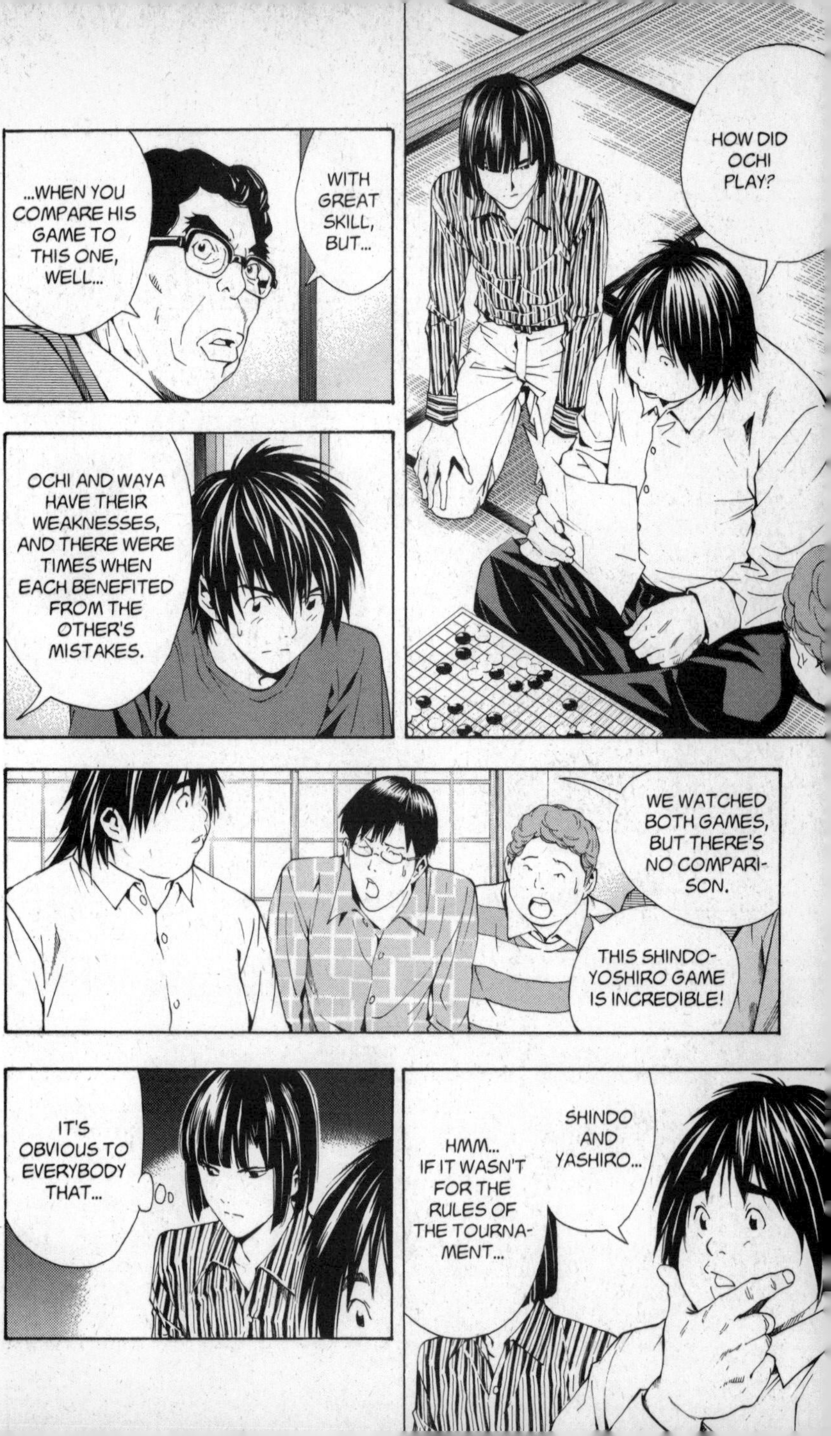
HOW DID OCHI PLAY?
WITH GREAT SKILL, BUT...
...WHEN YOU COMPARE HIS GAME TO THIS ONE, WELL...
OCHI AND WAYA HAVE THEIR WEAKNESSES, AND THERE WERE TIMES WHEN EACH BENEFITED FROM THE OTHER'S MISTAKES.
WE WATCHED BOTH GAMES, BUT THERE'S NO COMPARI-SON.
THIS SHINDO-YOSHIRO GAME IS INCREDIBLE!
SHINDO AND YASHIRO...
HMM... IF IT WASN'T FOR THE RULES OF THE TOURNA-MENT...
IT'S OBVIOUS TO EVERYBODY THAT...

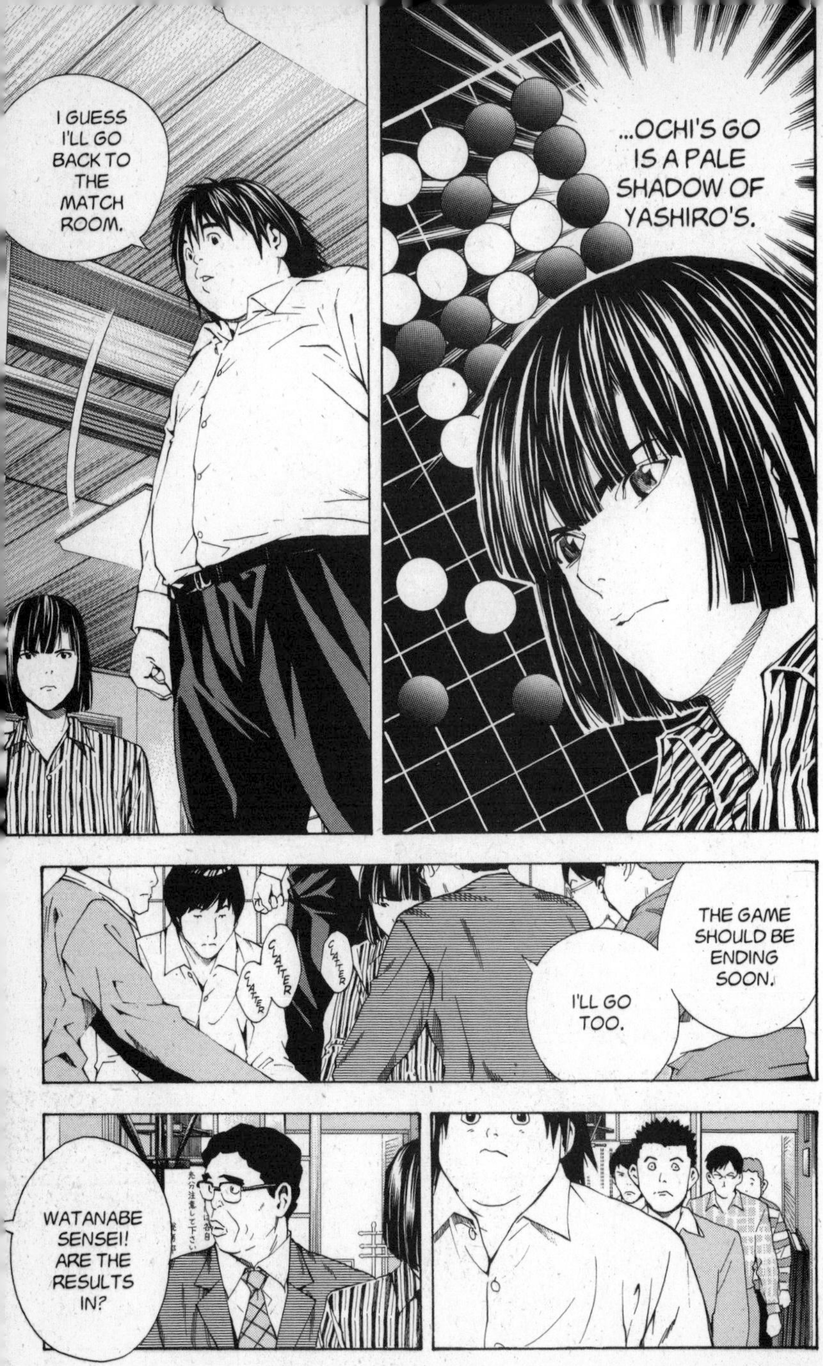
...OCHI'S GO IS A PALE SHADOW OF YASHIRO'S.
I GUESS I'LL GO BACK TO THE MATCH ROOM.
THE GAME SHOULD BE ENDING SOON.
I'LL GO TOO.
CLATTER
CLATTER
CLATTER
WATANABE SENSEI! ARE THE RESULTS IN?

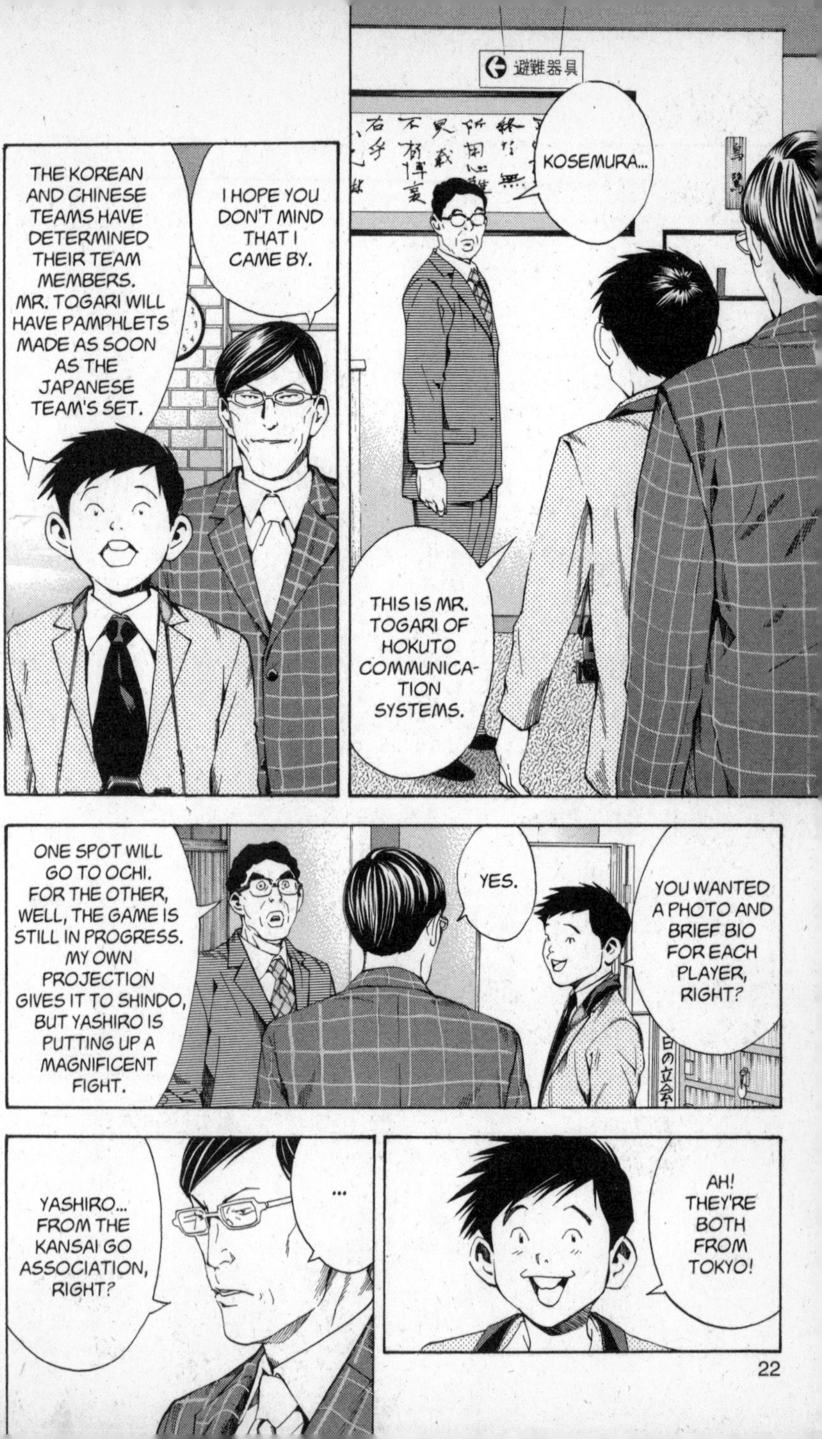
避難器具
KOSEMURA...
THIS IS MR. TOGARI OF HOKUTO COMMUNICATION SYSTEMS.
I HOPE YOU DON'T MIND THAT I CAME BY.
THE KOREAN AND CHINESE TEAMS HAVE DETERMINED THEIR TEAM MEMBERS. MR. TOGARI WILL HAVE PAMPHLETS MADE AS SOON AS THE JAPANESE TEAM'S SET.
YOU WANTED A PHOTO AND BRIEF BIO FOR EACH PLAYER, RIGHT?
YES.
ONE SPOT WILL GO TO OCHI. FOR THE OTHER, WELL, THE GAME IS STILL IN PROGRESS. MY OWN PROJECTION GIVES IT TO SHINDO, BUT YASHIRO IS PUTTING UP A MAGNIFICENT FIGHT.
AH! THEY'RE BOTH FROM TOKYO!
...
YASHIRO... FROM THE KANSAI GO ASSOCIATION, RIGHT?

READ THIS WAY

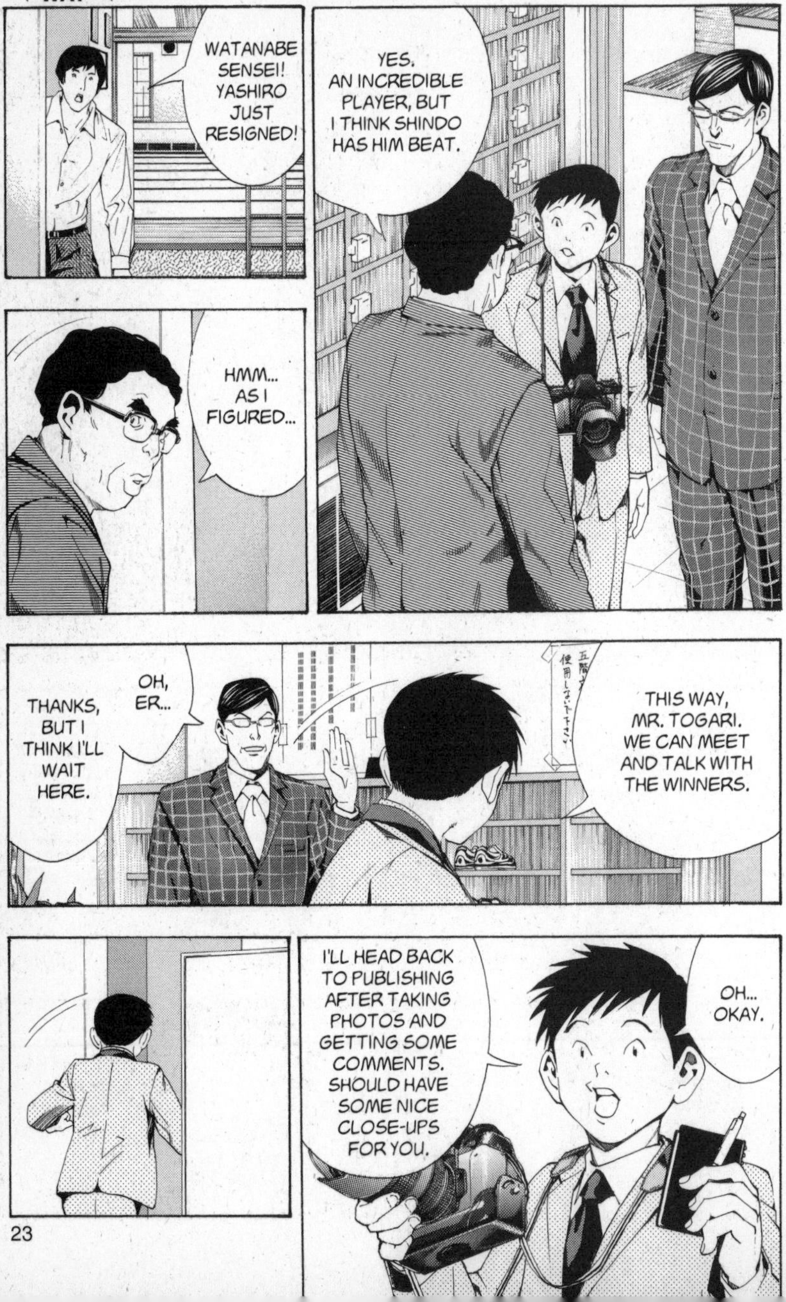
YES. AN INCREDIBLE PLAYER, BUT I THINK SHINDO HAS HIM BEAT.
WATANABE SENSEI! YASHIRO JUST RESIGNED!
HMM... AS I FIGURED...
THIS WAY, MR. TOGARI. WE CAN MEET AND TALK WITH THE WINNERS.
OH, ER...
THANKS, BUT I THINK I'LL WAIT HERE.
OH... OKAY.
I'LL HEAD BACK TO PUBLISHING AFTER TAKING PHOTOS AND GETTING SOME COMMENTS. SHOULD HAVE SOME NICE CLOSE-UPS FOR YOU.

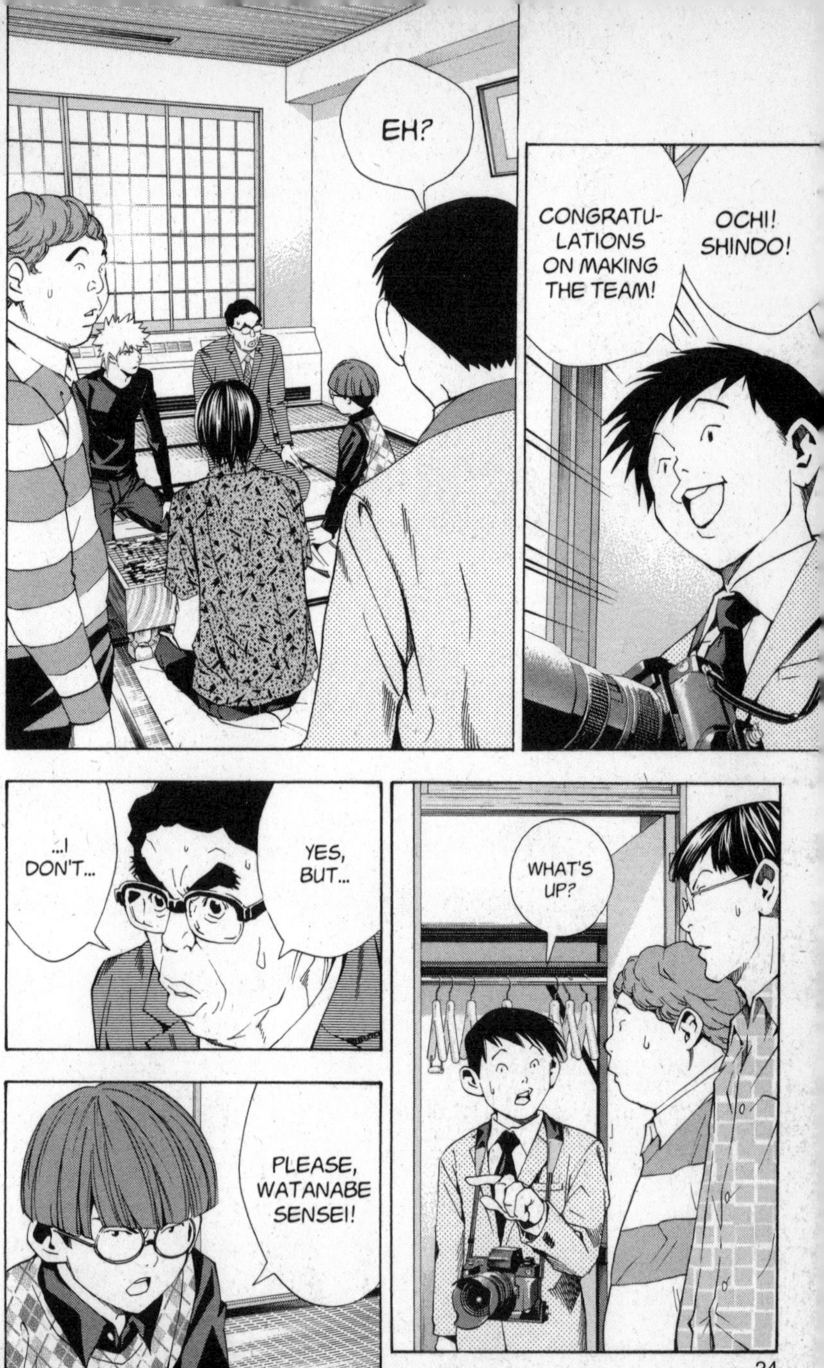
OCHI! SHINDO!
CONGRATU-LATIONS ON MAKING THE TEAM!
EH?
WHAT'S UP?
YES, BUT...
...I DON'T...
PLEASE, WATANABE SENSEI!

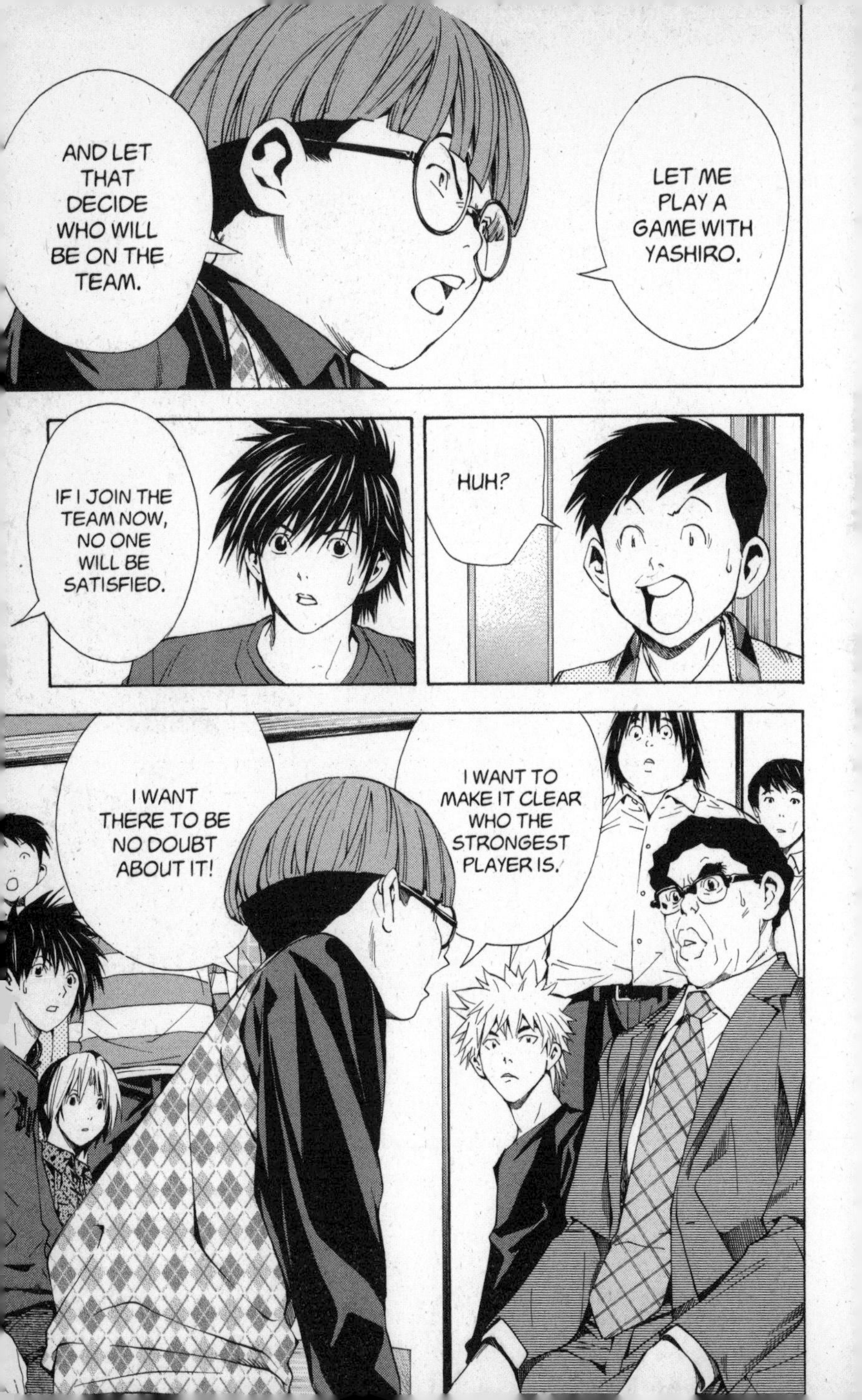
LET ME PLAY A GAME WITH YASHIRO.
AND LET THAT DECIDE WHO WILL BE ON THE TEAM.
HUH?
IF I JOIN THE TEAM NOW, NO ONE WILL BE SATISFIED.
I WANT TO MAKE IT CLEAR WHO THE STRONGEST PLAYER IS.
I WANT THERE TO BE NO DOUBT ABOUT IT!

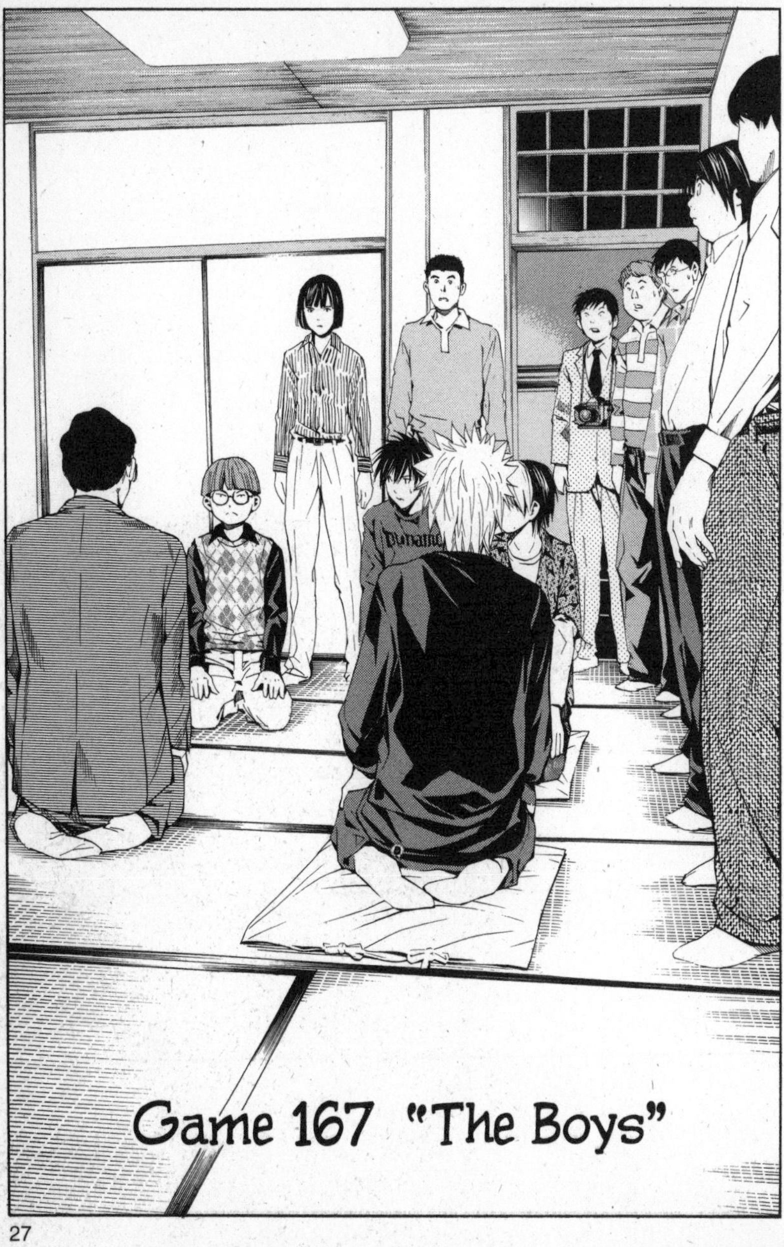
Game 167 "The Boys"

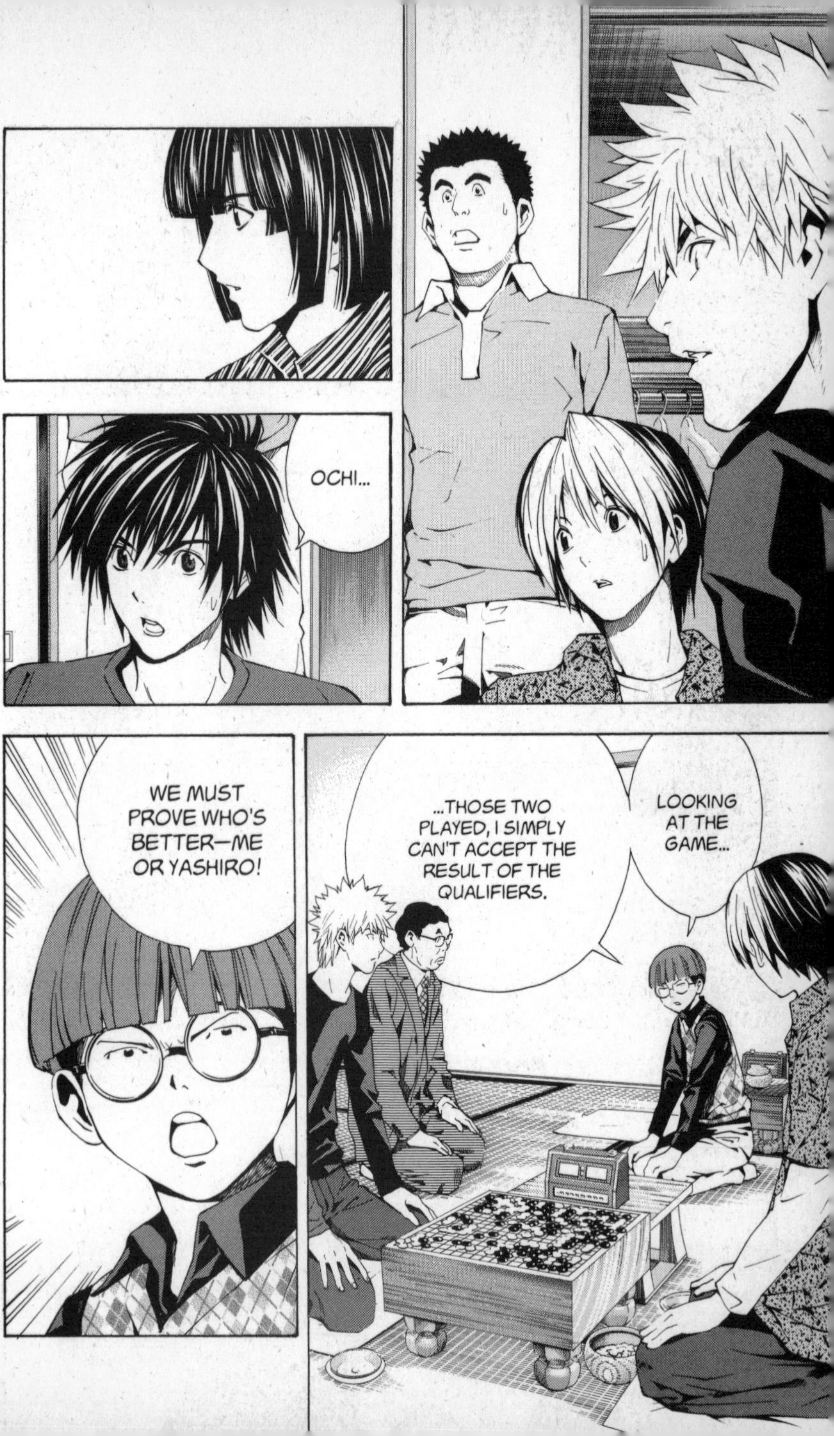
OCHI...
LOOKING AT THE GAME...
...THOSE TWO PLAYED, I SIMPLY CAN'T ACCEPT THE RESULT OF THE QUALIFIERS.
WE MUST PROVE WHO'S BETTER—ME OR YASHIRO!

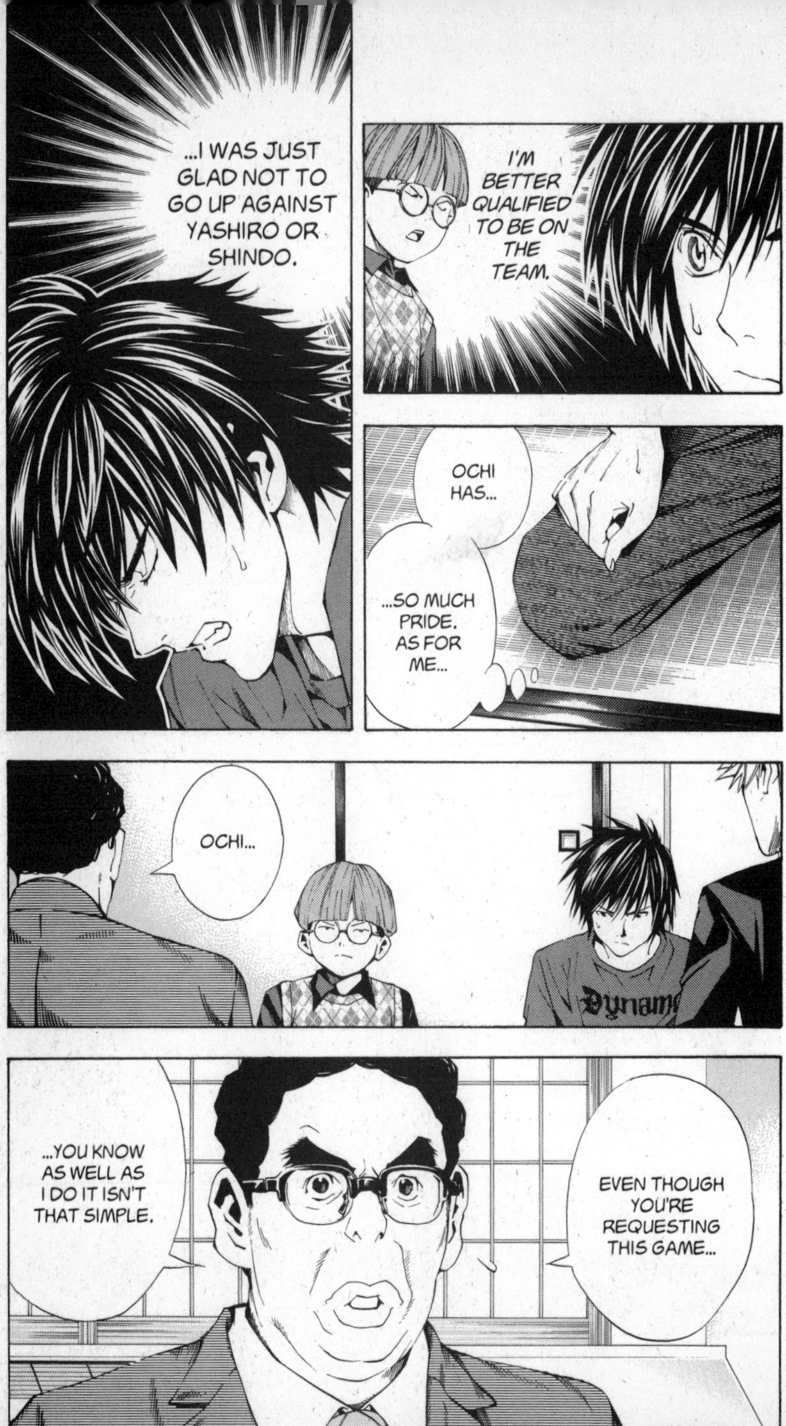
I'M BETTER QUALIFIED TO BE ON THE TEAM.
OCHI HAS...
...SO MUCH PRIDE. AS FOR ME...
...I WAS JUST GLAD NOT TO GO UP AGAINST YASHIRO OR SHINDO.
OCHI...
EVEN THOUGH YOU'RE REQUESTING THIS GAME...
...YOU KNOW AS WELL AS I DO IT ISN'T THAT SIMPLE.

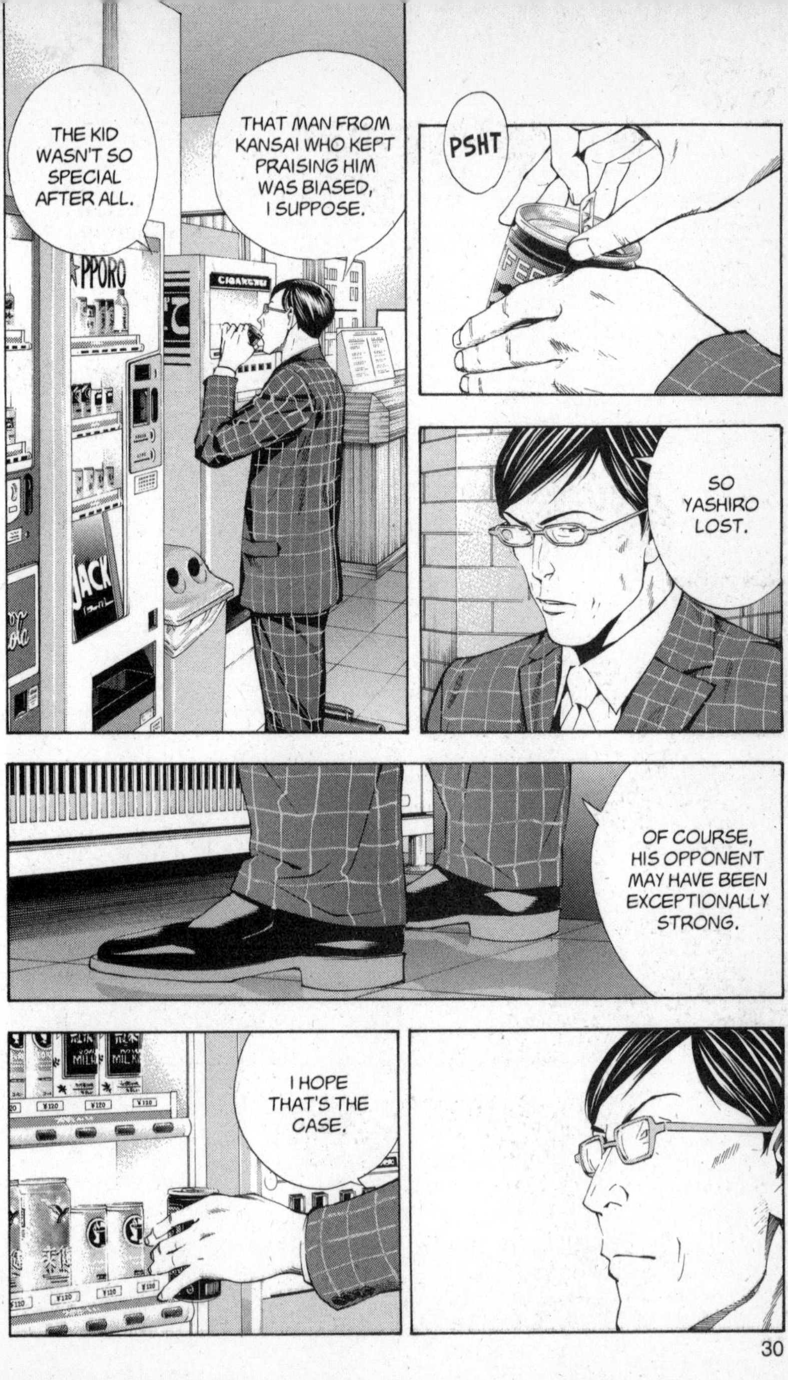
PSHT
SO YASHIRO LOST.
THAT MAN FROM KANSAI WHO KEPT PRAISING HIM WAS BIASED, I SUPPOSE.
THE KID WASN'T SO SPECIAL AFTER ALL.
OF COURSE, HIS OPPONENT MAY HAVE BEEN EXCEPTIONALLY STRONG.
I HOPE THAT'S THE CASE.

READ THIS WAY

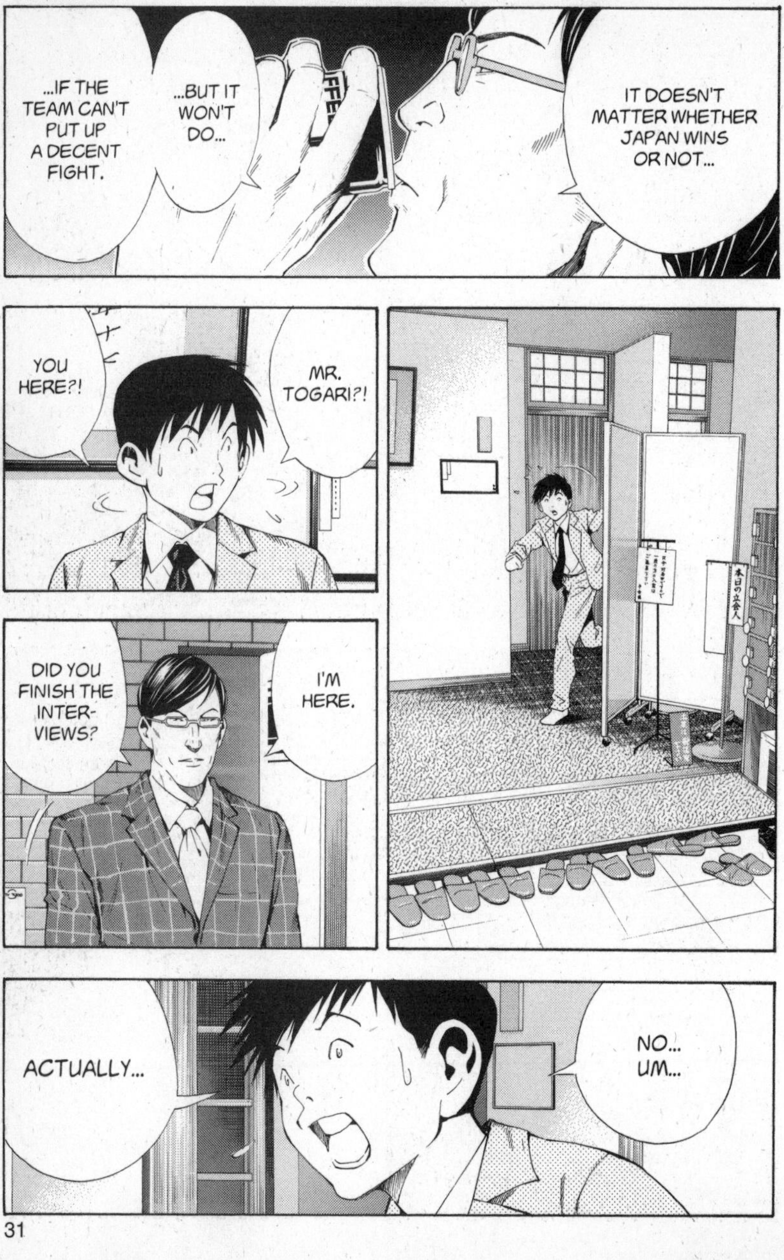

IT DOESN'T MATTER WHETHER JAPAN WINS OR NOT...
...BUT IT WON'T DO...
...IF THE TEAM CAN'T PUT UP A DECENT FIGHT.
MR. TOGARI?!
YOU HERE?!
I'M HERE.
DID YOU FINISH THE INTER-VIEWS?
NO... UM...
ACTUALLY...

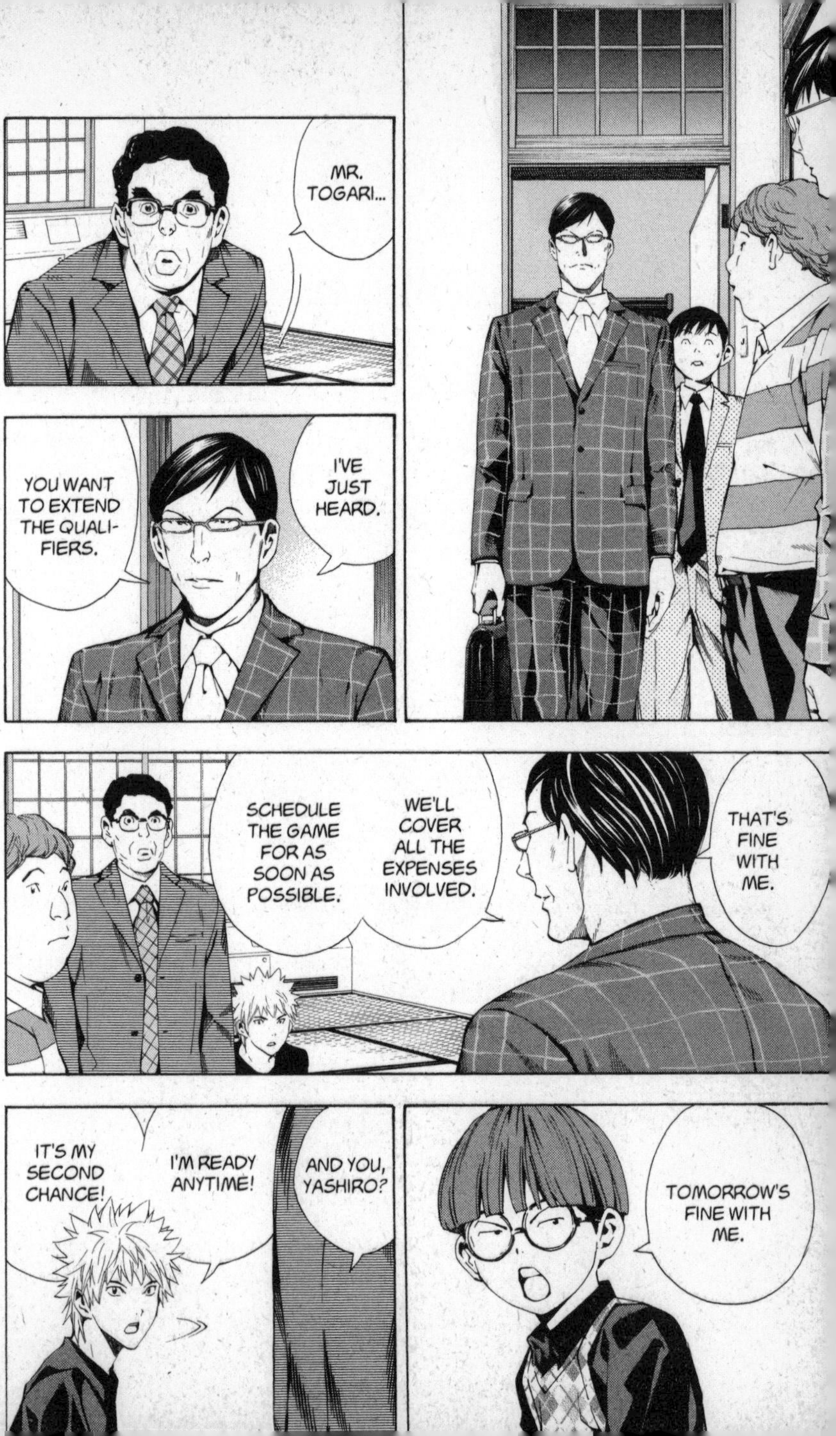

MR. TOGARI...
I'VE JUST HEARD.
YOU WANT TO EXTEND THE QUALIFIERS.
THAT'S FINE WITH ME.
WE'LL COVER ALL THE EXPENSES INVOLVED.
SCHEDULE THE GAME FOR AS SOON AS POSSIBLE.
TOMORROW'S FINE WITH ME.
AND YOU, YASHIRO?
I'M READY ANYTIME!
IT'S MY SECOND CHANCE!

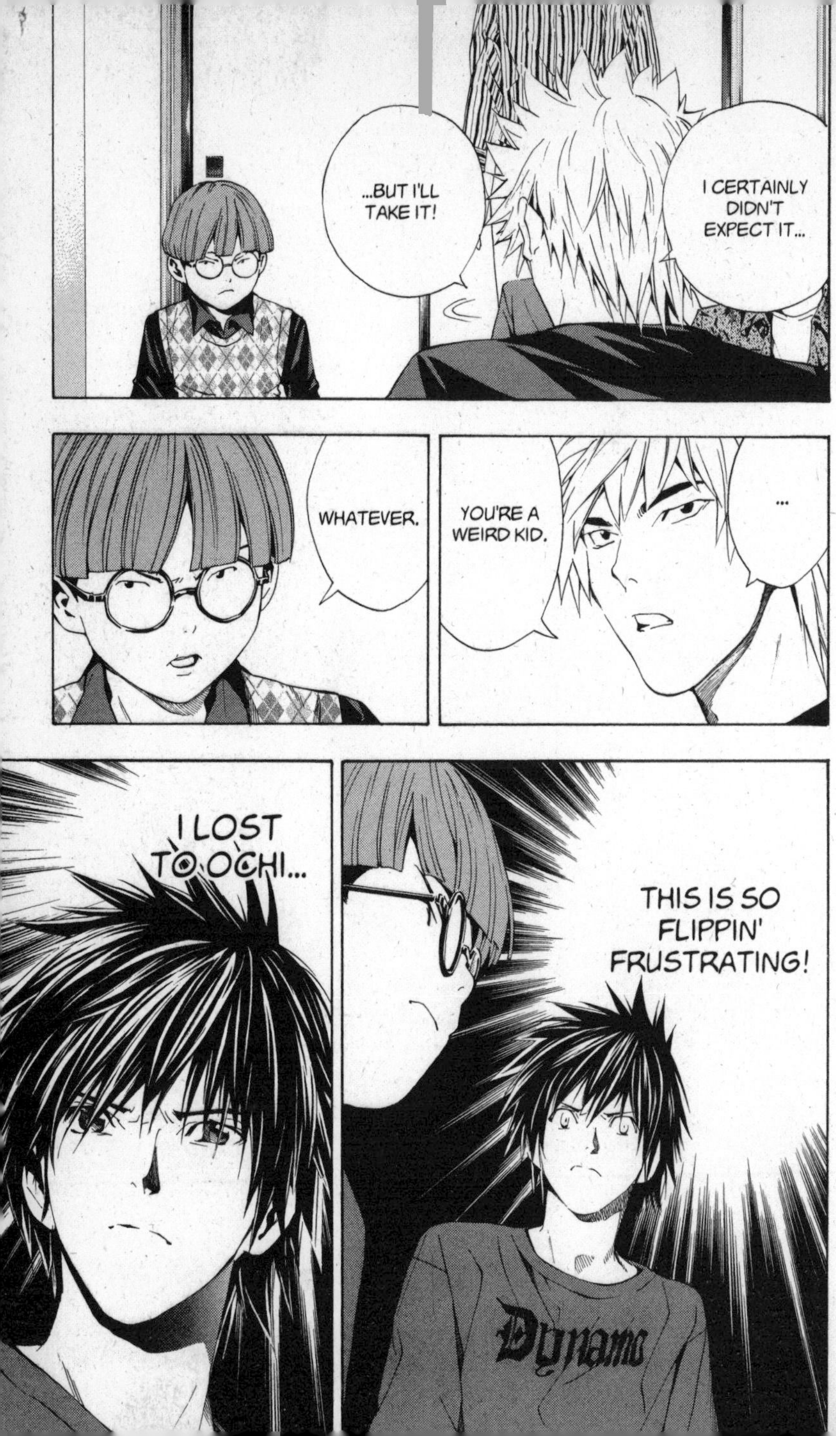
I CERTAINLY DIDN'T EXPECT IT...
...BUT I'LL TAKE IT!
...
YOU'RE A WEIRD KID.
WHATEVER.
THIS IS SO FLIPPIN' FRUSTRATING!
I LOST TO OCHI...

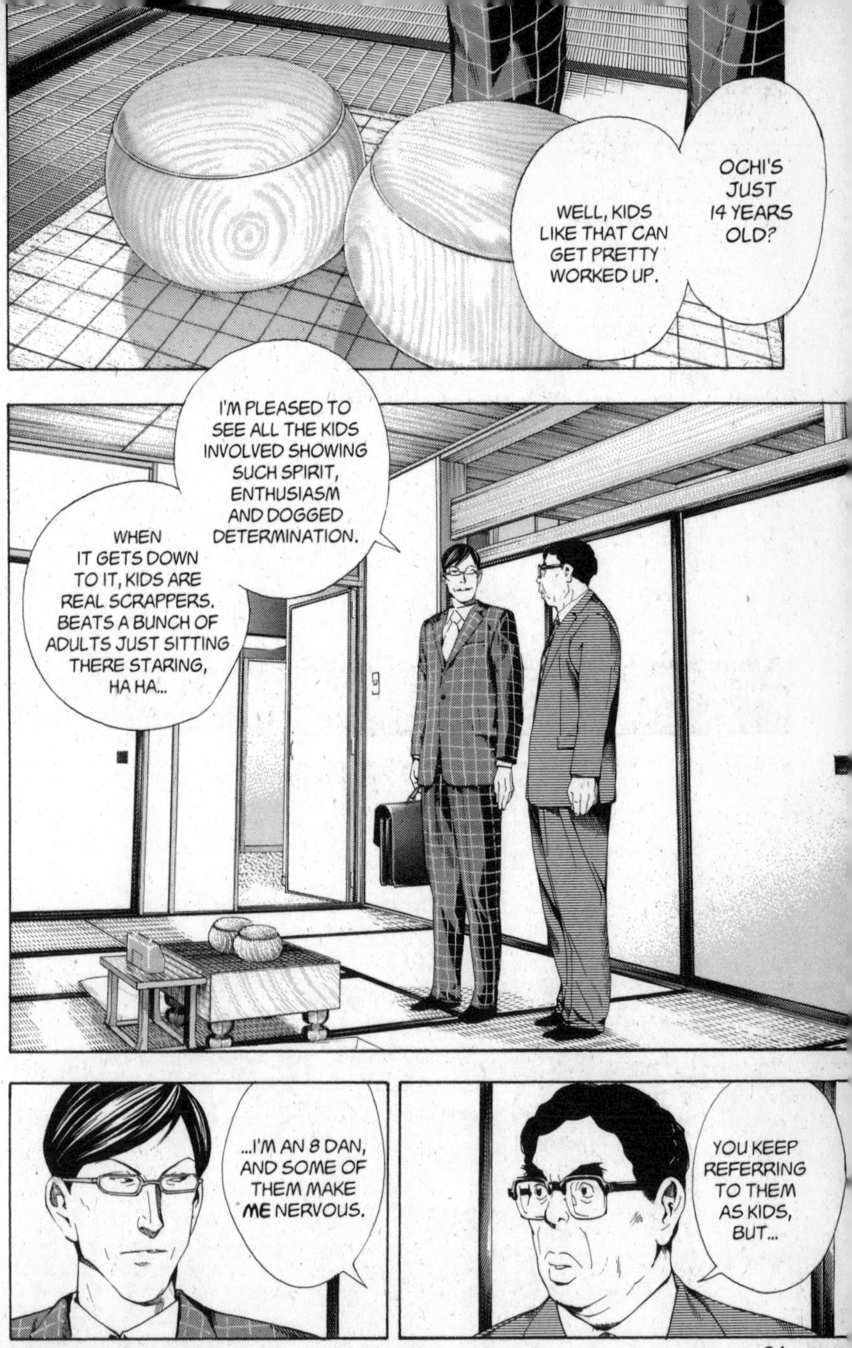
OCHI'S JUST 14 YEARS OLD?
WELL, KIDS LIKE THAT CAN GET PRETTY WORKED UP.
I'M PLEASED TO SEE ALL THE KIDS INVOLVED SHOWING SUCH SPIRIT, ENTHUSIASM AND DOGGED DETERMINATION.
WHEN IT GETS DOWN TO IT, KIDS ARE REAL SCRAPPERS. BEATS A BUNCH OF ADULTS JUST SITTING THERE STARING, HA HA...
YOU KEEP REFERRING TO THEM AS KIDS, BUT...
...I'M AN 8 DAN, AND SOME OF THEM MAKE **ME** NERVOUS.

READ THIS WAY

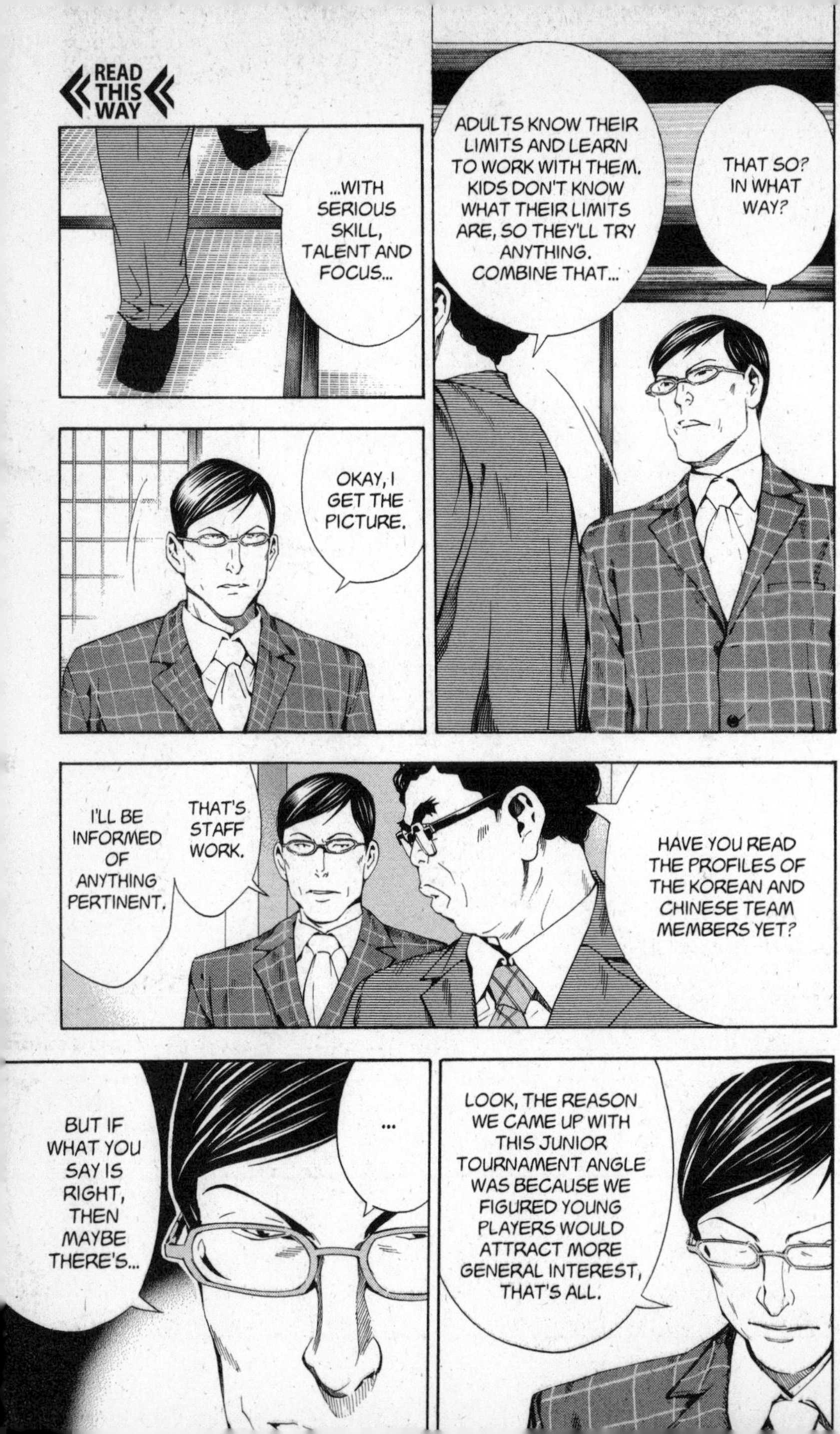
THAT SO? IN WHAT WAY?
ADULTS KNOW THEIR LIMITS AND LEARN TO WORK WITH THEM. KIDS DON'T KNOW WHAT THEIR LIMITS ARE, SO THEY'LL TRY ANYTHING. COMBINE THAT...
...WITH SERIOUS SKILL, TALENT AND FOCUS...
OKAY, I GET THE PICTURE.
HAVE YOU READ THE PROFILES OF THE KOREAN AND CHINESE TEAM MEMBERS YET?
THAT'S STAFF WORK.
I'LL BE INFORMED OF ANYTHING PERTINENT.
LOOK, THE REASON WE CAME UP WITH THIS JUNIOR TOURNAMENT ANGLE WAS BECAUSE WE FIGURED YOUNG PLAYERS WOULD ATTRACT MORE GENERAL INTEREST, THAT'S ALL.
...
BUT IF WHAT YOU SAY IS RIGHT, THEN MAYBE THERE'S...

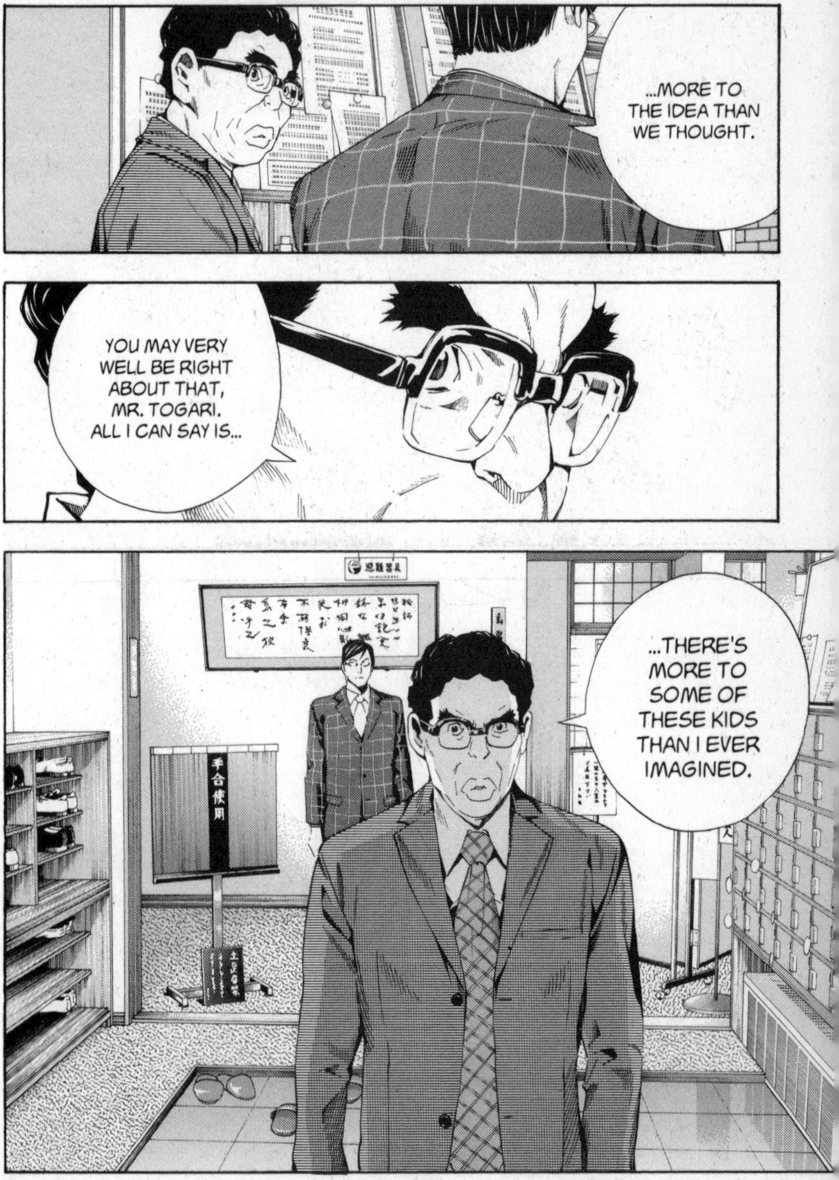
...MORE TO THE IDEA THAN WE THOUGHT.
YOU MAY VERY WELL BE RIGHT ABOUT THAT, MR. TOGARI. ALL I CAN SAY IS...
...THERE'S MORE TO SOME OF THESE KIDS THAN I EVER IMAGINED.

READ THIS WAY

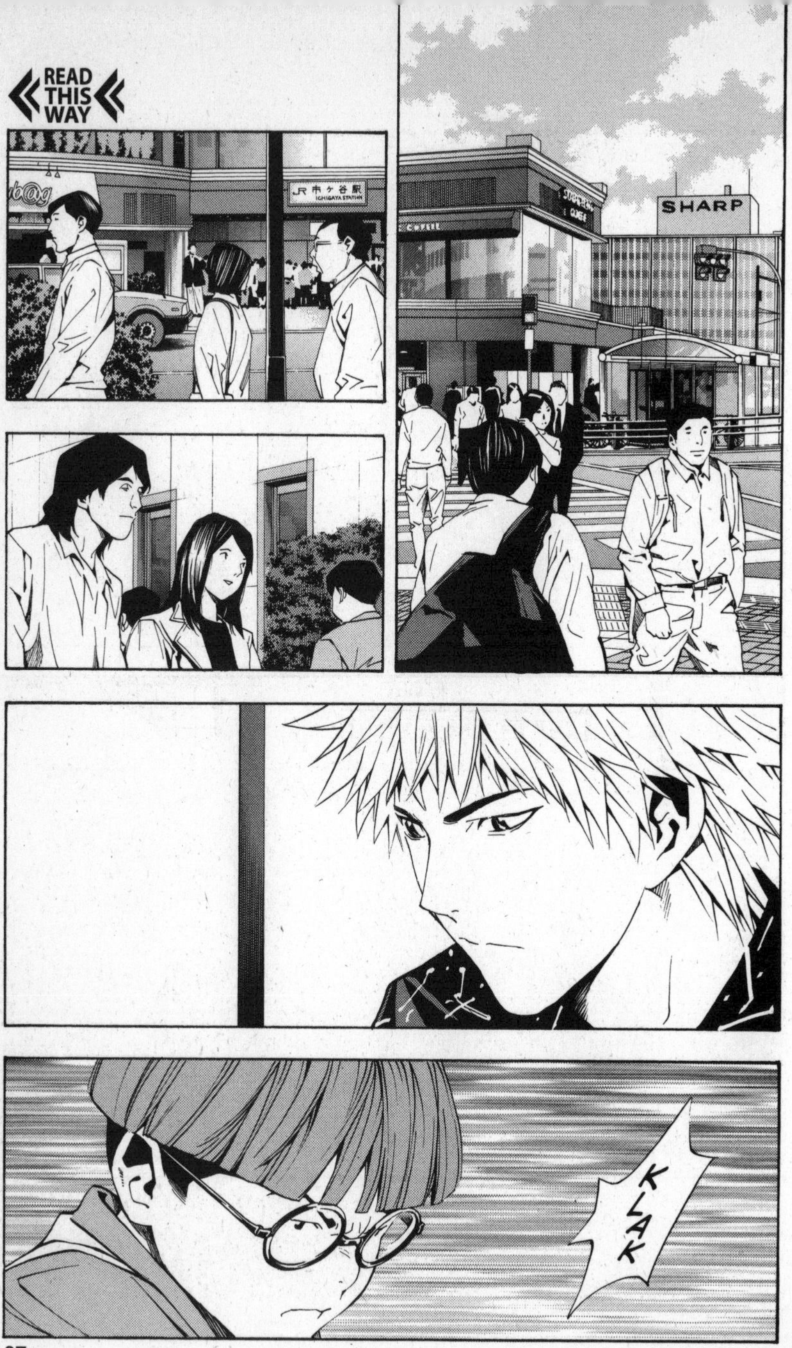
SHARP
JR 市ケ谷駅
ICHIGAYA STATION
KLAK

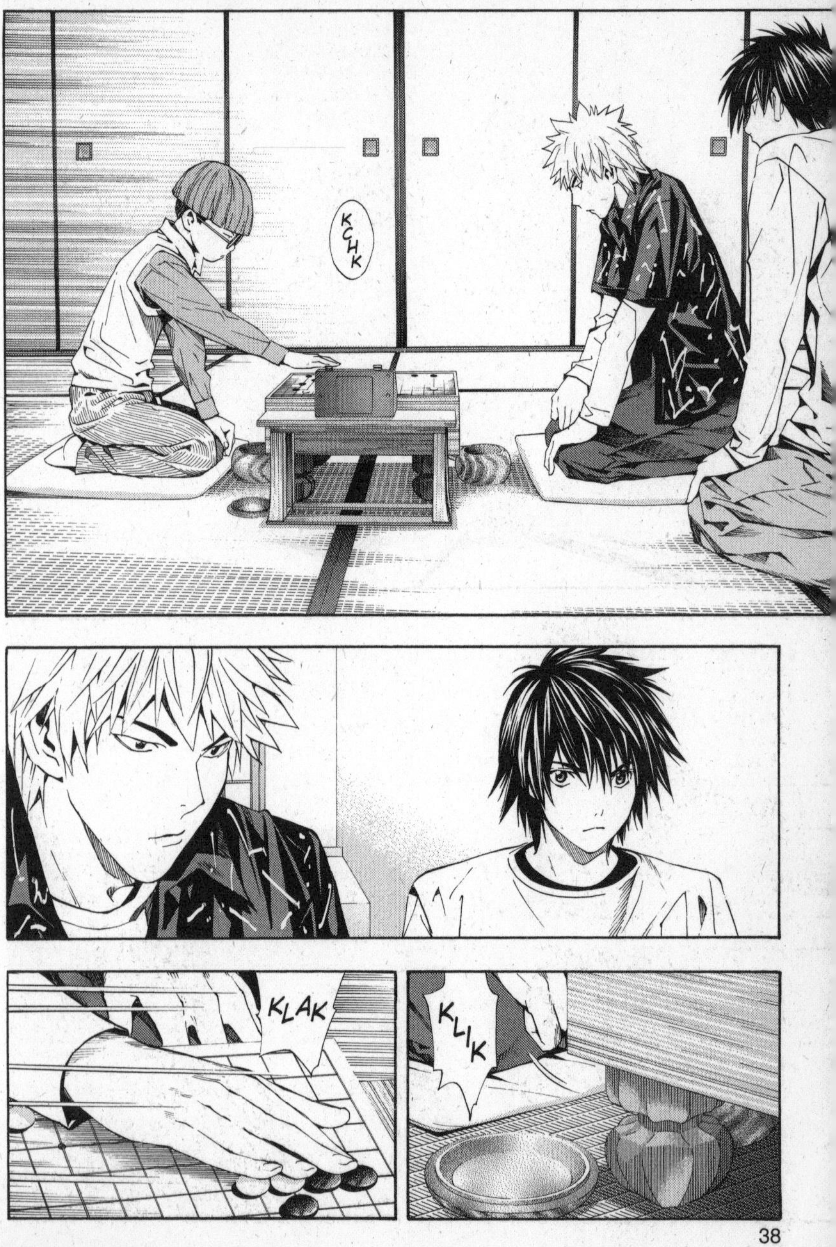
KCHK
KLIK
KLAK

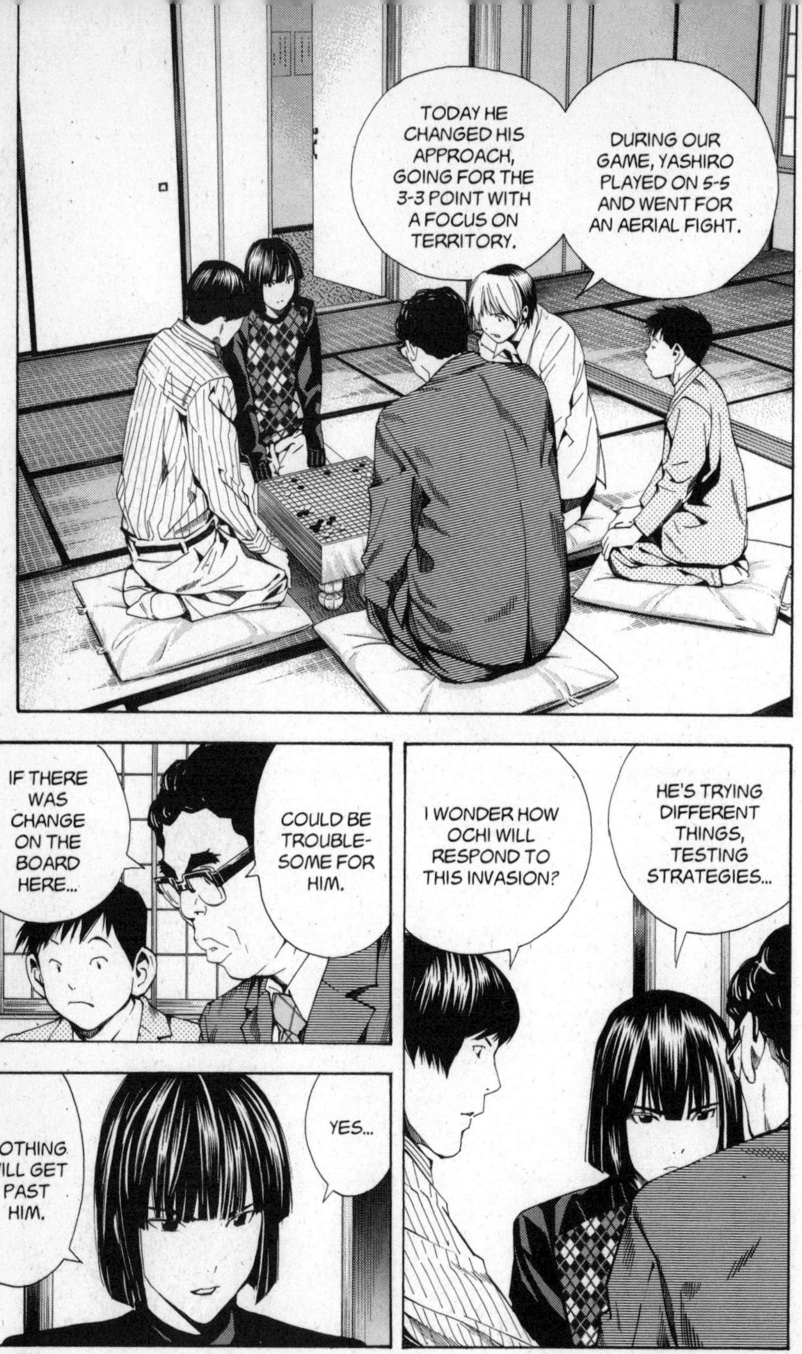
DURING OUR GAME, YASHIRO PLAYED ON 5-5 AND WENT FOR AN AERIAL FIGHT.
TODAY HE CHANGED HIS APPROACH, GOING FOR THE 3-3 POINT WITH A FOCUS ON TERRITORY.
HE'S TRYING DIFFERENT THINGS, TESTING STRATEGIES...
I WONDER HOW OCHI WILL RESPOND TO THIS INVASION?
IF THERE WAS CHANGE ON THE BOARD HERE...
COULD BE TROUBLE-SOME FOR HIM.
YES...
NOTHING WILL GET PAST HIM.

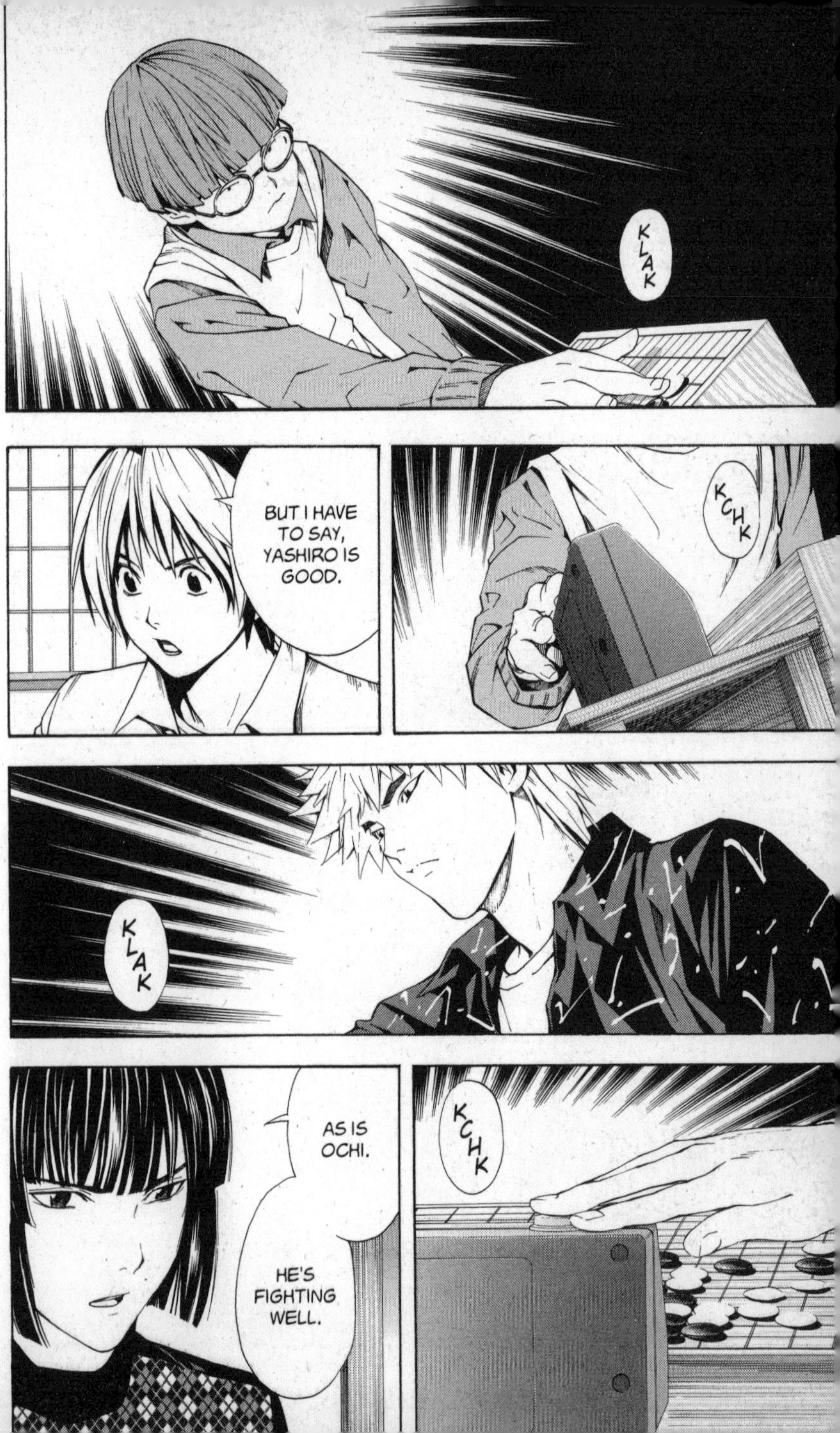
KLAK
KCHK
BUT I HAVE TO SAY, YASHIRO IS GOOD.
KLAK
KCHK
AS IS OCHI.
HE'S FIGHTING WELL.

◄◄ READ THIS WAY ◄◄

I DON'T SEE A COMEBACK FROM HERE.

HMM...

KLAK

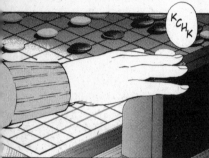

KCHK

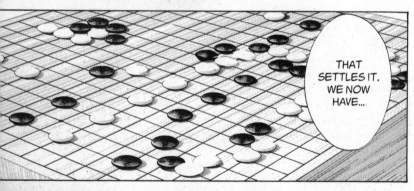

THAT SETTLES IT. WE NOW HAVE...

...OUR TEAM FOR THE HOKUTO CUP.

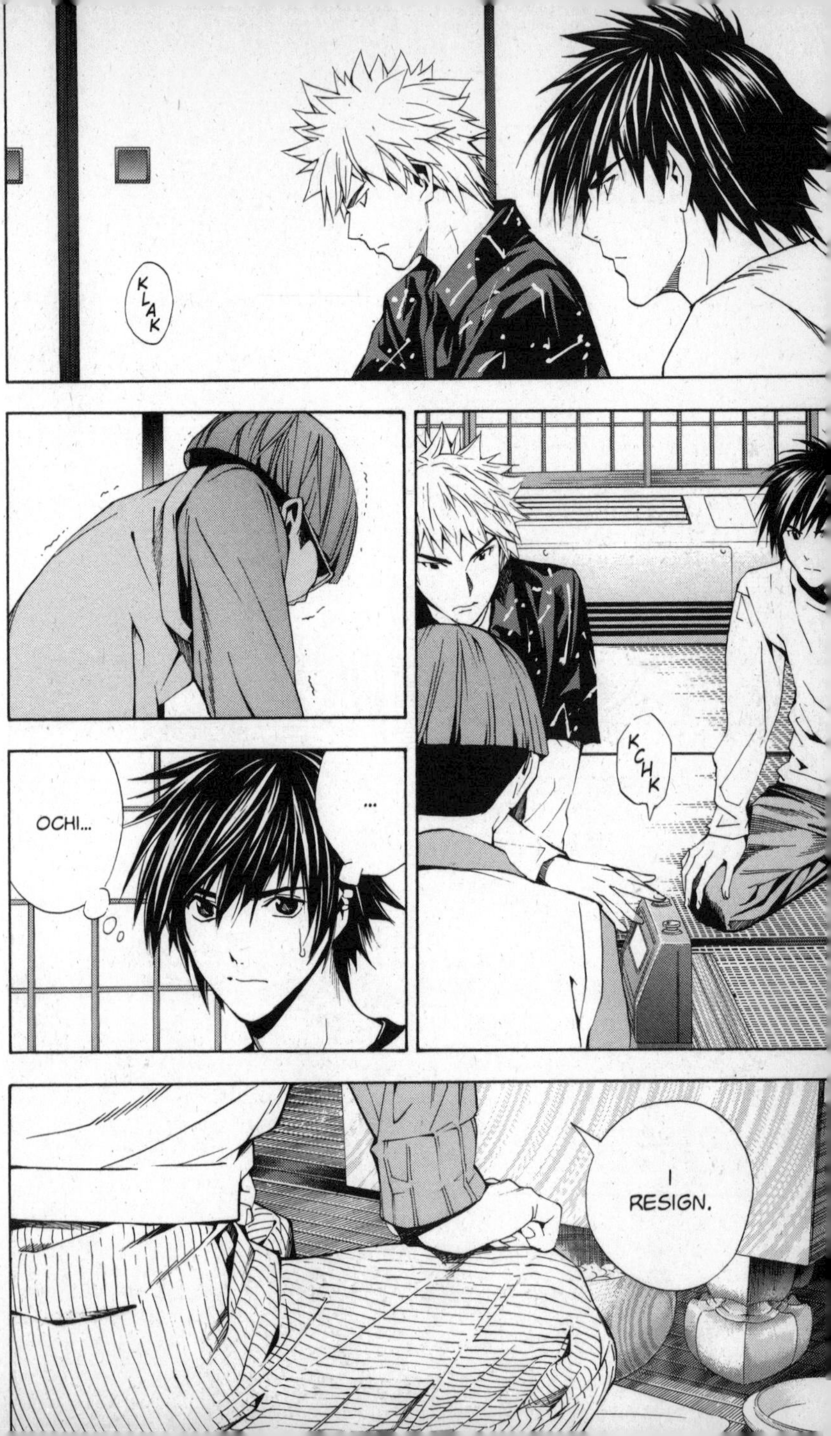
KLAK
KCHK
...
OCHI...
I RESIGN.

READ THIS WAY

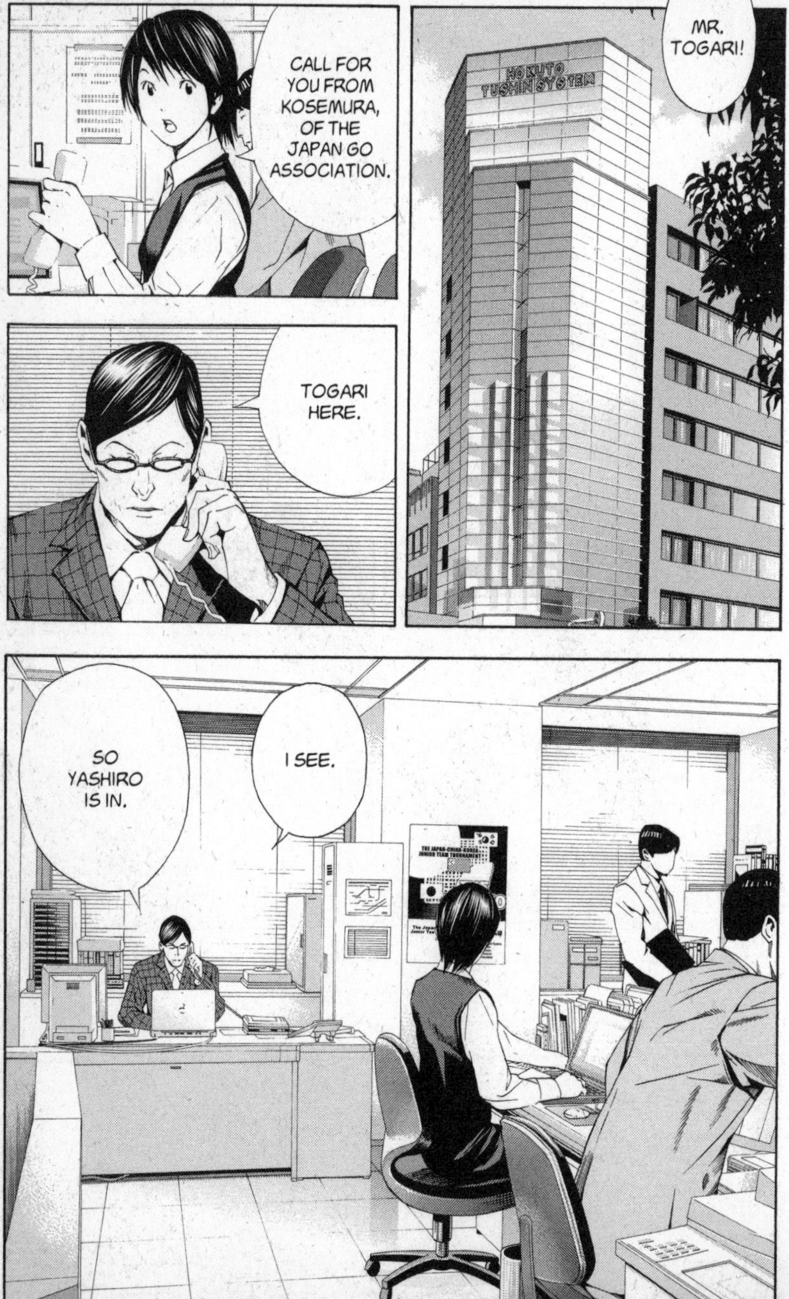
MR. TOGARI!
HOKUTO TUSHIN SYSTEM
CALL FOR YOU FROM KOSEMURA, OF THE JAPAN GO ASSOCIATION.
TOGARI HERE.
I SEE.
SO YASHIRO IS IN.

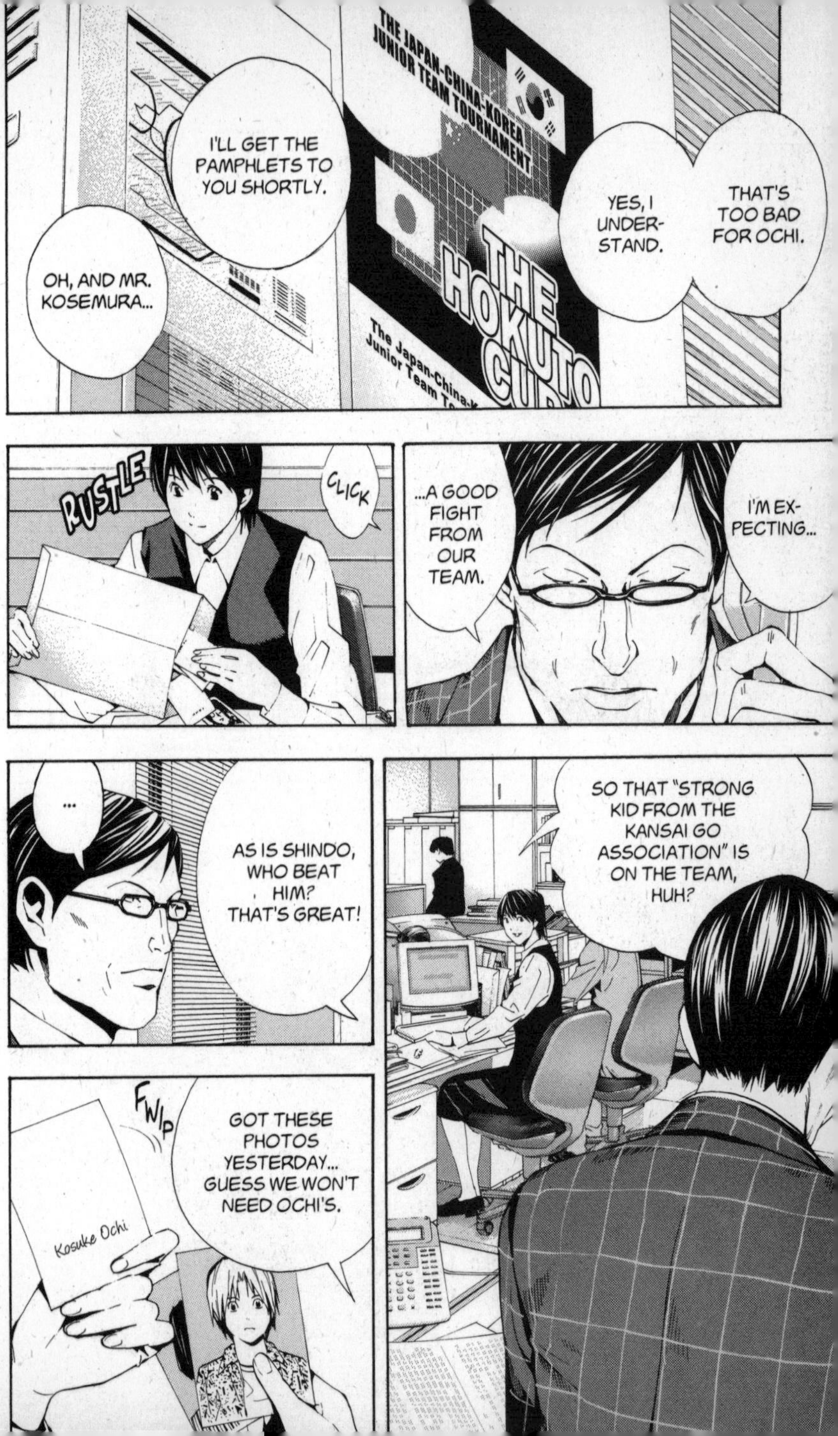
THAT'S TOO BAD FOR OCHI.
YES, I UNDERSTAND.
THE JAPAN-CHINA-KOREA JUNIOR TEAM TOURNAMENT
THE HOKUTO CUP
I'LL GET THE PAMPHLETS TO YOU SHORTLY.
OH, AND MR. KOSEMURA...
I'M EXPECTING...
...A GOOD FIGHT FROM OUR TEAM.
CLICK
RUSTLE
SO THAT "STRONG KID FROM THE KANSAI GO ASSOCIATION" IS ON THE TEAM, HUH?
AS IS SHINDO, WHO BEAT HIM? THAT'S GREAT!
...
GOT THESE PHOTOS YESTERDAY... GUESS WE WON'T NEED OCHI'S.
FWIP
Kosuke Ochi

READ THIS WAY

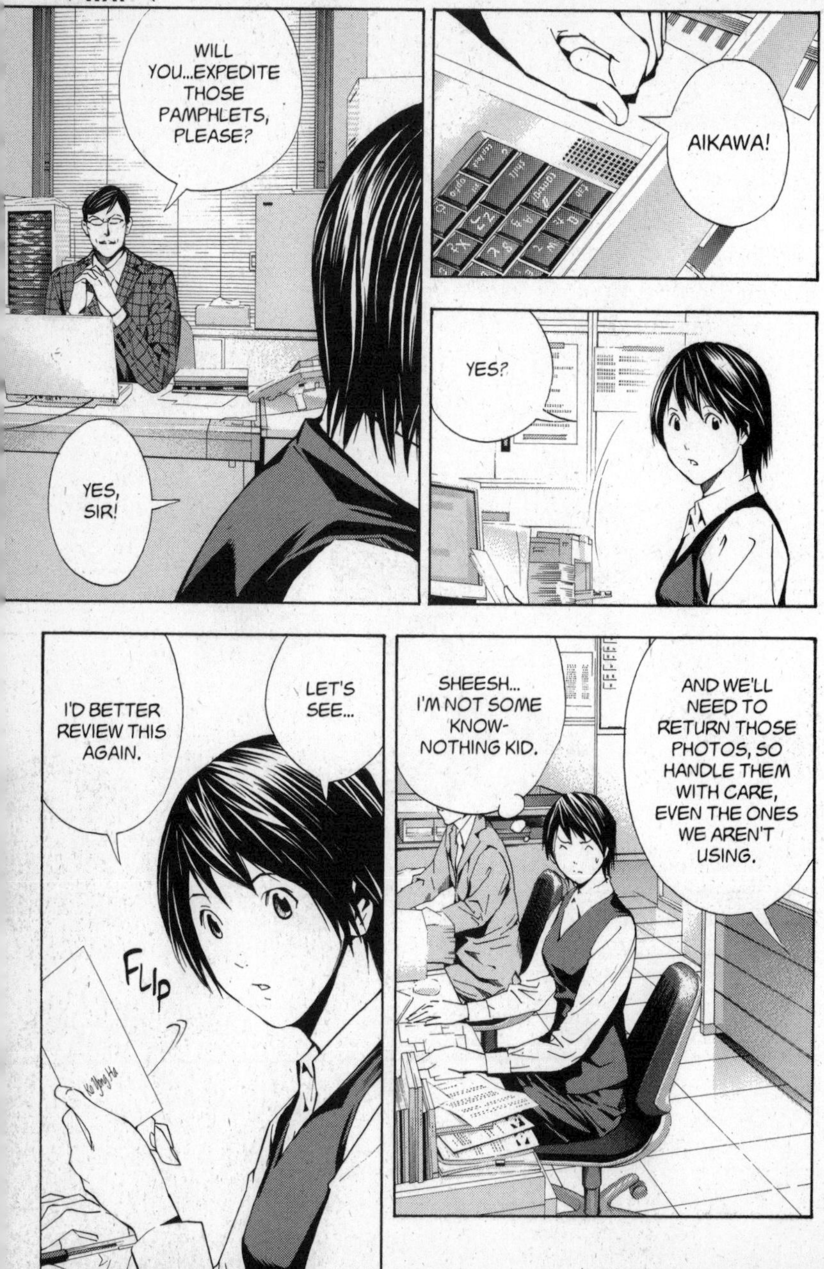
AIKAWA!
YES?
WILL YOU...EXPEDITE THOSE PAMPHLETS, PLEASE?
YES, SIR!
AND WE'LL NEED TO RETURN THOSE PHOTOS, SO HANDLE THEM WITH CARE, EVEN THE ONES WE AREN'T USING.
SHEESH... I'M NOT SOME KNOW-NOTHING KID.
LET'S SEE...
I'D BETTER REVIEW THIS AGAIN.
FLIP
Ko Yong Ha

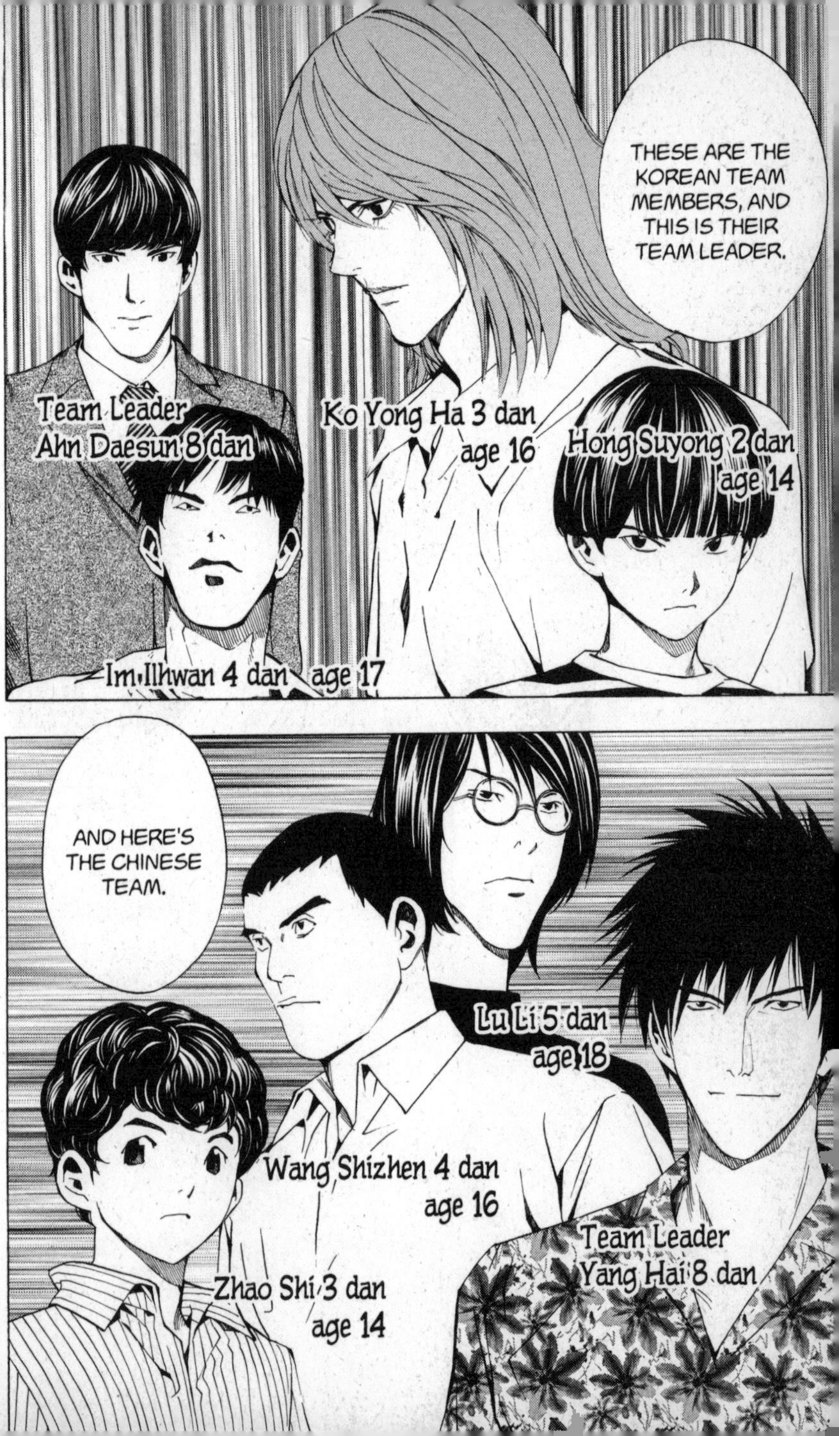
THESE ARE THE KOREAN TEAM MEMBERS, AND THIS IS THEIR TEAM LEADER.
Hong Suyong 2 dan age 14
Ko Yong Ha 3 dan age 16
Team Leader Ahn Daesun 8 dan
Im Ilhwan 4 dan age 17
AND HERE'S THE CHINESE TEAM.
Lu Li 5 dan age 18
Wang Shizhen 4 dan age 16
Team Leader Yang Hai 8 dan
Zhao Shi 3 dan age 14

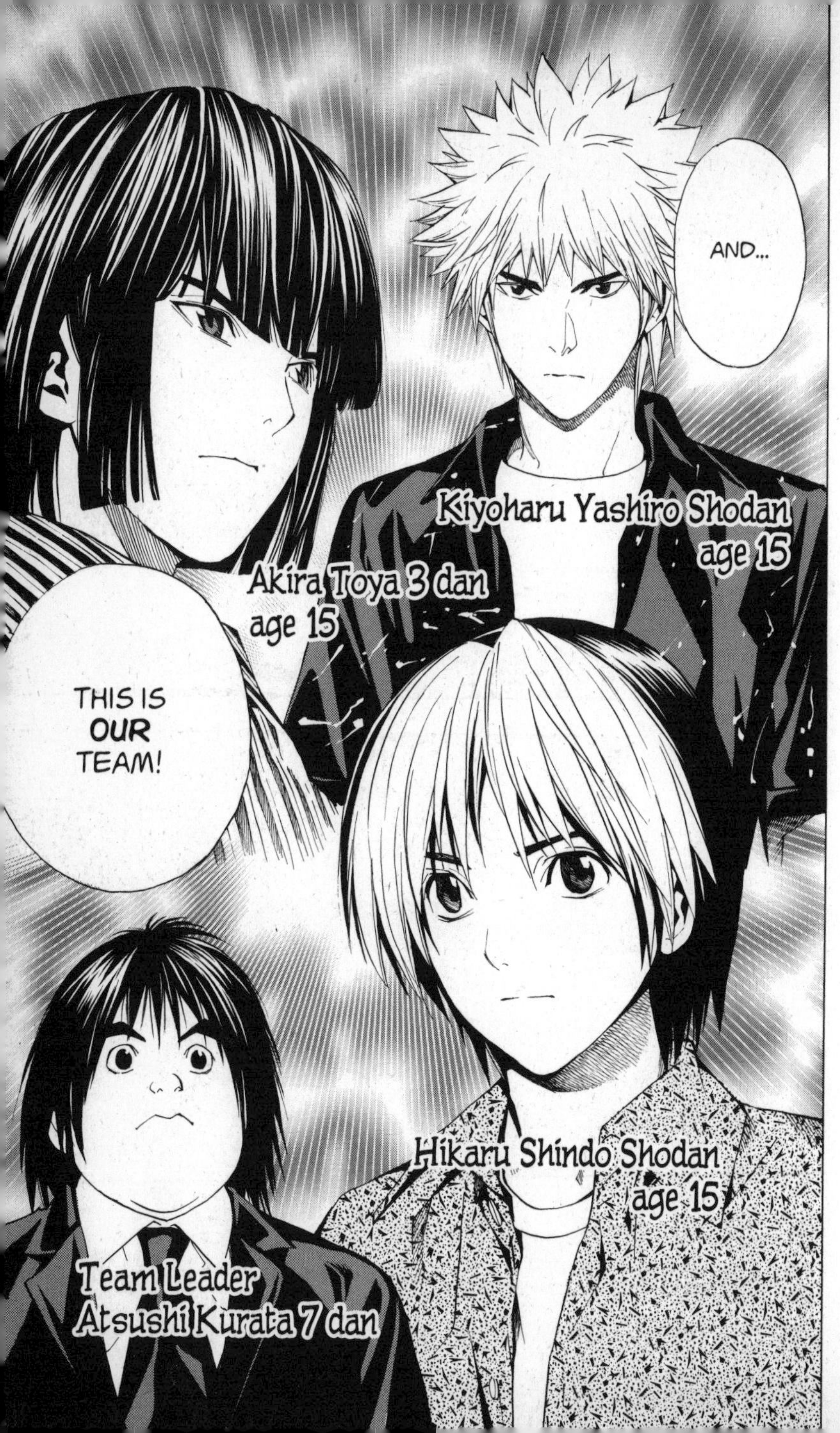
AND...
Kiyoharu Yashiro Shodan age 15
Akira Toya 3 dan age 15
THIS IS OUR TEAM!
Hikaru Shindo Shodan age 15
Team Leader Atsushi Kurata 7 dan

A WORD ABOUT HIKARU NO GO

● DOUBLE ROLES IN THE ANIME ●

C A S T

Hikaru Shindo... Tomoko Kawakami (Production Baobab)

Akira Toya... Sanae Kobayashi (Production Baobab)

Akari Fujisawa... Yumi Kakazu (Genki Project)

Yoshitaka Waya... Reiko Takagi (Sigma Seven)

Kosuke Ochi... Yoko Matsuoka (81 Produce)

Atsushi Kurata 6 dan... Mitsuo Iwata (Osawa Jimusho)

Shinoda Insei Instructor... Naoki Bando (Mausu Promotion)

Amano... Yoshito Ishinami (Gekidan Subaru)

Hikaru's mother... Yurika Hirano (Gekidan Subaru)

Hiroyuki Ashiwara 4 dan... Katsuyuki Konishi (Ken Production)

Mitsuru Mashiba... Hiroyuki Yoshino (Sigma Seven)

Morishita 9 dan... Katsuhiro Kitagawa (Gekidan Subaru)

Michio Shirakawa 7 dan... Koji Yusa (Free Agent)

Koji Saeki 4 dan... Toshitaka Shimizu (Mausu Promotion)

Sakamaki... Shouto Kashii (Mausu Promotion)

Female student A... (Sanae Kobayashi)

Female student B... (Reiko Takagi)

ON THE BACK FLAP OF THIS VOLUME I WROTE
ABOUT ANIME EPISODE 73. THE ABOVE IS FROM THE
CAST PAGE OF THE SCRIPT.

THERE'S ALSO EPISODE 64, WHERE CHIBA-SAN, WHO
VOICES SAI, DOES THE VOICE FOR A BASEBALL
PLAYER AND EPISODE 53, WHERE KOBAYASHI-SAN,
AKIRA'S VOICE, PROVIDES THE VOICE OF A NURSE.

EVEN KAWAKAMI-SAN, WHO VOICES HIKARU, DOES
A FEW WORDS IN THE VOICE OF A CUTE GIRL WHO
SAYS, "OKAY, I'M SORRY."

Game 168

"One Month Before the Hokuto Cup"

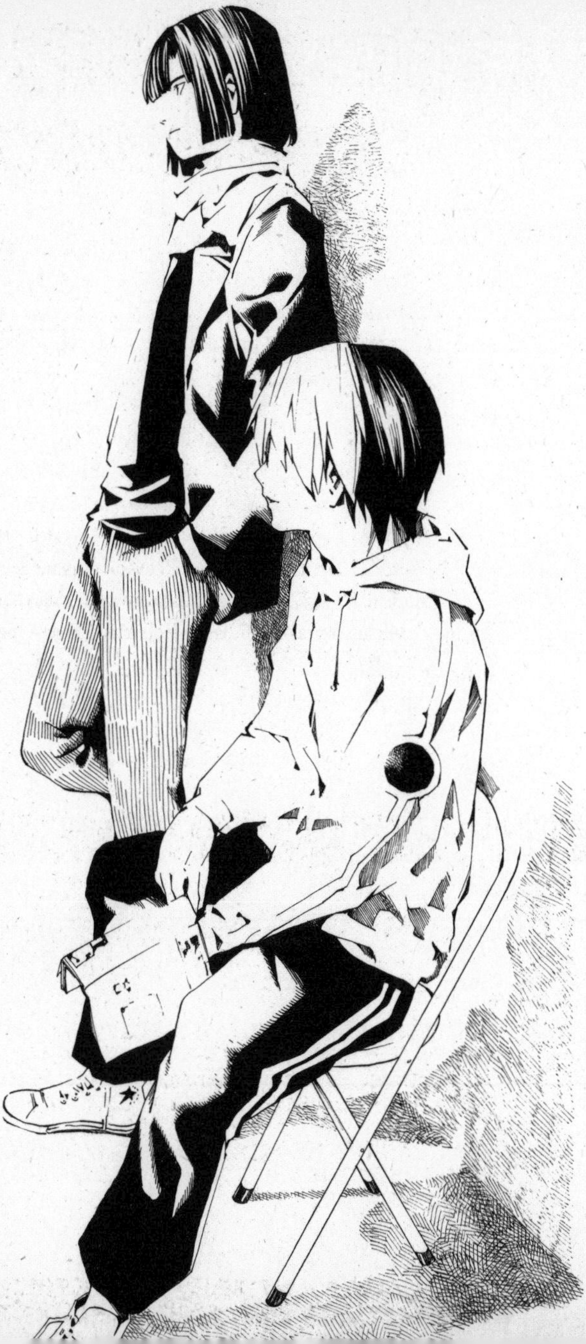

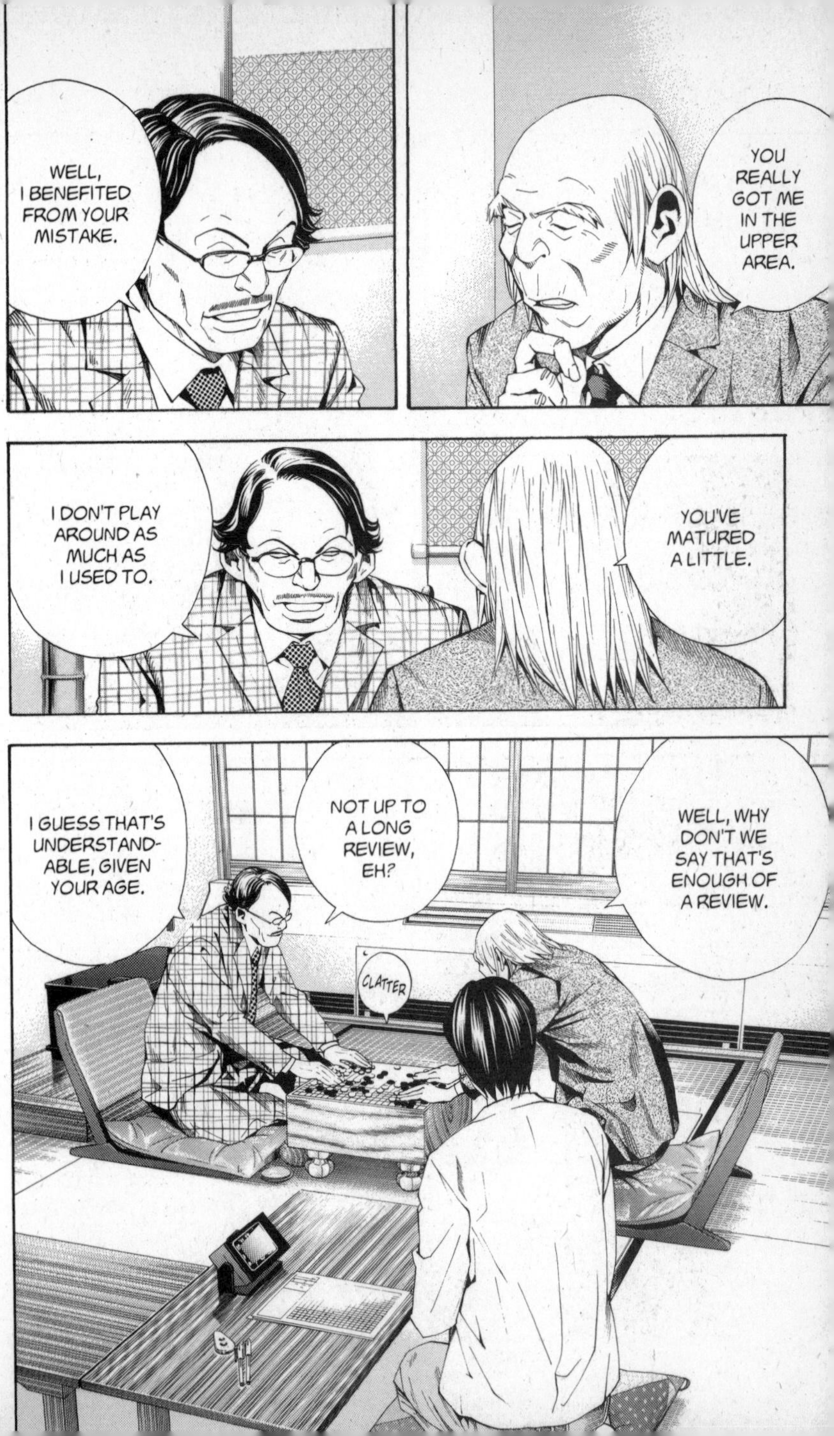
YOU REALLY GOT ME IN THE UPPER AREA.
WELL, I BENEFITED FROM YOUR MISTAKE.
YOU'VE MATURED A LITTLE.
I DON'T PLAY AROUND AS MUCH AS I USED TO.
WELL, WHY DON'T WE SAY THAT'S ENOUGH OF A REVIEW.
NOT UP TO A LONG REVIEW, EH?
I GUESS THAT'S UNDERSTAND-ABLE, GIVEN YOUR AGE.
CLATTER

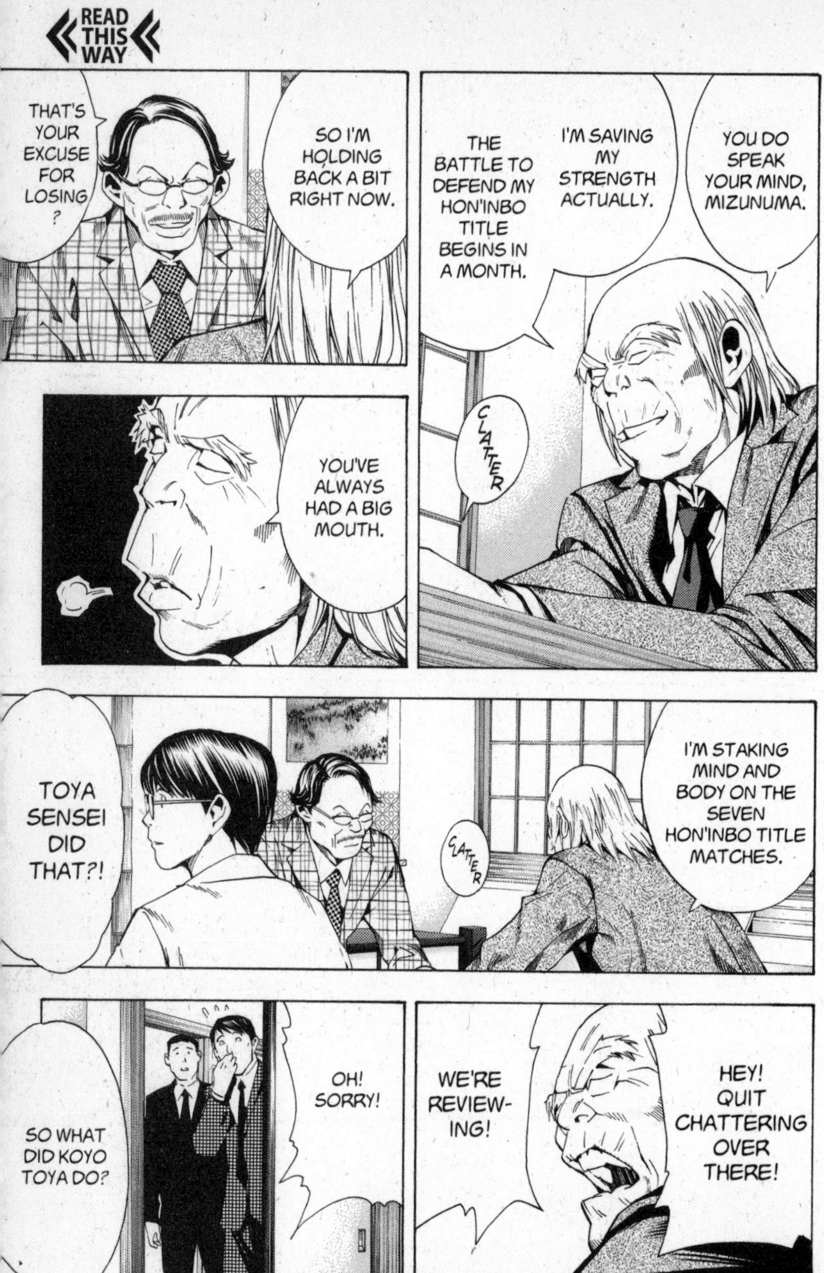
READ THIS WAY
YOU DO SPEAK YOUR MIND, MIZUNUMA.
I'M SAVING MY STRENGTH ACTUALLY.
THE BATTLE TO DEFEND MY HON'INBO TITLE BEGINS IN A MONTH.
CLATTER
SO I'M HOLDING BACK A BIT RIGHT NOW.
THAT'S YOUR EXCUSE FOR LOSING?
YOU'VE ALWAYS HAD A BIG MOUTH.
I'M STAKING MIND AND BODY ON THE SEVEN HON'INBO TITLE MATCHES.
CLATTER
TOYA SENSEI DID THAT?!
HEY! QUIT CHATTERING OVER THERE!
WE'RE REVIEW-ING!
OH! SORRY!
SO WHAT DID KOYO TOYA DO?

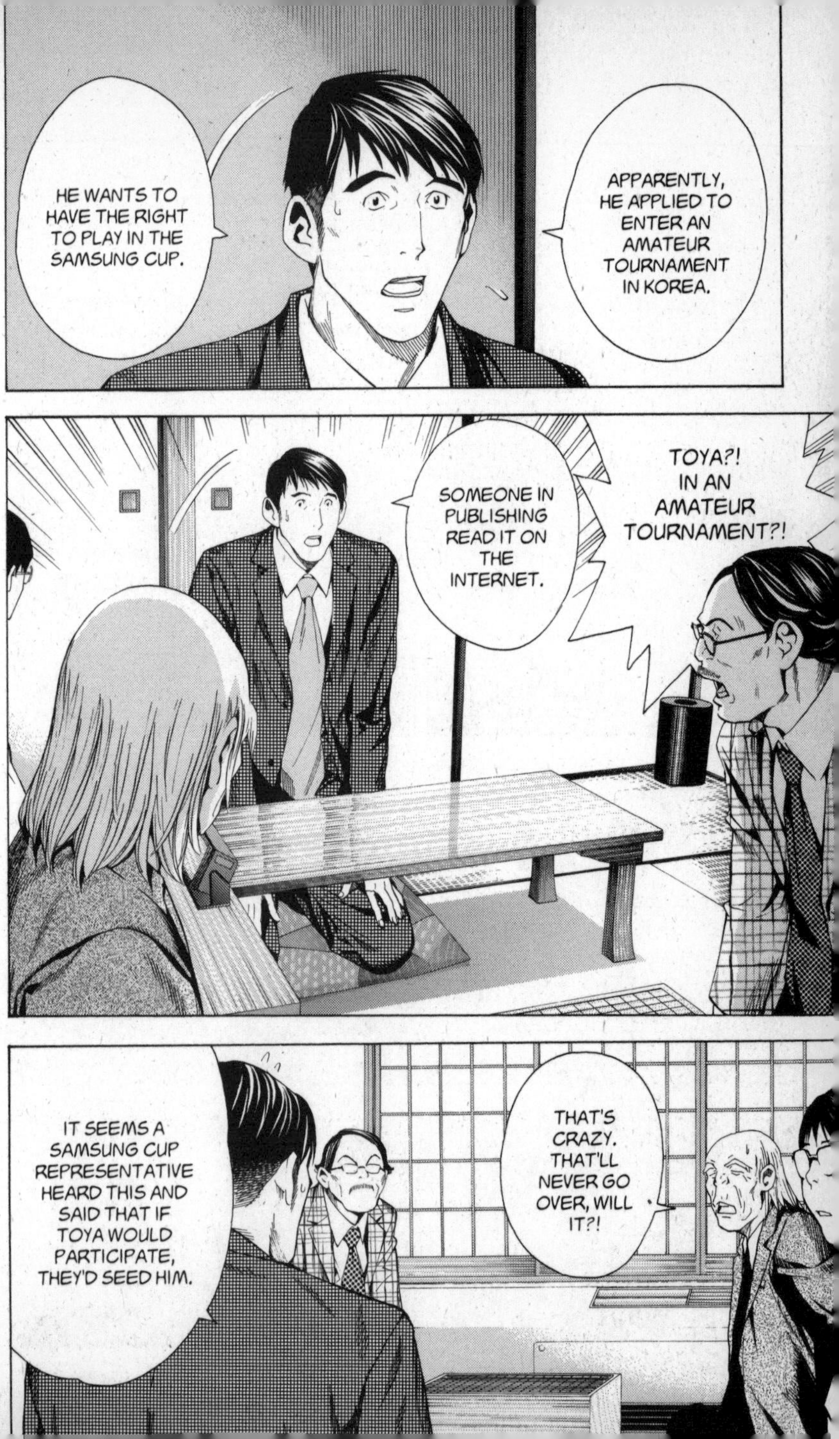
APPARENTLY, HE APPLIED TO ENTER AN AMATEUR TOURNAMENT IN KOREA.
HE WANTS TO HAVE THE RIGHT TO PLAY IN THE SAMSUNG CUP.
TOYA?! IN AN AMATEUR TOURNAMENT?!
SOMEONE IN PUBLISHING READ IT ON THE INTERNET.
THAT'S CRAZY. THAT'LL NEVER GO OVER, WILL IT?!
IT SEEMS A SAMSUNG CUP REPRESENTATIVE HEARD THIS AND SAID THAT IF TOYA WOULD PARTICIPATE, THEY'D SEED HIM.

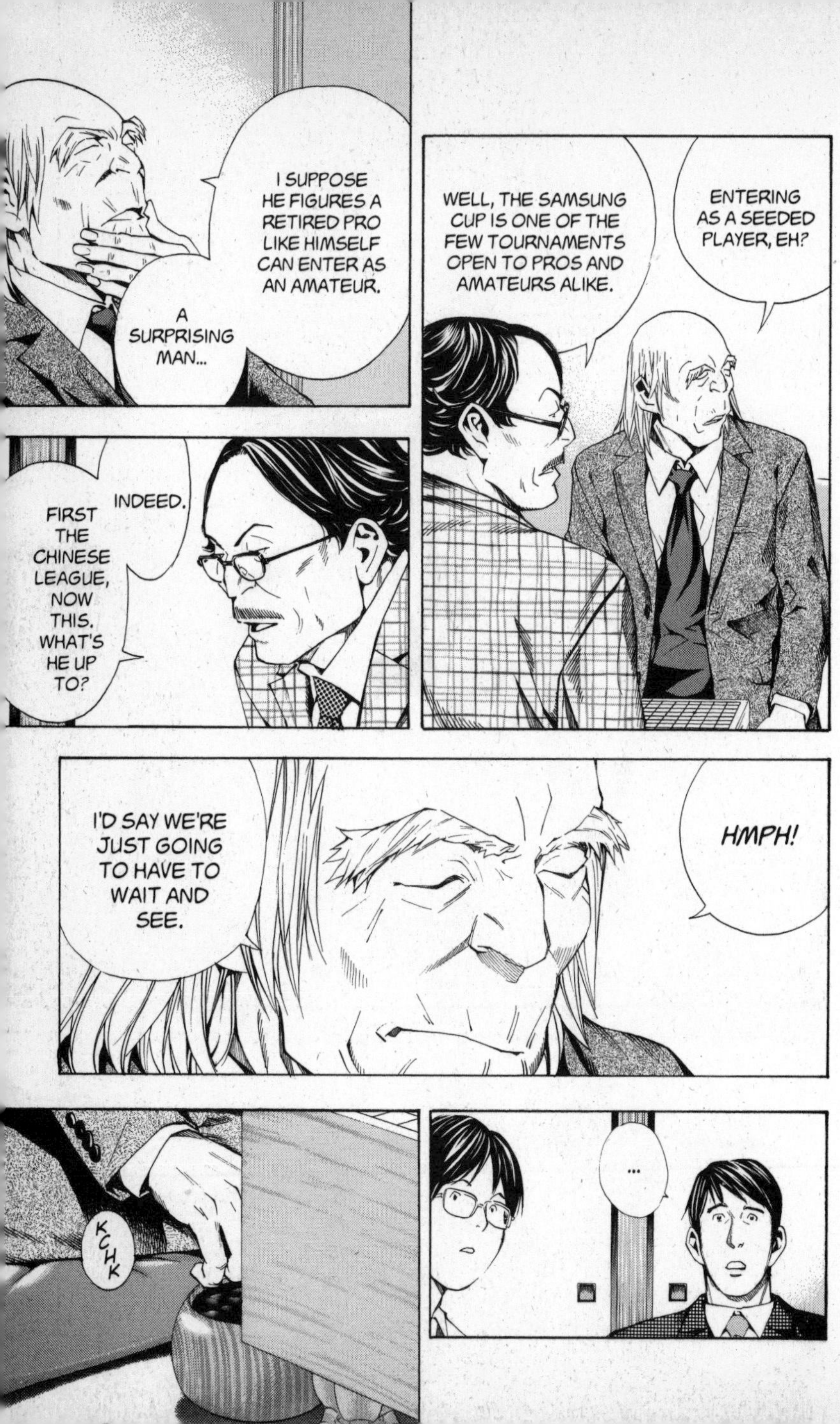
ENTERING AS A SEEDED PLAYER, EH?
WELL, THE SAMSUNG CUP IS ONE OF THE FEW TOURNAMENTS OPEN TO PROS AND AMATEURS ALIKE.
I SUPPOSE HE FIGURES A RETIRED PRO LIKE HIMSELF CAN ENTER AS AN AMATEUR.
A SURPRISING MAN...
INDEED.
FIRST THE CHINESE LEAGUE, NOW THIS. WHAT'S HE UP TO?
HMPH!
I'D SAY WE'RE JUST GOING TO HAVE TO WAIT AND SEE.
...
KCHK

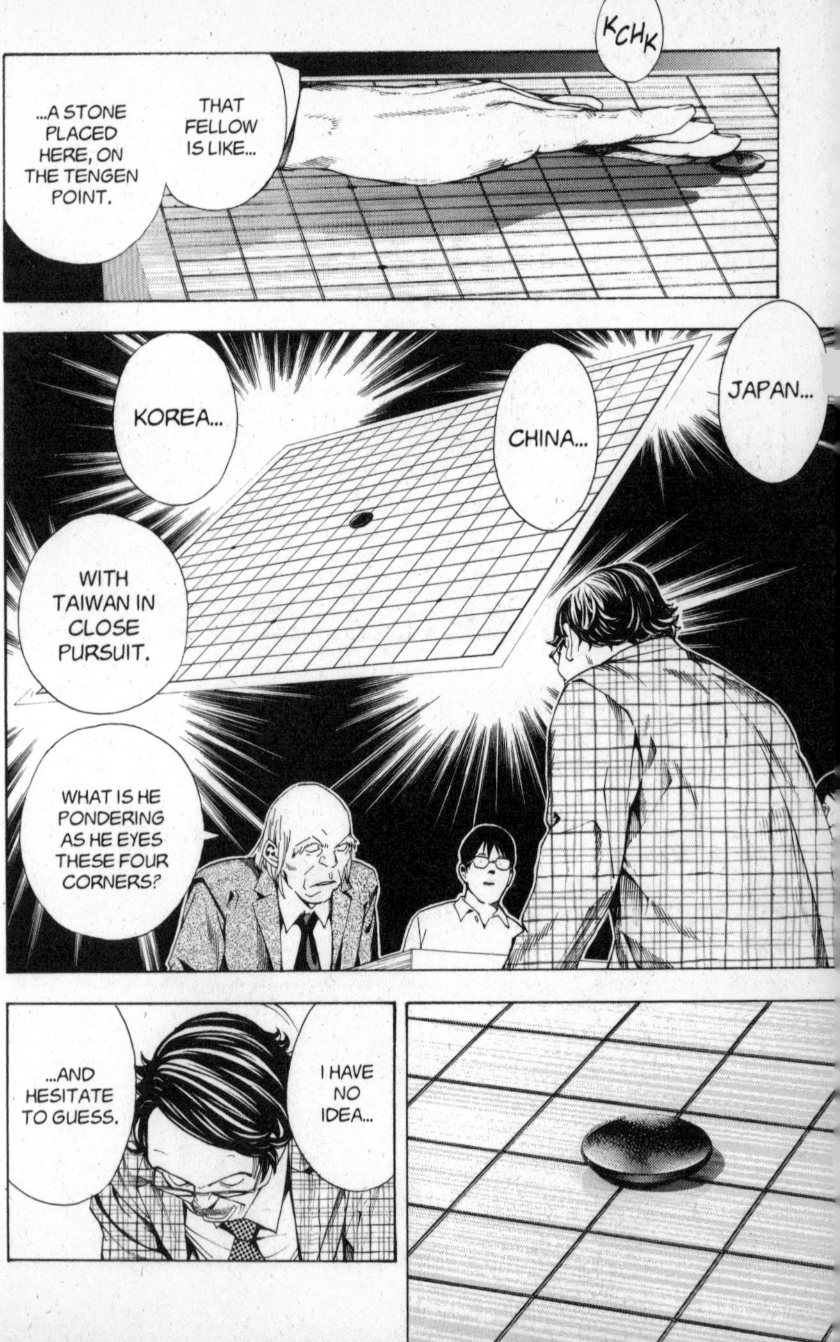
KCHK
THAT FELLOW IS LIKE...
...A STONE PLACED HERE, ON THE TENGEN POINT.
JAPAN...
CHINA...
KOREA...
WITH TAIWAN IN CLOSE PURSUIT.
WHAT IS HE PONDERING AS HE EYES THESE FOUR CORNERS?
I HAVE NO IDEA...
...AND HESITATE TO GUESS.

READ THIS WAY

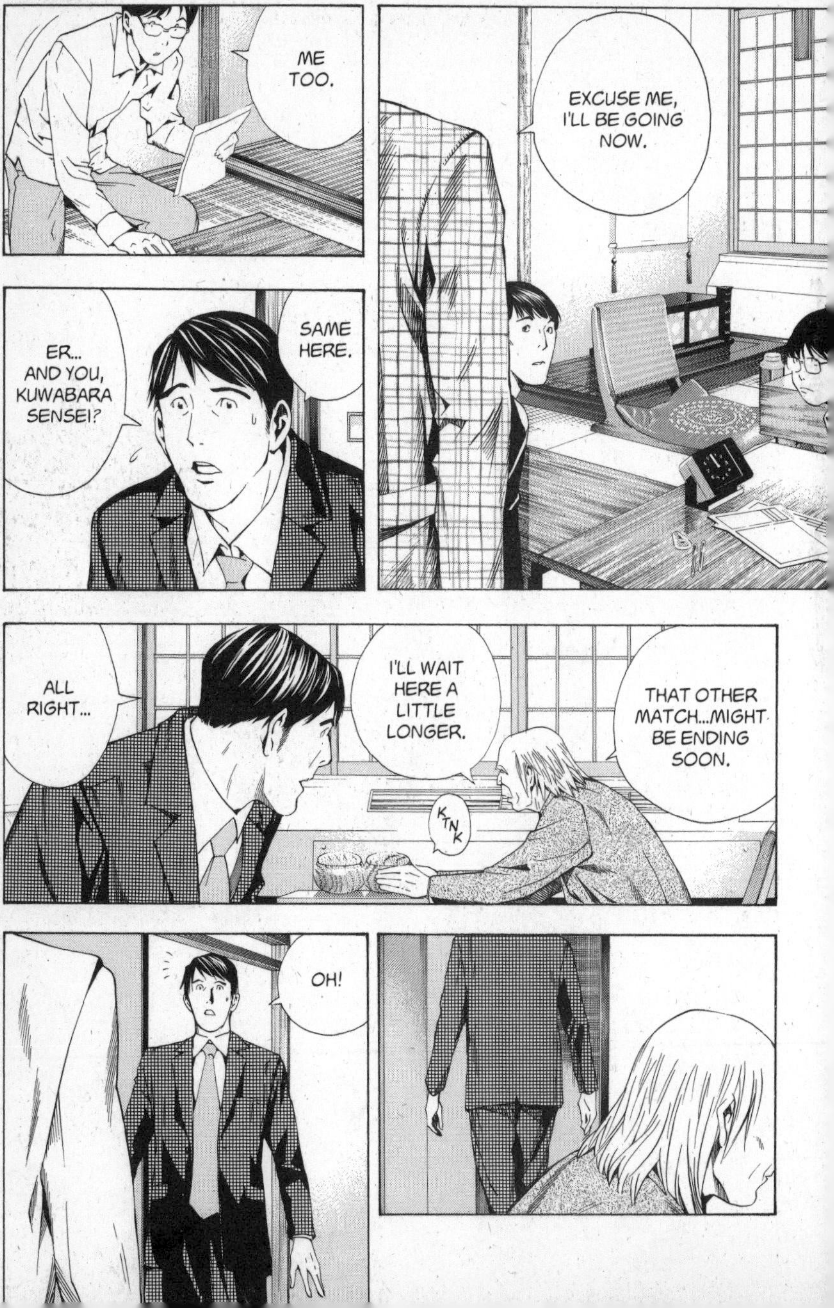
EXCUSE ME, I'LL BE GOING NOW.
ME TOO.
SAME HERE.
ER... AND YOU, KUWABARA SENSEI?
THAT OTHER MATCH...MIGHT BE ENDING SOON.
I'LL WAIT HERE A LITTLE LONGER.
KTNK
ALL RIGHT...
OH!

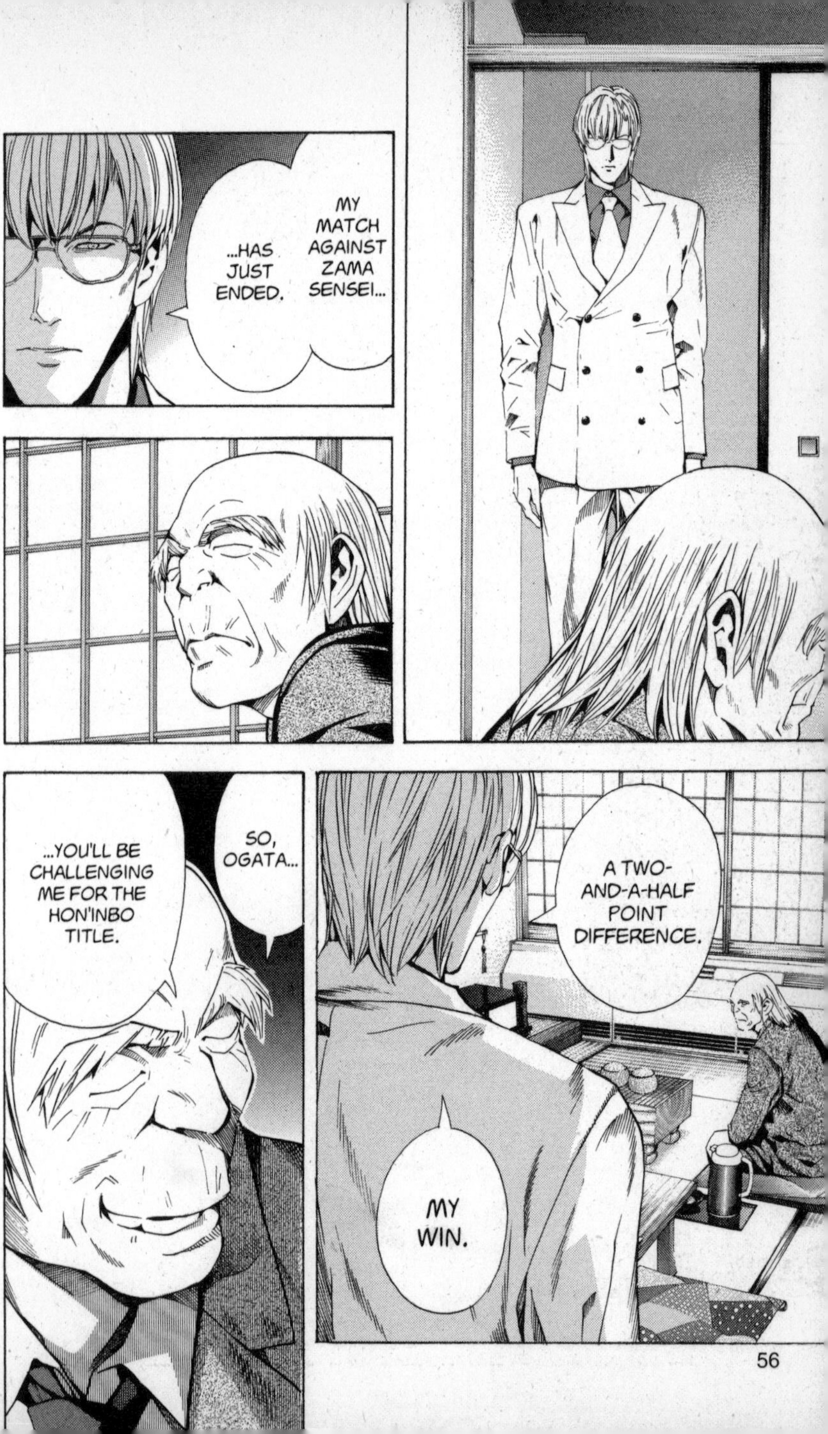
MY MATCH AGAINST ZAMA SENSEI...
...HAS JUST ENDED.
A TWO-AND-A-HALF POINT DIFFERENCE.
MY WIN.
SO, OGATA...
...YOU'LL BE CHALLENGING ME FOR THE HON'INBO TITLE.

READ THIS WAY

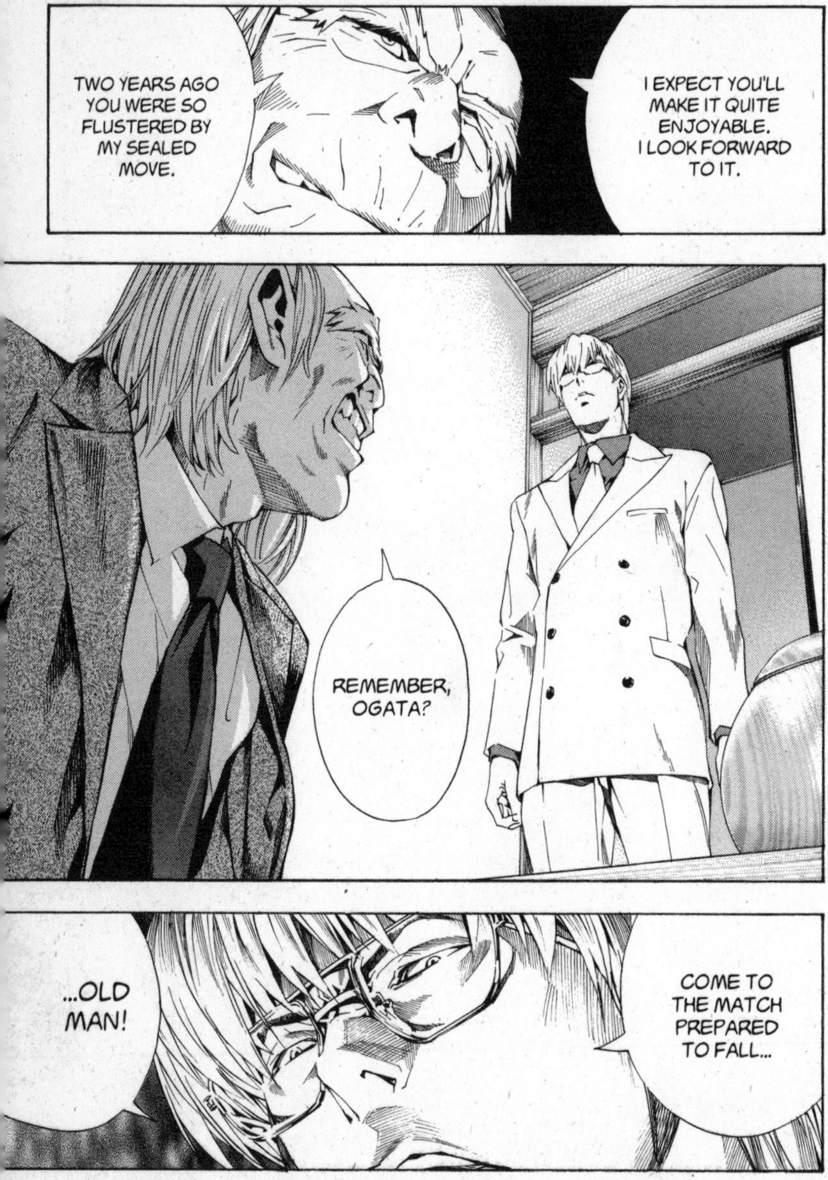
I EXPECT YOU'LL MAKE IT QUITE ENJOYABLE. I LOOK FORWARD TO IT.
TWO YEARS AGO YOU WERE SO FLUSTERED BY MY SEALED MOVE.
REMEMBER, OGATA?
COME TO THE MATCH PREPARED TO FALL...
...OLD MAN!

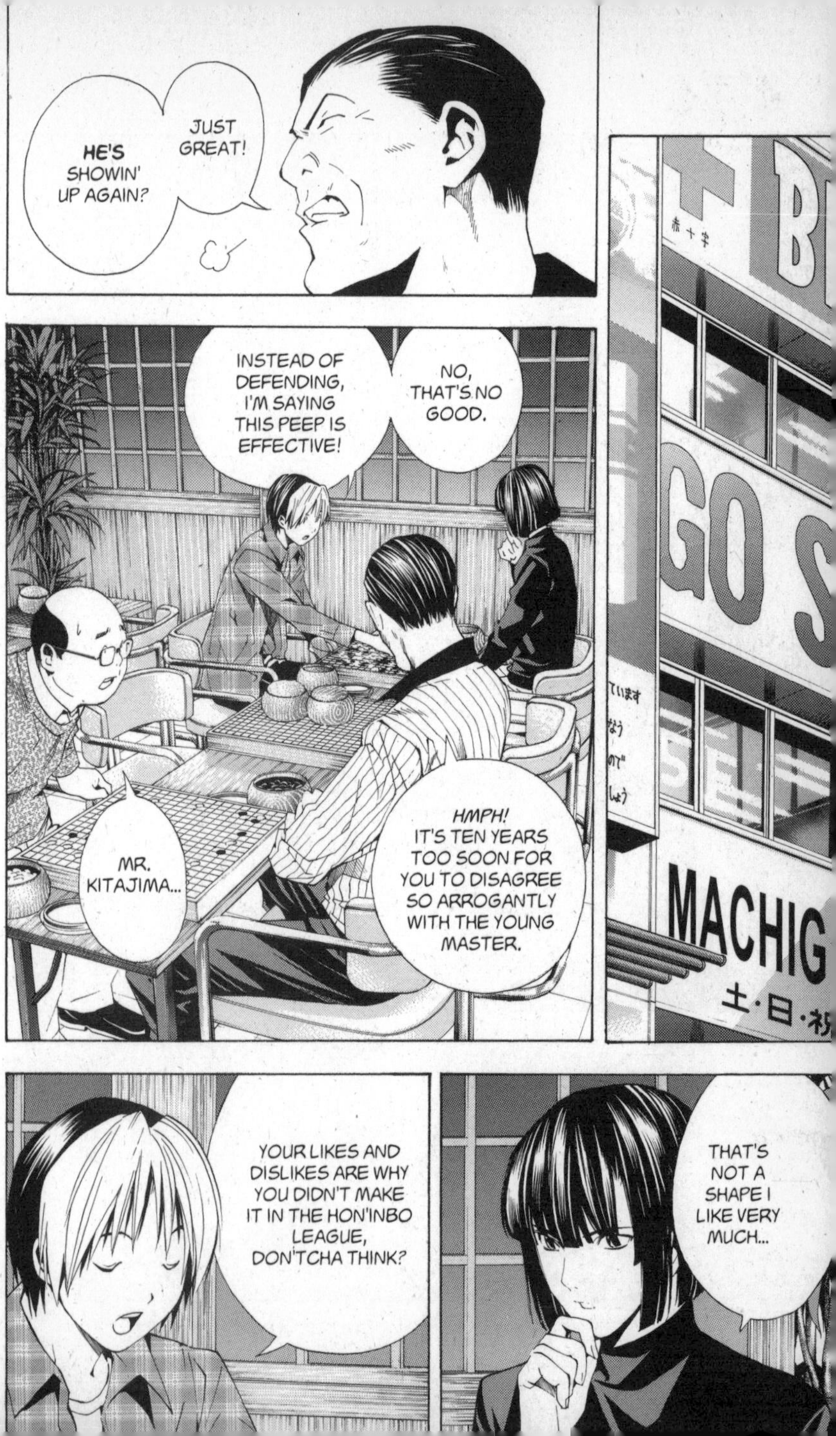
赤十字
JUST GREAT!
HE'S SHOWIN' UP AGAIN?
NO, THAT'S NO GOOD.
INSTEAD OF DEFENDING, I'M SAYING THIS PEEP IS EFFECTIVE!
HMPH! IT'S TEN YEARS TOO SOON FOR YOU TO DISAGREE SO ARROGANTLY WITH THE YOUNG MASTER.
MR. KITAJIMA...
THAT'S NOT A SHAPE I LIKE VERY MUCH...
YOUR LIKES AND DISLIKES ARE WHY YOU DIDN'T MAKE IT IN THE HON'INBO LEAGUE, DON'TCHA THINK?

READ THIS WAY

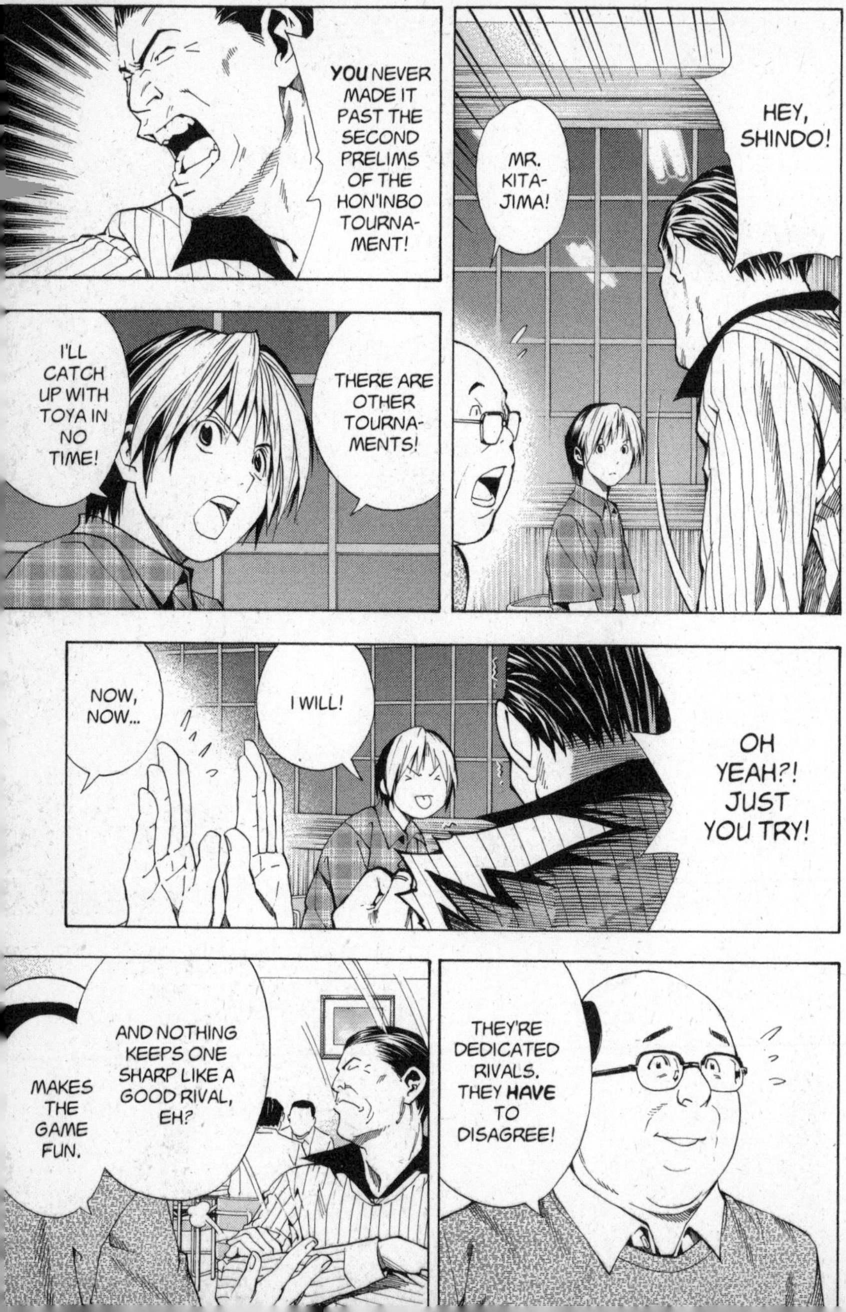
HEY, SHINDO!
MR. KITA-JIMA!
YOU NEVER MADE IT PAST THE SECOND PRELIMS OF THE HON'INBO TOURNA-MENT!
THERE ARE OTHER TOURNA-MENTS!
I'LL CATCH UP WITH TOYA IN NO TIME!
OH YEAH?! JUST YOU TRY!
I WILL!
NOW, NOW...
THEY'RE DEDICATED RIVALS. THEY HAVE TO DISAGREE!
AND NOTHING KEEPS ONE SHARP LIKE A GOOD RIVAL, EH?
MAKES THE GAME FUN.

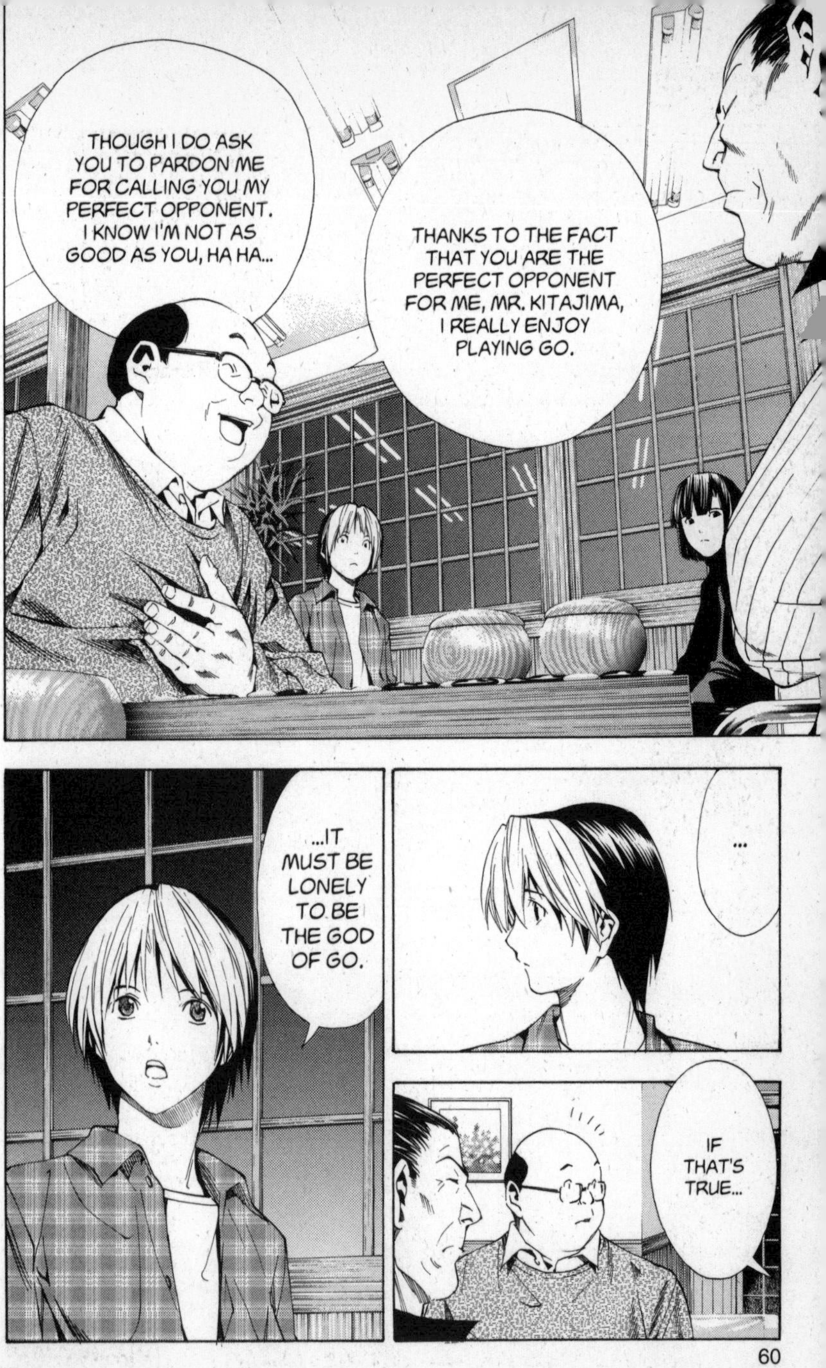
THANKS TO THE FACT THAT YOU ARE THE PERFECT OPPONENT FOR ME, MR. KITAJIMA, I REALLY ENJOY PLAYING GO.
THOUGH I DO ASK YOU TO PARDON ME FOR CALLING YOU MY PERFECT OPPONENT. I KNOW I'M NOT AS GOOD AS YOU, HA HA...
...
IF THAT'S TRUE...
...IT MUST BE LONELY TO BE THE GOD OF GO.

READ THIS WAY

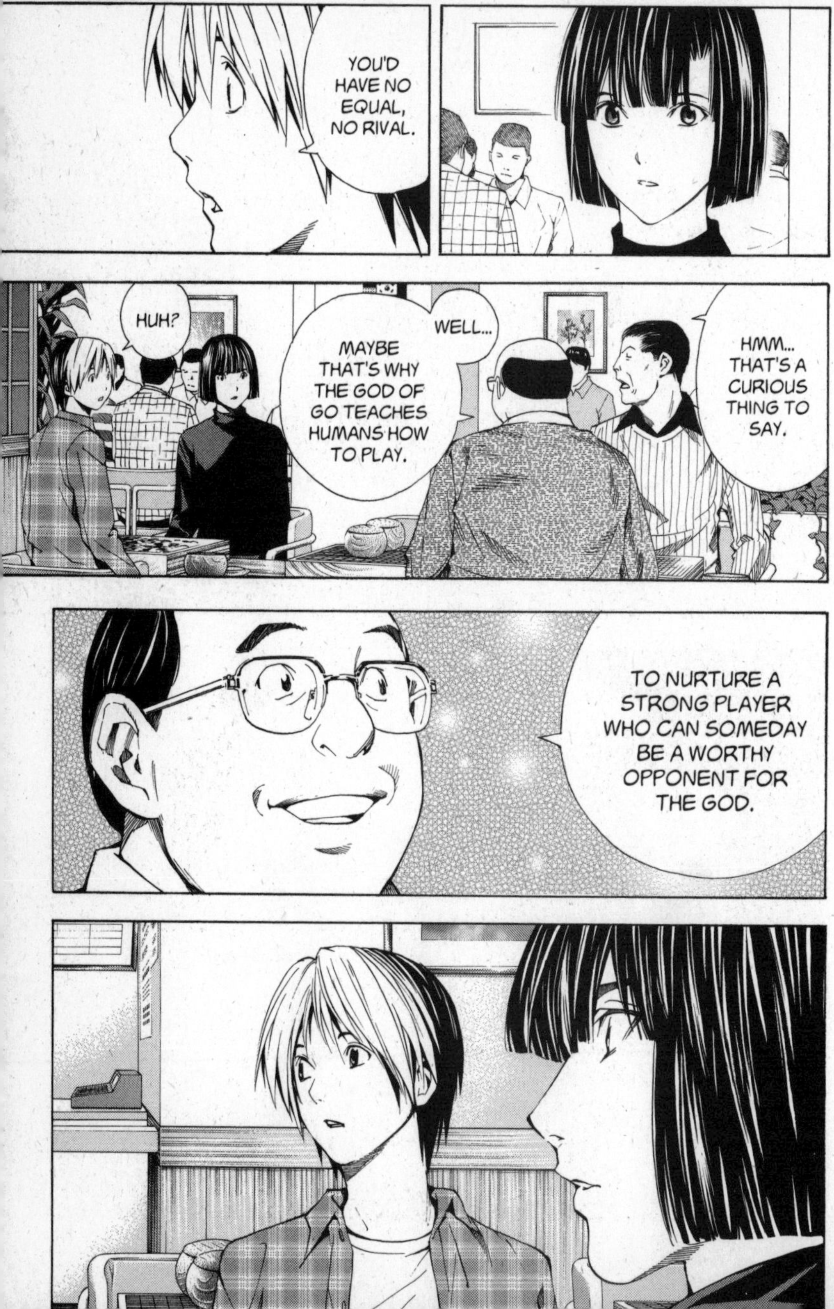
YOU'D HAVE NO EQUAL, NO RIVAL.
HMM... THAT'S A CURIOUS THING TO SAY.
WELL...
MAYBE THAT'S WHY THE GOD OF GO TEACHES HUMANS HOW TO PLAY.
HUH?
TO NURTURE A STRONG PLAYER WHO CAN SOMEDAY BE A WORTHY OPPONENT FOR THE GOD.

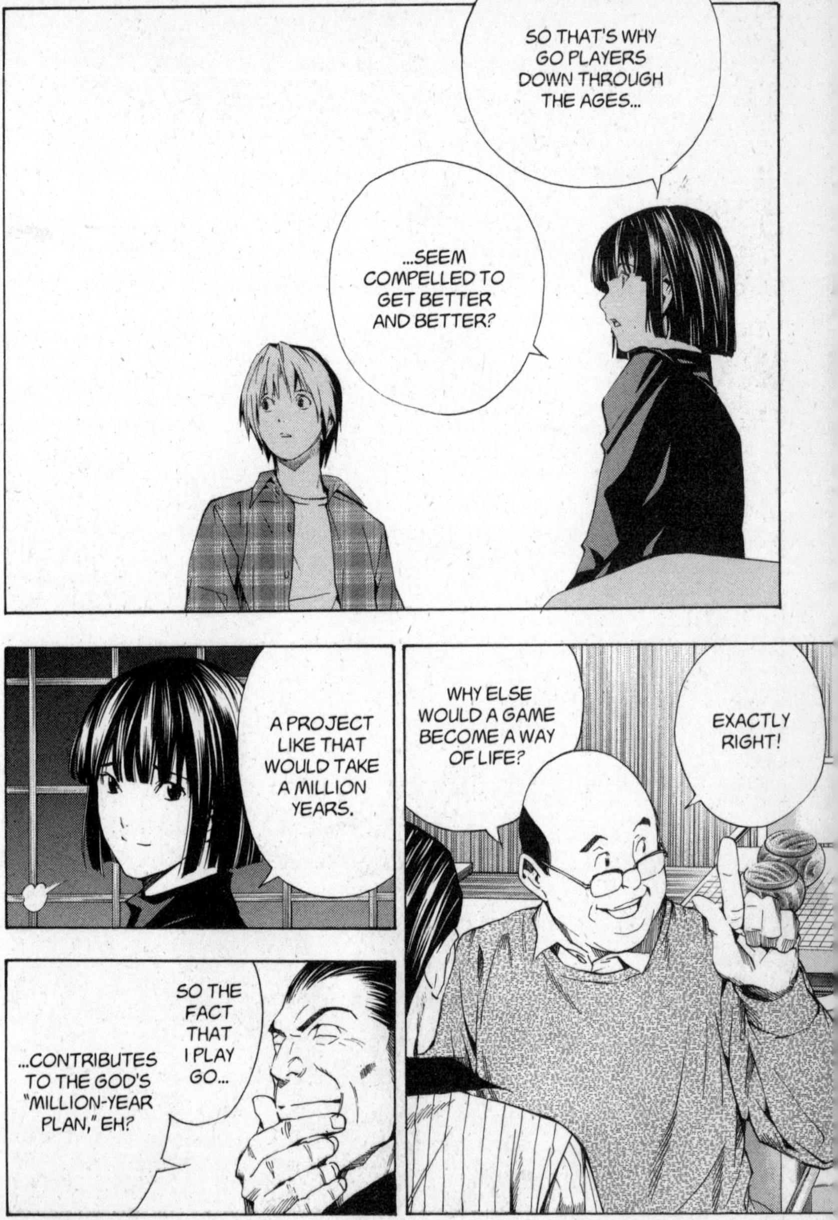
SO THAT'S WHY GO PLAYERS DOWN THROUGH THE AGES...
...SEEM COMPELLED TO GET BETTER AND BETTER?
EXACTLY RIGHT!
WHY ELSE WOULD A GAME BECOME A WAY OF LIFE?
A PROJECT LIKE THAT WOULD TAKE A MILLION YEARS.
SO THE FACT THAT I PLAY GO...
...CONTRIBUTES TO THE GOD'S "MILLION-YEAR PLAN," EH?

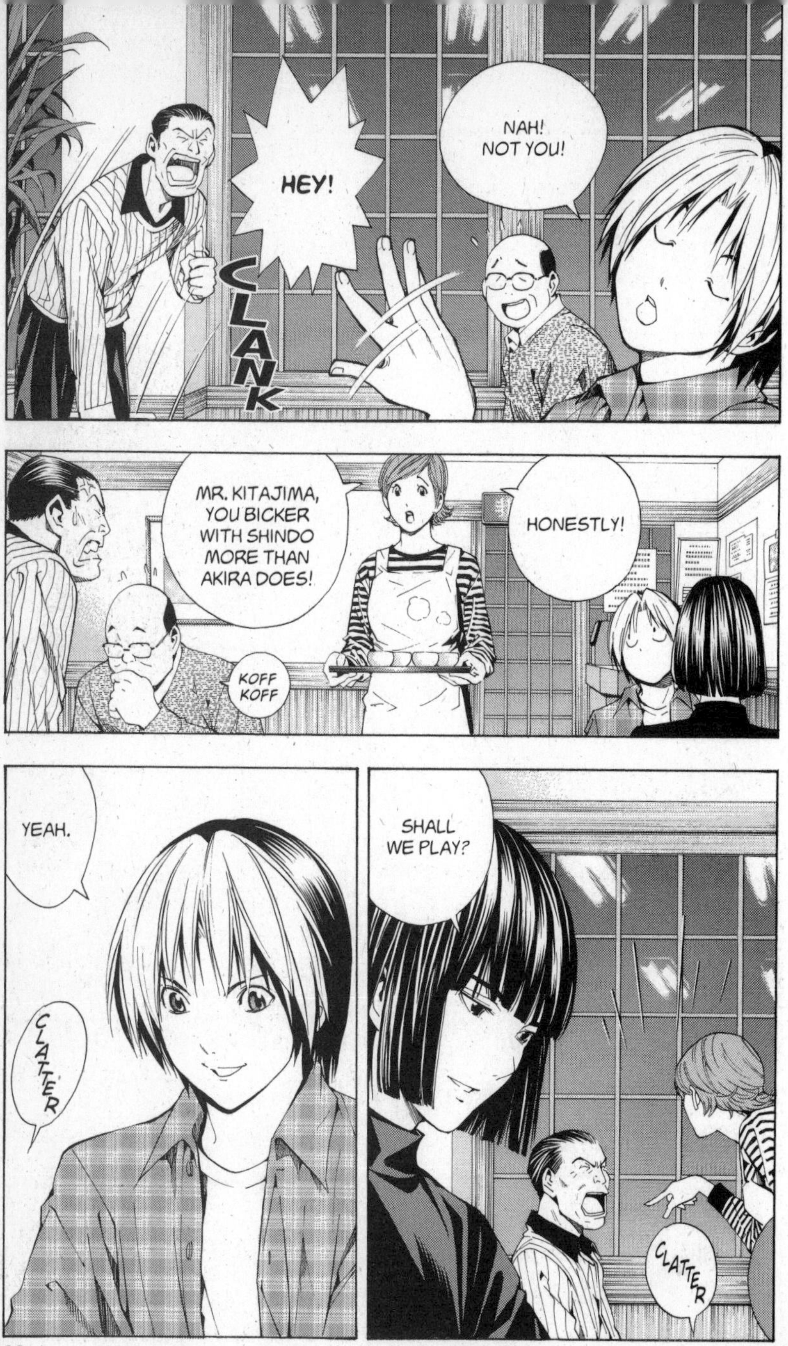
NAH! NOT YOU!
HEY!
CLANK
HONESTLY!
MR. KITAJIMA, YOU BICKER WITH SHINDO MORE THAN AKIRA DOES!
KOFF KOFF
SHALL WE PLAY?
CLATTER
YEAH.
CLATTER

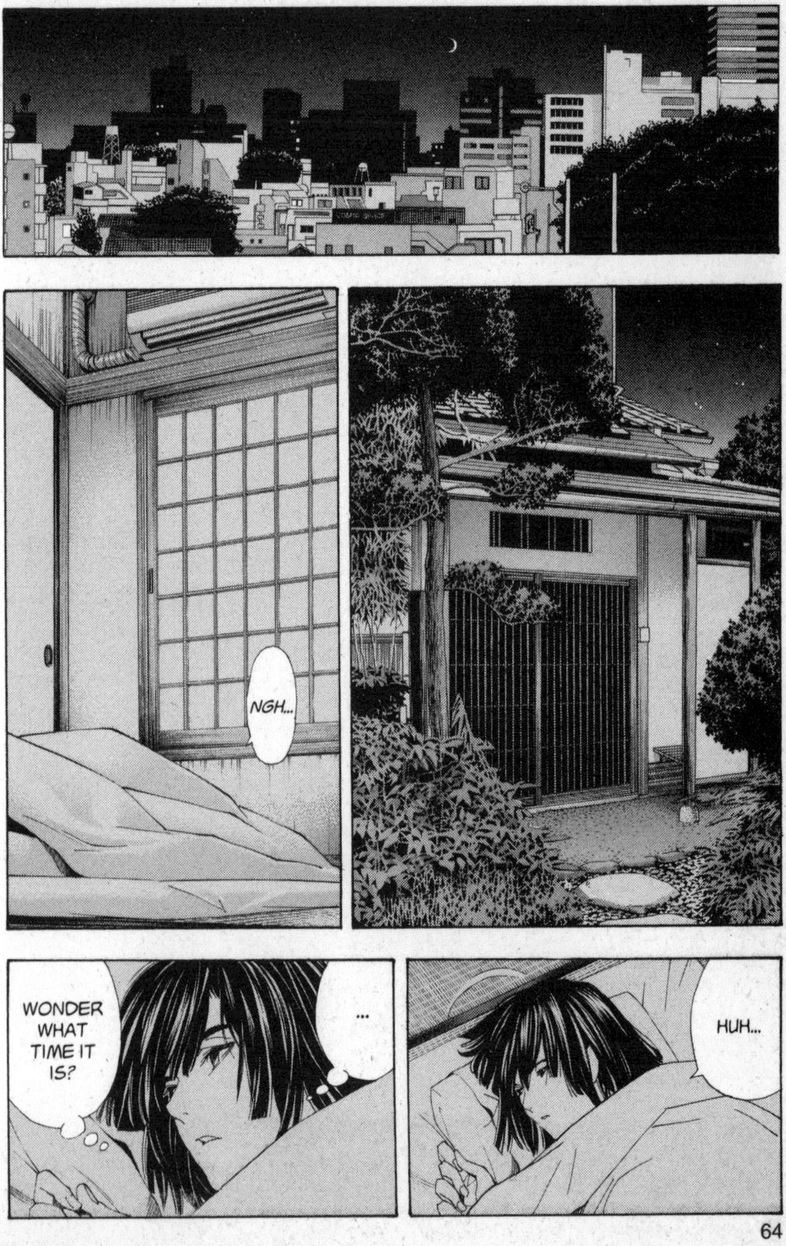
NGH...
HUH...
...
WONDER WHAT TIME IT IS?

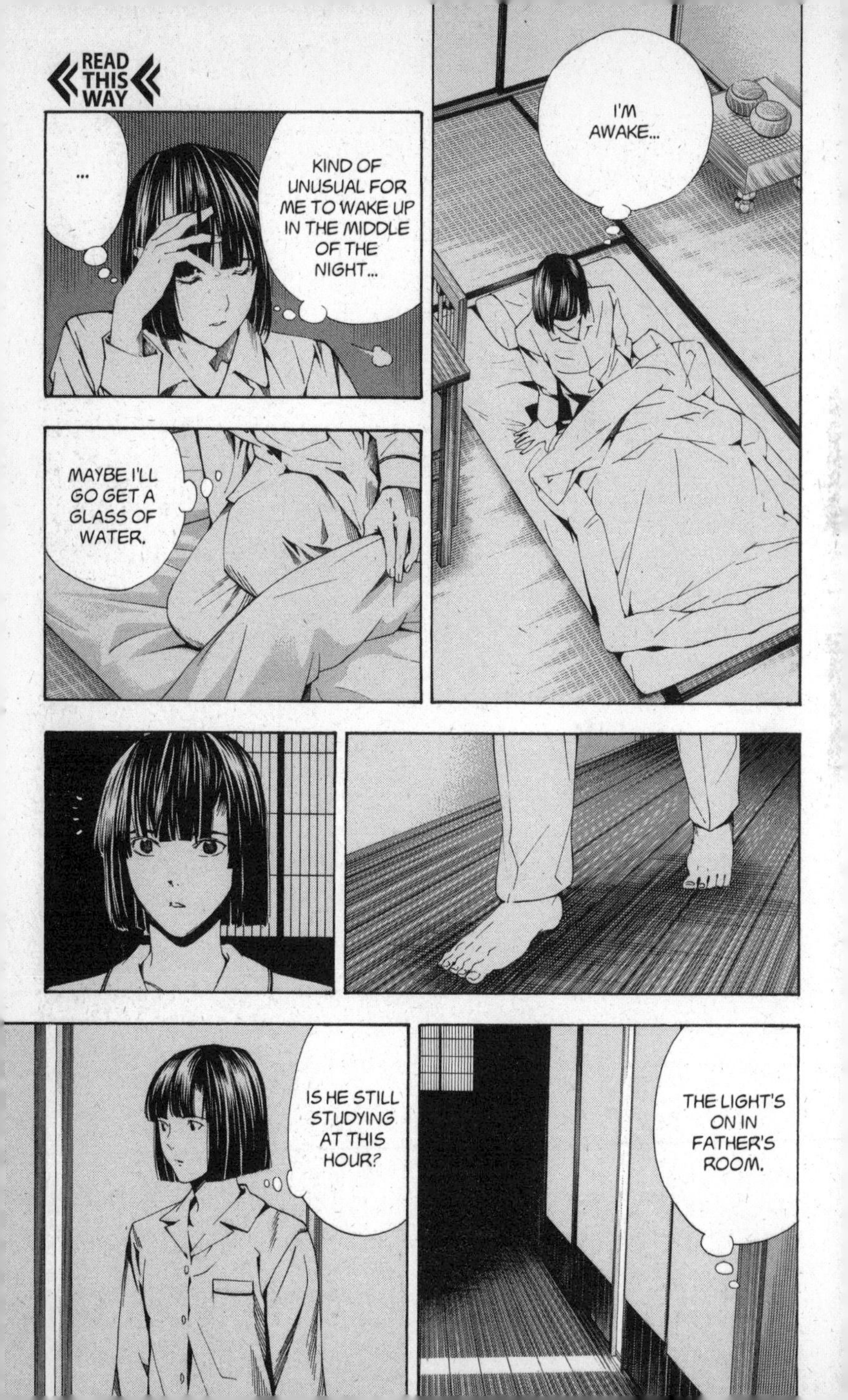
READ THIS WAY
I'M AWAKE...
KIND OF UNUSUAL FOR ME TO WAKE UP IN THE MIDDLE OF THE NIGHT...
...
MAYBE I'LL GO GET A GLASS OF WATER.
THE LIGHT'S ON IN FATHER'S ROOM.
IS HE STILL STUDYING AT THIS HOUR?

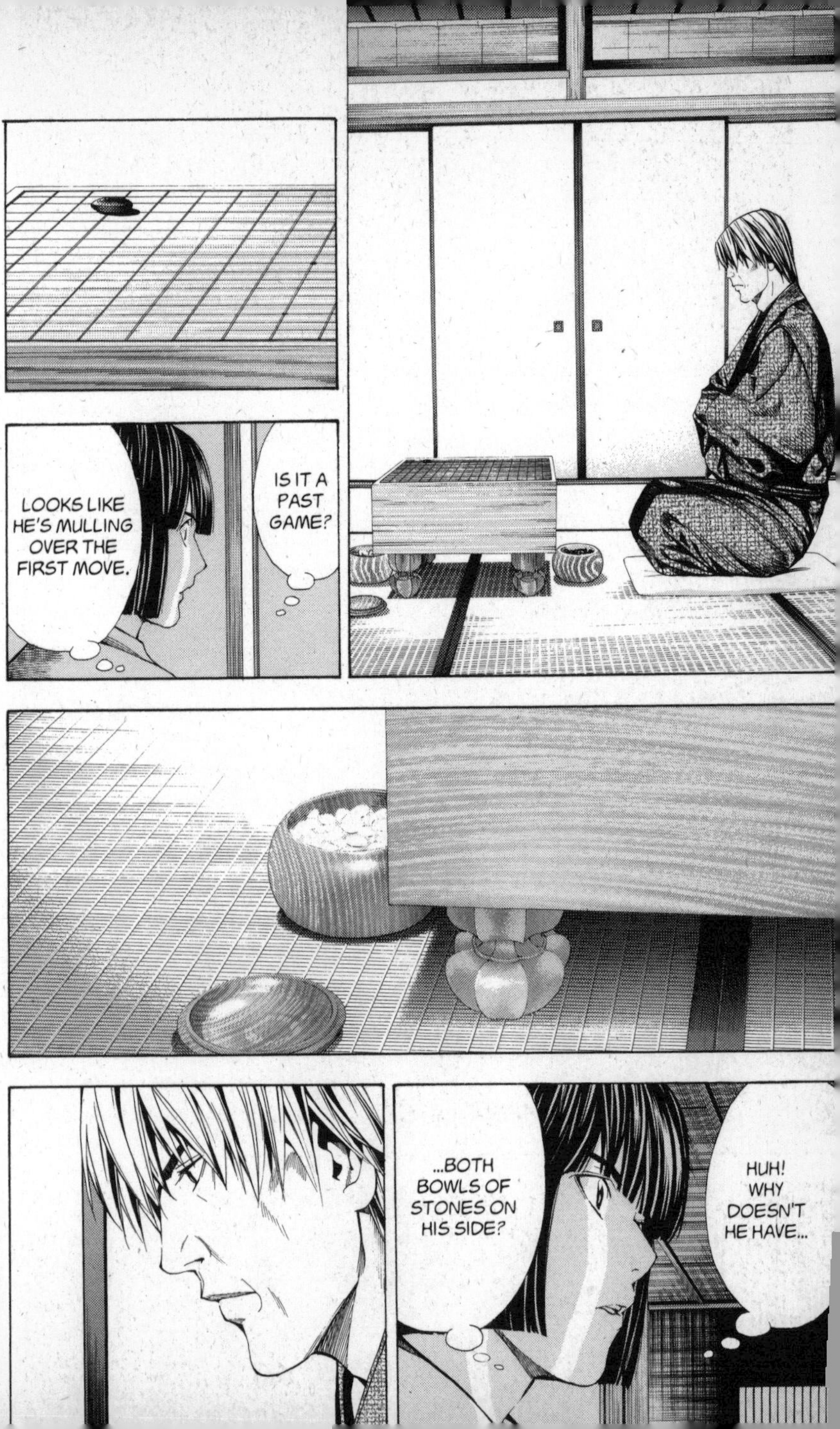
IS IT A PAST GAME?
LOOKS LIKE HE'S MULLING OVER THE FIRST MOVE.
HUH! WHY DOESN'T HE HAVE...
...BOTH BOWLS OF STONES ON HIS SIDE?

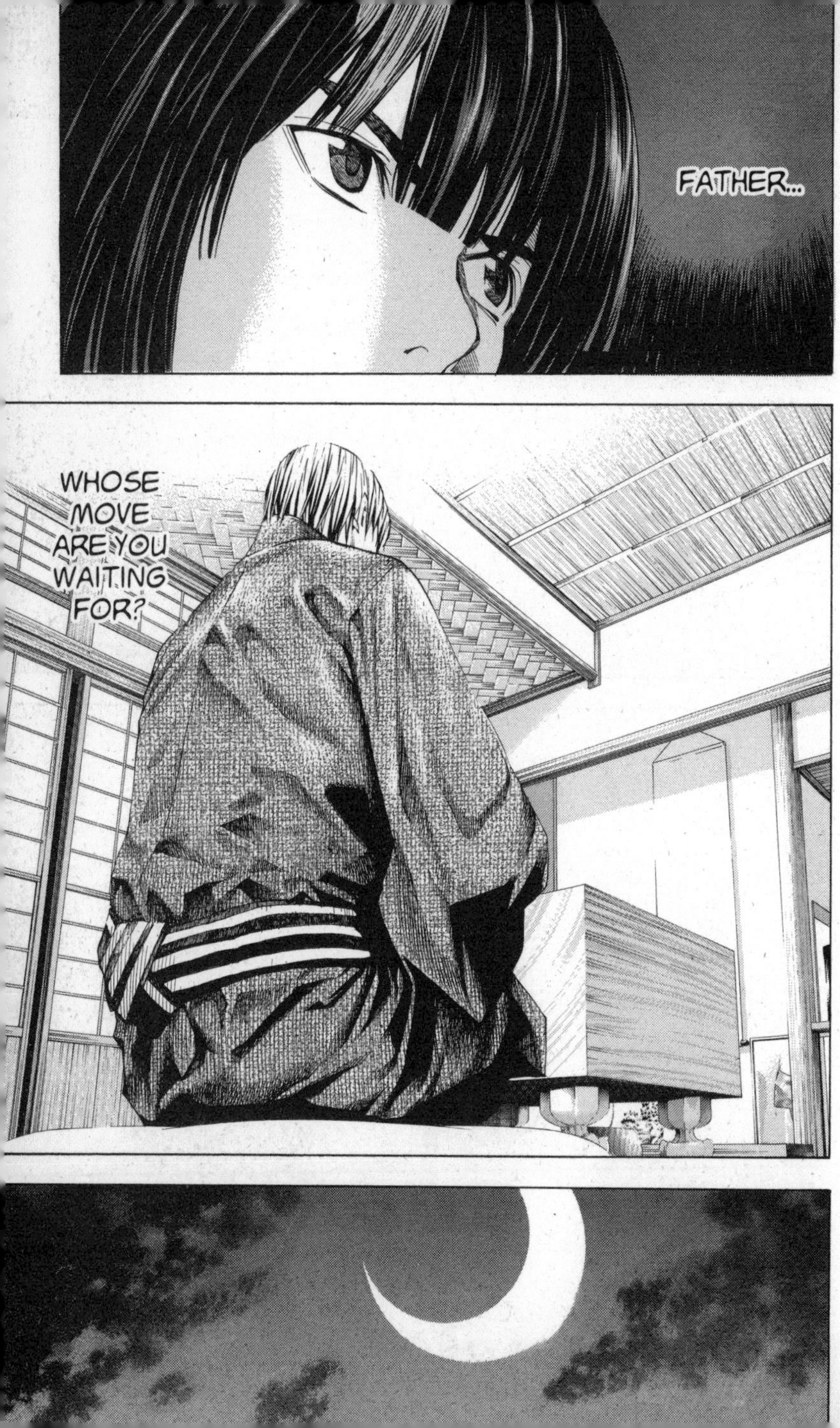
FATHER...
WHOSE MOVE ARE YOU WAITING FOR?

HIKARU **5** SHINDO

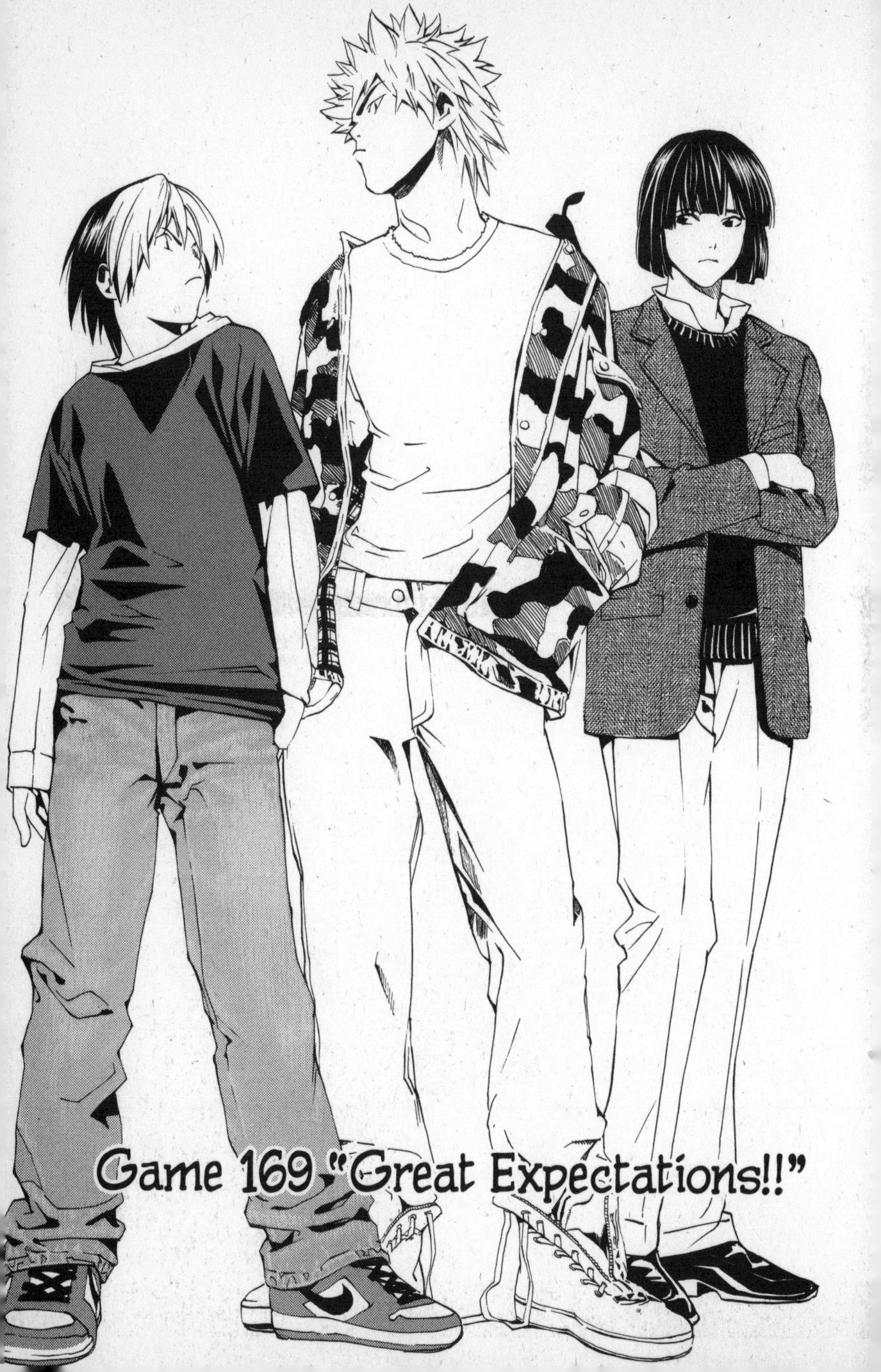
Game 169 "Great Expectations!!"

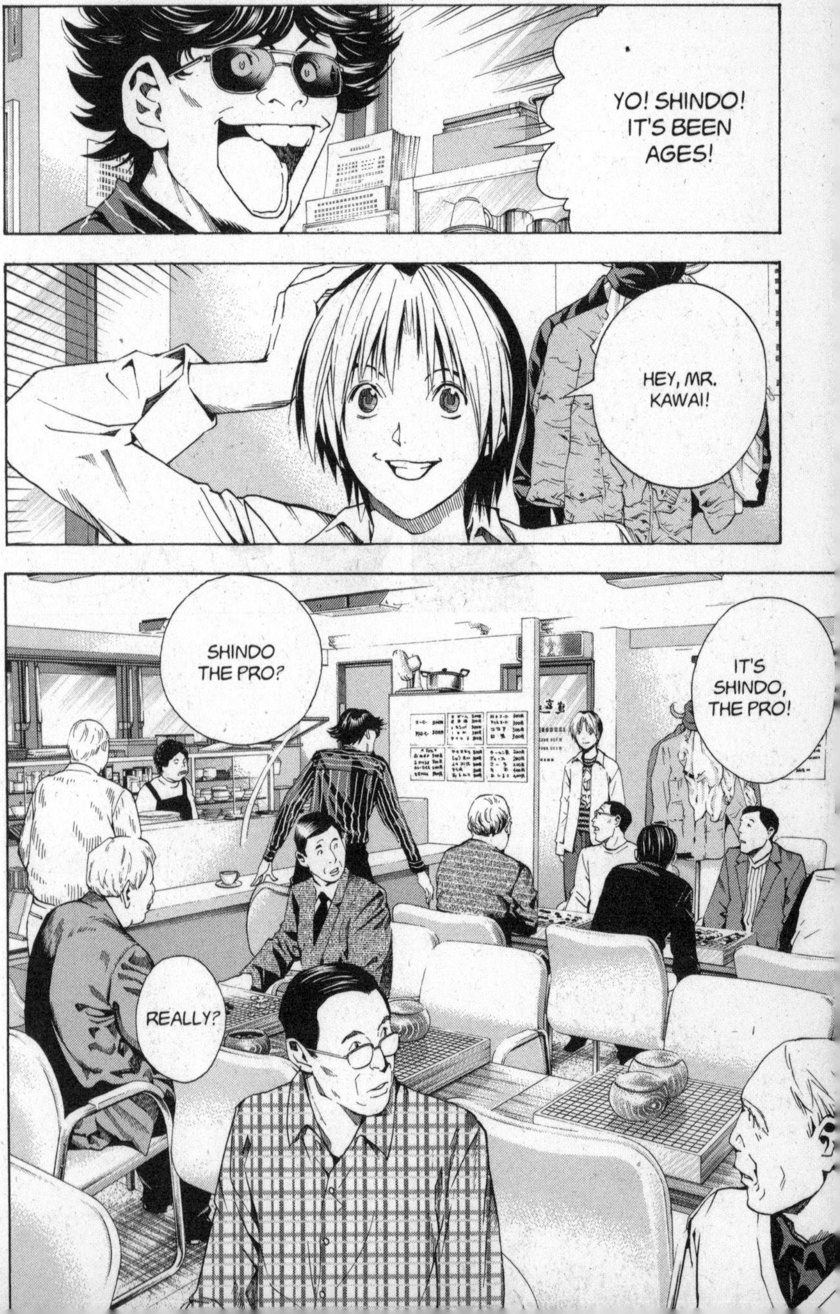
YO! SHINDO! IT'S BEEN AGES!
HEY, MR. KAWAI!
IT'S SHINDO, THE PRO!
SHINDO THE PRO?
REALLY?

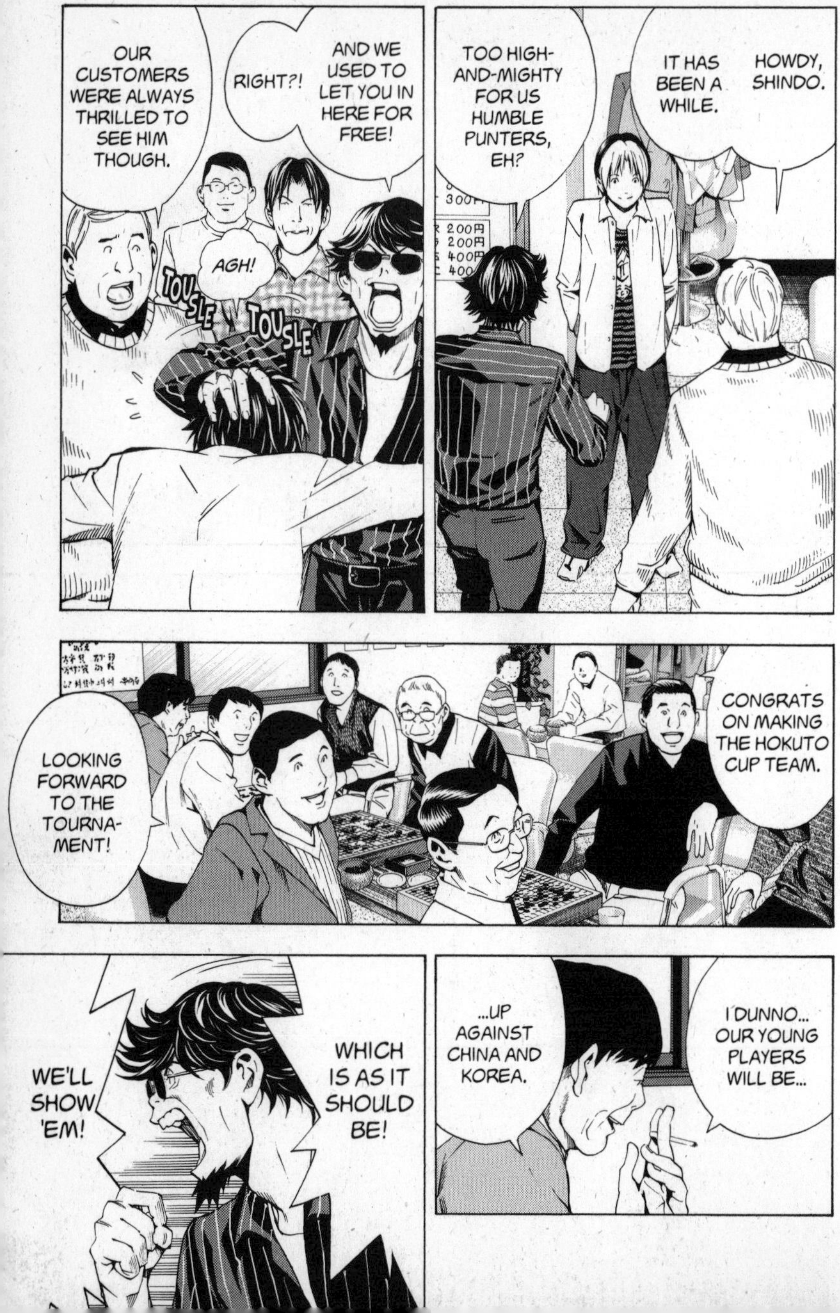
HOWDY, SHINDO.
IT HAS BEEN A WHILE.
TOO HIGH-AND-MIGHTY FOR US HUMBLE PUNTERS, EH?
AND WE USED TO LET YOU IN HERE FOR FREE!
RIGHT?!
OUR CUSTOMERS WERE ALWAYS THRILLED TO SEE HIM THOUGH.
AGH!
TOUSLE
TOUSLE
CONGRATS ON MAKING THE HOKUTO CUP TEAM.
LOOKING FORWARD TO THE TOURNA-MENT!
I DUNNO... OUR YOUNG PLAYERS WILL BE...
...UP AGAINST CHINA AND KOREA.
WHICH IS AS IT SHOULD BE!
WE'LL SHOW 'EM!

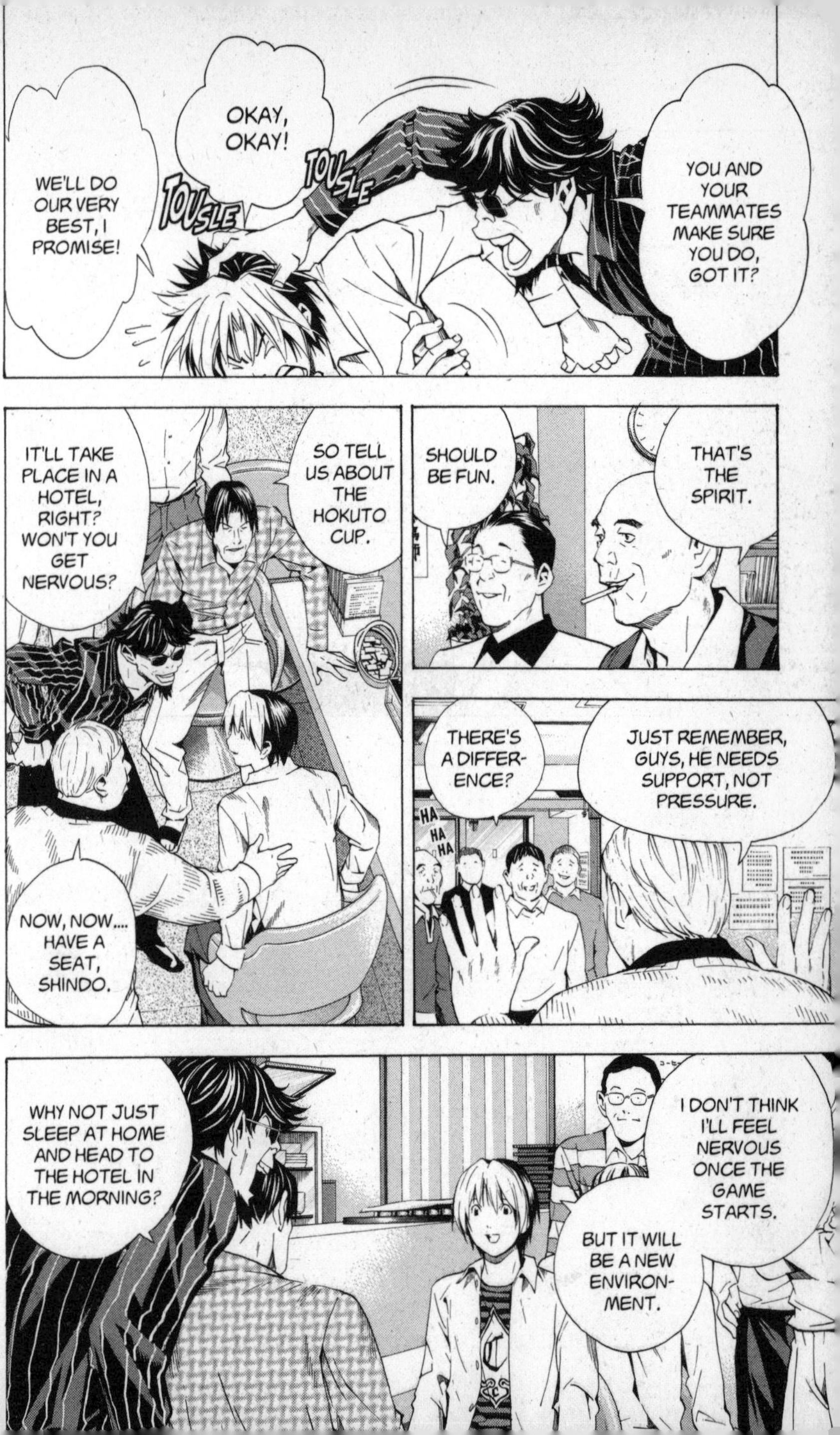
YOU AND YOUR TEAMMATES MAKE SURE YOU DO, GOT IT?
TOUSLE
OKAY, OKAY!
TOUSLE
WE'LL DO OUR VERY BEST, I PROMISE!
THAT'S THE SPIRIT.
SHOULD BE FUN.
JUST REMEMBER, GUYS, HE NEEDS SUPPORT, NOT PRESSURE.
THERE'S A DIFFERENCE?
HA HA HA
SO TELL US ABOUT THE HOKUTO CUP.
IT'LL TAKE PLACE IN A HOTEL, RIGHT? WON'T YOU GET NERVOUS?
NOW, NOW.... HAVE A SEAT, SHINDO.
I DON'T THINK I'LL FEEL NERVOUS ONCE THE GAME STARTS.
BUT IT WILL BE A NEW ENVIRONMENT.
WHY NOT JUST SLEEP AT HOME AND HEAD TO THE HOTEL IN THE MORNING?

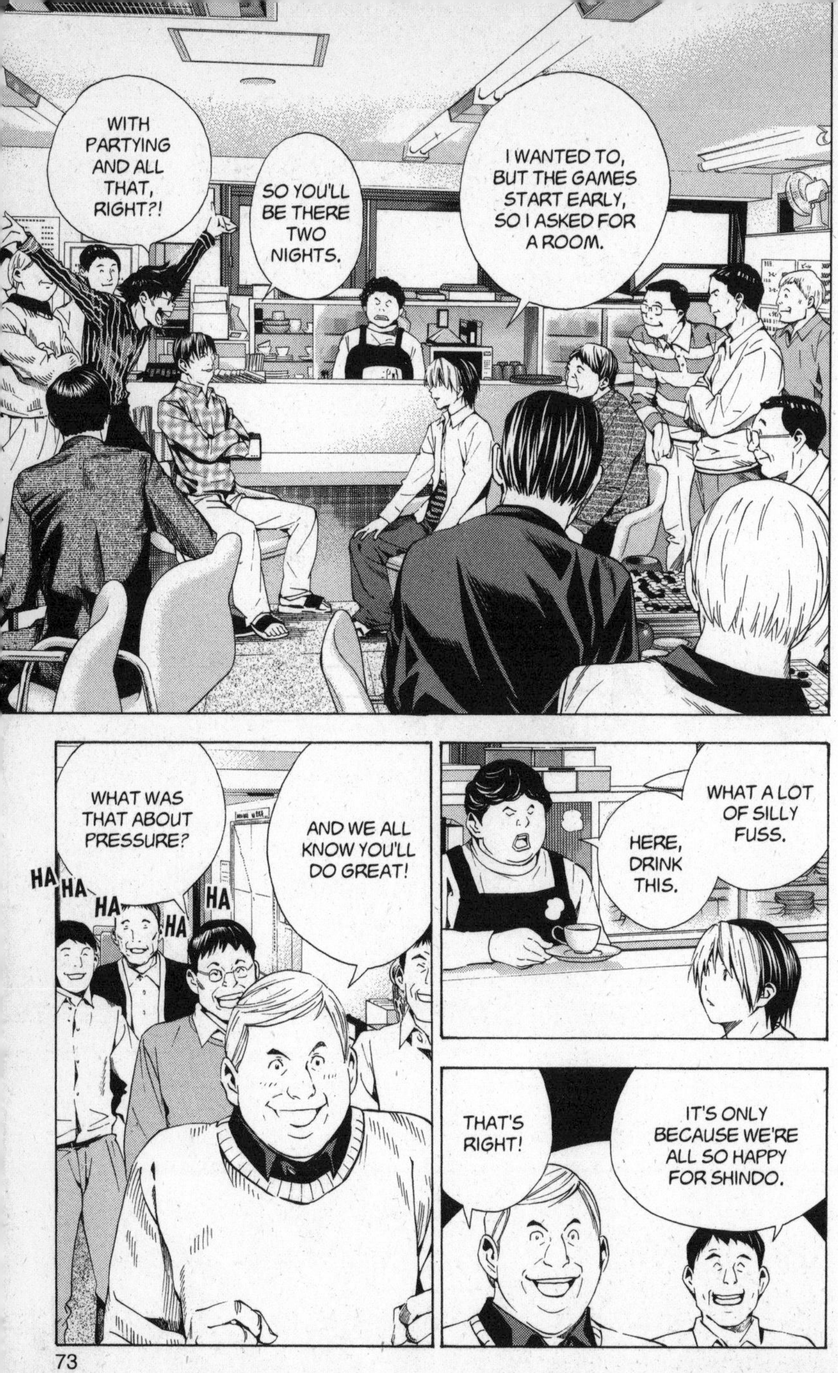
I WANTED TO, BUT THE GAMES START EARLY, SO I ASKED FOR A ROOM.
SO YOU'LL BE THERE TWO NIGHTS.
WITH PARTYING AND ALL THAT, RIGHT?!
WHAT A LOT OF SILLY FUSS.
HERE, DRINK THIS.
IT'S ONLY BECAUSE WE'RE ALL SO HAPPY FOR SHINDO.
THAT'S RIGHT!
AND WE ALL KNOW YOU'LL DO GREAT!
WHAT WAS THAT ABOUT PRESSURE?
HA
HA
HA
HA
HA

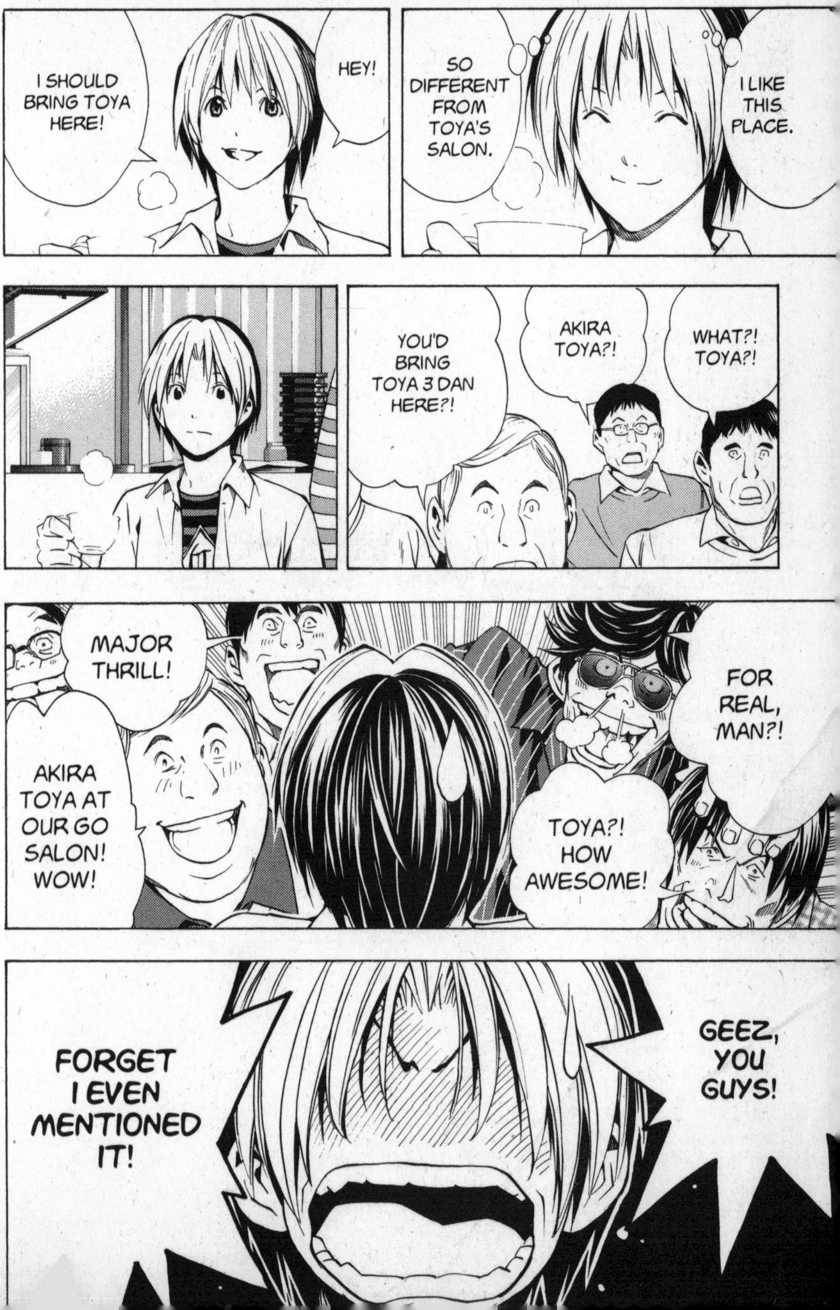
I LIKE THIS PLACE.
SO DIFFERENT FROM TOYA'S SALON.
HEY!
I SHOULD BRING TOYA HERE!
WHAT?! TOYA?!
AKIRA TOYA?!
YOU'D BRING TOYA 3 DAN HERE?!
FOR REAL, MAN?!
TOYA?! HOW AWESOME!
MAJOR THRILL!
AKIRA TOYA AT OUR GO SALON! WOW!
GEEZ, YOU GUYS!
FORGET I EVEN MENTIONED IT!

READ THIS WAY

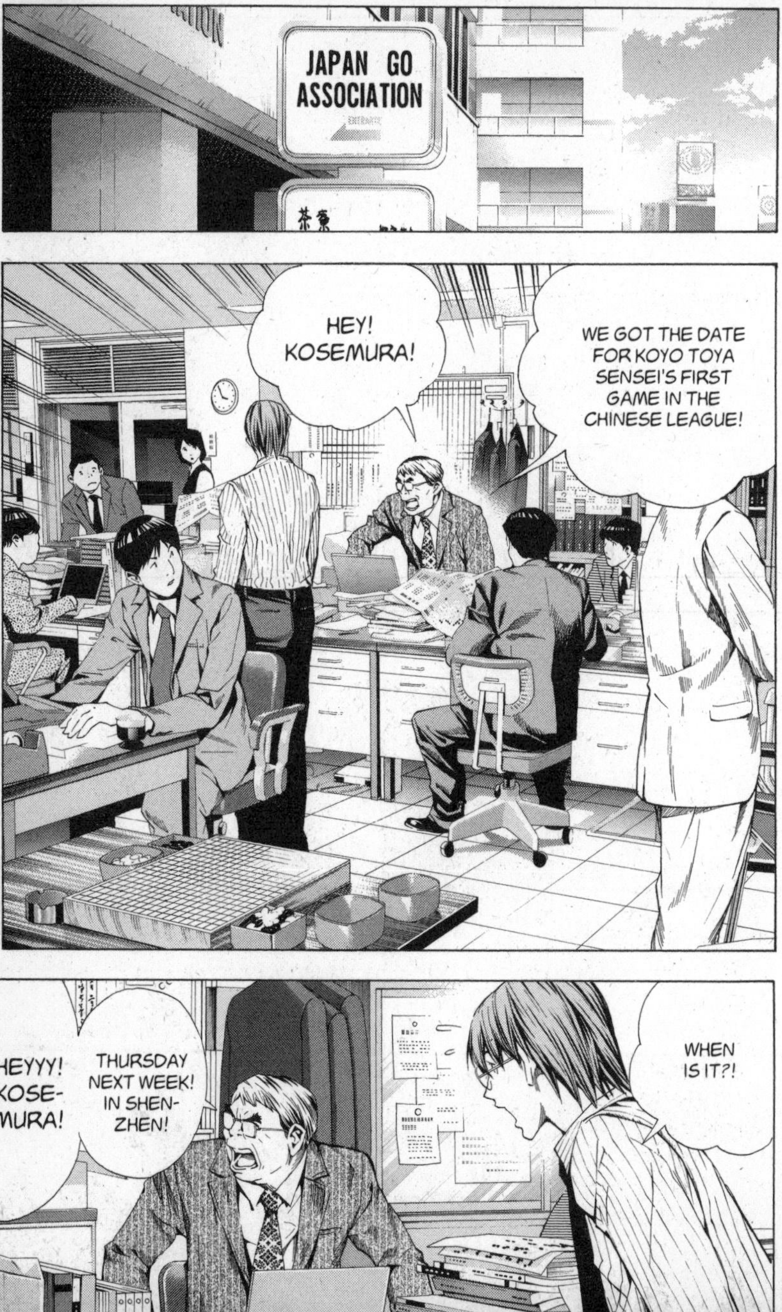
JAPAN GO ASSOCIATION
WE GOT THE DATE FOR KOYO TOYA SENSEI'S FIRST GAME IN THE CHINESE LEAGUE!
HEY! KOSEMURA!
WHEN IS IT?!
THURSDAY NEXT WEEK! IN SHEN-ZHEN!
HEYYY! KOSE-MURA!

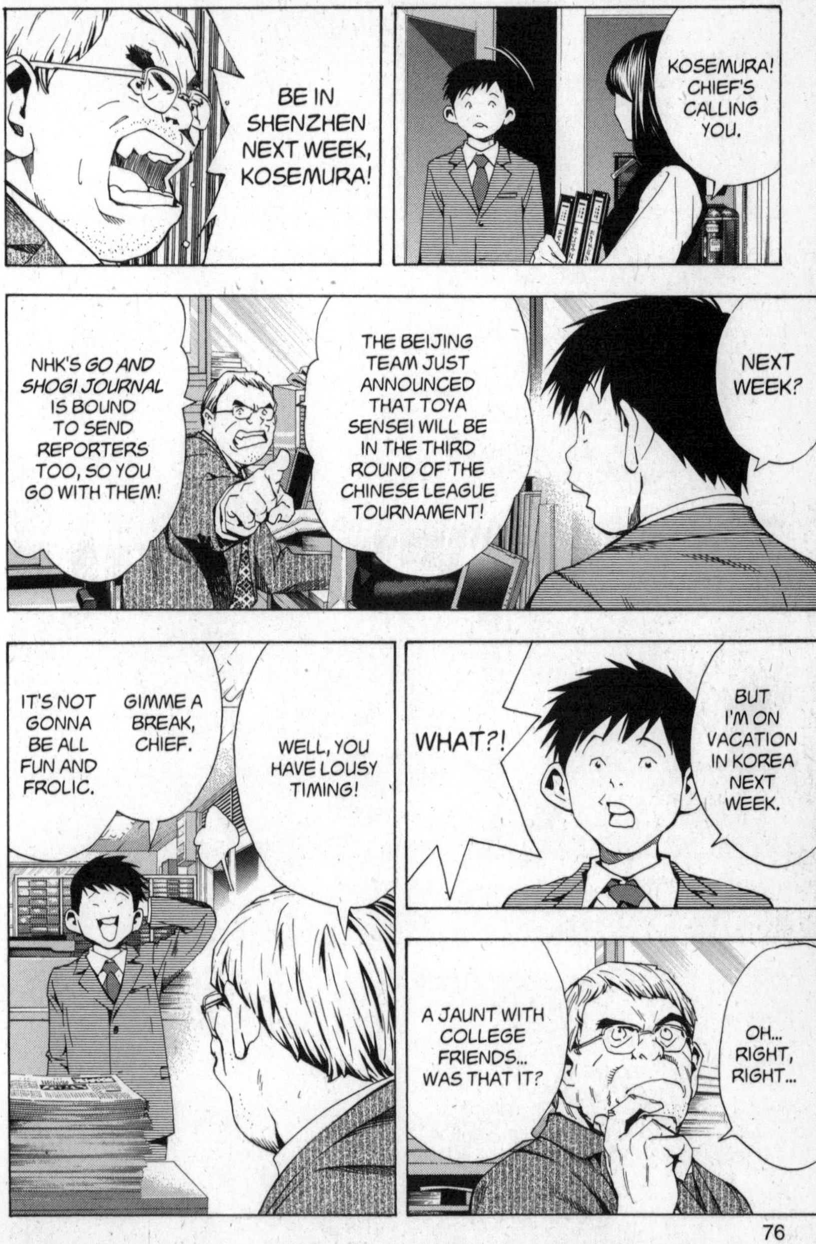
KOSEMURA! CHIEF'S CALLING YOU.
BE IN SHENZHEN NEXT WEEK, KOSEMURA!
NEXT WEEK?
THE BEIJING TEAM JUST ANNOUNCED THAT TOYA SENSEI WILL BE IN THE THIRD ROUND OF THE CHINESE LEAGUE TOURNAMENT!
NHK'S *GO AND SHOGI JOURNAL* IS BOUND TO SEND REPORTERS TOO, SO YOU GO WITH THEM!
WHAT?!
BUT I'M ON VACATION IN KOREA NEXT WEEK.
OH... RIGHT, RIGHT...
A JAUNT WITH COLLEGE FRIENDS... WAS THAT IT?
WELL, YOU HAVE LOUSY TIMING!
GIMME A BREAK, CHIEF.
IT'S NOT GONNA BE ALL FUN AND FROLIC.

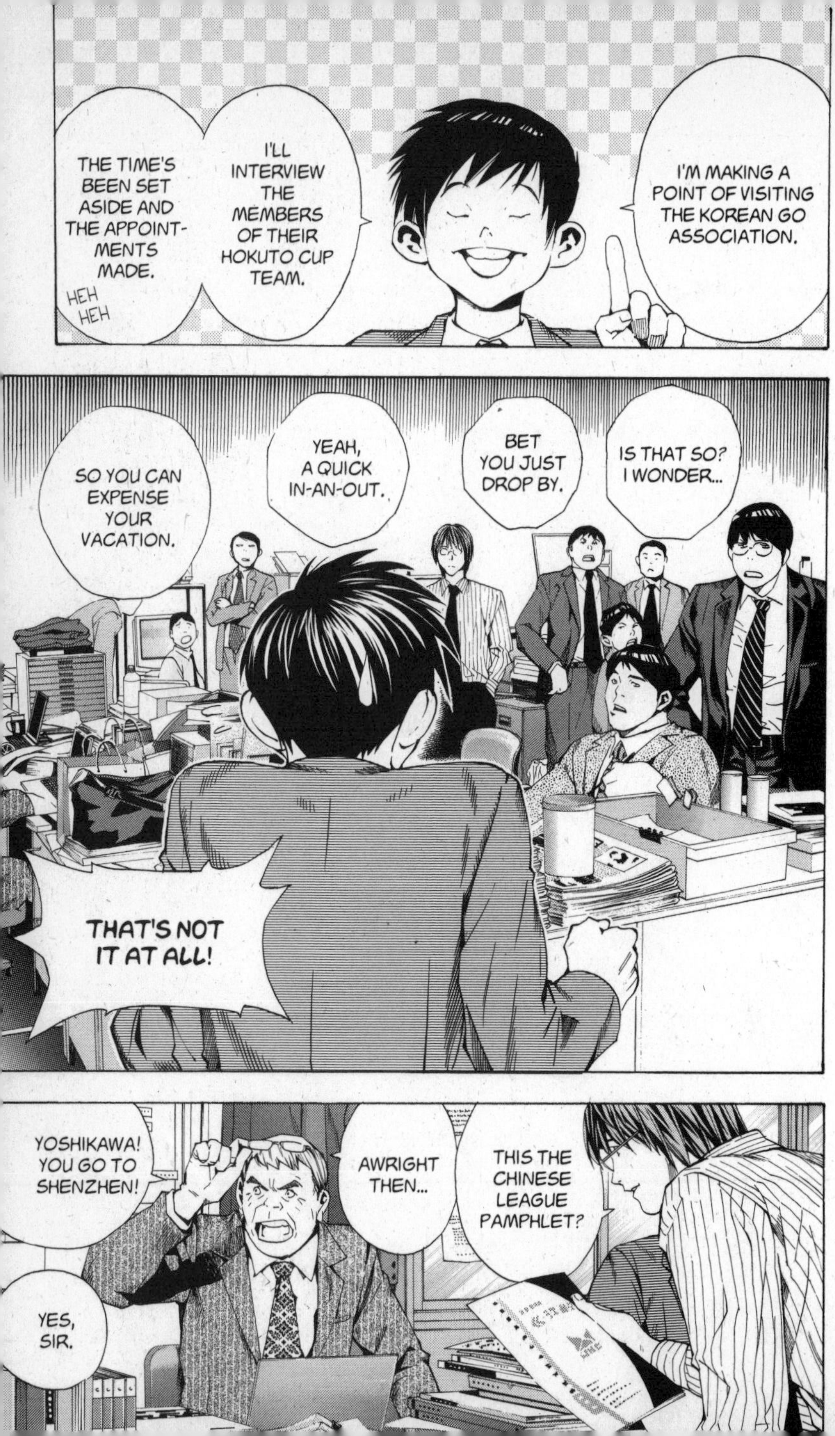
I'M MAKING A POINT OF VISITING THE KOREAN GO ASSOCIATION.
I'LL INTERVIEW THE MEMBERS OF THEIR HOKUTO CUP TEAM.
THE TIME'S BEEN SET ASIDE AND THE APPOINT-MENTS MADE.
HEH HEH
IS THAT SO? I WONDER...
BET YOU JUST DROP BY.
YEAH, A QUICK IN-AN-OUT.
SO YOU CAN EXPENSE YOUR VACATION.
THAT'S NOT IT AT ALL!
THIS THE CHINESE LEAGUE PAMPHLET?
AWRIGHT THEN...
YOSHIKAWA! YOU GO TO SHENZHEN!
YES, SIR.

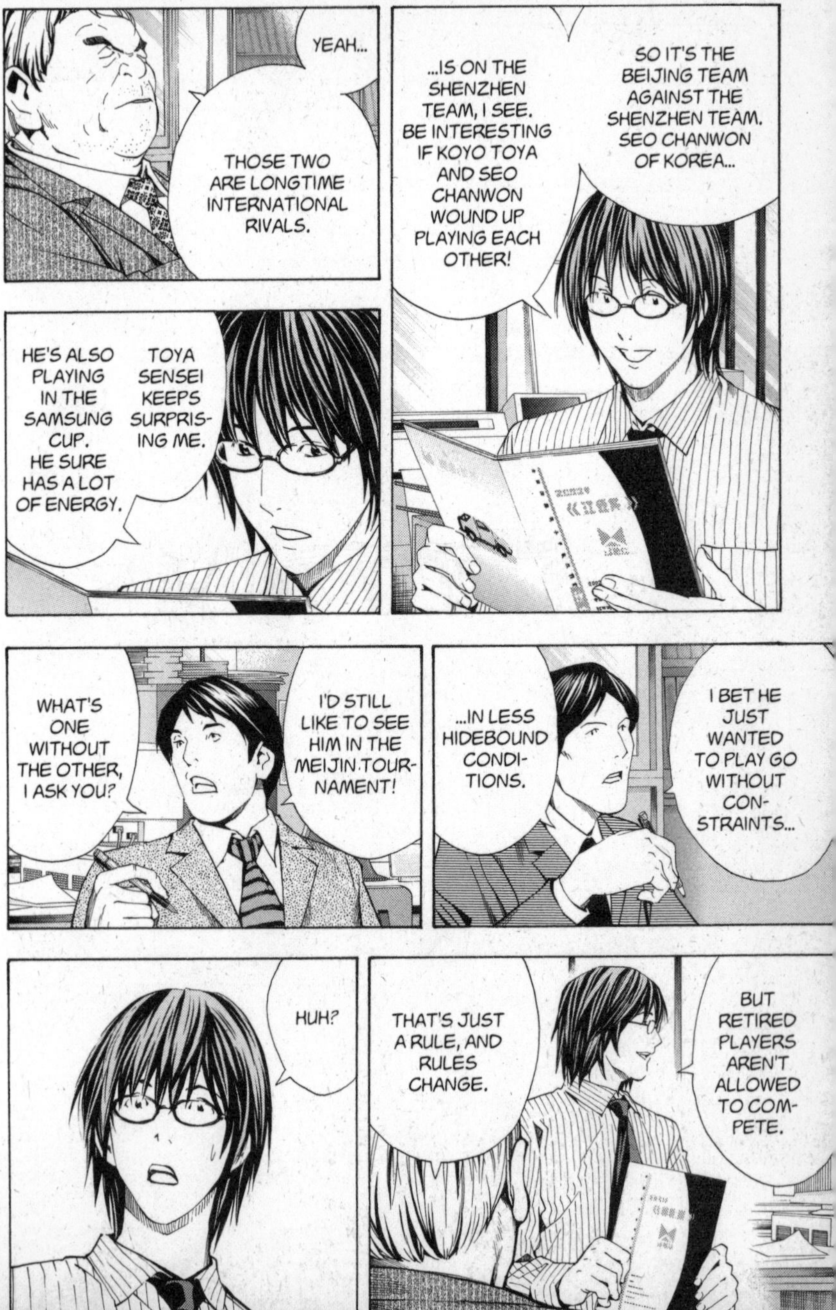
SO IT'S THE BEIJING TEAM AGAINST THE SHENZHEN TEAM. SEO CHANWON OF KOREA...
...IS ON THE SHENZHEN TEAM, I SEE. BE INTERESTING IF KOYO TOYA AND SEO CHANWON WOUND UP PLAYING EACH OTHER!
YEAH...
THOSE TWO ARE LONGTIME INTERNATIONAL RIVALS.
TOYA SENSEI KEEPS SURPRIS-ING ME.
HE'S ALSO PLAYING IN THE SAMSUNG CUP. HE SURE HAS A LOT OF ENERGY.
I BET HE JUST WANTED TO PLAY GO WITHOUT CON-STRAINTS...
...IN LESS HIDEBOUND CONDI-TIONS.
I'D STILL LIKE TO SEE HIM IN THE MEIJIN TOUR-NAMENT!
WHAT'S ONE WITHOUT THE OTHER, I ASK YOU?
BUT RETIRED PLAYERS AREN'T ALLOWED TO COM-PETE.
THAT'S JUST A RULE, AND RULES CHANGE.
HUH?

READ THIS WAY

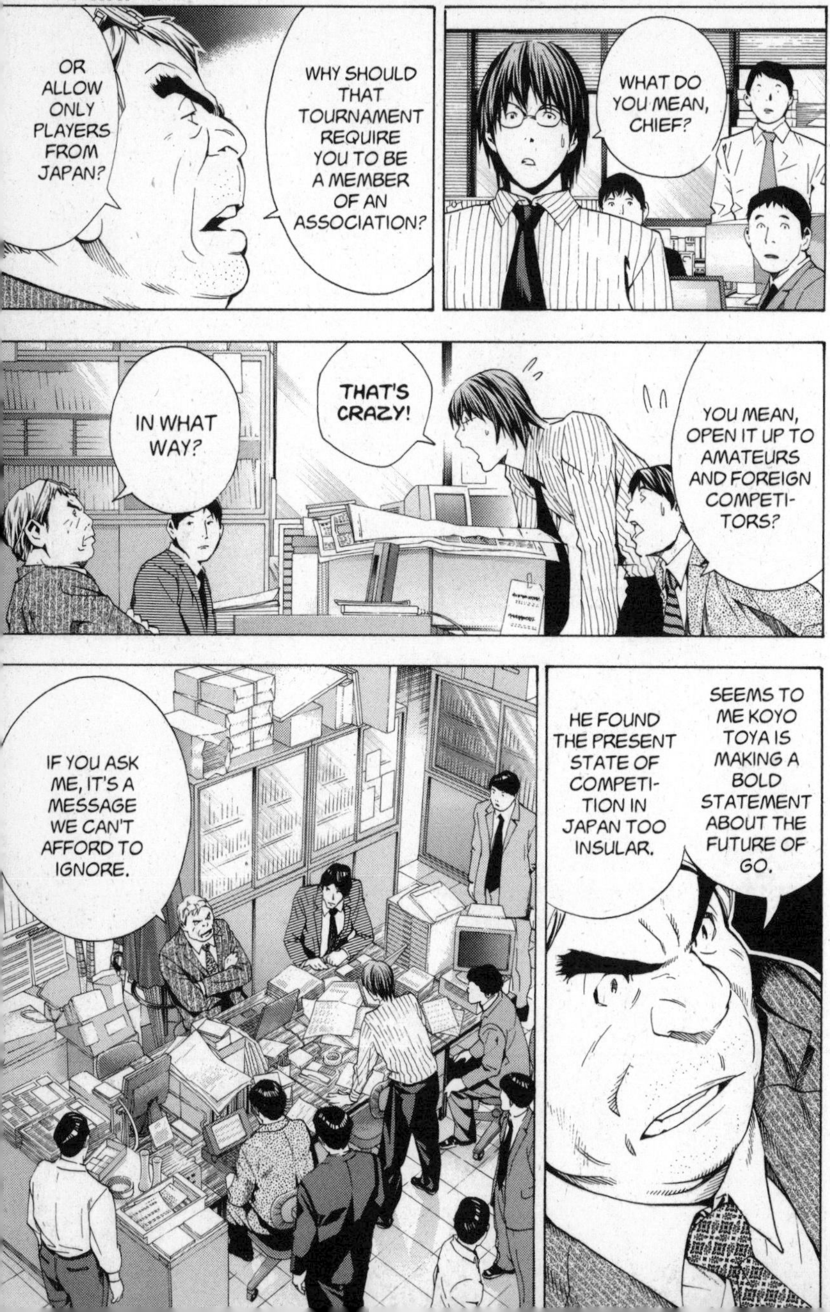
WHAT DO YOU MEAN, CHIEF?
WHY SHOULD THAT TOURNAMENT REQUIRE YOU TO BE A MEMBER OF AN ASSOCIATION?
OR ALLOW ONLY PLAYERS FROM JAPAN?
YOU MEAN, OPEN IT UP TO AMATEURS AND FOREIGN COMPETI-TORS?
THAT'S CRAZY!
IN WHAT WAY?
SEEMS TO ME KOYO TOYA IS MAKING A BOLD STATEMENT ABOUT THE FUTURE OF GO.
HE FOUND THE PRESENT STATE OF COMPETI-TION IN JAPAN TOO INSULAR.
IF YOU ASK ME, IT'S A MESSAGE WE CAN'T AFFORD TO IGNORE.

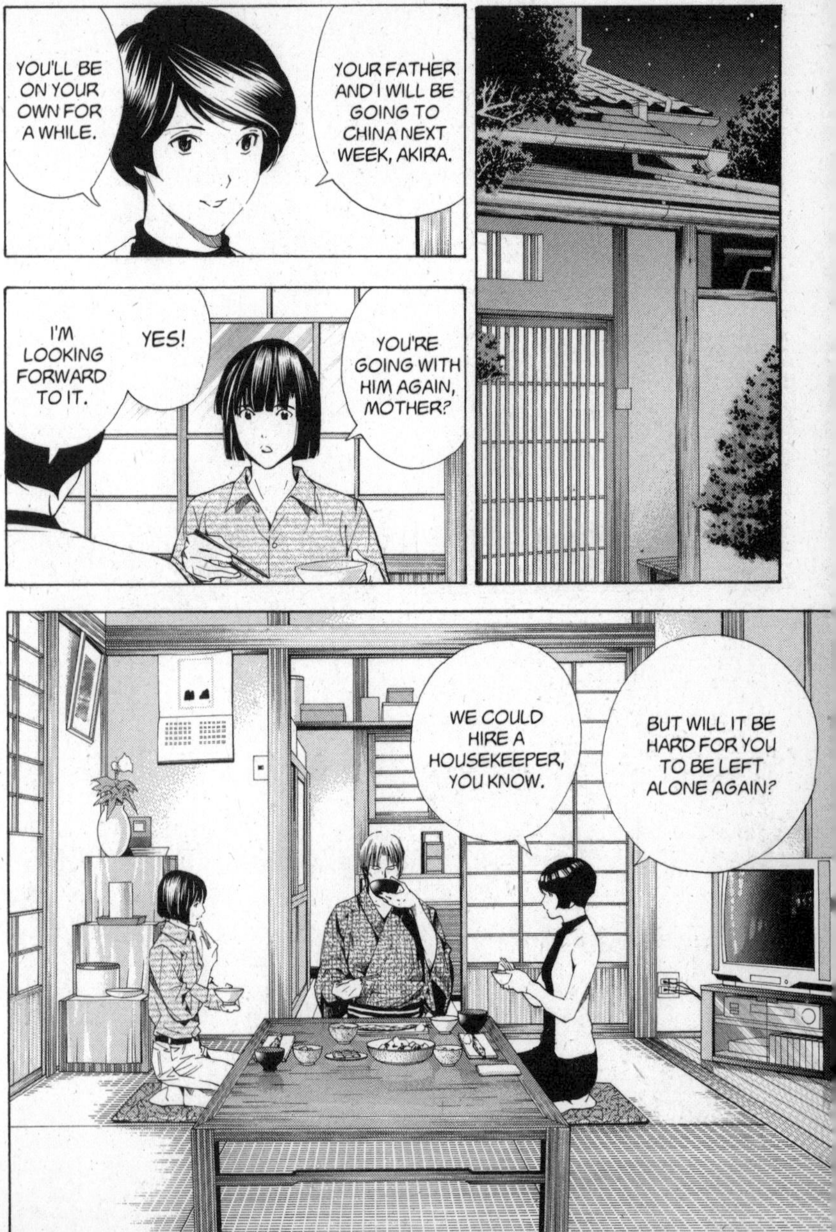
YOUR FATHER AND I WILL BE GOING TO CHINA NEXT WEEK, AKIRA.
YOU'LL BE ON YOUR OWN FOR A WHILE.
YOU'RE GOING WITH HIM AGAIN, MOTHER?
YES!
I'M LOOKING FORWARD TO IT.
BUT WILL IT BE HARD FOR YOU TO BE LEFT ALONE AGAIN?
WE COULD HIRE A HOUSEKEEPER, YOU KNOW.

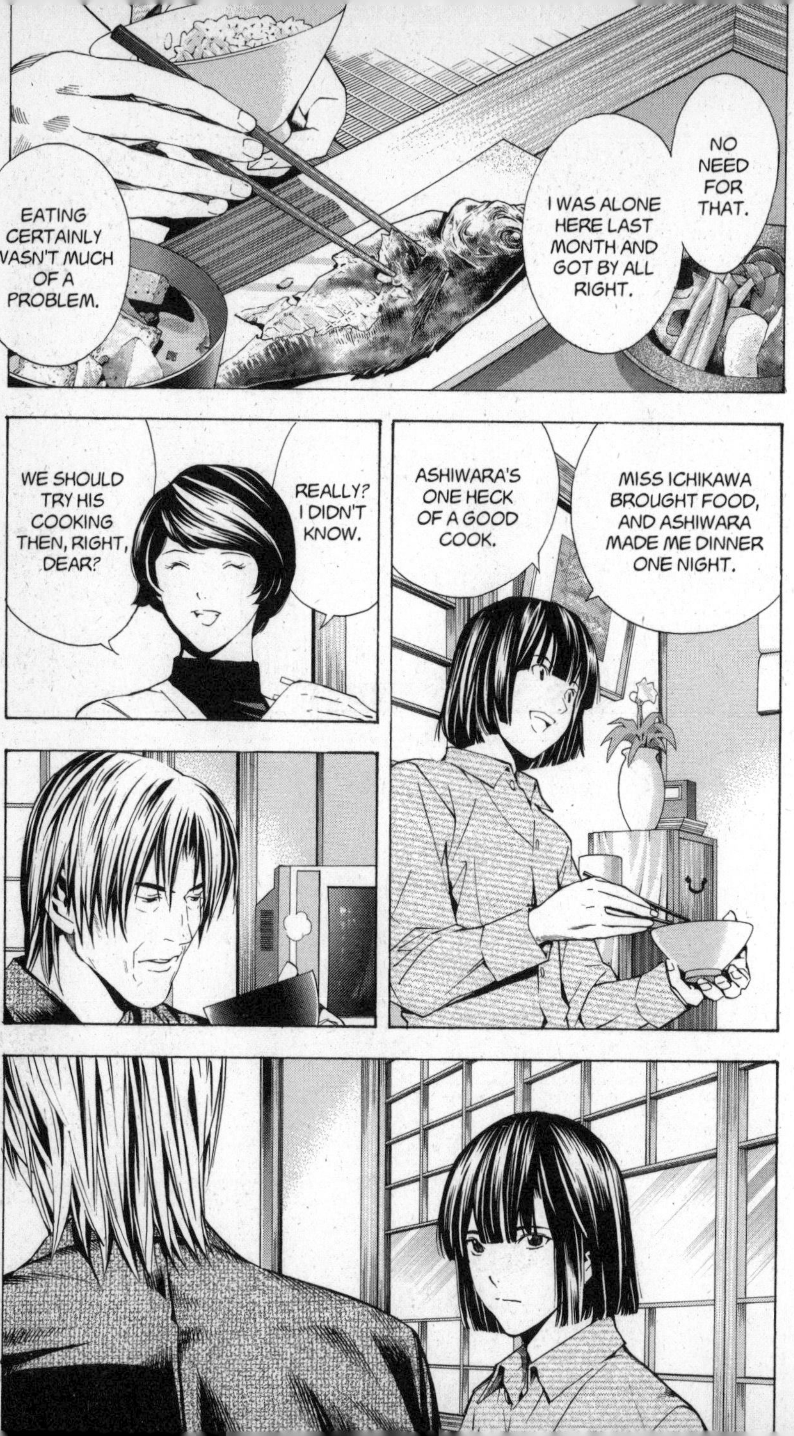
NO NEED FOR THAT.
I WAS ALONE HERE LAST MONTH AND GOT BY ALL RIGHT.
EATING CERTAINLY WASN'T MUCH OF A PROBLEM.
MISS ICHIKAWA BROUGHT FOOD, AND ASHIWARA MADE ME DINNER ONE NIGHT.
ASHIWARA'S ONE HECK OF A GOOD COOK.
REALLY? I DIDN'T KNOW.
WE SHOULD TRY HIS COOKING THEN, RIGHT, DEAR?

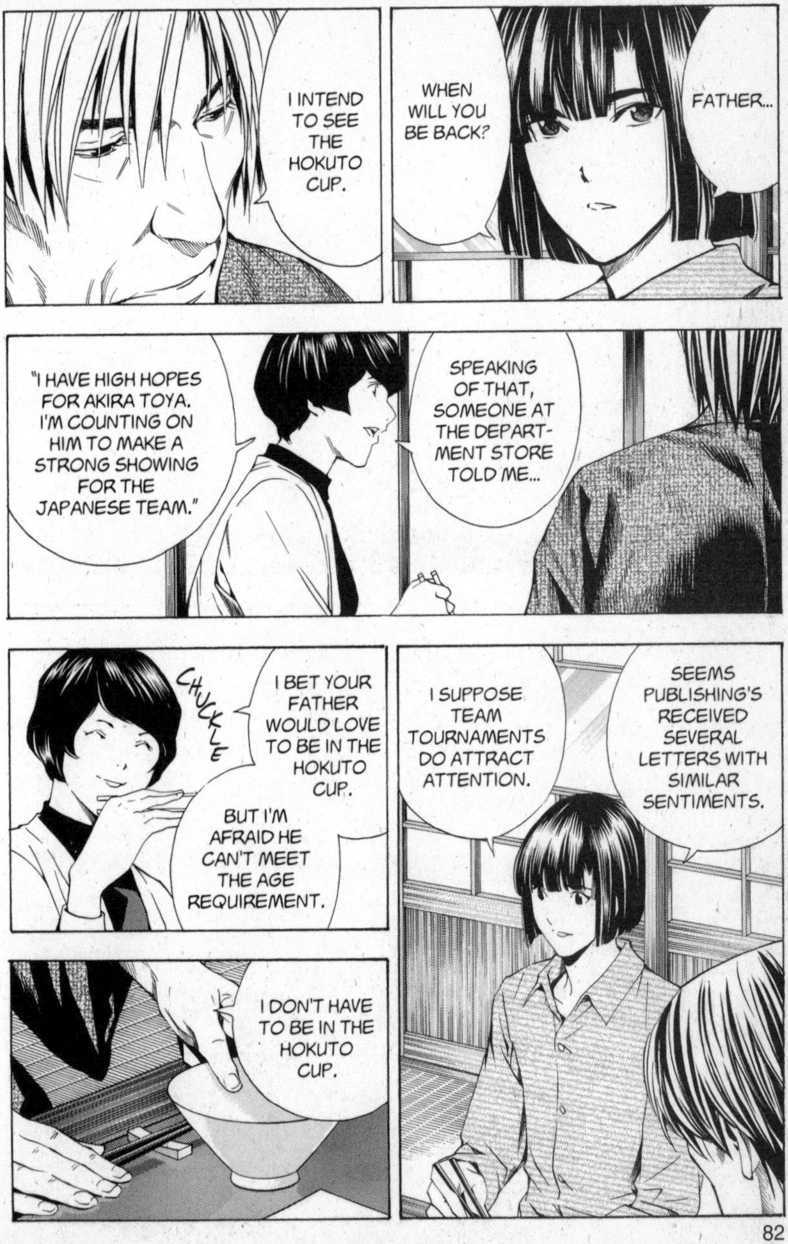
FATHER...
WHEN WILL YOU BE BACK?
I INTEND TO SEE THE HOKUTO CUP.
SPEAKING OF THAT, SOMEONE AT THE DEPART-MENT STORE TOLD ME...
"I HAVE HIGH HOPES FOR AKIRA TOYA. I'M COUNTING ON HIM TO MAKE A STRONG SHOWING FOR THE JAPANESE TEAM."
SEEMS PUBLISHING'S RECEIVED SEVERAL LETTERS WITH SIMILAR SENTIMENTS.
I SUPPOSE TEAM TOURNAMENTS DO ATTRACT ATTENTION.
CHUCKLE
I BET YOUR FATHER WOULD LOVE TO BE IN THE HOKUTO CUP.
BUT I'M AFRAID HE CAN'T MEET THE AGE REQUIREMENT.
I DON'T HAVE TO BE IN THE HOKUTO CUP.

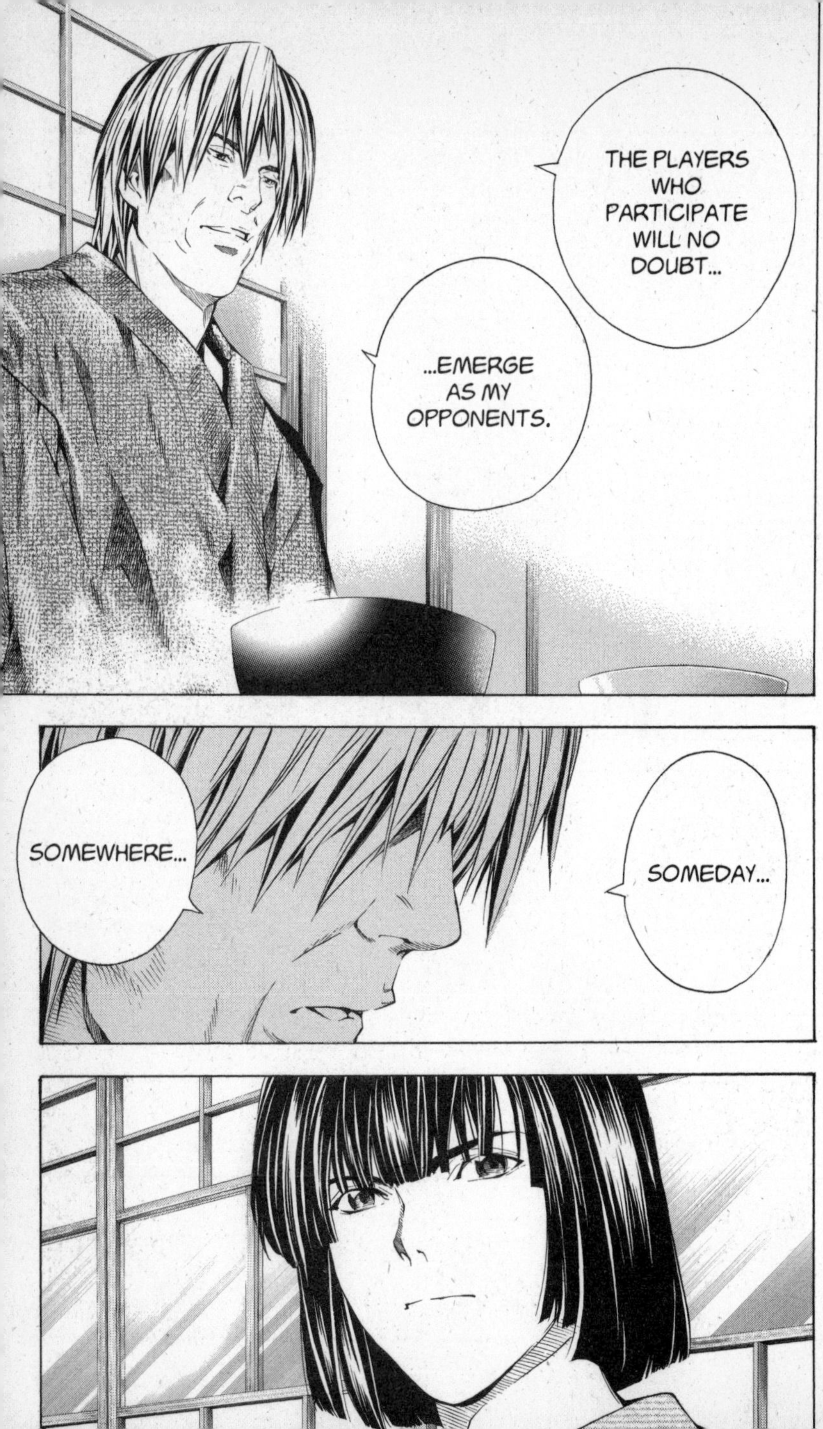
THE PLAYERS WHO PARTICIPATE WILL NO DOUBT...
...EMERGE AS MY OPPONENTS.
SOMEDAY...
SOMEWHERE...

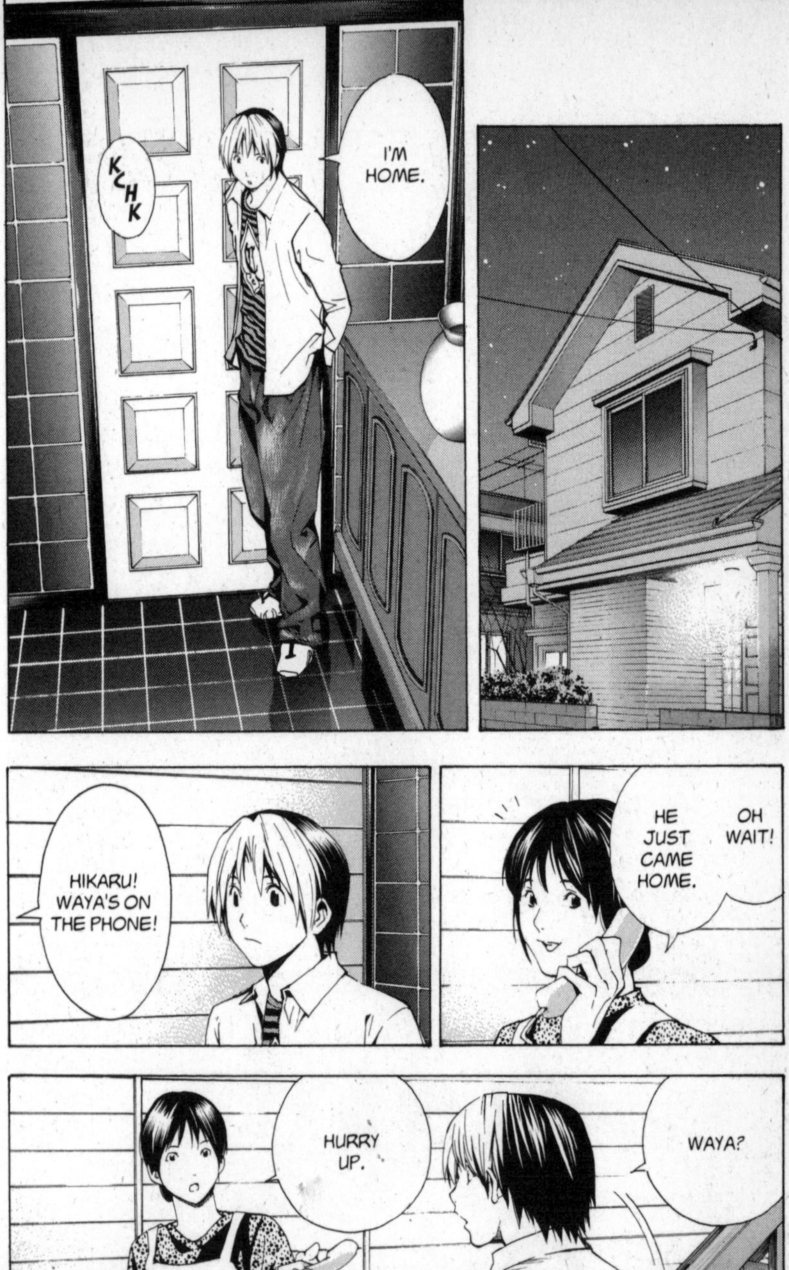
I'M HOME.
KCHK
OH WAIT!
HE JUST CAME HOME.
HIKARU! WAYA'S ON THE PHONE!
WAYA?
HURRY UP.

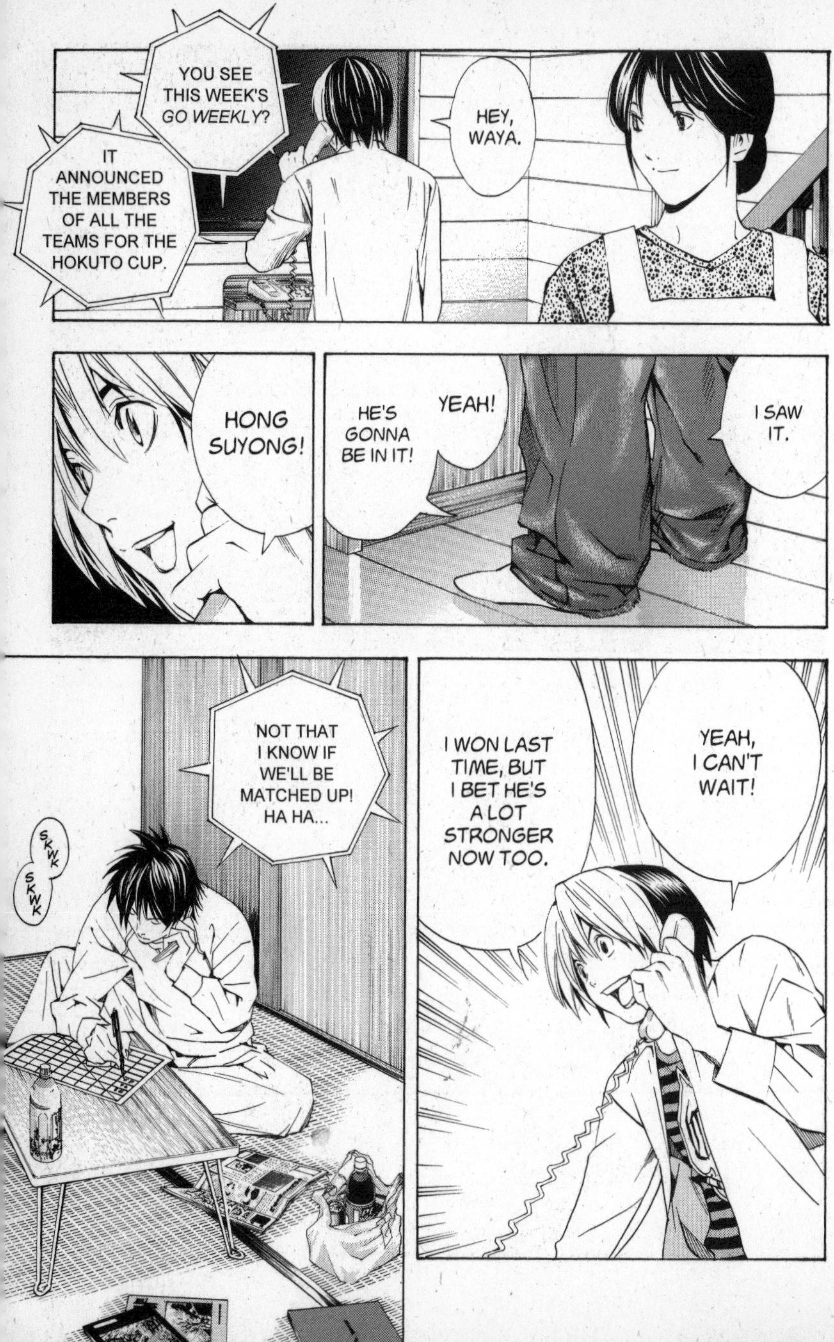
HEY, WAYA.
YOU SEE THIS WEEK'S GO WEEKLY?
IT ANNOUNCED THE MEMBERS OF ALL THE TEAMS FOR THE HOKUTO CUP.
I SAW IT.
YEAH!
HE'S GONNA BE IN IT!
HONG SUYONG!
YEAH, I CAN'T WAIT!
I WON LAST TIME, BUT I BET HE'S A LOT STRONGER NOW TOO.
NOT THAT I KNOW IF WE'LL BE MATCHED UP! HA HA...
SKWK SKWK

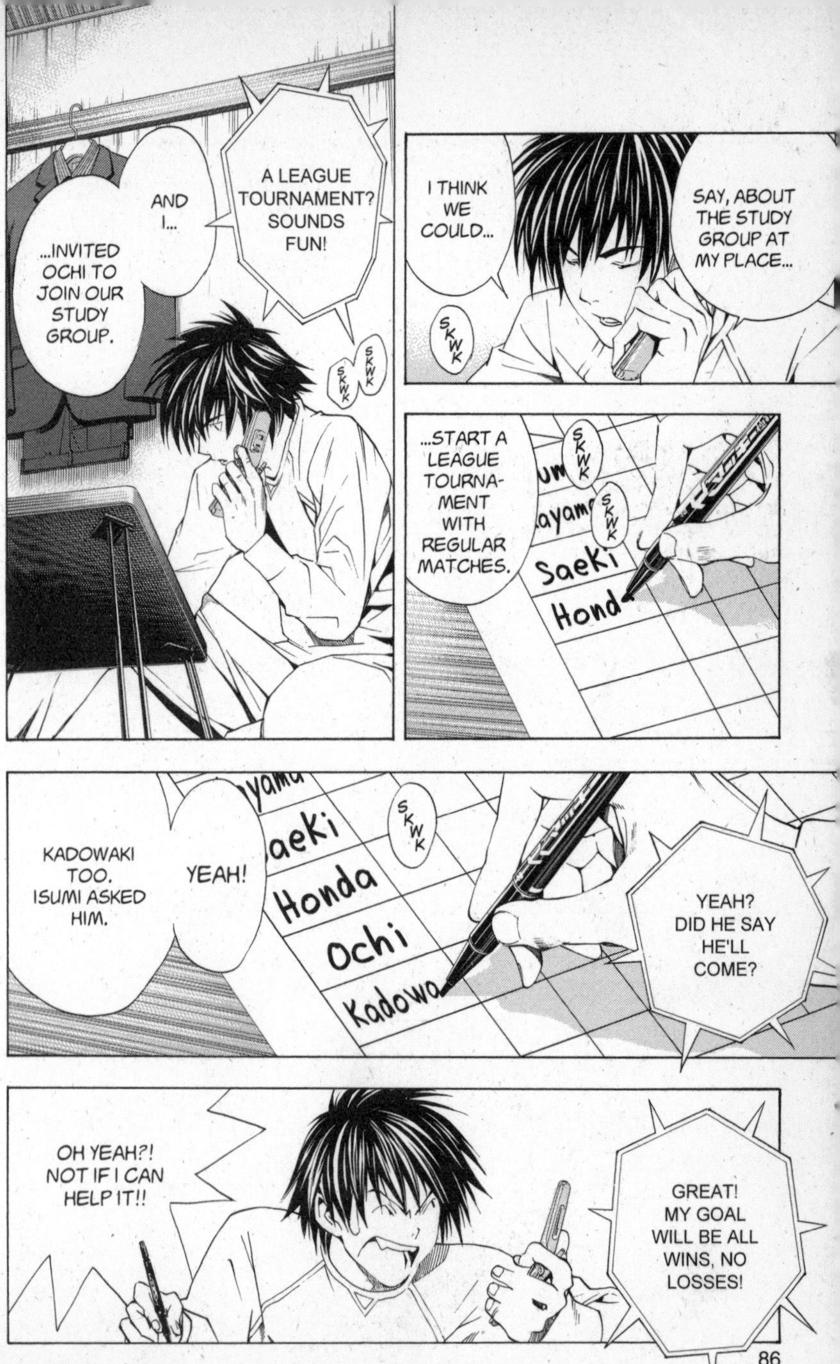
SAY, ABOUT THE STUDY GROUP AT MY PLACE...
I THINK WE COULD...
SKWK
...START A LEAGUE TOURNAMENT WITH REGULAR MATCHES.
SKWK
SKWK
Saeki
Hond
A LEAGUE TOURNAMENT? SOUNDS FUN!
AND I...
...INVITED OCHI TO JOIN OUR STUDY GROUP.
SKWK
SKWK
YEAH? DID HE SAY HE'LL COME?
SKWK
Saeki
Honda
Ochi
Kadowa
YEAH!
KADOWAKI TOO. ISUMI ASKED HIM.
GREAT! MY GOAL WILL BE ALL WINS, NO LOSSES!
OH YEAH?! NOT IF I CAN HELP IT!!

READ THIS WAY

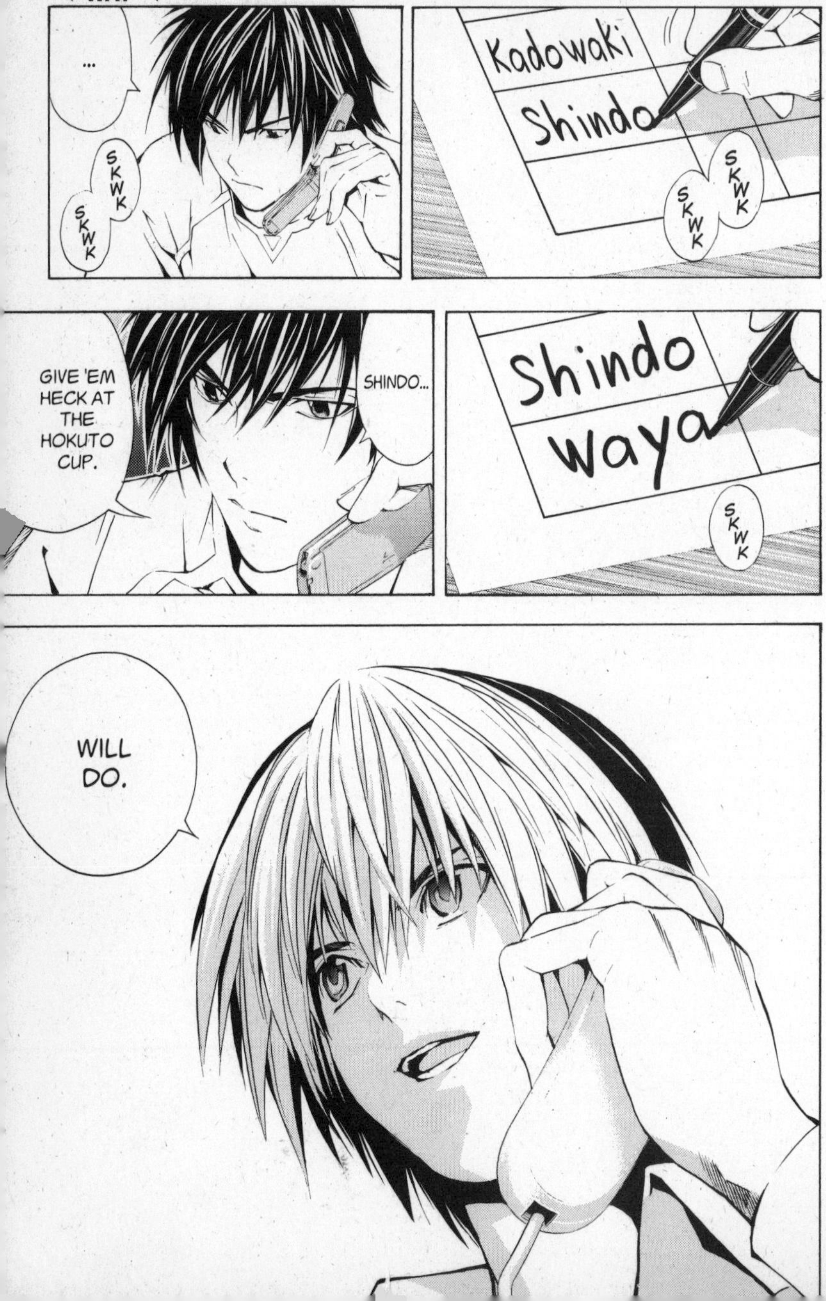
Kadowaki
Shindo
SKWK
SKWK
...
SKWK
SKWK
Shindo
waya
SKWK
SHINDO...
GIVE 'EM HECK AT THE HOKUTO CUP.
WILL DO.

HIKARU NO GO STORYBOARDS

49

YUMI HOTTA

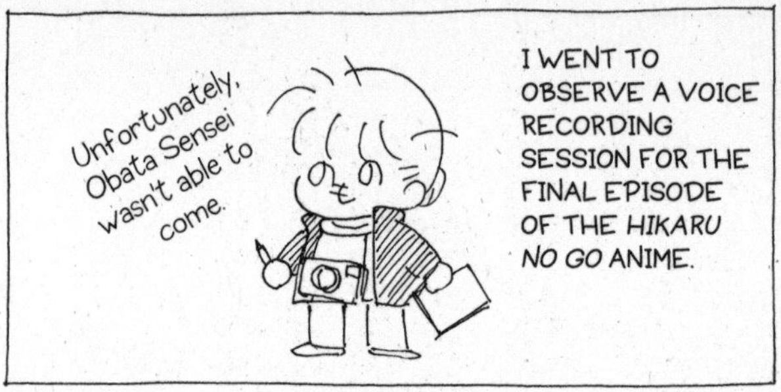
I WENT TO OBSERVE A VOICE RECORDING SESSION FOR THE FINAL EPISODE OF THE *HIKARU NO GO* ANIME.
Unfortunately, Obata Sensei wasn't able to come.

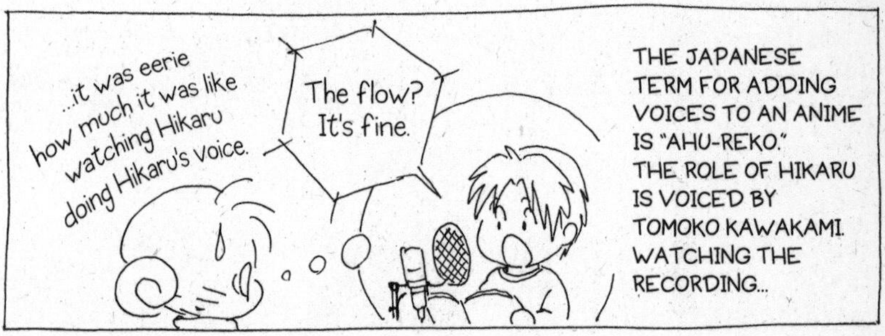
THE JAPANESE TERM FOR ADDING VOICES TO AN ANIME IS "AHU-REKO." THE ROLE OF HIKARU IS VOICED BY TOMOKO KAWAKAMI. WATCHING THE RECORDING...
The flow? It's fine.
...it was eerie how much it was like watching Hikaru doing Hikaru's voice.

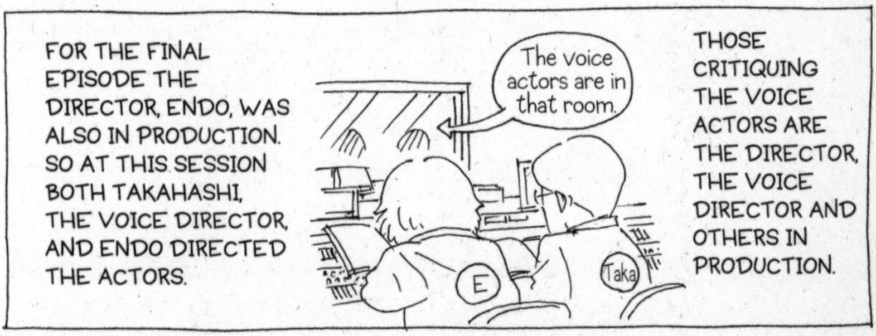
THOSE CRITIQUING THE VOICE ACTORS ARE THE DIRECTOR, THE VOICE DIRECTOR AND OTHERS IN PRODUCTION.
The voice actors are in that room.
FOR THE FINAL EPISODE THE DIRECTOR, ENDO, WAS ALSO IN PRODUCTION. SO AT THIS SESSION BOTH TAKAHASHI, THE VOICE DIRECTOR, AND ENDO DIRECTED THE ACTORS.
Taka
E

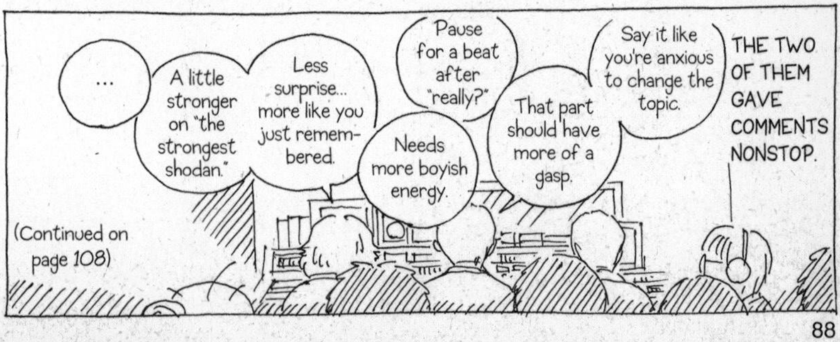
THE TWO OF THEM GAVE COMMENTS NONSTOP.
Say it like you're anxious to change the topic.
Pause for a beat after "really?"
That part should have more of a gasp.
Needs more boyish energy.
Less surprise... more like you just remembered.
A little stronger on "the strongest shodan."
...

(Continued on page 108)

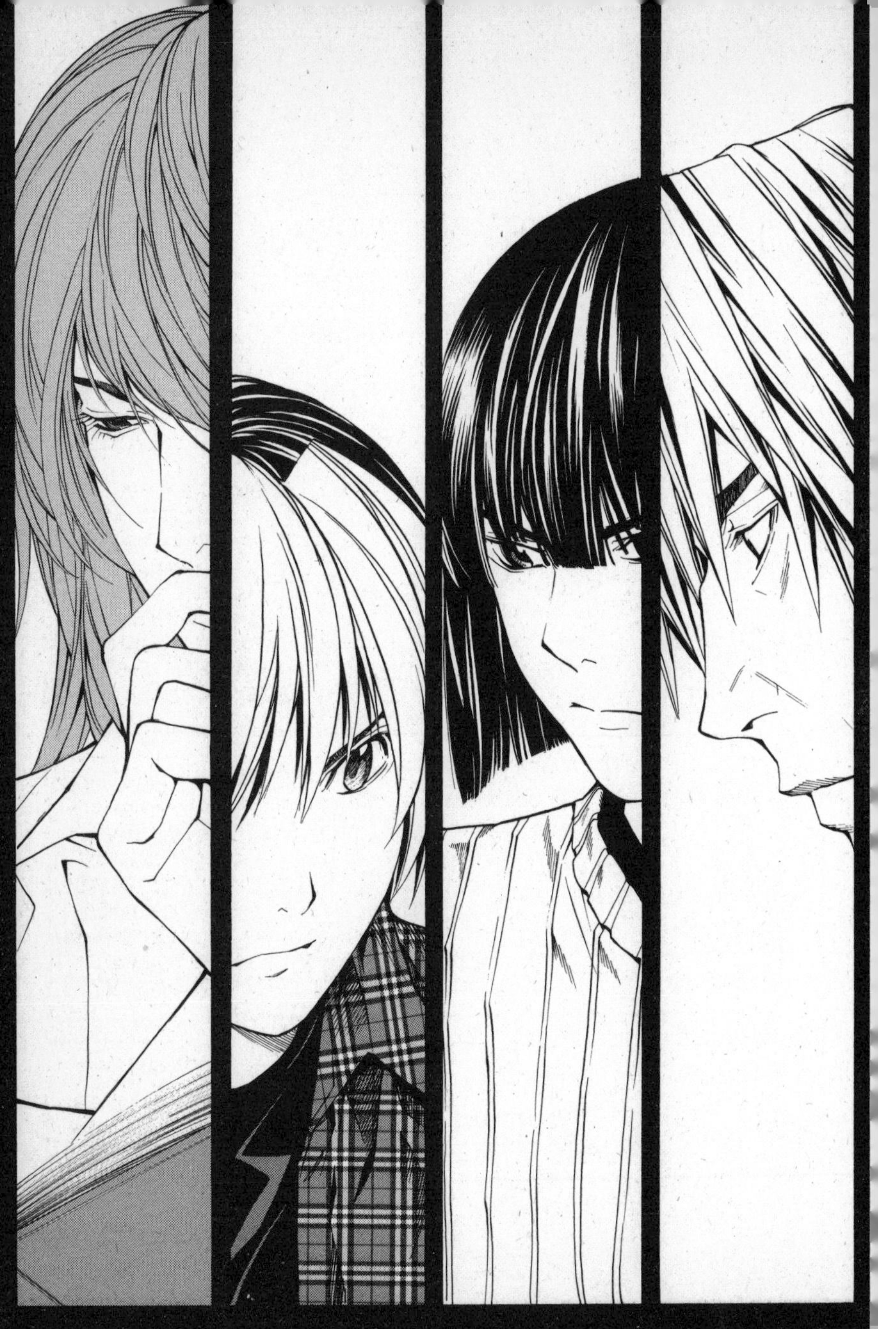

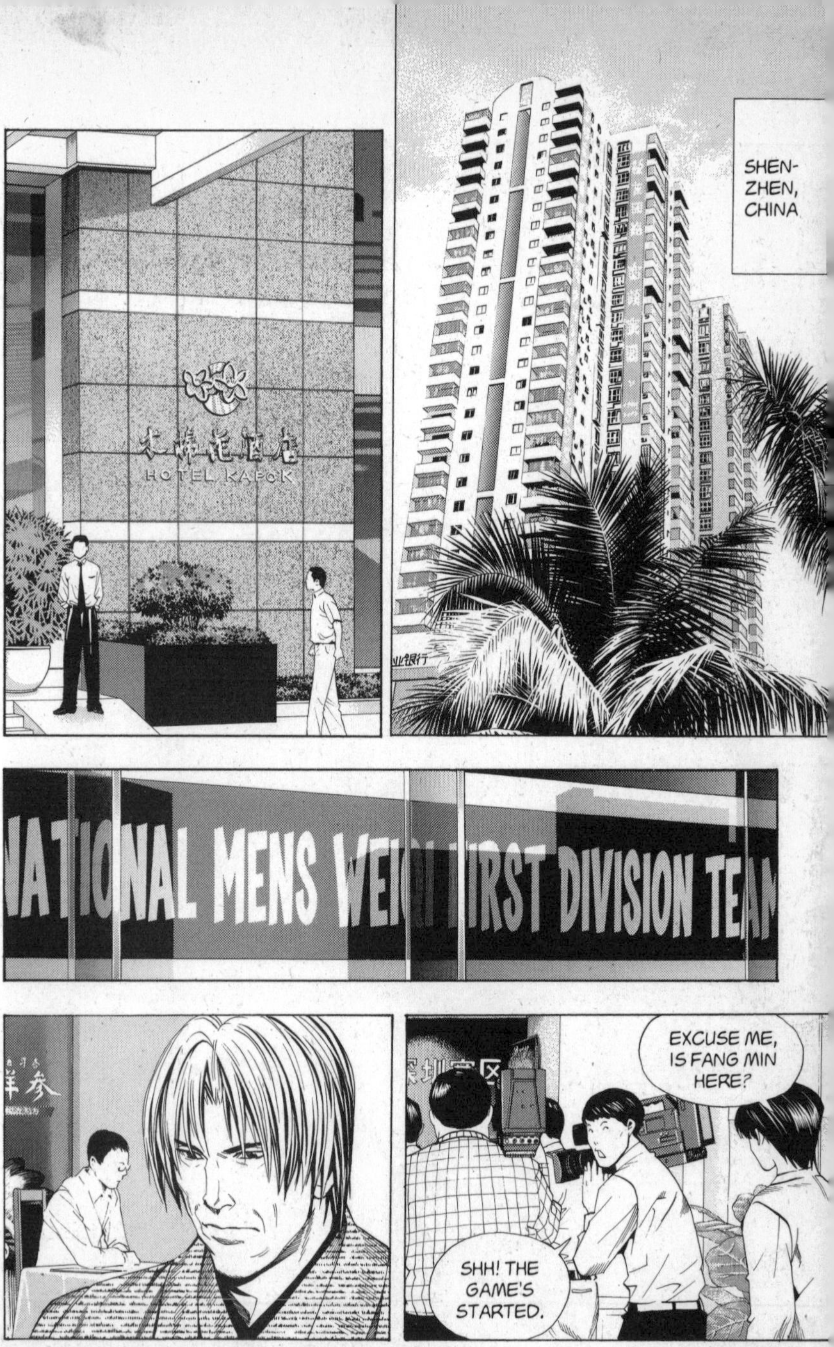
SHEN-
ZHEN,
CHINA
木棉花酒店
HOTEL KAPOK
NATIONAL MENS WEIQI FIRST DIVISION TEA
EXCUSE ME, IS FANG MIN HERE?
SHH! THE GAME'S STARTED.

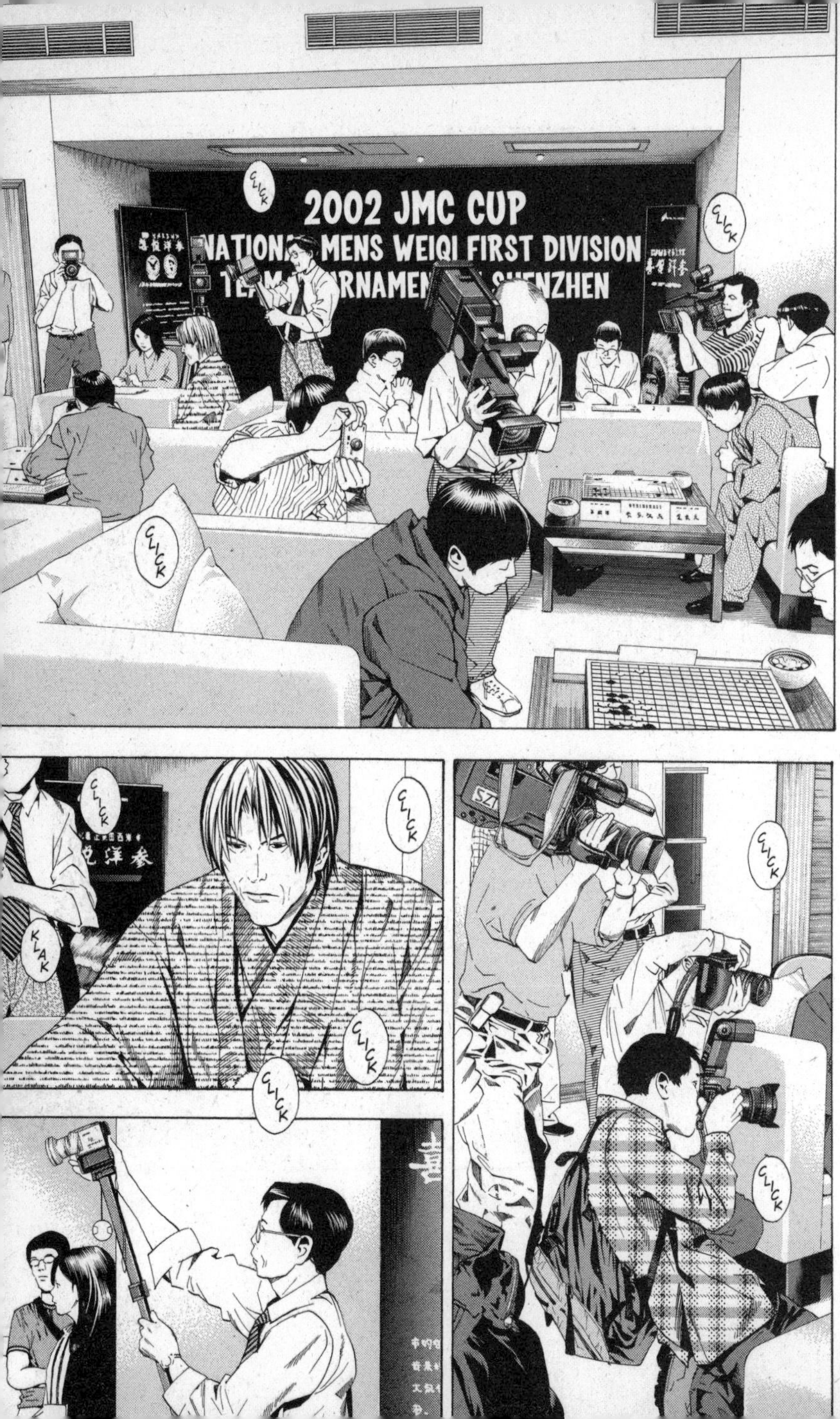
2002 JMC CUP
NATIONA MENS WEIQI FIRST DIVISION
TEA RNAMEN SHENZHEN
CLICK
CLICK
CLICK
CLICK
CLICK
CLICK
CLICK
KLAK
CLICK
CLICK

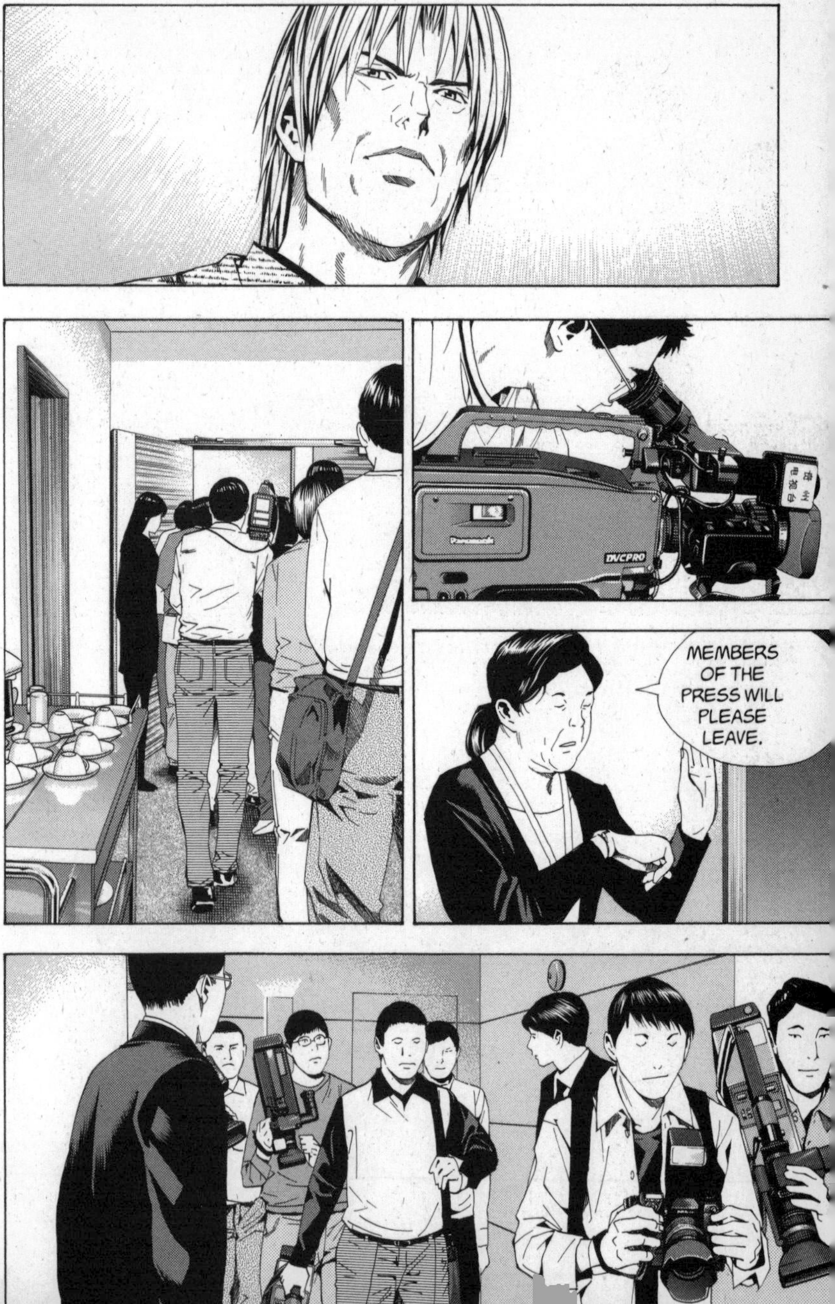
MEMBERS OF THE PRESS WILL PLEASE LEAVE.

READ THIS WAY

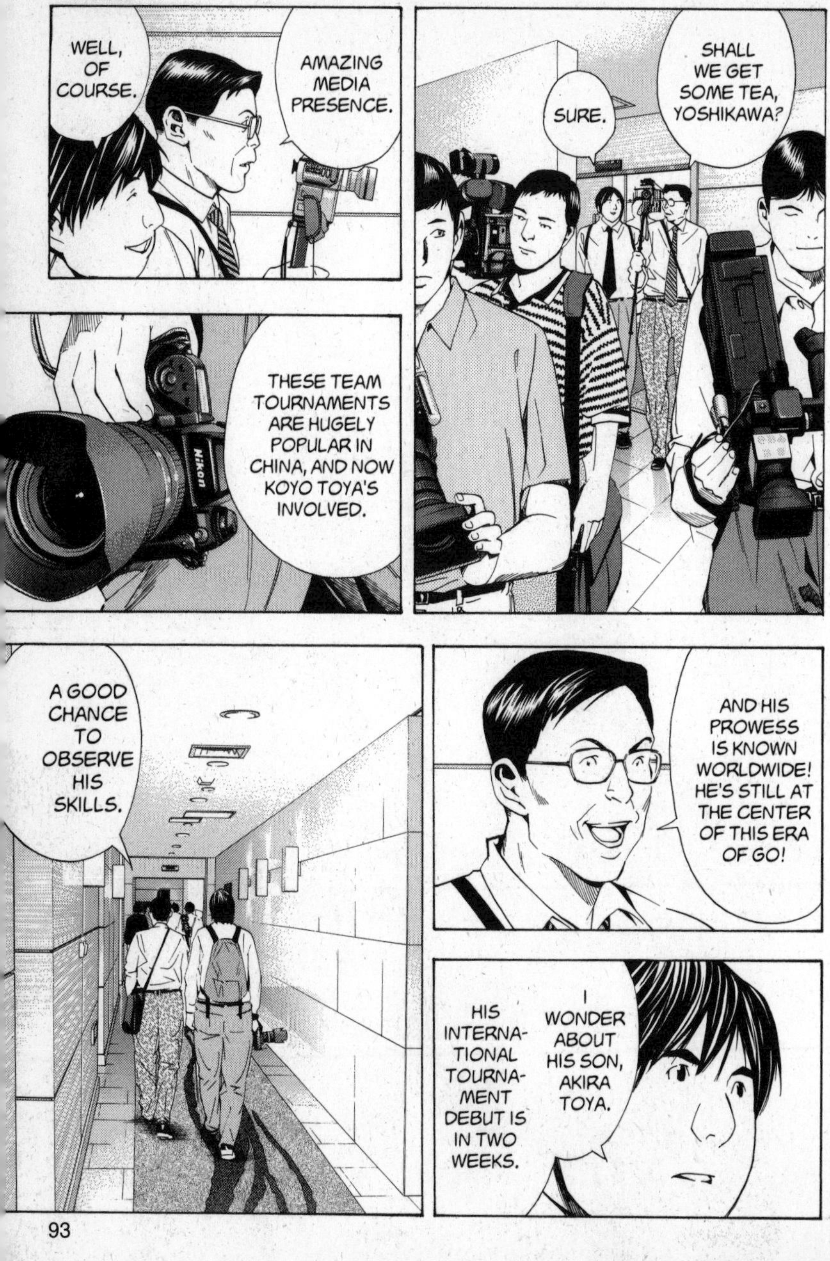
SHALL WE GET SOME TEA, YOSHIKAWA?
SURE.
AMAZING MEDIA PRESENCE.
WELL, OF COURSE.
THESE TEAM TOURNAMENTS ARE HUGELY POPULAR IN CHINA, AND NOW KOYO TOYA'S INVOLVED.
Nikon
AND HIS PROWESS IS KNOWN WORLDWIDE! HE'S STILL AT THE CENTER OF THIS ERA OF GO!
I WONDER ABOUT HIS SON, AKIRA TOYA.
HIS INTERNATIONAL TOURNAMENT DEBUT IS IN TWO WEEKS.
A GOOD CHANCE TO OBSERVE HIS SKILLS.

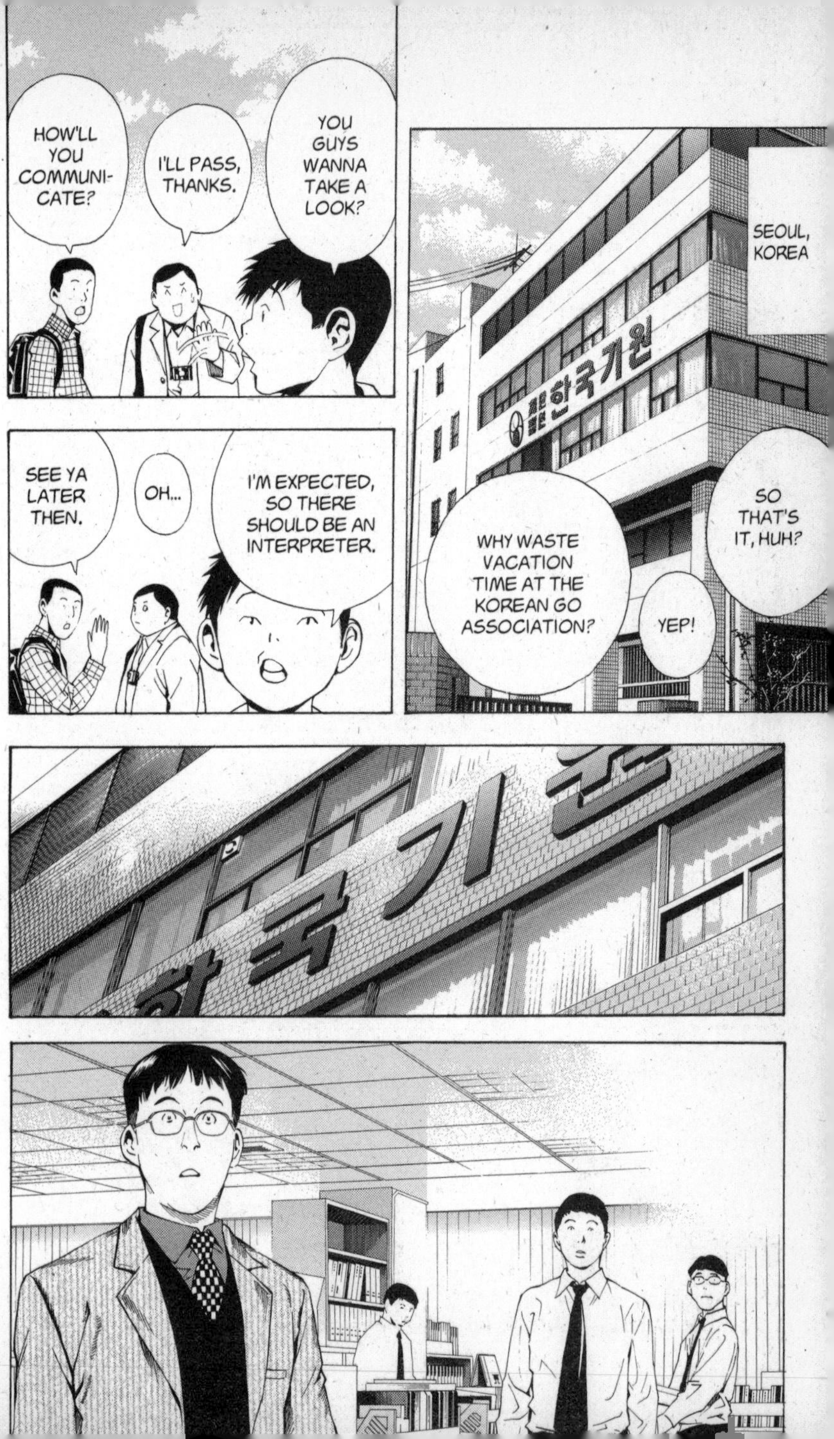
SEOUL, KOREA
한국기원
SO THAT'S IT, HUH?
YEP!
WHY WASTE VACATION TIME AT THE KOREAN GO ASSOCIATION?
YOU GUYS WANNA TAKE A LOOK?
I'LL PASS, THANKS.
HOW'LL YOU COMMUNICATE?
I'M EXPECTED, SO THERE SHOULD BE AN INTERPRETER.
OH...
SEE YA LATER THEN.

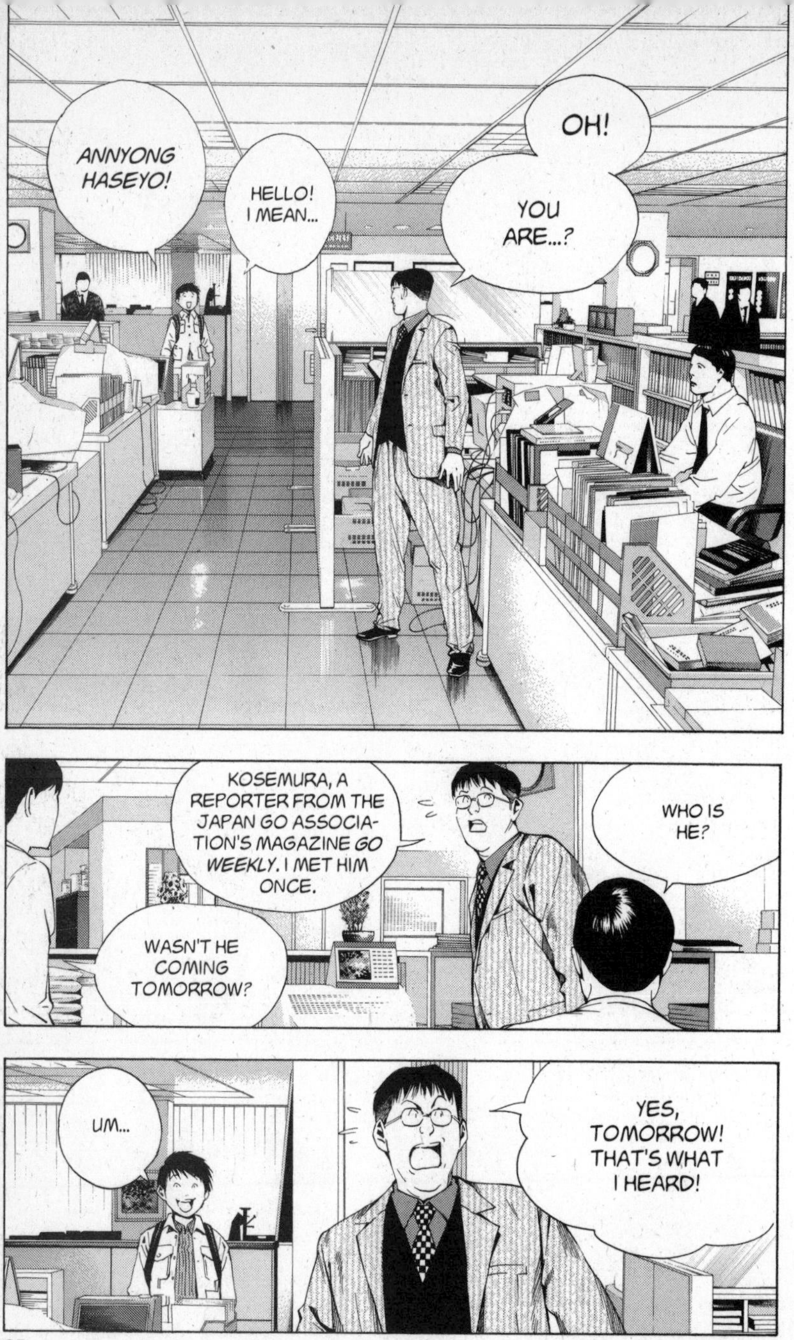
OH!
YOU ARE...?
HELLO! I MEAN...
ANNYONG HASEYO!
WHO IS HE?
KOSEMURA, A REPORTER FROM THE JAPAN GO ASSOCIATION'S MAGAZINE *GO WEEKLY*. I MET HIM ONCE.
WASN'T HE COMING TOMORROW?
YES, TOMORROW! THAT'S WHAT I HEARD!
UM...

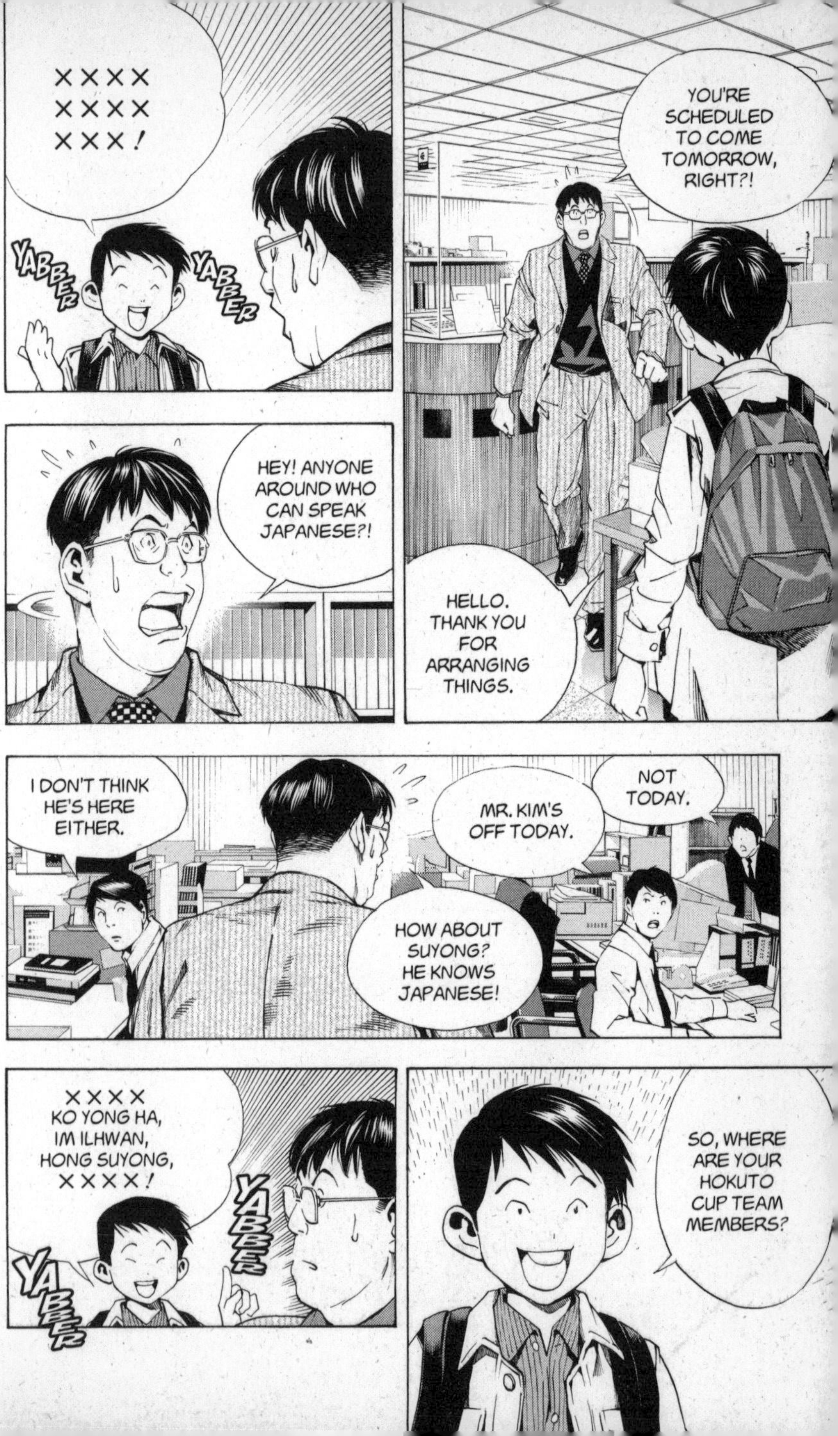
YOU'RE SCHEDULED TO COME TOMORROW, RIGHT?!
HELLO. THANK YOU FOR ARRANGING THINGS.
× × × × × × × × × × × !
YABBER
YABBER
HEY! ANYONE AROUND WHO CAN SPEAK JAPANESE?!
NOT TODAY.
MR. KIM'S OFF TODAY.
HOW ABOUT SUYONG? HE KNOWS JAPANESE!
I DON'T THINK HE'S HERE EITHER.
SO, WHERE ARE YOUR HOKUTO CUP TEAM MEMBERS?
× × × × KO YONG HA, IM ILHWAN, HONG SUYONG, × × × × !
YABBER
YABBER

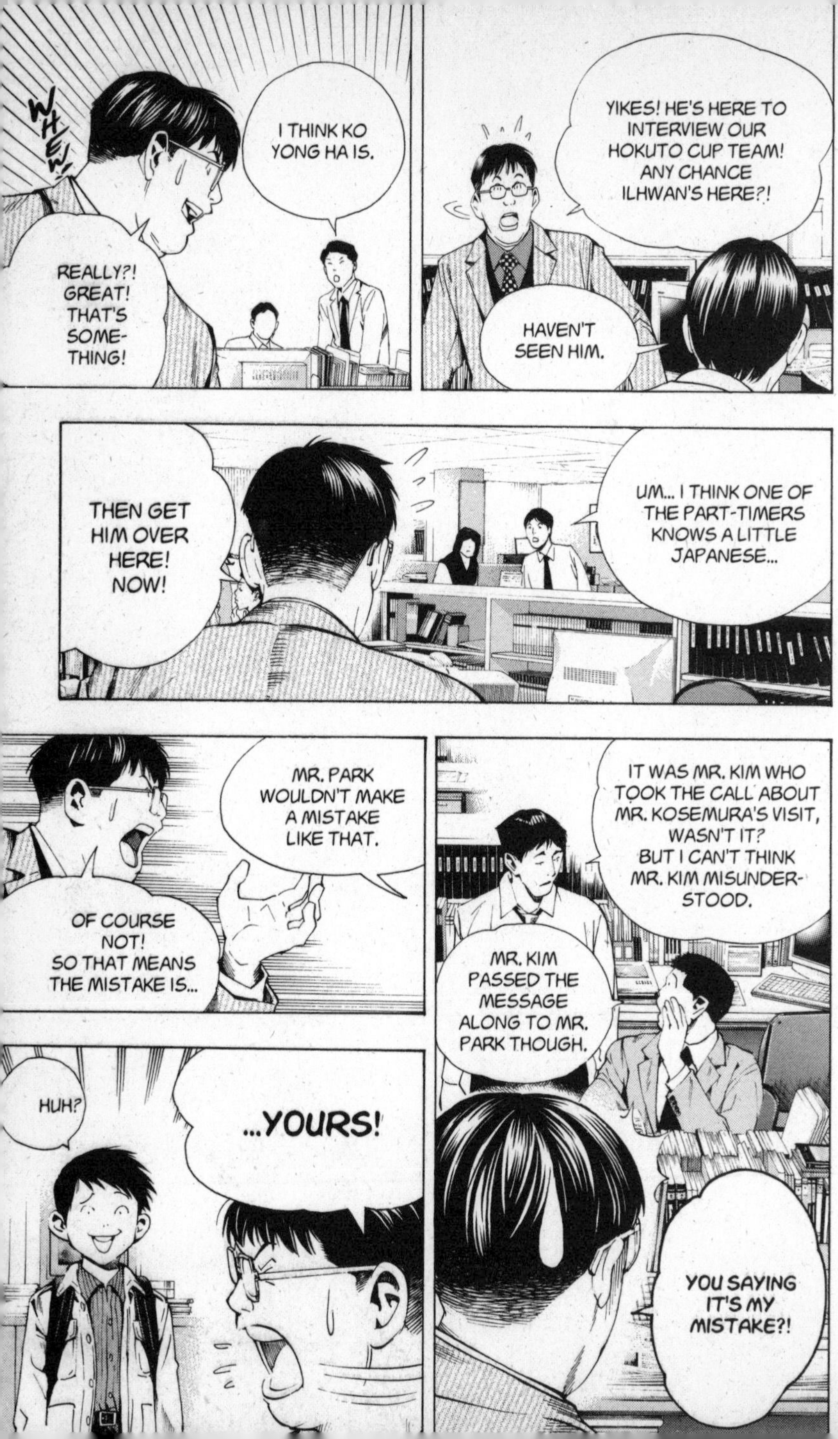
YIKES! HE'S HERE TO INTERVIEW OUR HOKUTO CUP TEAM! ANY CHANCE ILHWAN'S HERE?!
HAVEN'T SEEN HIM.
WHEW
I THINK KO YONG HA IS.
REALLY?! GREAT! THAT'S SOME-THING!
UM... I THINK ONE OF THE PART-TIMERS KNOWS A LITTLE JAPANESE...
THEN GET HIM OVER HERE! NOW!
IT WAS MR. KIM WHO TOOK THE CALL ABOUT MR. KOSEMURA'S VISIT, WASN'T IT? BUT I CAN'T THINK MR. KIM MISUNDER-STOOD.
MR. KIM PASSED THE MESSAGE ALONG TO MR. PARK THOUGH.
YOU SAYING IT'S MY MISTAKE?!
MR. PARK WOULDN'T MAKE A MISTAKE LIKE THAT.
OF COURSE NOT! SO THAT MEANS THE MISTAKE IS...
...YOURS!
HUH?

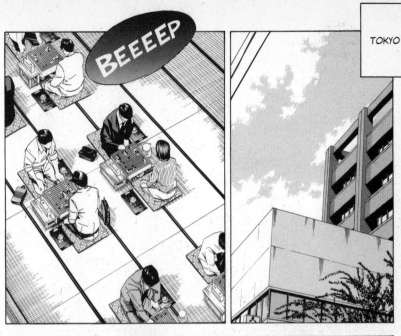

BEEEEP

SOUNDS GOOD.

LUNCH, NAKA-MURA?

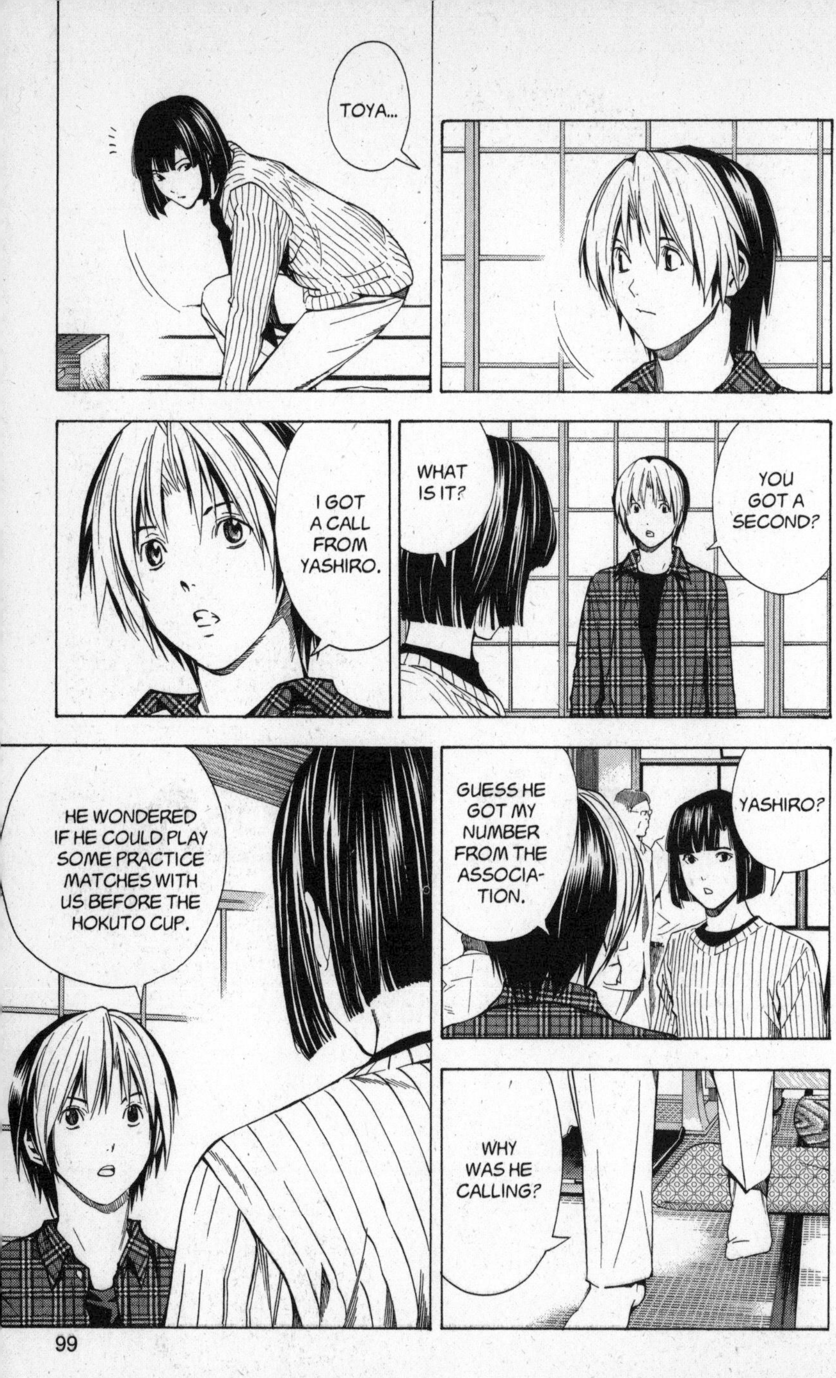
TOYA...
YOU GOT A SECOND?
WHAT IS IT?
I GOT A CALL FROM YASHIRO.
YASHIRO?
GUESS HE GOT MY NUMBER FROM THE ASSOCIA-TION.
WHY WAS HE CALLING?
HE WONDERED IF HE COULD PLAY SOME PRACTICE MATCHES WITH US BEFORE THE HOKUTO CUP.

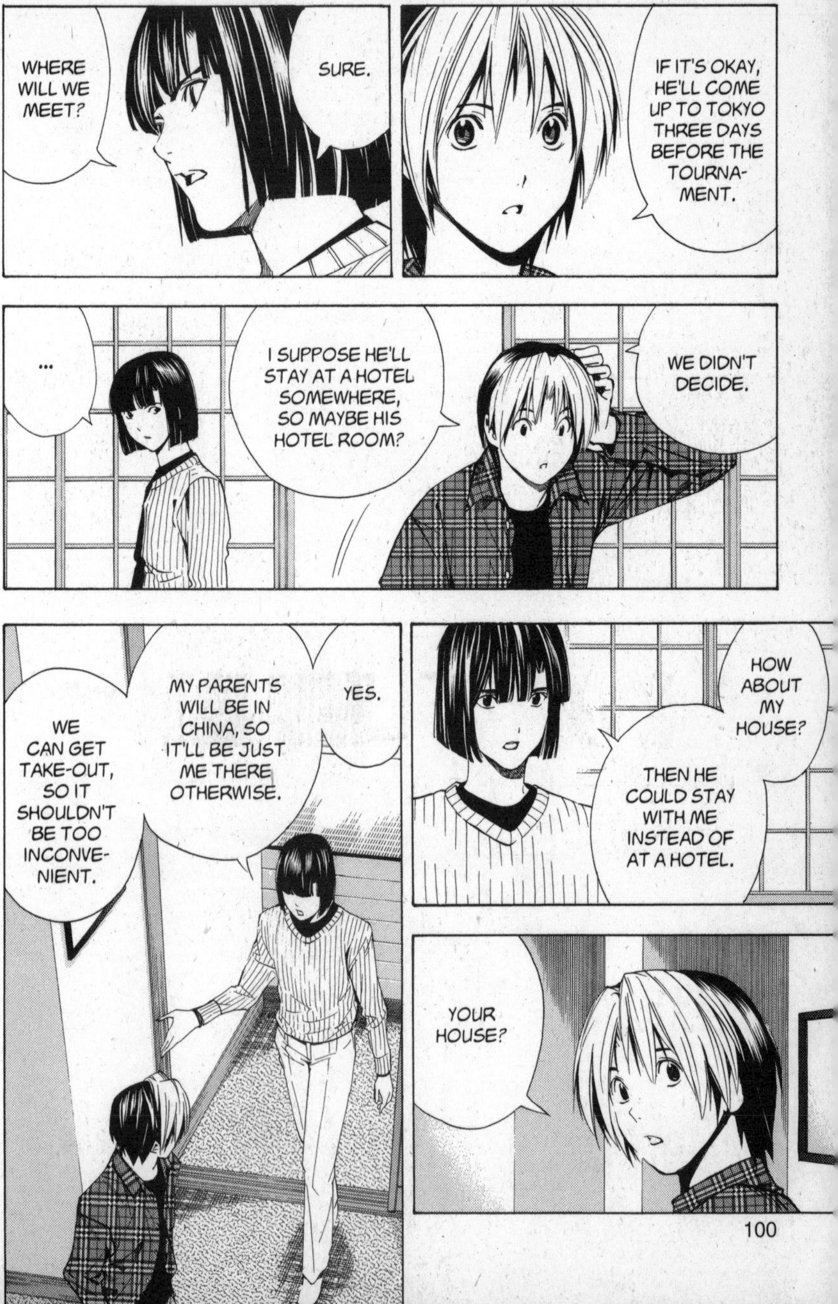
IF IT'S OKAY, HE'LL COME UP TO TOKYO THREE DAYS BEFORE THE TOURNA- MENT.
SURE.
WHERE WILL WE MEET?
WE DIDN'T DECIDE.
I SUPPOSE HE'LL STAY AT A HOTEL SOMEWHERE, SO MAYBE HIS HOTEL ROOM?
...
HOW ABOUT MY HOUSE?
THEN HE COULD STAY WITH ME INSTEAD OF AT A HOTEL.
YOUR HOUSE?
YES.
MY PARENTS WILL BE IN CHINA, SO IT'LL BE JUST ME THERE OTHERWISE.
WE CAN GET TAKE-OUT, SO IT SHOULDN'T BE TOO INCONVE- NIENT.

READ THIS WAY

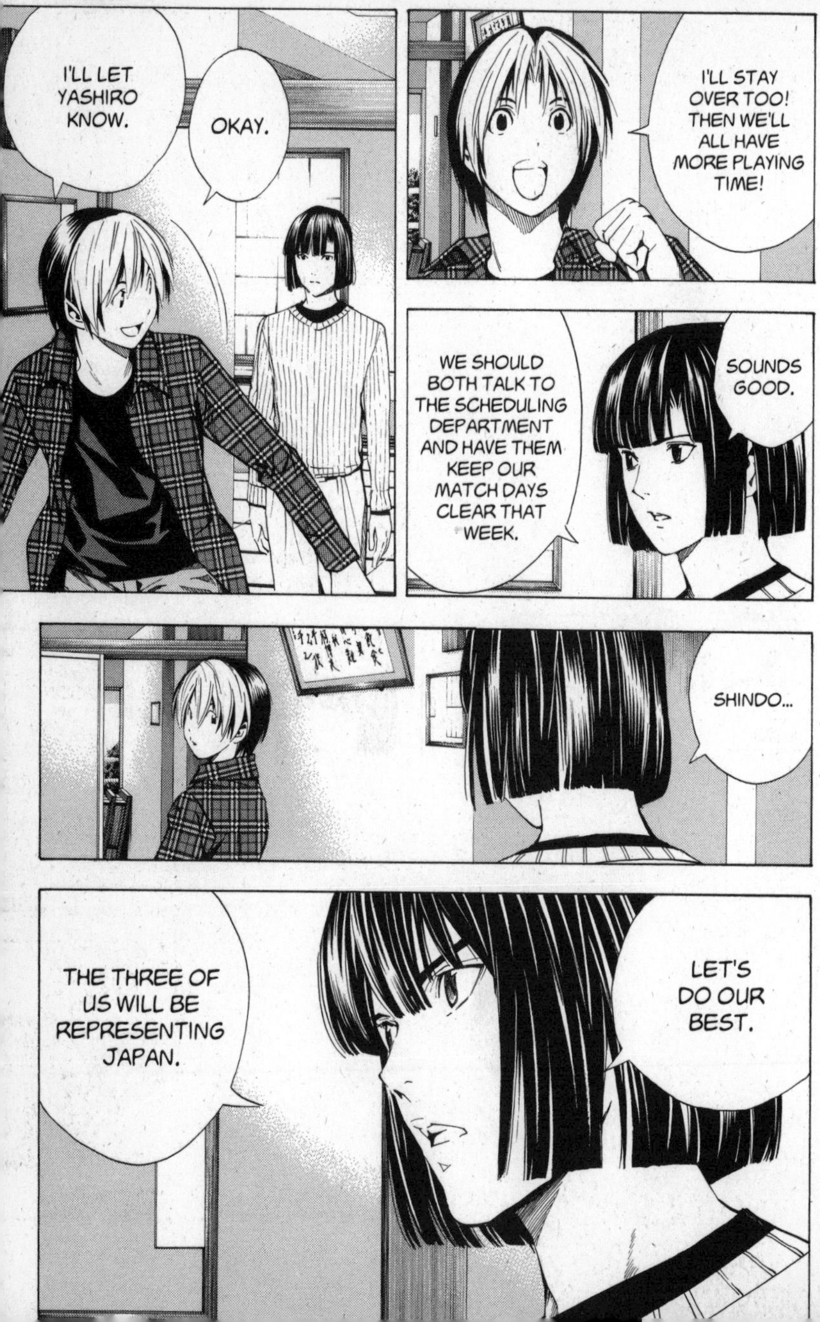
I'LL STAY OVER TOO! THEN WE'LL ALL HAVE MORE PLAYING TIME!
SOUNDS GOOD.
WE SHOULD BOTH TALK TO THE SCHEDULING DEPARTMENT AND HAVE THEM KEEP OUR MATCH DAYS CLEAR THAT WEEK.
OKAY.
I'LL LET YASHIRO KNOW.
SHINDO...
LET'S DO OUR BEST.
THE THREE OF US WILL BE REPRESENTING JAPAN.

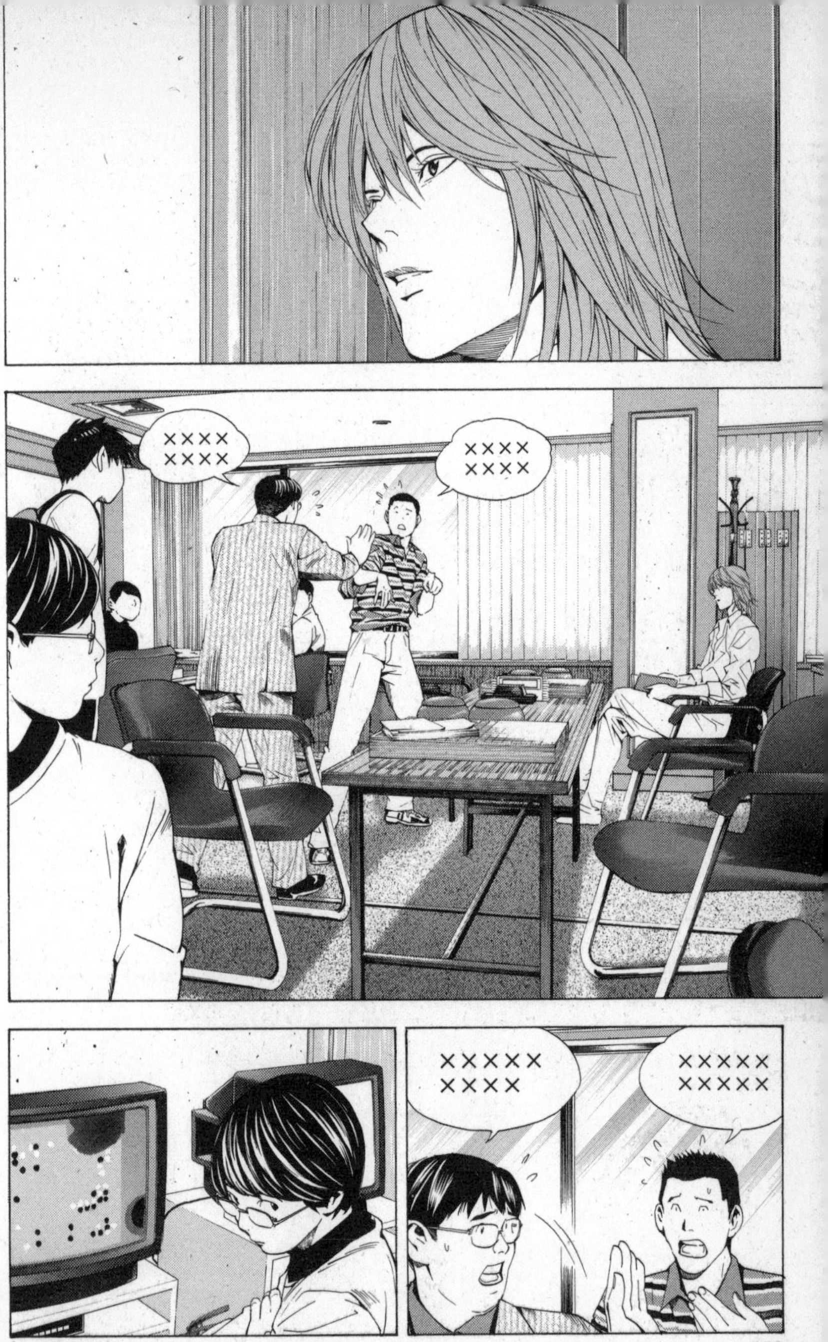
××××
××××
××××
××××
×××××
×××××
×××××
××××

READ THIS WAY

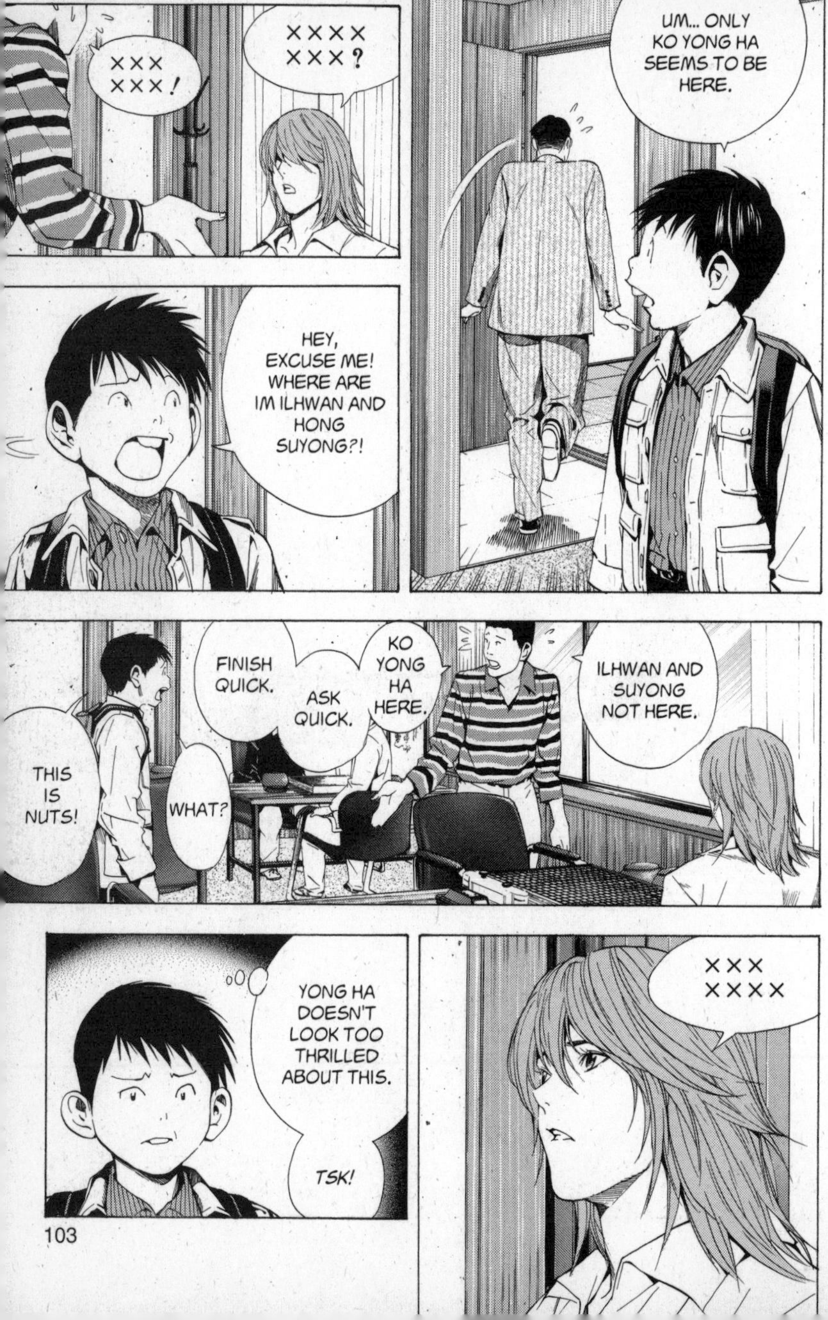

UM... ONLY KO YONG HA SEEMS TO BE HERE.
×××× ×××?
××× ×××!
HEY, EXCUSE ME! WHERE ARE IM ILHWAN AND HONG SUYONG?!
ILHWAN AND SUYONG NOT HERE.
KO YONG HA HERE.
ASK QUICK.
FINISH QUICK.
WHAT?
THIS IS NUTS!
××× ××××
YONG HA DOESN'T LOOK TOO THRILLED ABOUT THIS.
TSK!

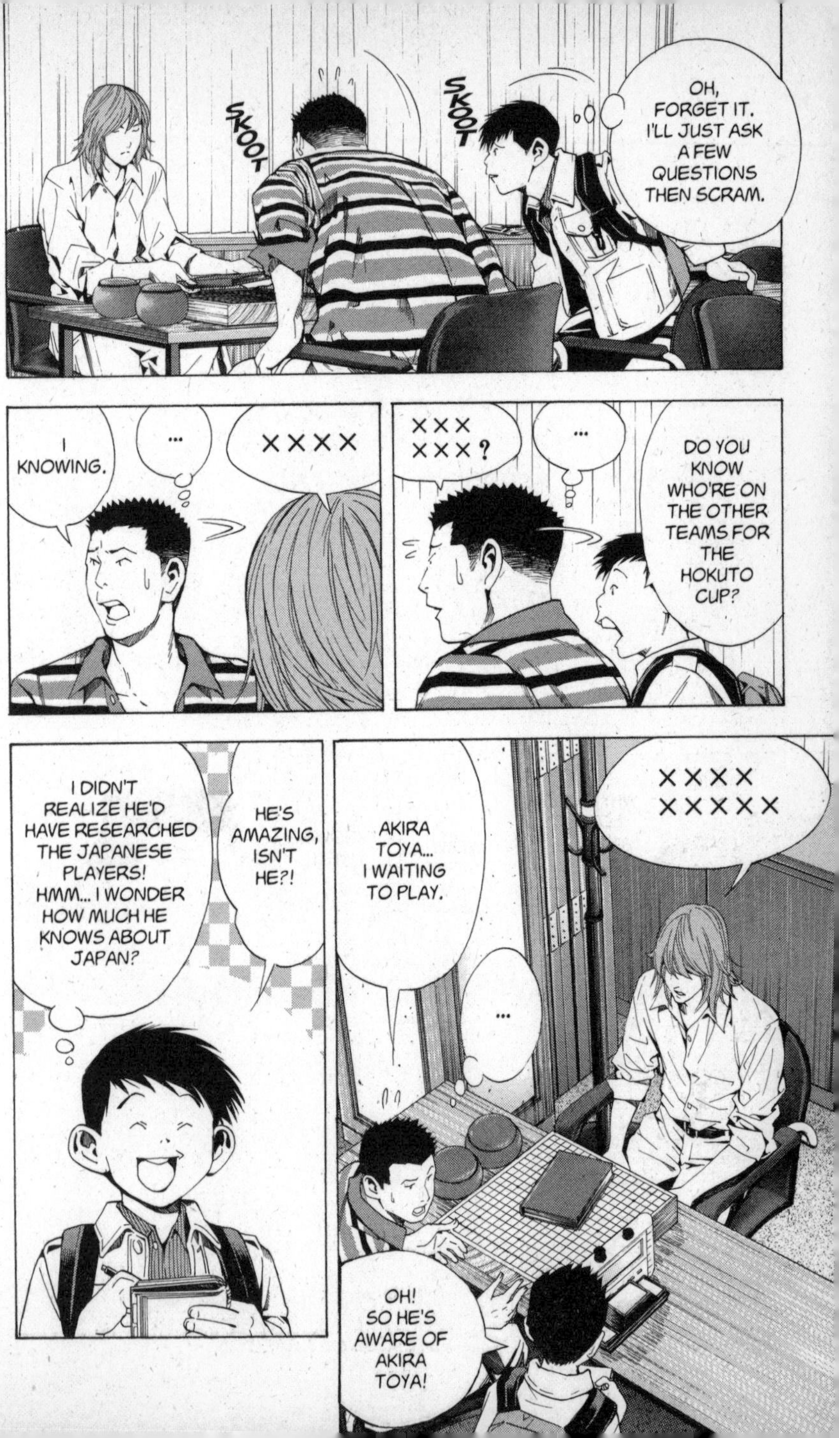
SKOOT
SKOOT
OH, FORGET IT. I'LL JUST ASK A FEW QUESTIONS THEN SCRAM.
DO YOU KNOW WHO'RE ON THE OTHER TEAMS FOR THE HOKUTO CUP?
...
××× ×××?
××××
...
I KNOWING.
×××× ×××××
...
AKIRA TOYA... I WAITING TO PLAY.
OH! SO HE'S AWARE OF AKIRA TOYA!
HE'S AMAZING, ISN'T HE?!
I DIDN'T REALIZE HE'D HAVE RESEARCHED THE JAPANESE PLAYERS! HMM... I WONDER HOW MUCH HE KNOWS ABOUT JAPAN?

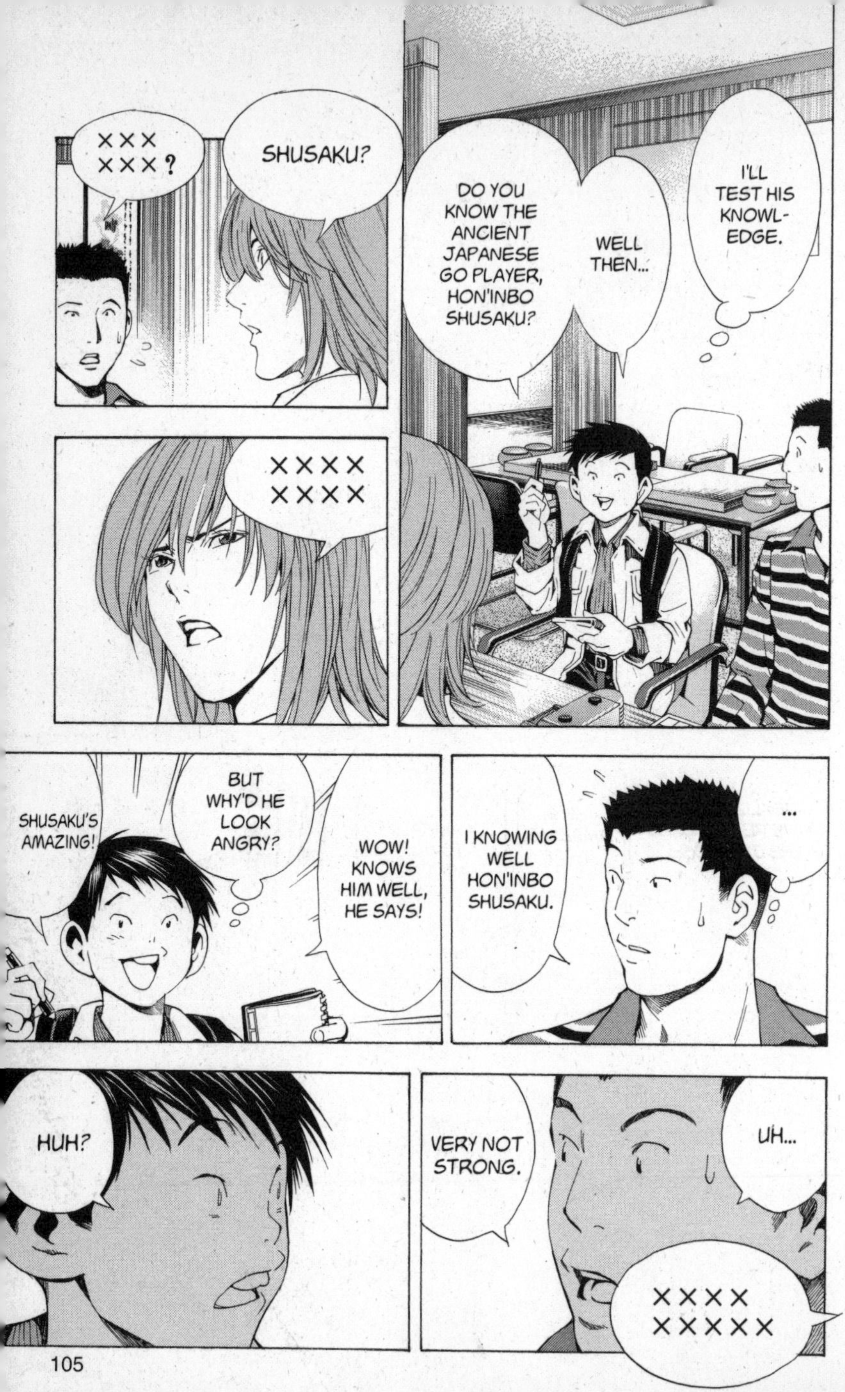
I'LL TEST HIS KNOWL-EDGE.
WELL THEN...
DO YOU KNOW THE ANCIENT JAPANESE GO PLAYER, HON'INBO SHUSAKU?
SHUSAKU?
××× ××× ?
×××× ××××
...
I KNOWING WELL HON'INBO SHUSAKU.
WOW! KNOWS HIM WELL, HE SAYS!
BUT WHY'D HE LOOK ANGRY?
SHUSAKU'S AMAZING!
UH...
VERY NOT STRONG.
×××× ×××××
HUH?

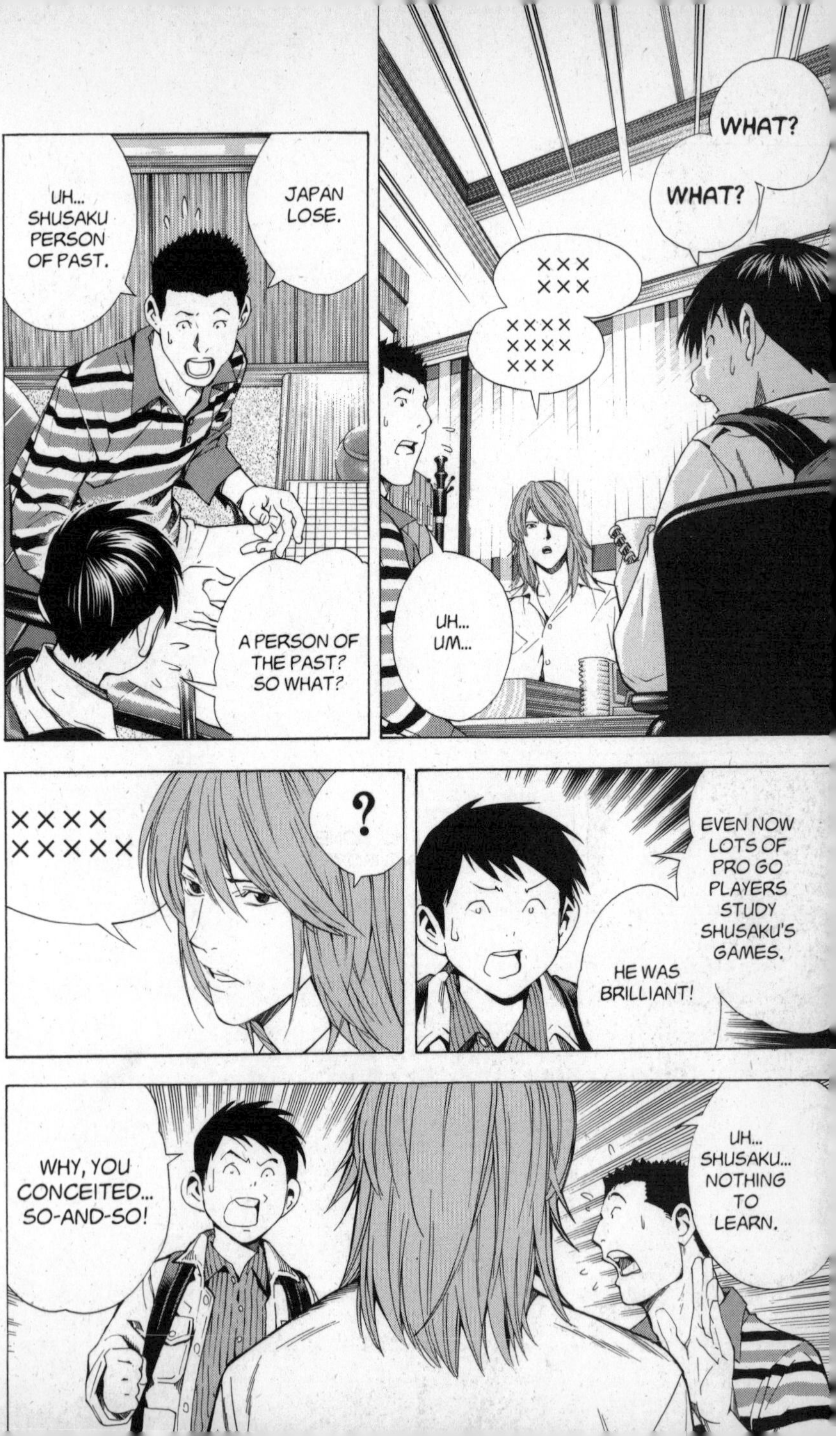
WHAT?
WHAT?
××× ×××
×××× ×××× ×××
UH... UM...
JAPAN LOSE.
UH... SHUSAKU PERSON OF PAST.
A PERSON OF THE PAST? SO WHAT?
EVEN NOW LOTS OF PRO GO PLAYERS STUDY SHUSAKU'S GAMES.
HE WAS BRILLIANT!
?
×××× ×××××
UH... SHUSAKU... NOTHING TO LEARN.
WHY, YOU CONCEITED... SO-AND-SO!

READ THIS WAY

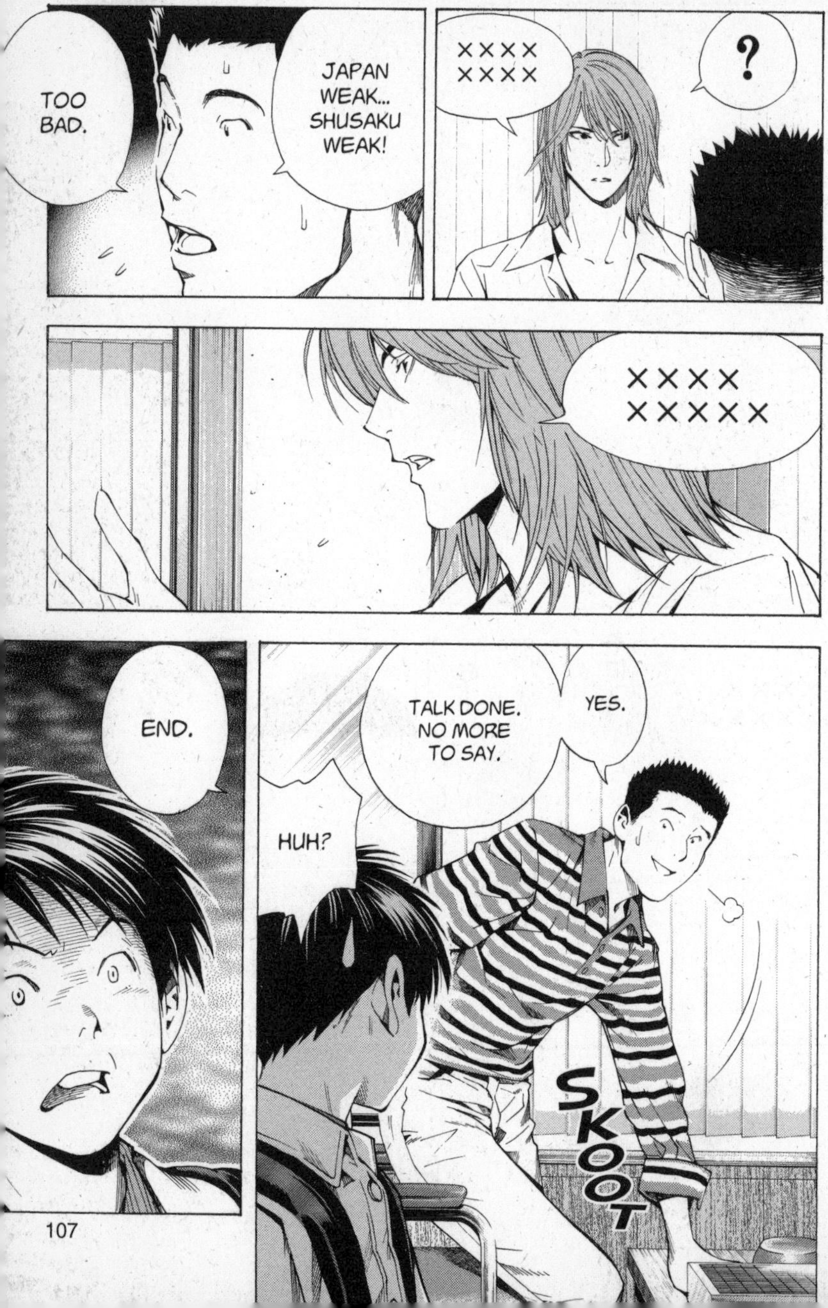

?
×××× ××××
JAPAN WEAK... SHUSAKU WEAK!
TOO BAD.
×××× ×××××
YES.
TALK DONE. NO MORE TO SAY.
HUH?
SKOOT
END.

HIKARU NO GO STORYBOARDS

⑸⓪

YUMI HOTTA

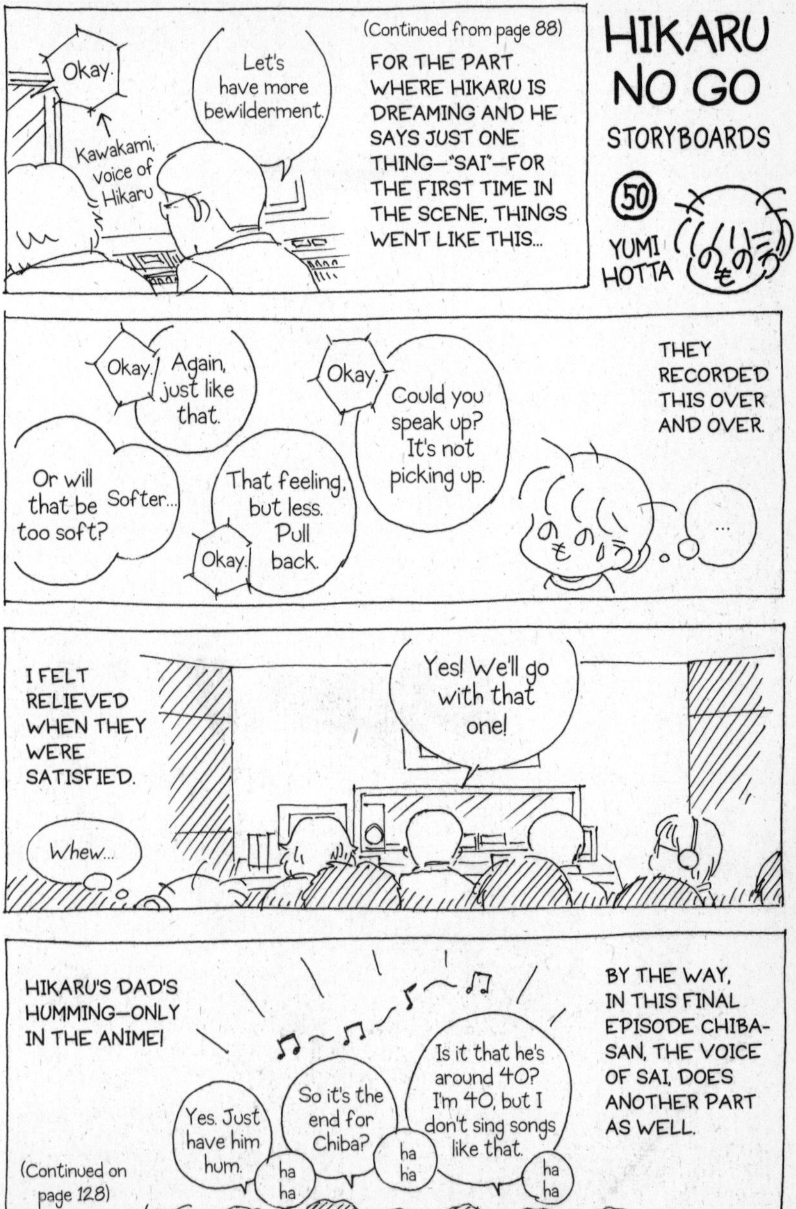
(Continued from page 88)
FOR THE PART WHERE HIKARU IS DREAMING AND HE SAYS JUST ONE THING—"SAI"—FOR THE FIRST TIME IN THE SCENE, THINGS WENT LIKE THIS...
Let's have more bewilderment.
Okay.
Kawakami, voice of Hikaru
THEY RECORDED THIS OVER AND OVER.
...
Okay.
Could you speak up? It's not picking up.
Okay.
Again, just like that.
That feeling, but less. Pull back.
Okay.
Softer...
Or will that be too soft?
Yes! We'll go with that one!
I FELT RELIEVED WHEN THEY WERE SATISFIED.
Whew...
BY THE WAY, IN THIS FINAL EPISODE CHIBA-SAN, THE VOICE OF SAI, DOES ANOTHER PART AS WELL.
Is it that he's around 40? I'm 40, but I don't sing songs like that.
ha ha
ha ha
HIKARU'S DAD'S HUMMING—ONLY IN THE ANIME!
So it's the end for Chiba?
Yes. Just have him hum.
ha ha
(Continued on page 128)

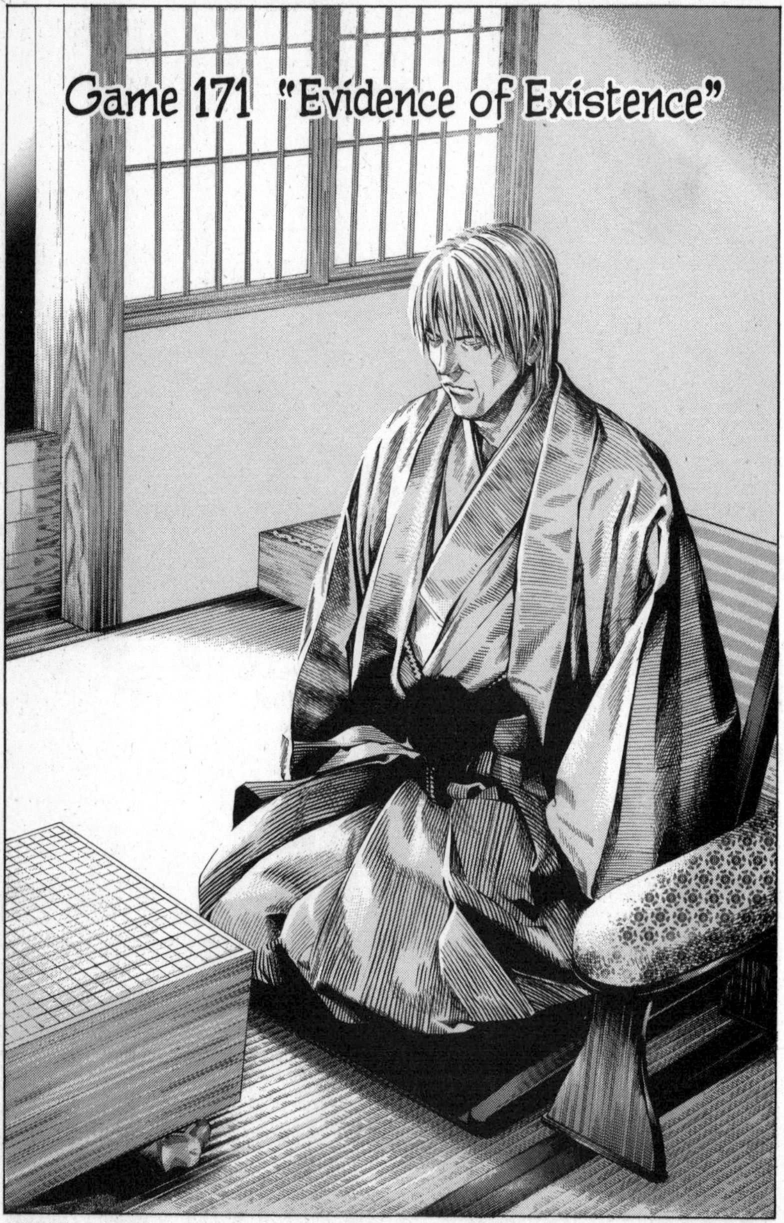
Game 171 "Evidence of Existence"

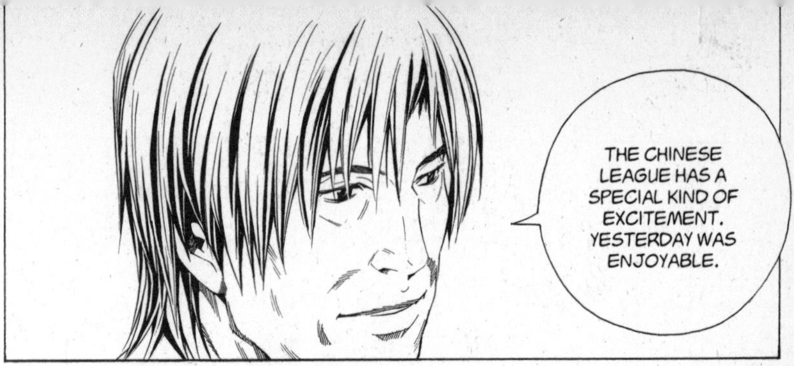
THE CHINESE LEAGUE HAS A SPECIAL KIND OF EXCITEMENT. YESTERDAY WAS ENJOYABLE.

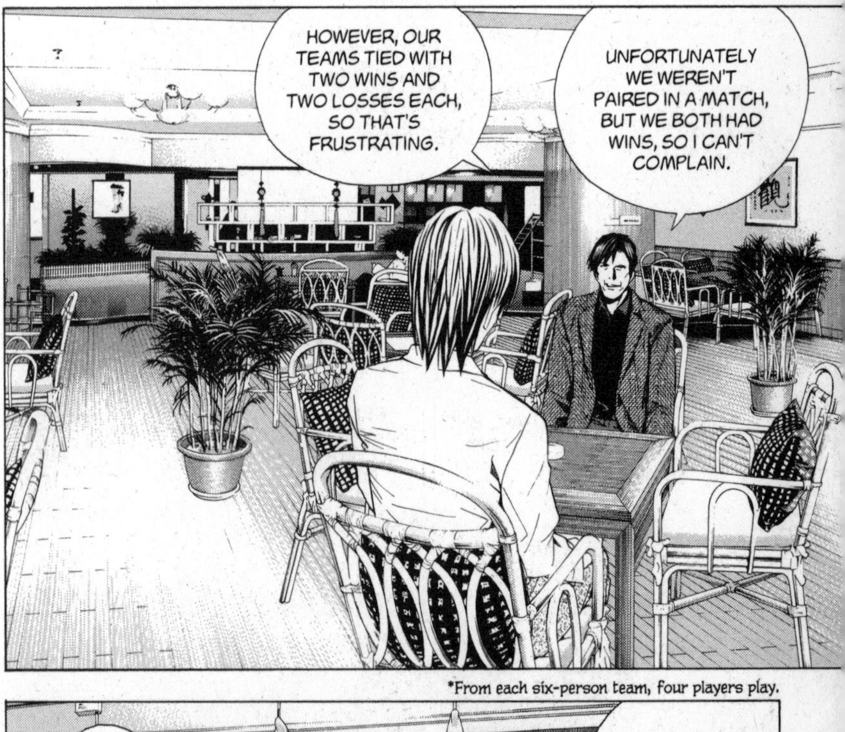
UNFORTUNATELY WE WEREN'T PAIRED IN A MATCH, BUT WE BOTH HAD WINS, SO I CAN'T COMPLAIN.
HOWEVER, OUR TEAMS TIED WITH TWO WINS AND TWO LOSSES EACH, SO THAT'S FRUSTRATING.

*From each six-person team, four players play.

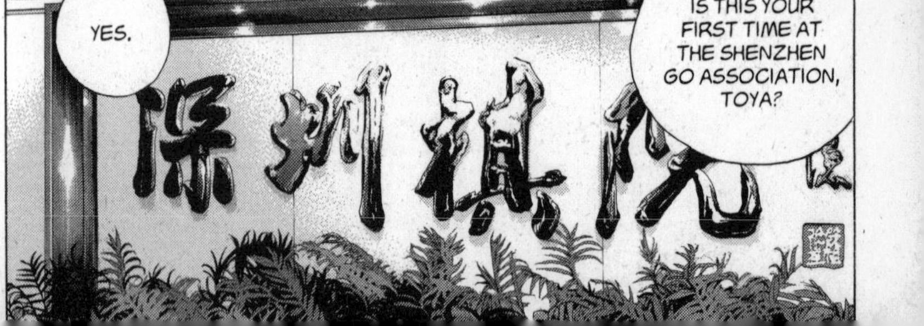
IS THIS YOUR FIRST TIME AT THE SHENZHEN GO ASSOCIATION, TOYA?
YES.
深圳棋院

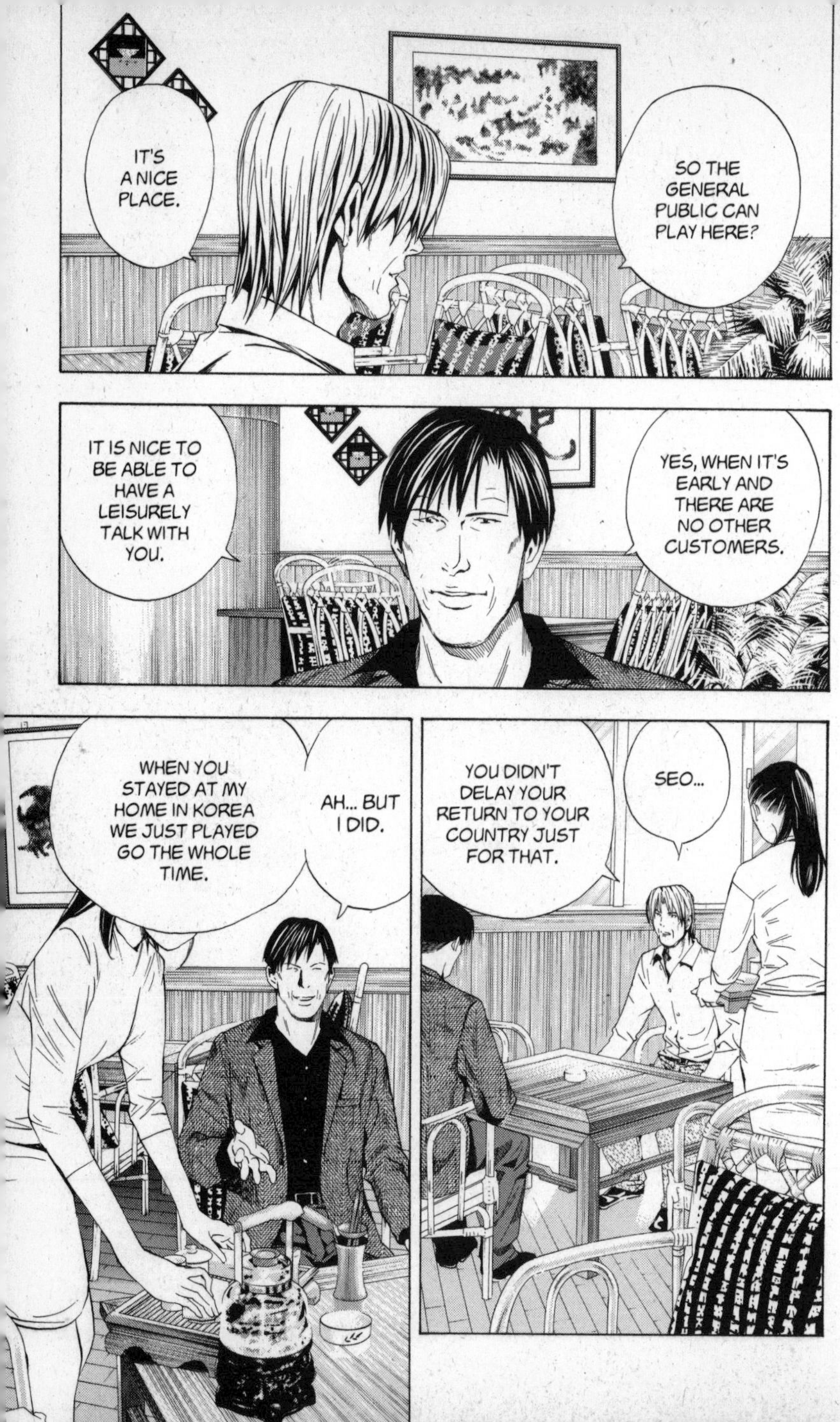
SO THE GENERAL PUBLIC CAN PLAY HERE?
IT'S A NICE PLACE.
YES, WHEN IT'S EARLY AND THERE ARE NO OTHER CUSTOMERS.
IT IS NICE TO BE ABLE TO HAVE A LEISURELY TALK WITH YOU.
SEO...
YOU DIDN'T DELAY YOUR RETURN TO YOUR COUNTRY JUST FOR THAT.
AH... BUT I DID.
WHEN YOU STAYED AT MY HOME IN KOREA WE JUST PLAYED GO THE WHOLE TIME.

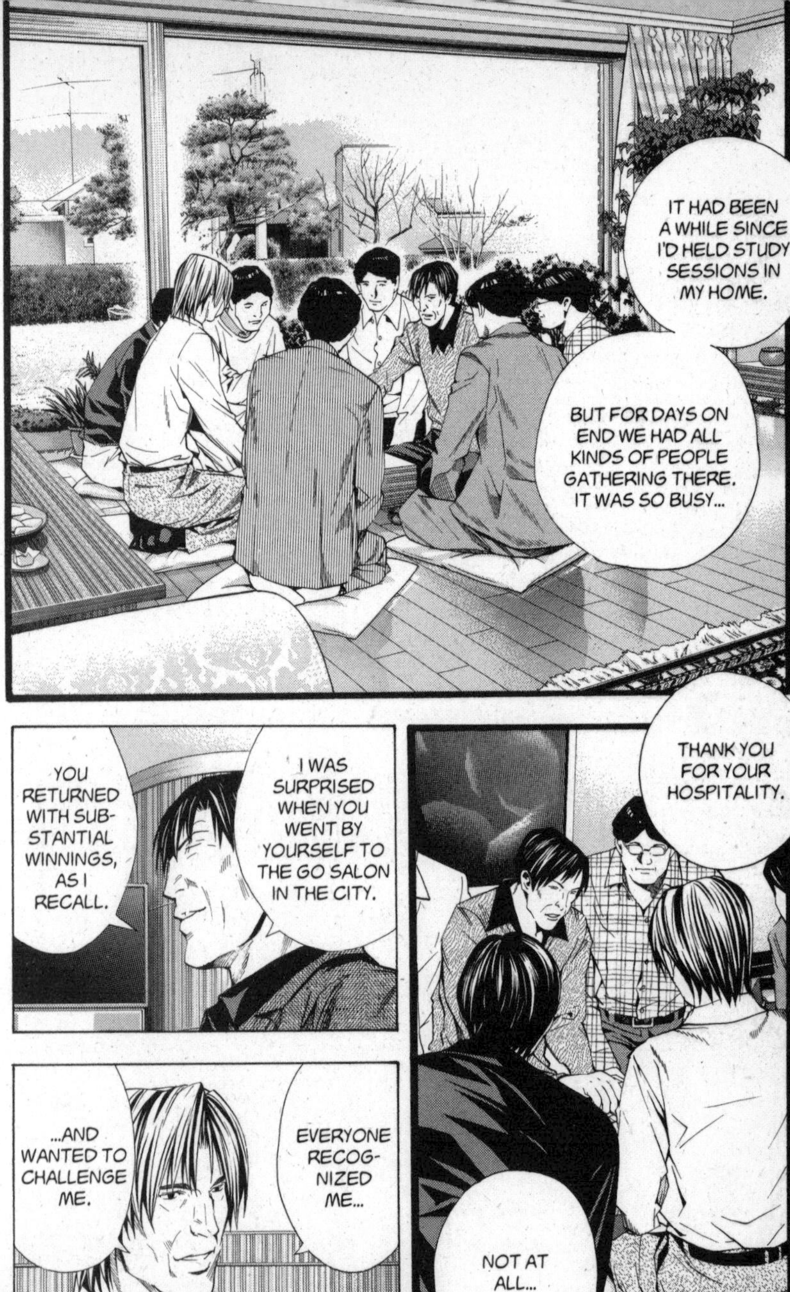
IT HAD BEEN A WHILE SINCE I'D HELD STUDY SESSIONS IN MY HOME.
BUT FOR DAYS ON END WE HAD ALL KINDS OF PEOPLE GATHERING THERE. IT WAS SO BUSY...
THANK YOU FOR YOUR HOSPITALITY.
NOT AT ALL...
I WAS SURPRISED WHEN YOU WENT BY YOURSELF TO THE GO SALON IN THE CITY.
YOU RETURNED WITH SUB-STANTIAL WINNINGS, AS I RECALL.
EVERYONE RECOG-NIZED ME...
...AND WANTED TO CHALLENGE ME.

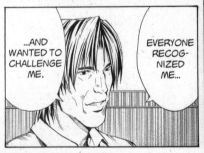

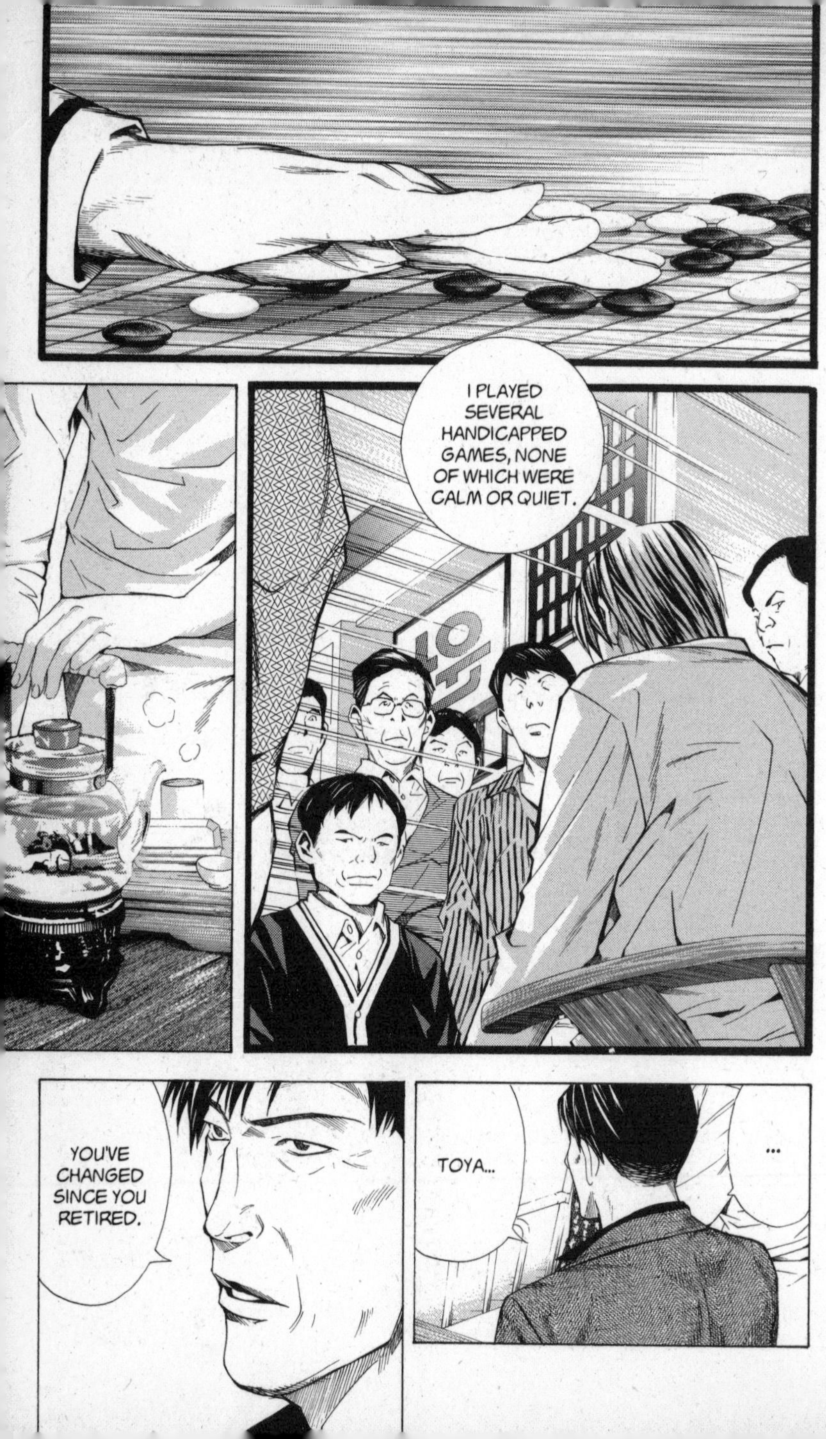
I PLAYED SEVERAL HANDICAPPED GAMES, NONE OF WHICH WERE CALM OR QUIET.
...
TOYA...
YOU'VE CHANGED SINCE YOU RETIRED.

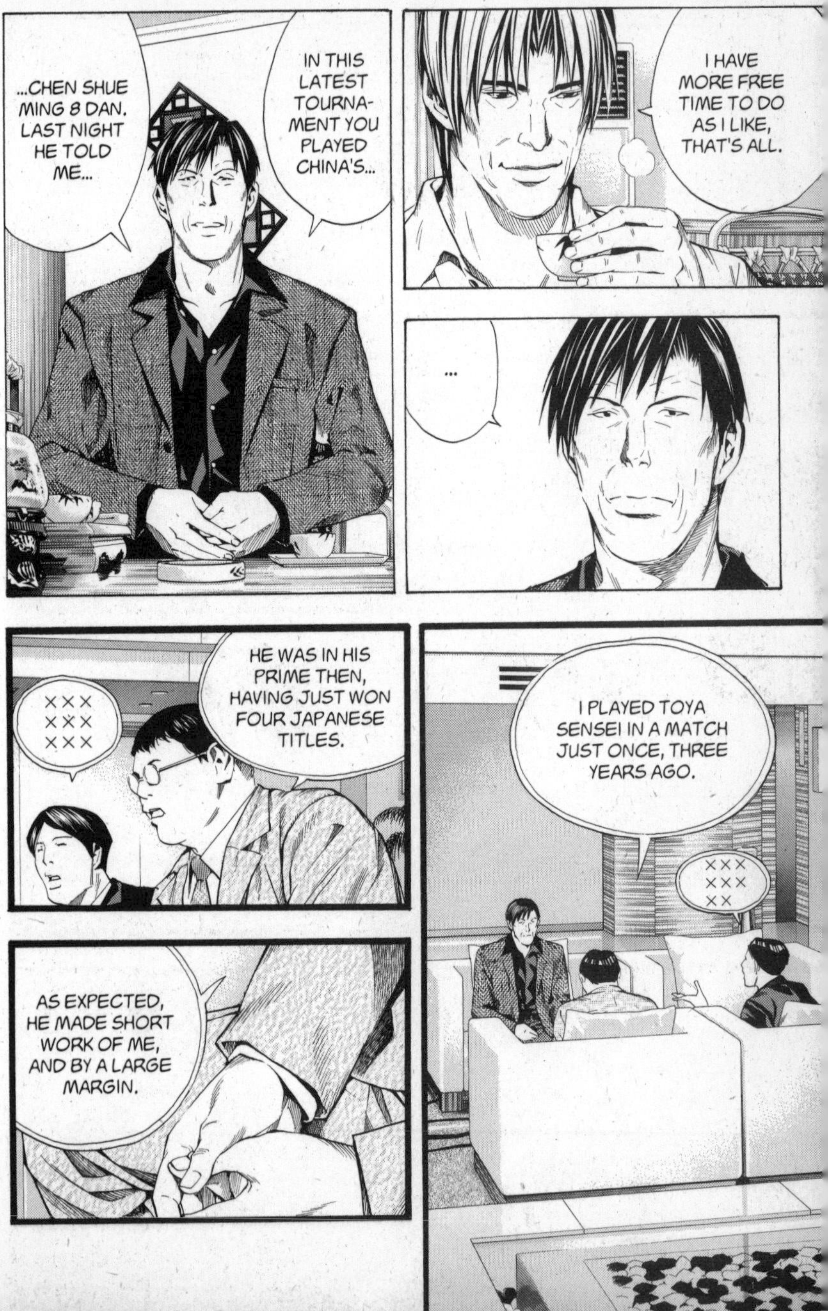
I HAVE MORE FREE TIME TO DO AS I LIKE, THAT'S ALL.
...
IN THIS LATEST TOURNAMENT YOU PLAYED CHINA'S...
...CHEN SHUE MING 8 DAN. LAST NIGHT HE TOLD ME...
I PLAYED TOYA SENSEI IN A MATCH JUST ONCE, THREE YEARS AGO.
XXX XXX XX
HE WAS IN HIS PRIME THEN, HAVING JUST WON FOUR JAPANESE TITLES.
XXX XXX XXX
AS EXPECTED, HE MADE SHORT WORK OF ME, AND BY A LARGE MARGIN.

READ THIS WAY

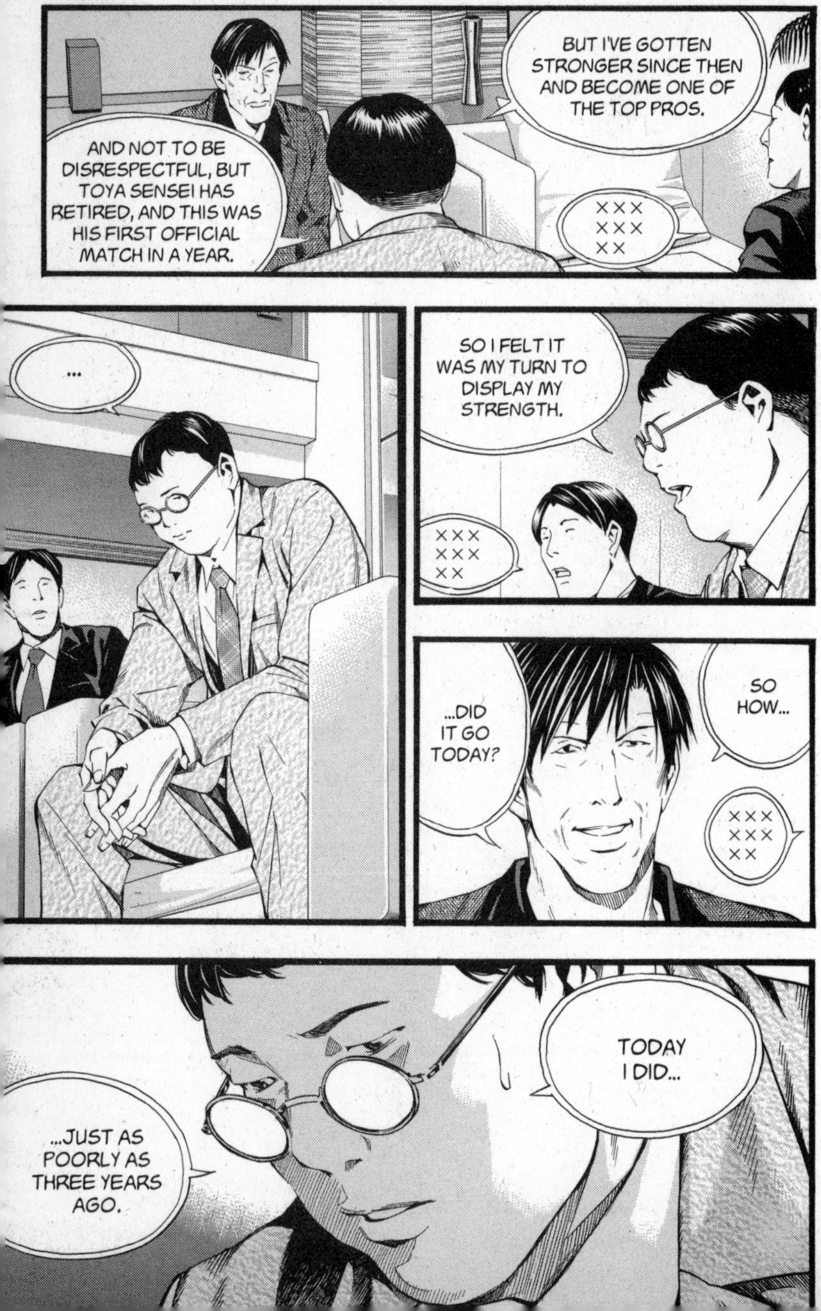

BUT I'VE GOTTEN STRONGER SINCE THEN AND BECOME ONE OF THE TOP PROS.
AND NOT TO BE DISRESPECTFUL, BUT TOYA SENSEI HAS RETIRED, AND THIS WAS HIS FIRST OFFICIAL MATCH IN A YEAR.
××× ××× ××
SO I FELT IT WAS MY TURN TO DISPLAY MY STRENGTH.
××× ××× ××
SO HOW...
...DID IT GO TODAY?
××× ××× ××
...
TODAY I DID...
...JUST AS POORLY AS THREE YEARS AGO.

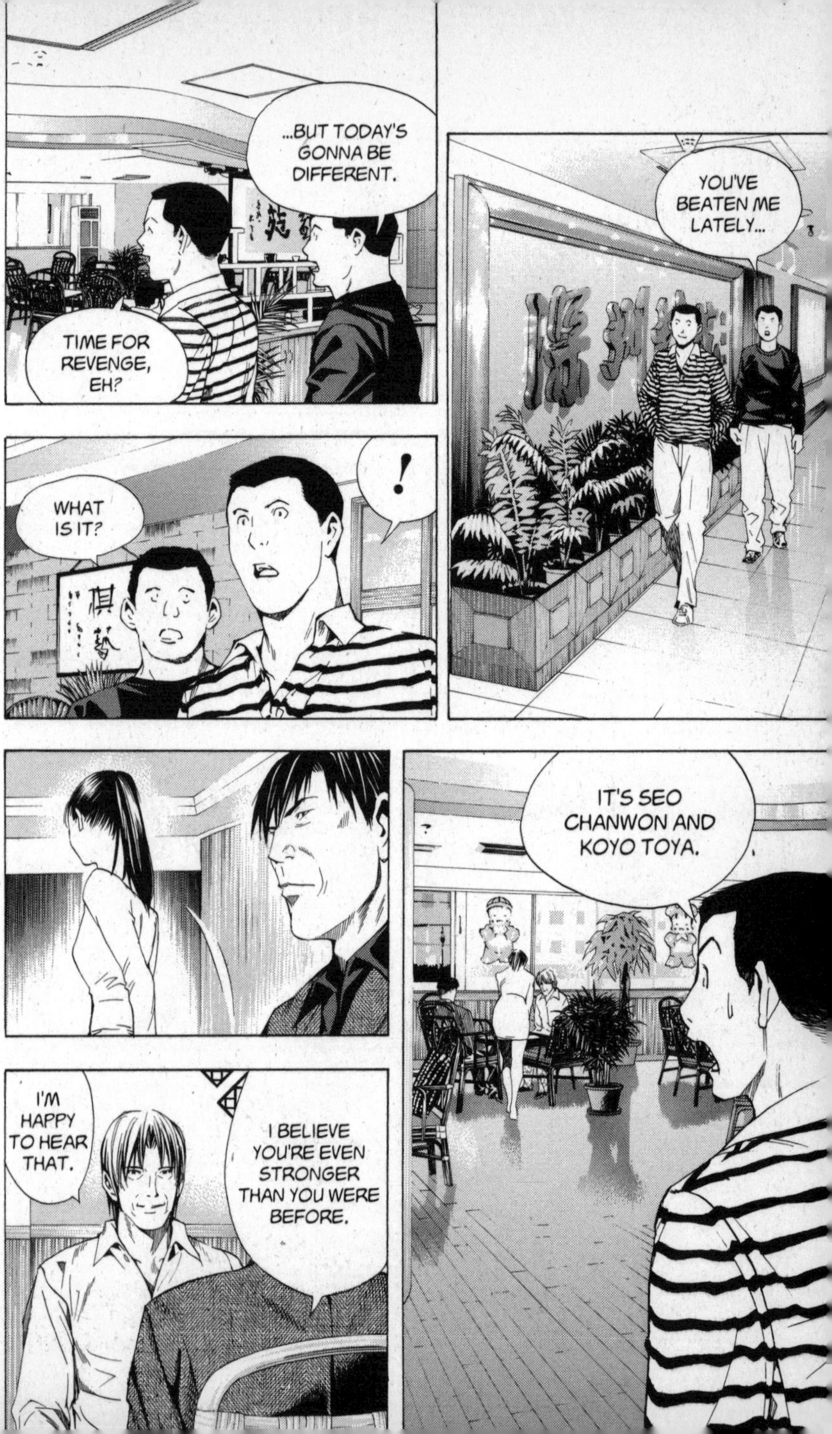
YOU'VE BEATEN ME LATELY...
...BUT TODAY'S GONNA BE DIFFERENT.
TIME FOR REVENGE, EH?
!
WHAT IS IT?
IT'S SEO CHANWON AND KOYO TOYA.
I BELIEVE YOU'RE EVEN STRONGER THAN YOU WERE BEFORE.
I'M HAPPY TO HEAR THAT.

READ THIS WAY

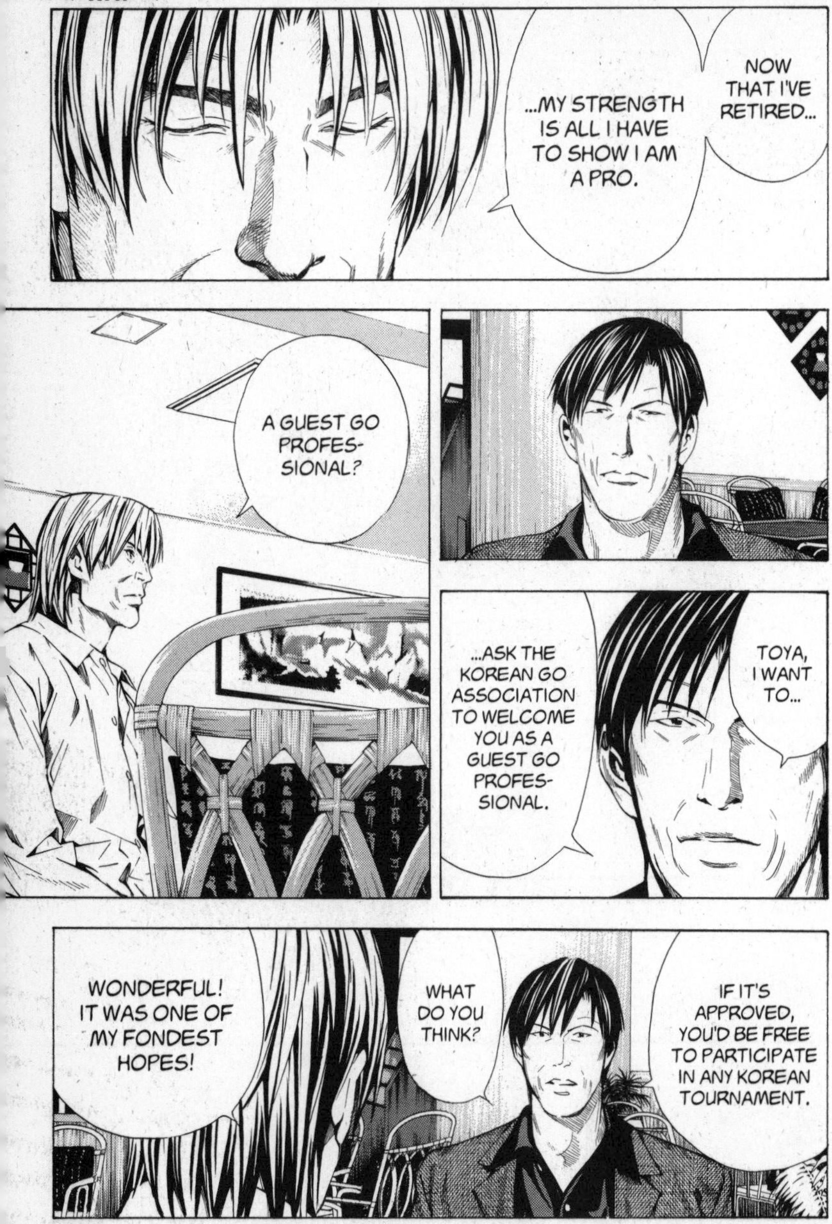
NOW THAT I'VE RETIRED...
...MY STRENGTH IS ALL I HAVE TO SHOW I AM A PRO.
TOYA, I WANT TO...
...ASK THE KOREAN GO ASSOCIATION TO WELCOME YOU AS A GUEST GO PROFES-SIONAL.
A GUEST GO PROFES-SIONAL?
IF IT'S APPROVED, YOU'D BE FREE TO PARTICIPATE IN ANY KOREAN TOURNAMENT.
WHAT DO YOU THINK?
WONDERFUL! IT WAS ONE OF MY FONDEST HOPES!

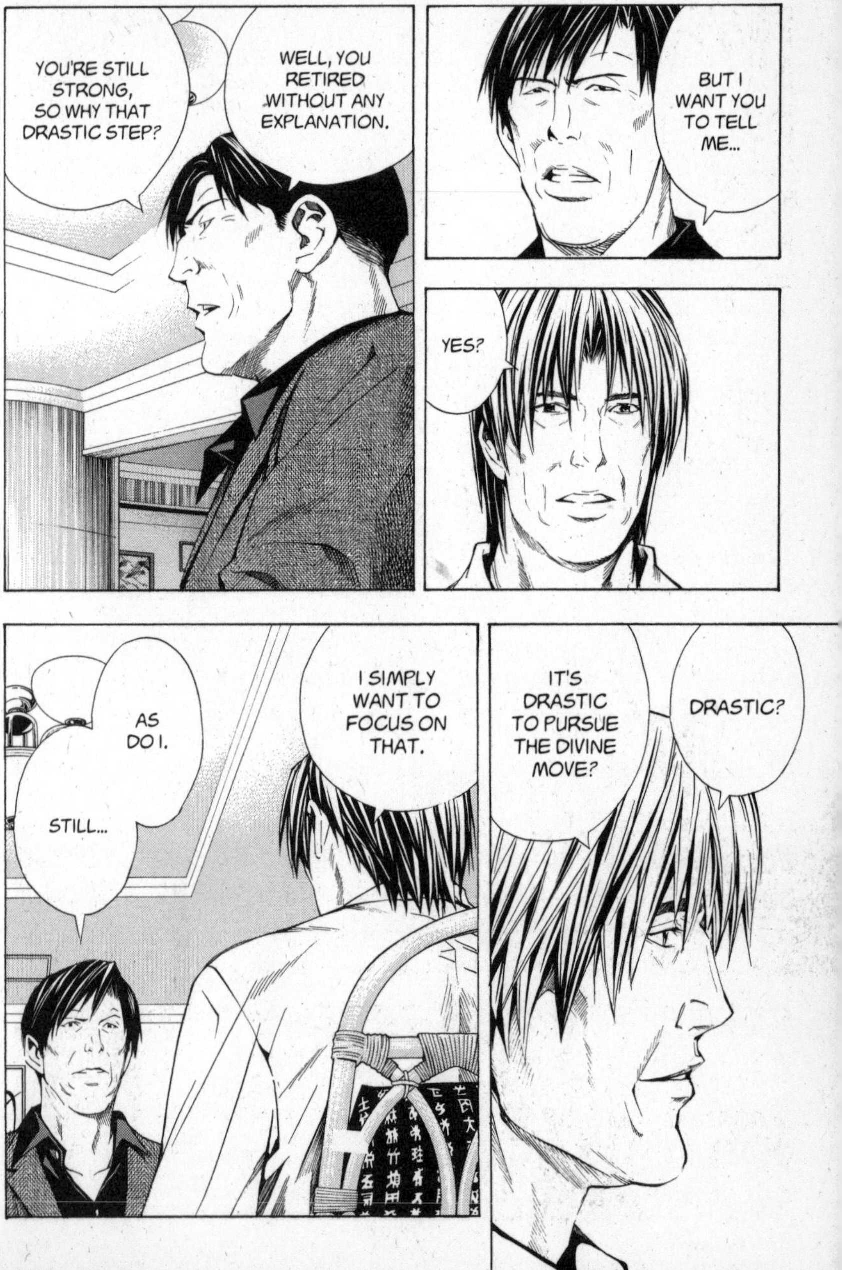
BUT I WANT YOU TO TELL ME...
YES?
WELL, YOU RETIRED WITHOUT ANY EXPLANATION.
YOU'RE STILL STRONG, SO WHY THAT DRASTIC STEP?
DRASTIC?
IT'S DRASTIC TO PURSUE THE DIVINE MOVE?
I SIMPLY WANT TO FOCUS ON THAT.
AS DO I.
STILL...

READ THIS WAY

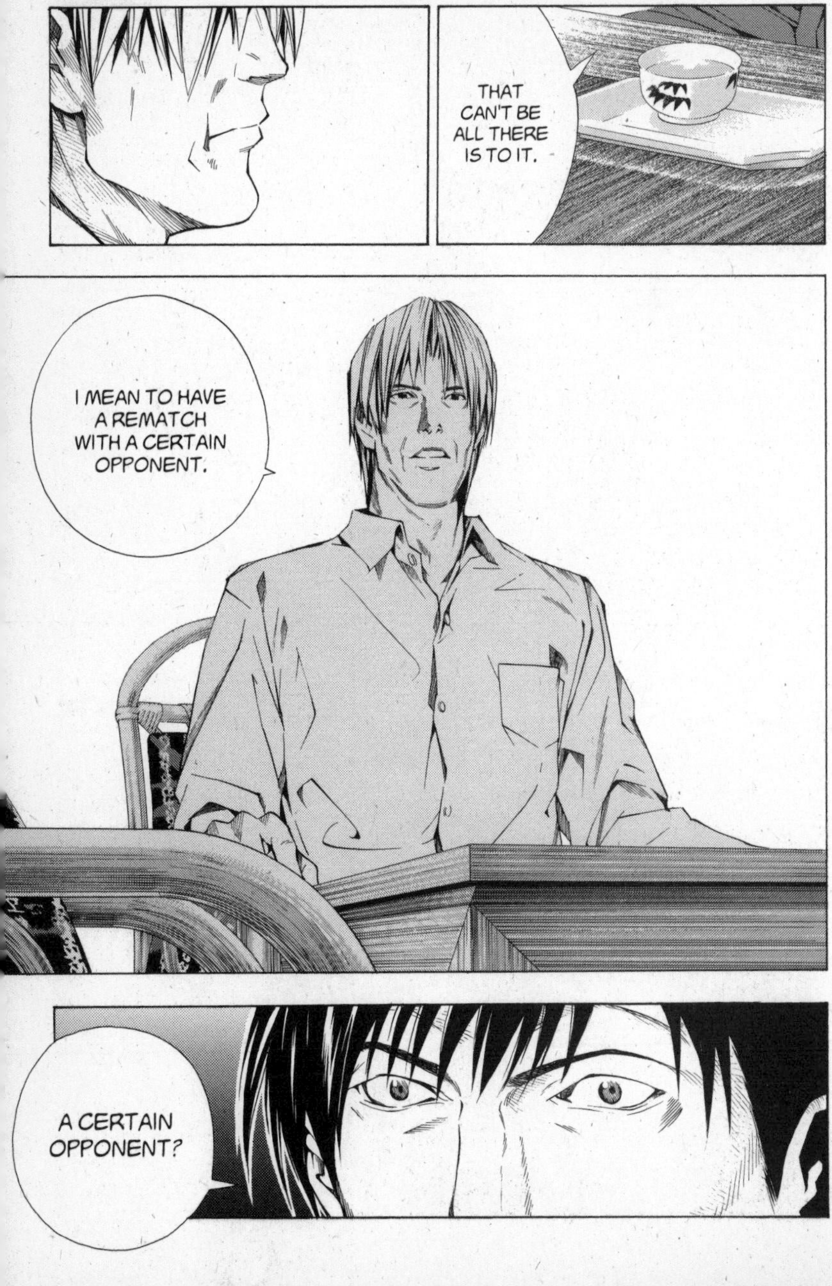
THAT CAN'T BE ALL THERE IS TO IT.
I MEAN TO HAVE A REMATCH WITH A CERTAIN OPPONENT.
A CERTAIN OPPONENT?

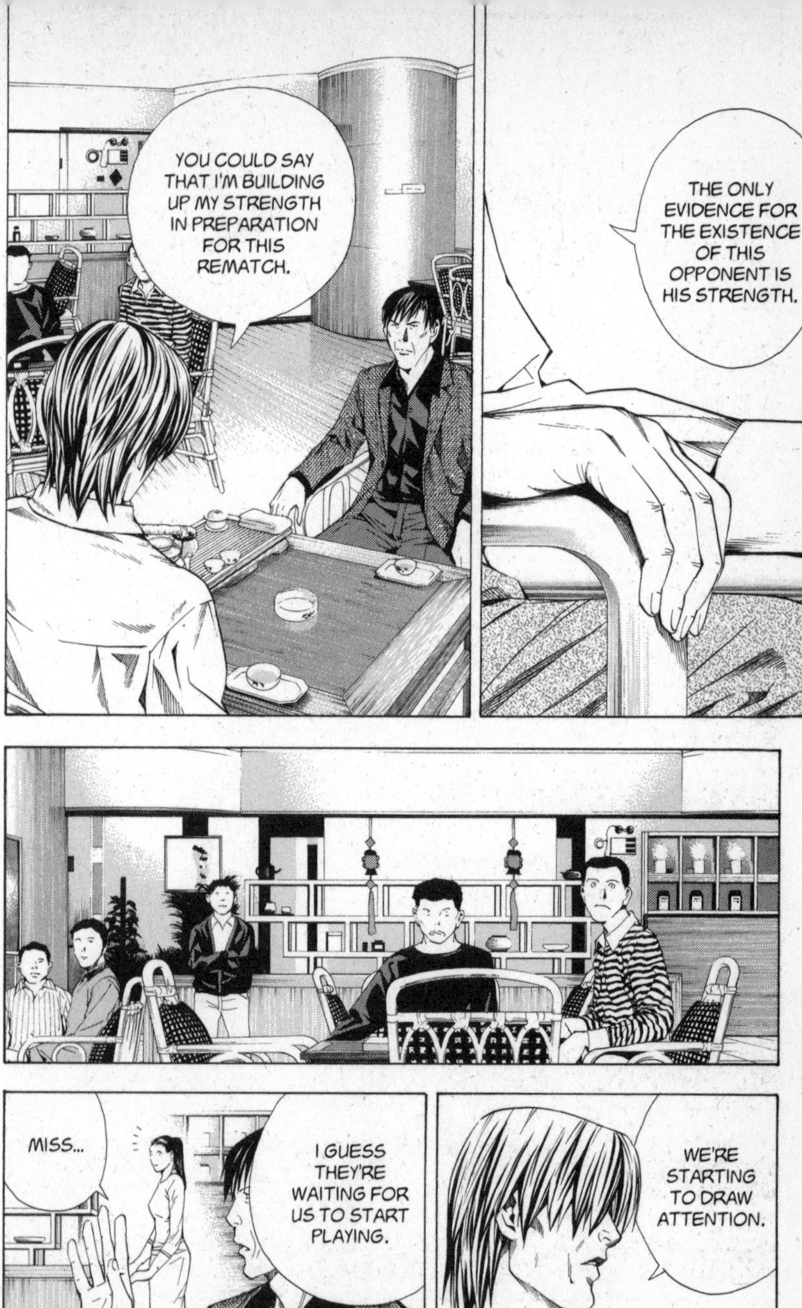
THE ONLY EVIDENCE FOR THE EXISTENCE OF THIS OPPONENT IS HIS STRENGTH.
YOU COULD SAY THAT I'M BUILDING UP MY STRENGTH IN PREPARATION FOR THIS REMATCH.
WE'RE STARTING TO DRAW ATTENTION.
I GUESS THEY'RE WAITING FOR US TO START PLAYING.
MISS...

THERE
THEY GO.

MURMUR

SKOOT

AH!

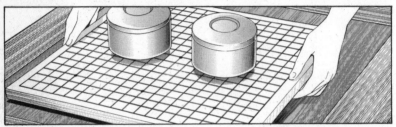

WHO
IS IT?

TOYA... THIS
OPPONENT
OF YOURS...

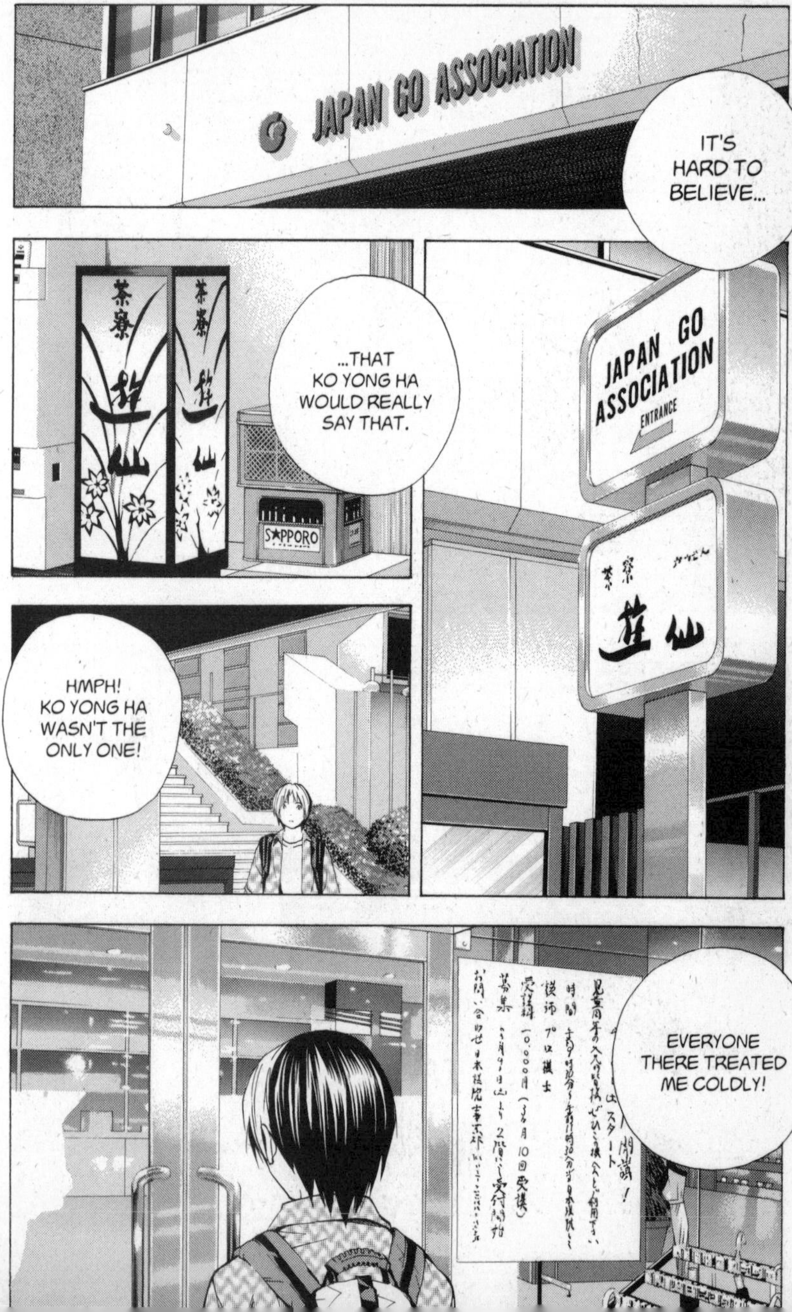
JAPAN GO ASSOCIATION
IT'S HARD TO BELIEVE...
JAPAN GO ASSOCIATION
ENTRANCE
...THAT KO YONG HA WOULD REALLY SAY THAT.
SAPPORO
HMPH! KO YONG HA WASN'T THE ONLY ONE!
EVERYONE THERE TREATED ME COLDLY!

READ THIS WAY

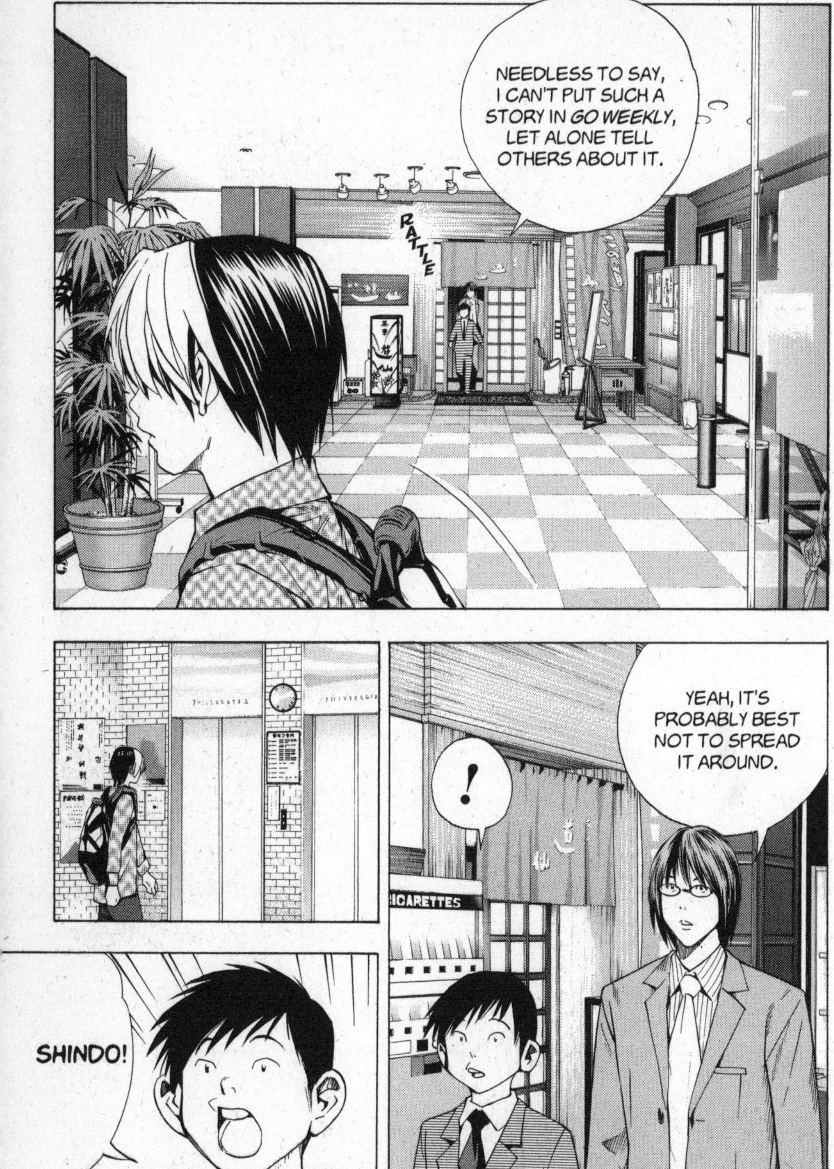

NEEDLESS TO SAY, I CAN'T PUT SUCH A STORY IN *GO WEEKLY*, LET ALONE TELL OTHERS ABOUT IT.
RATTLE
YEAH, IT'S PROBABLY BEST NOT TO SPREAD IT AROUND.
!
CIGARETTES
SHINDO!

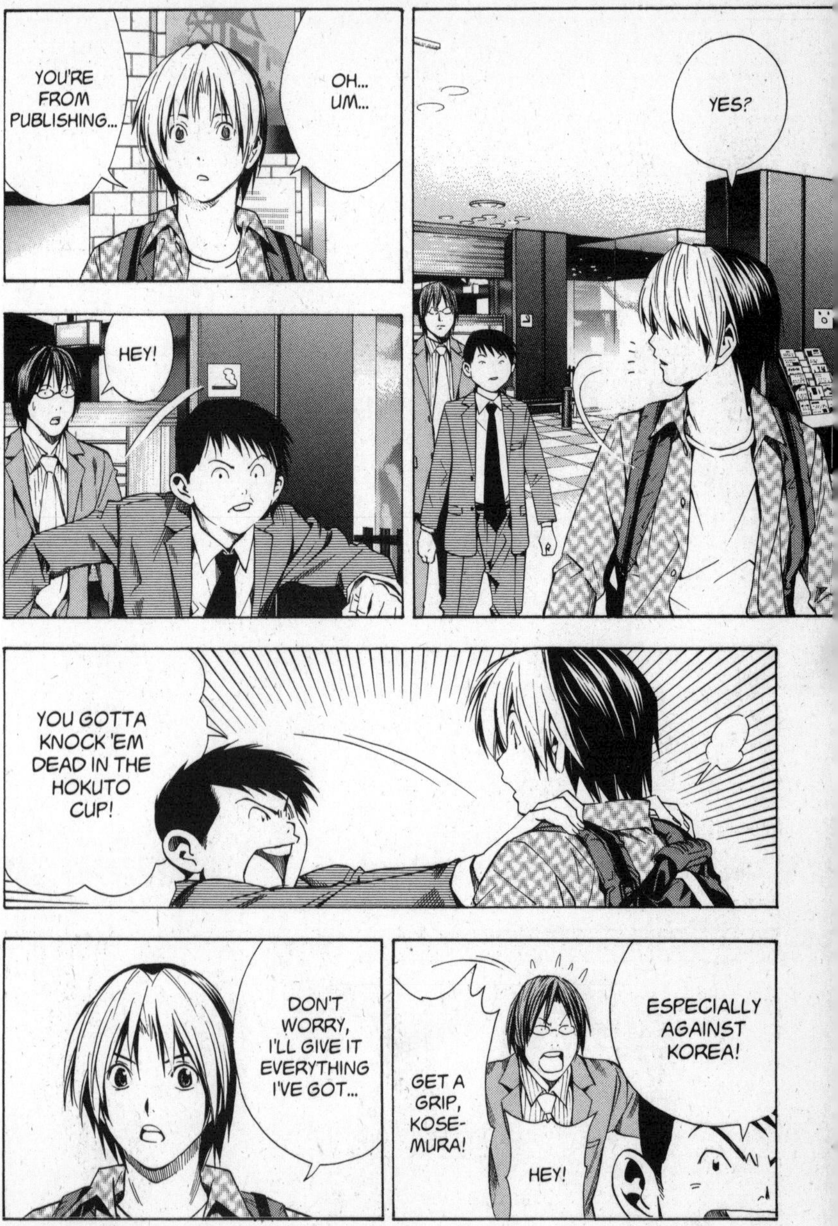
YES?
OH... UM...
YOU'RE FROM PUBLISHING...
HEY!
YOU GOTTA KNOCK 'EM DEAD IN THE HOKUTO CUP!
ESPECIALLY AGAINST KOREA!
GET A GRIP, KOSE-MURA!
HEY!
DON'T WORRY, I'LL GIVE IT EVERYTHING I'VE GOT...

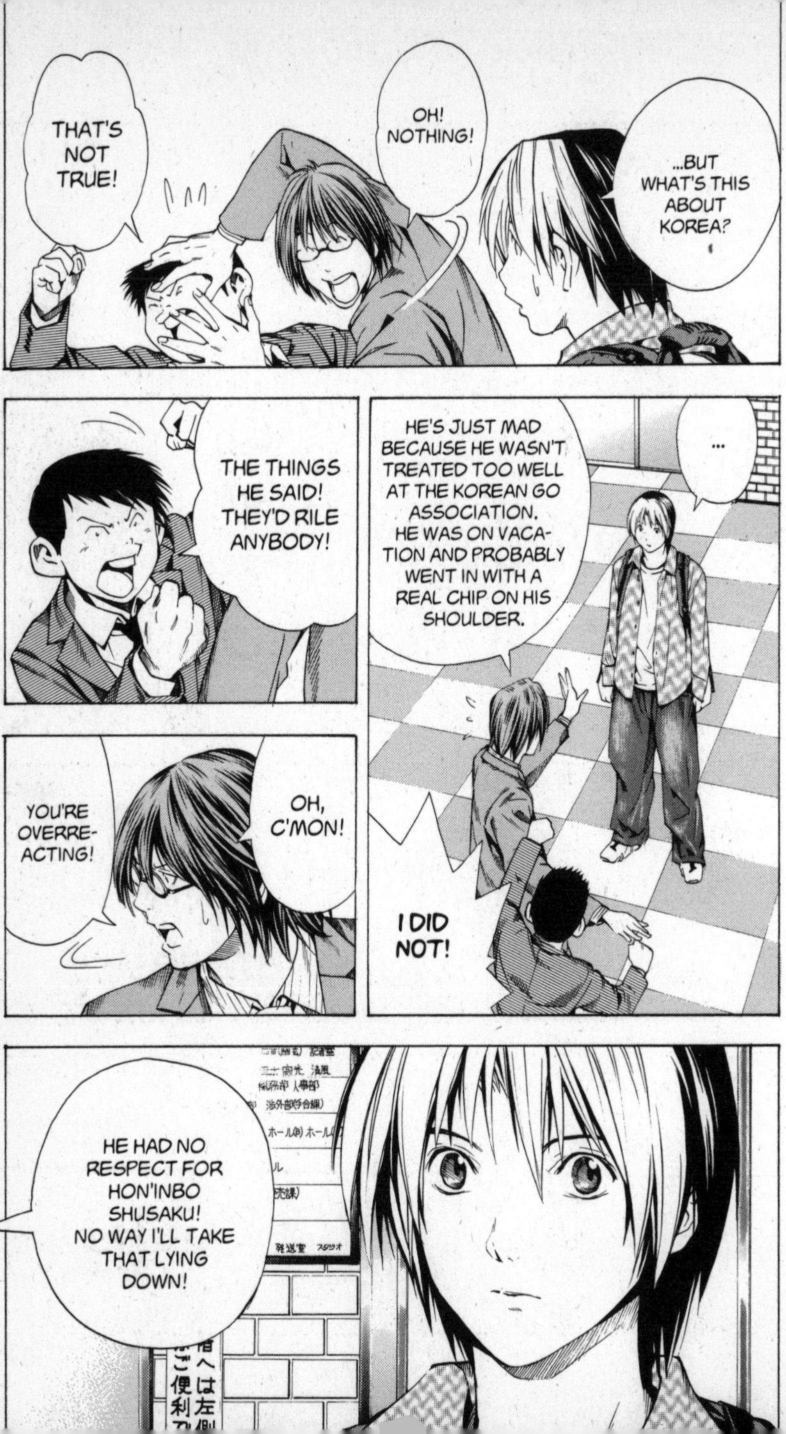
...BUT WHAT'S THIS ABOUT KOREA?
OH! NOTHING!
THAT'S NOT TRUE!
...
HE'S JUST MAD BECAUSE HE WASN'T TREATED TOO WELL AT THE KOREAN GO ASSOCIATION. HE WAS ON VACA-TION AND PROBABLY WENT IN WITH A REAL CHIP ON HIS SHOULDER.
I DID NOT!
THE THINGS HE SAID! THEY'D RILE ANYBODY!
OH, C'MON!
YOU'RE OVERRE-ACTING!
HE HAD NO RESPECT FOR HON'INBO SHUSAKU! NO WAY I'LL TAKE THAT LYING DOWN!

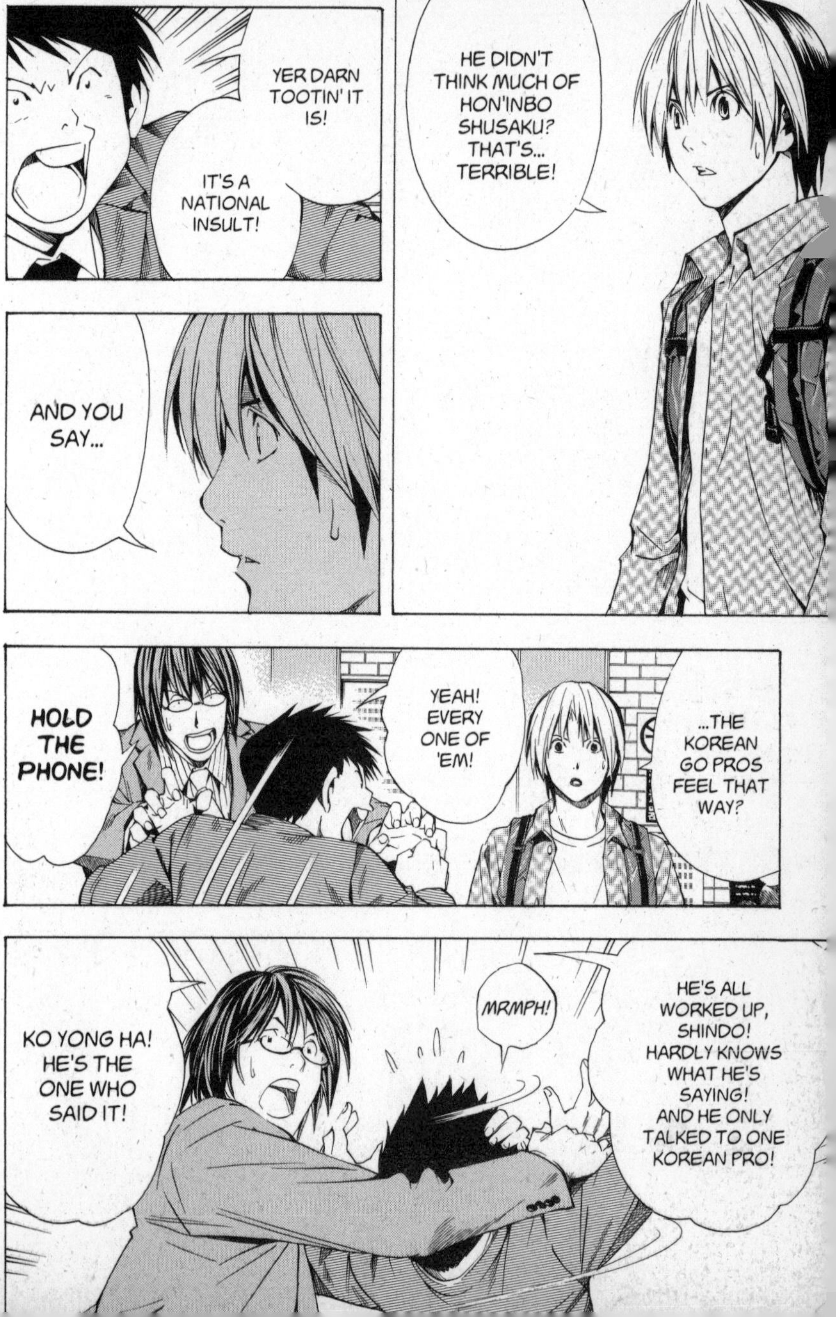
HE DIDN'T THINK MUCH OF HON'INBO SHUSAKU? THAT'S... TERRIBLE!
YER DARN TOOTIN' IT IS!
IT'S A NATIONAL INSULT!
AND YOU SAY...
...THE KOREAN GO PROS FEEL THAT WAY?
YEAH! EVERY ONE OF 'EM!
HOLD THE PHONE!
HE'S ALL WORKED UP, SHINDO! HARDLY KNOWS WHAT HE'S SAYING! AND HE ONLY TALKED TO ONE KOREAN PRO!
MRMPH!
KO YONG HA! HE'S THE ONE WHO SAID IT!

READ THIS WAY

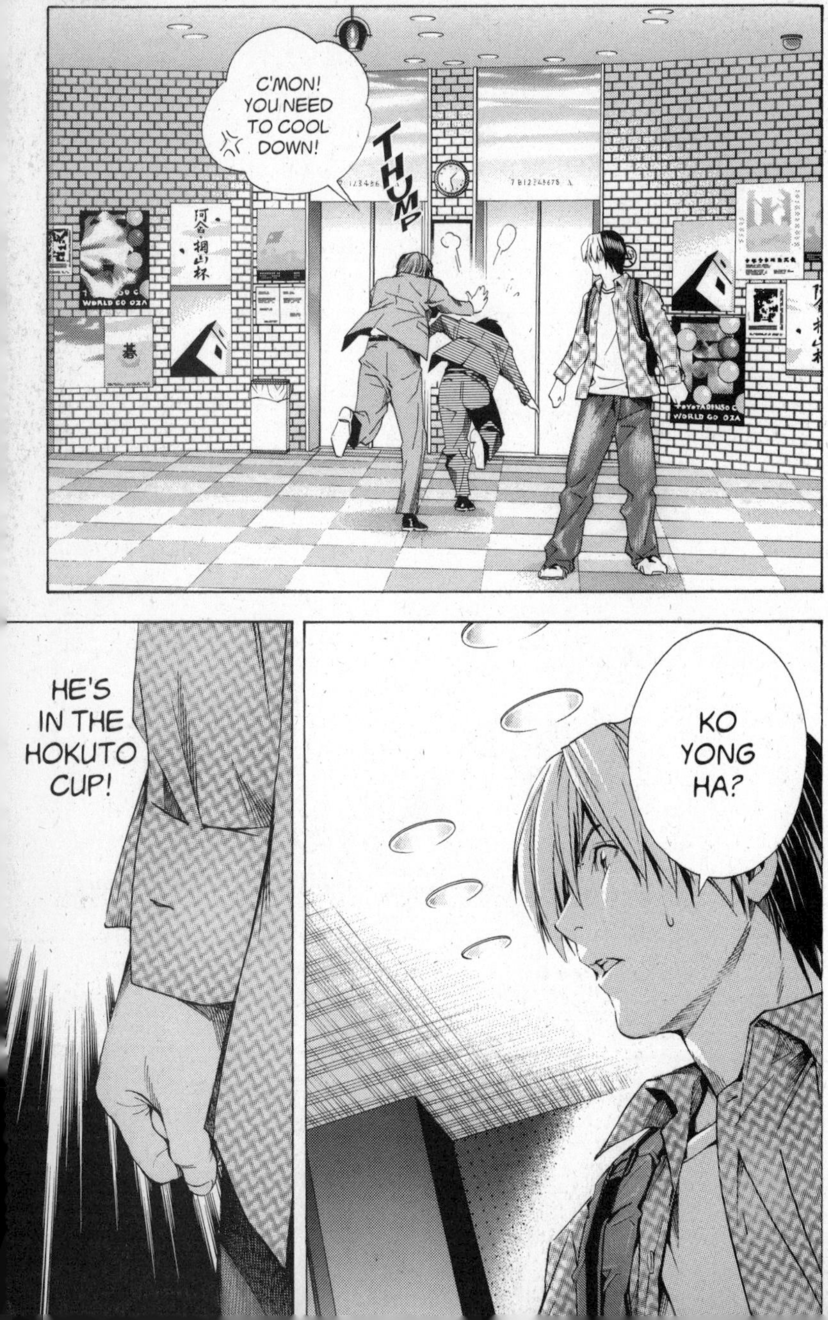
C'MON! YOU NEED TO COOL DOWN!
THUMP
KO YONG HA?
HE'S IN THE HOKUTO CUP!

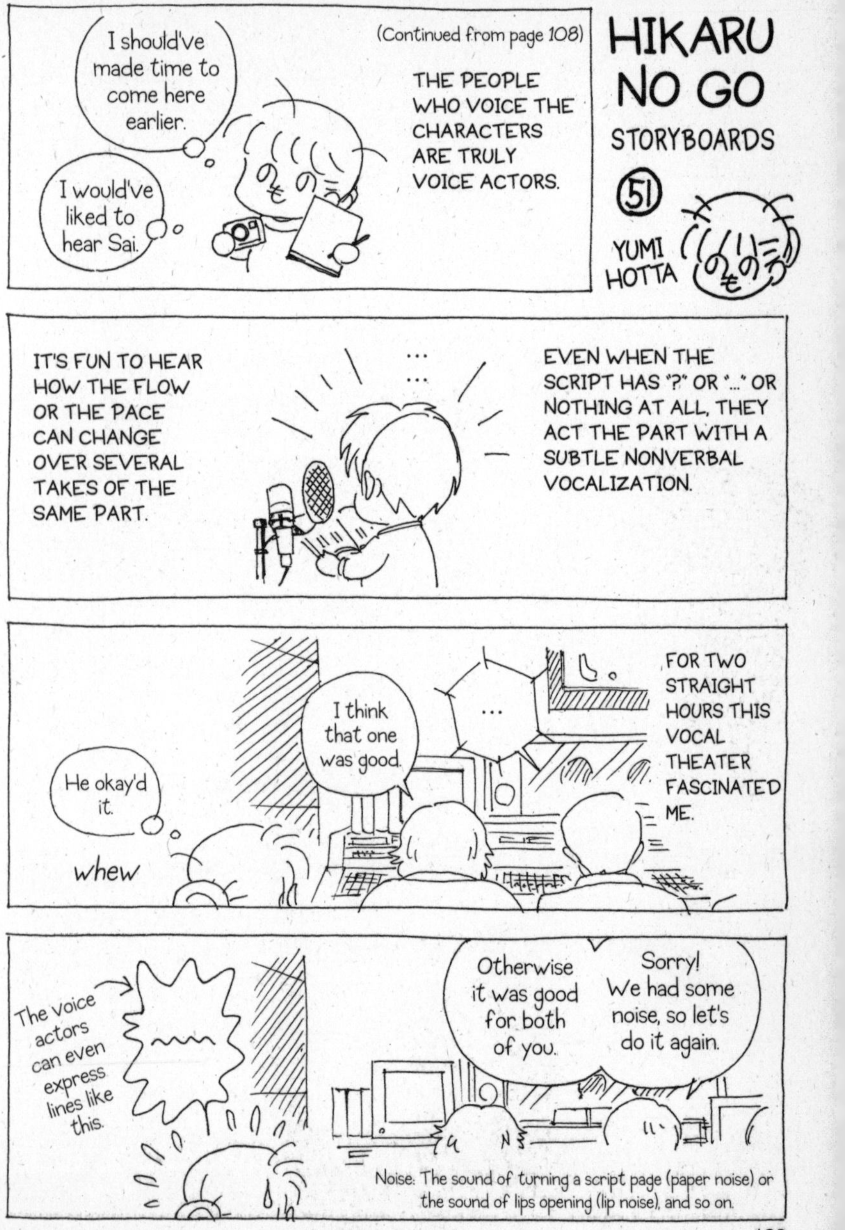
HIKARU NO GO
STORYBOARDS
51
YUMI HOTTA
(Continued from page 108)
THE PEOPLE WHO VOICE THE CHARACTERS ARE TRULY VOICE ACTORS.
I should've made time to come here earlier.
I would've liked to hear Sai.
EVEN WHEN THE SCRIPT HAS "?" OR "..." OR NOTHING AT ALL, THEY ACT THE PART WITH A SUBTLE NONVERBAL VOCALIZATION.
...
...
IT'S FUN TO HEAR HOW THE FLOW OR THE PACE CAN CHANGE OVER SEVERAL TAKES OF THE SAME PART.
FOR TWO STRAIGHT HOURS THIS VOCAL THEATER FASCINATED ME.
...
I think that one was good.
He okay'd it.
whew
Sorry! We had some noise, so let's do it again.
Otherwise it was good for both of you.
The voice actors can even express lines like this.
Noise: The sound of turning a script page (paper noise) or the sound of lips opening (lip noise), and so on.

Game 172 "The Toya Residence"

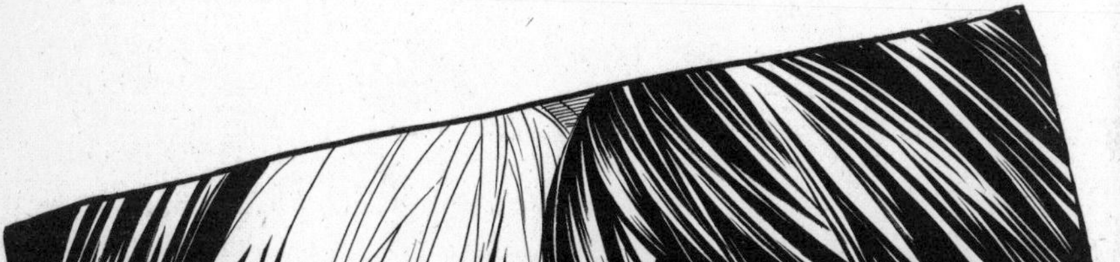

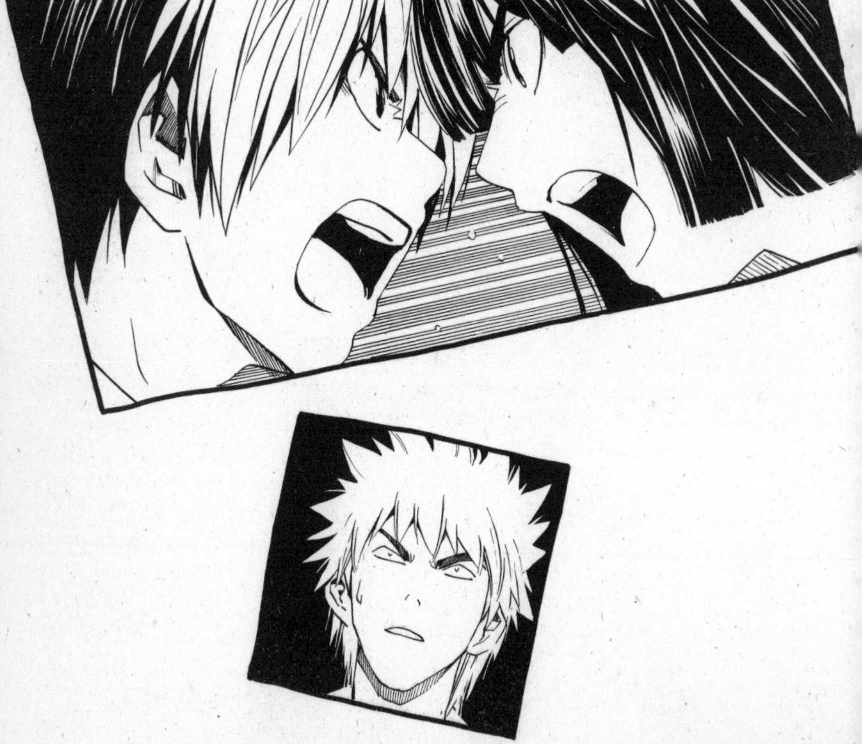

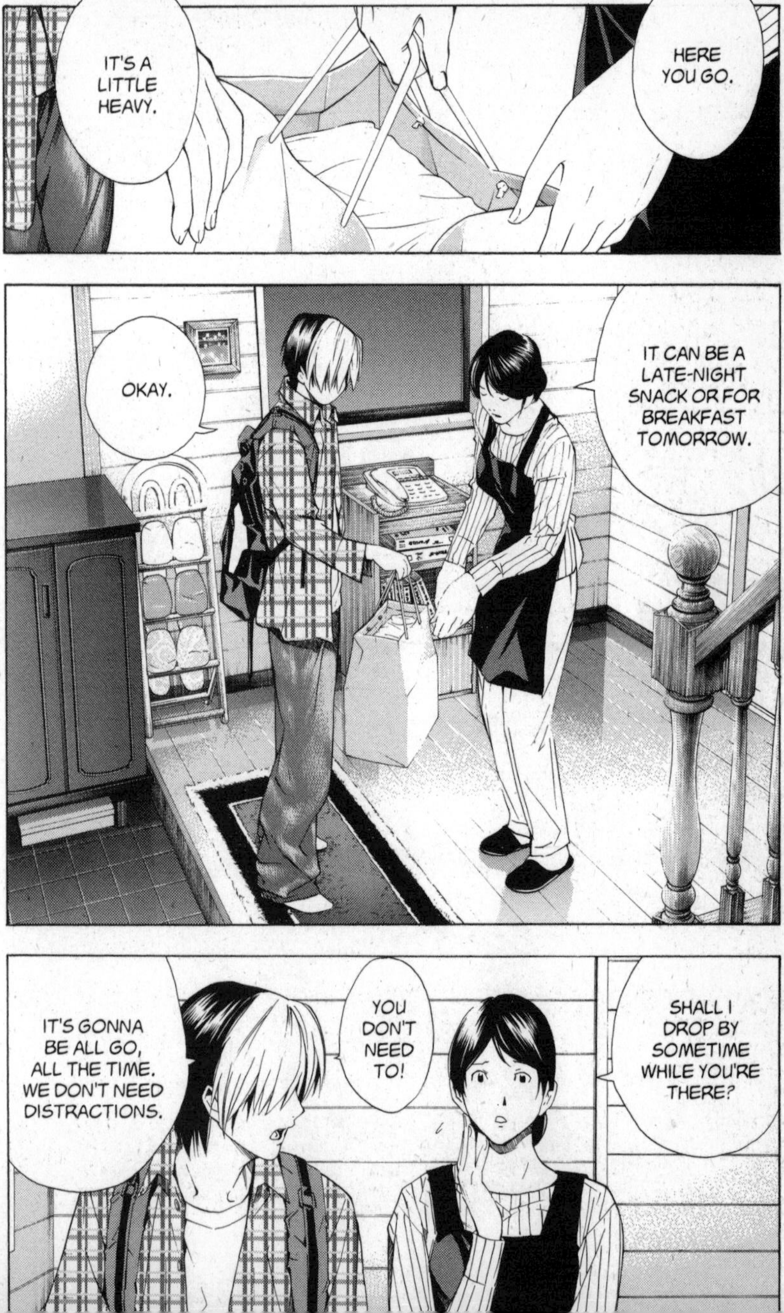
HERE YOU GO.
IT'S A LITTLE HEAVY.
IT CAN BE A LATE-NIGHT SNACK OR FOR BREAKFAST TOMORROW.
OKAY.
SHALL I DROP BY SOMETIME WHILE YOU'RE THERE?
YOU DON'T NEED TO!
IT'S GONNA BE ALL GO, ALL THE TIME. WE DON'T NEED DISTRACTIONS.

READ THIS WAY

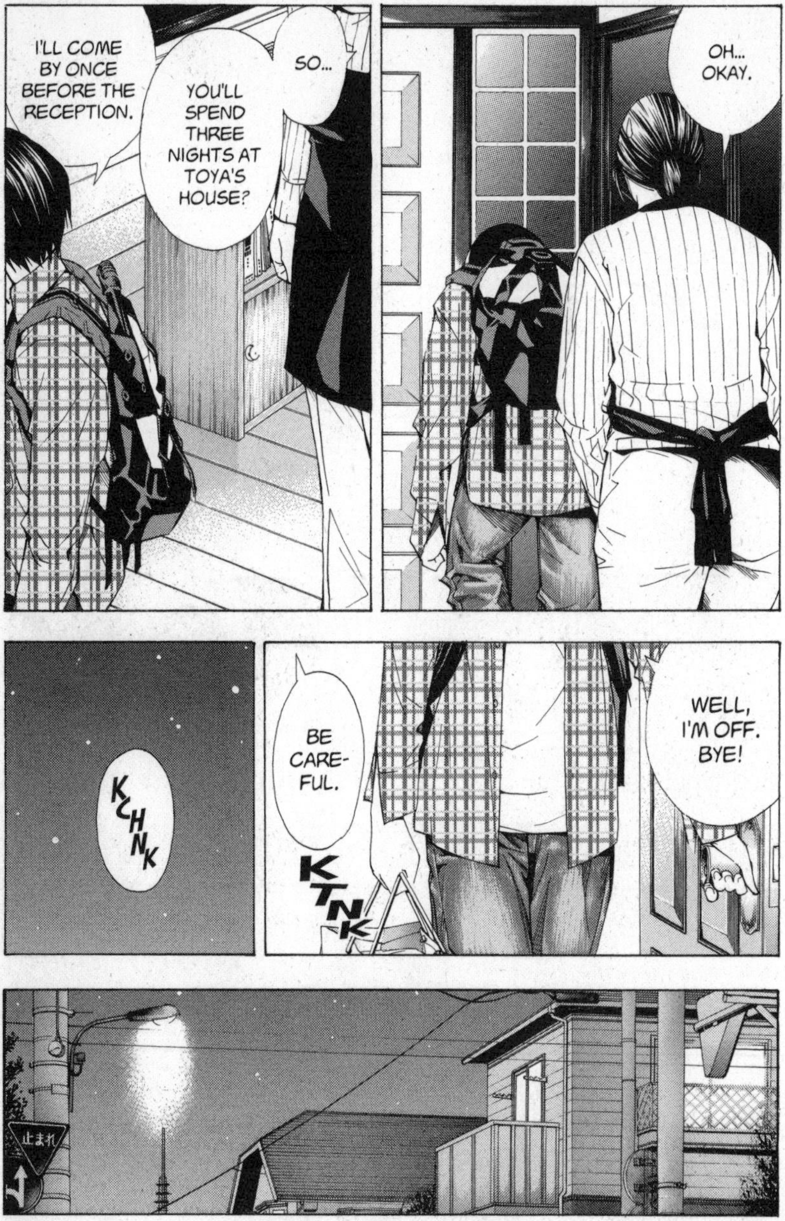
OH... OKAY.
SO...
YOU'LL SPEND THREE NIGHTS AT TOYA'S HOUSE?
I'LL COME BY ONCE BEFORE THE RECEPTION.
WELL, I'M OFF. BYE!
BE CARE-FUL.
KTNK
KCHNK
止まれ

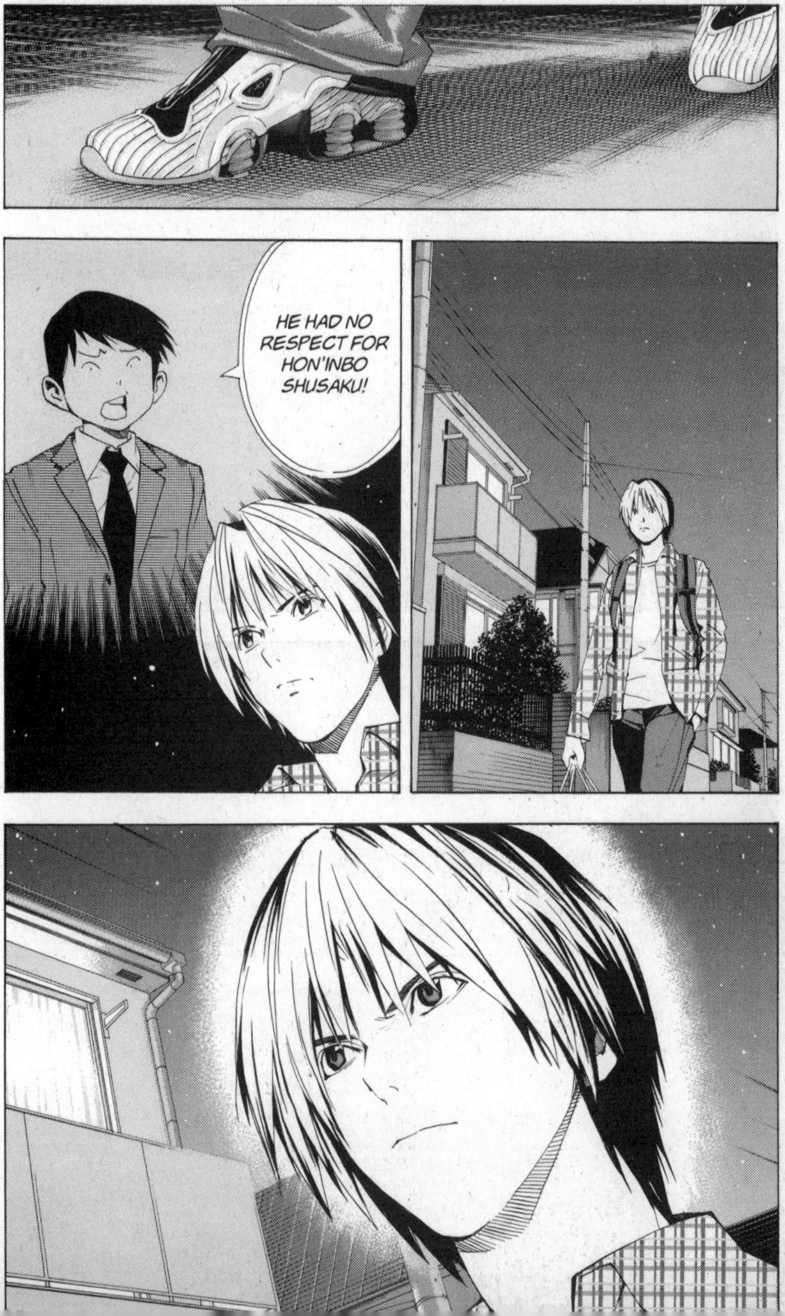
HE HAD NO RESPECT FOR HON'INBO SHUSAKU!

READ THIS WAY

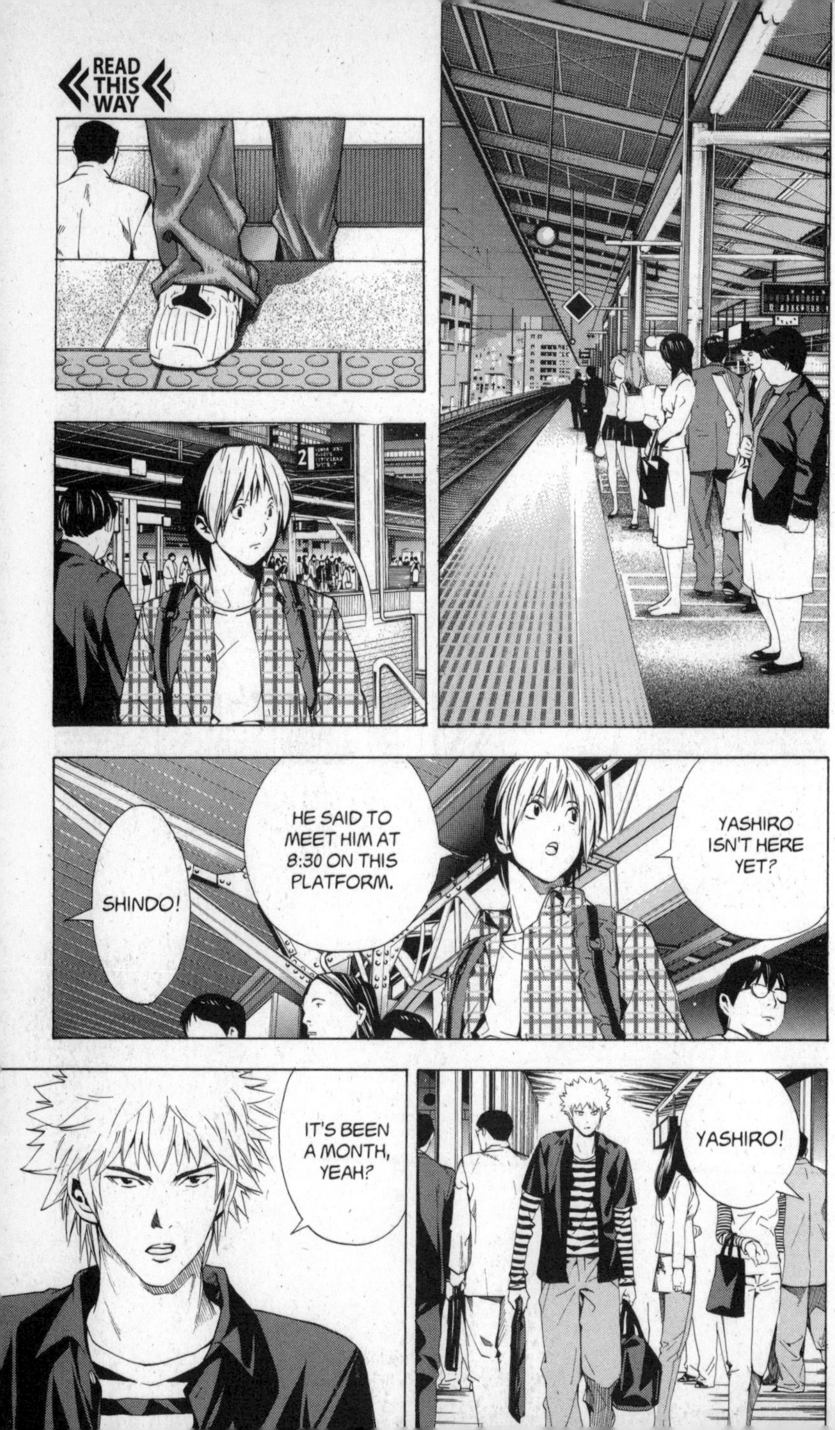
YASHIRO ISN'T HERE YET?
HE SAID TO MEET HIM AT 8:30 ON THIS PLATFORM.
SHINDO!
YASHIRO!
IT'S BEEN A MONTH, YEAH?

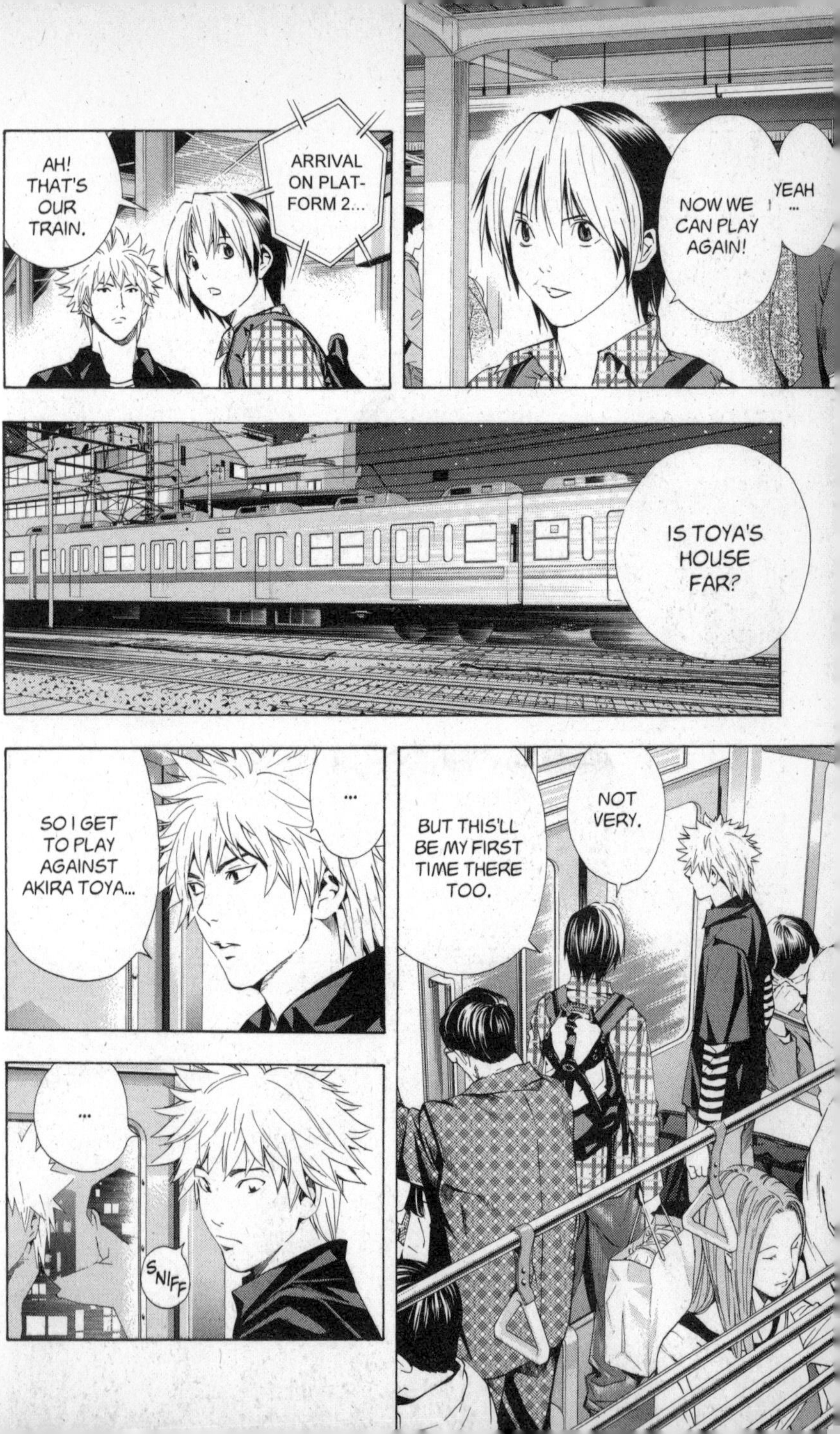
YEAH ...
NOW WE CAN PLAY AGAIN!
ARRIVAL ON PLATFORM 2...
AH! THAT'S OUR TRAIN.
IS TOYA'S HOUSE FAR?
NOT VERY.
BUT THIS'LL BE MY FIRST TIME THERE TOO.
...
SO I GET TO PLAY AGAINST AKIRA TOYA...
...
SNIFF

READ THIS WAY

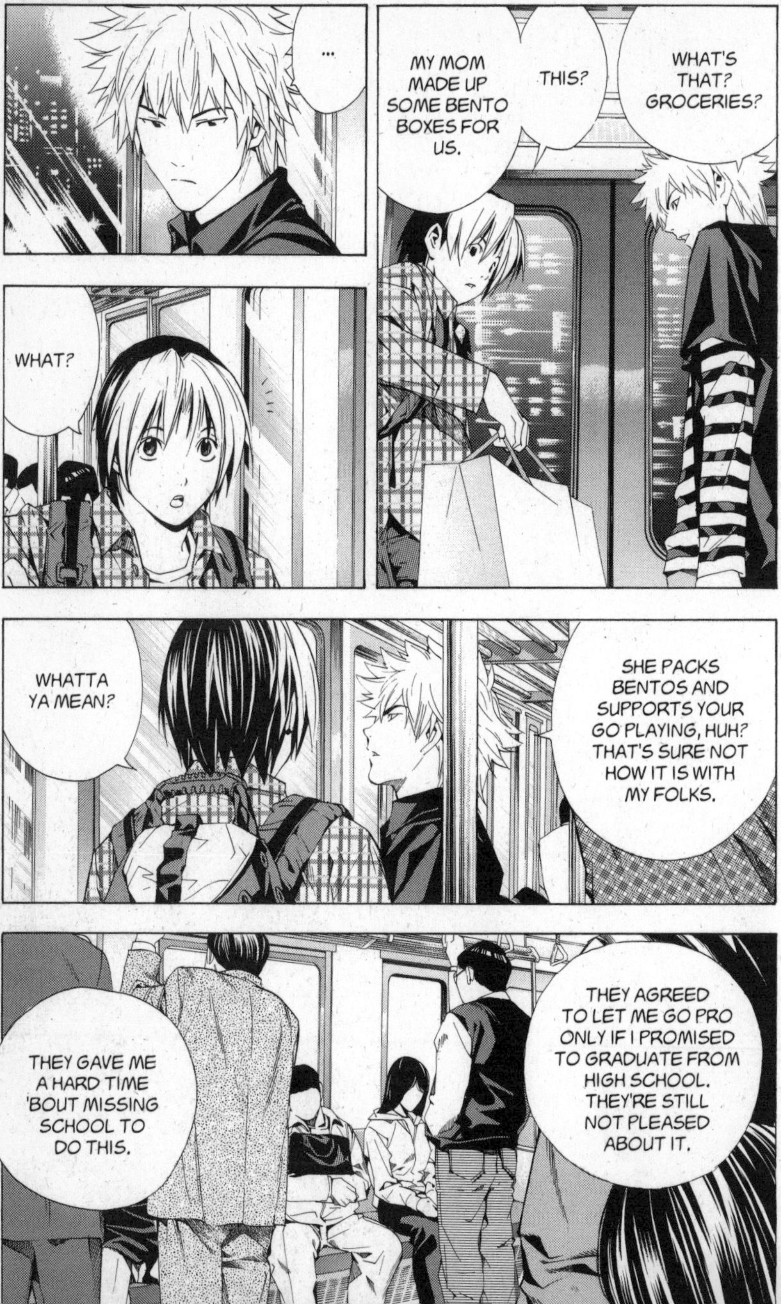
WHAT'S THAT? GROCERIES?
THIS?
MY MOM MADE UP SOME BENTO BOXES FOR US.
...
WHAT?
SHE PACKS BENTOS AND SUPPORTS YOUR GO PLAYING, HUH? THAT'S SURE NOT HOW IT IS WITH MY FOLKS.
WHATTA YA MEAN?
THEY AGREED TO LET ME GO PRO ONLY IF I PROMISED TO GRADUATE FROM HIGH SCHOOL. THEY'RE STILL NOT PLEASED ABOUT IT.
THEY GAVE ME A HARD TIME 'BOUT MISSING SCHOOL TO DO THIS.

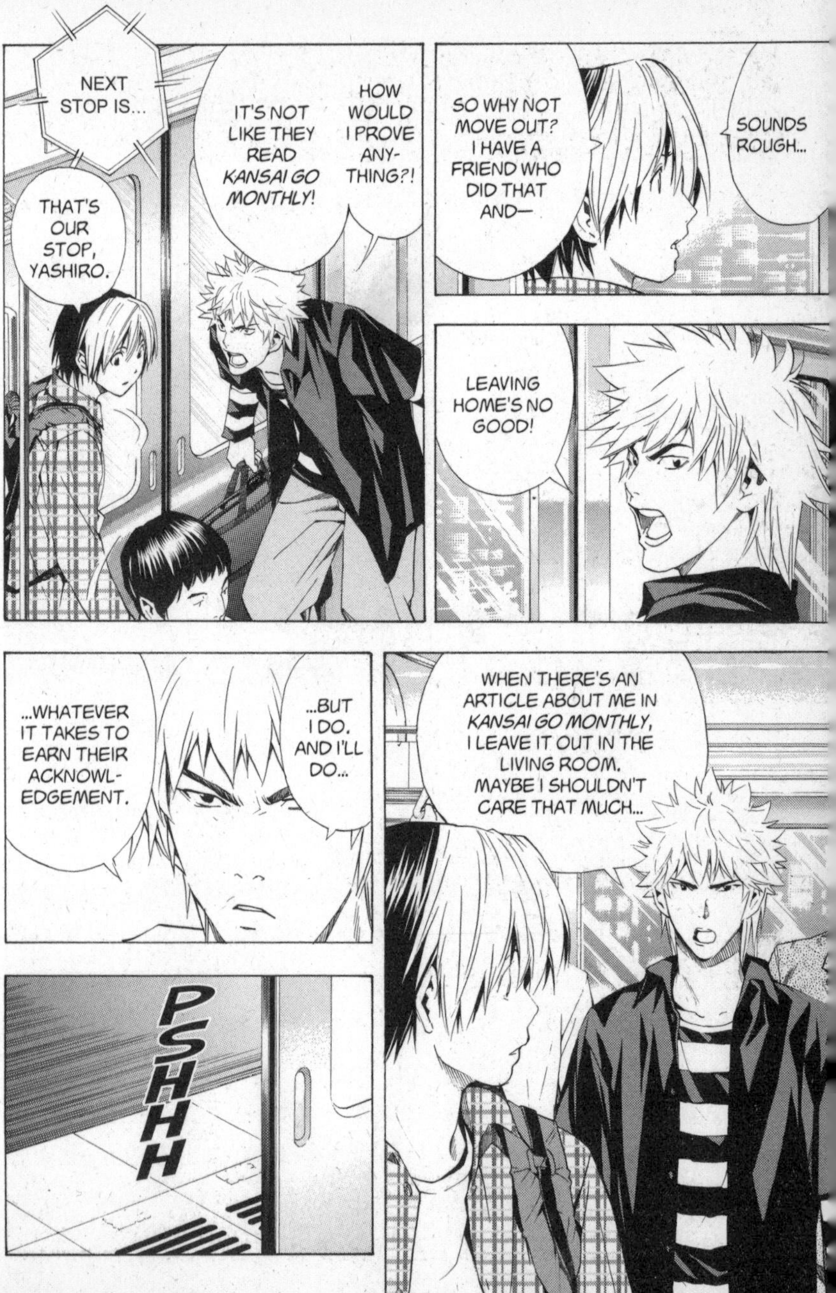
SOUNDS ROUGH...
SO WHY NOT MOVE OUT? I HAVE A FRIEND WHO DID THAT AND—
LEAVING HOME'S NO GOOD!
HOW WOULD I PROVE ANYTHING?!
IT'S NOT LIKE THEY READ *KANSAI GO MONTHLY*!
NEXT STOP IS...
THAT'S OUR STOP, YASHIRO.
WHEN THERE'S AN ARTICLE ABOUT ME IN *KANSAI GO MONTHLY*, I LEAVE IT OUT IN THE LIVING ROOM. MAYBE I SHOULDN'T CARE THAT MUCH...
...BUT I DO. AND I'LL DO...
...WHATEVER IT TAKES TO EARN THEIR ACKNOWL-EDGEMENT.
PSHHH

READ THIS WAY

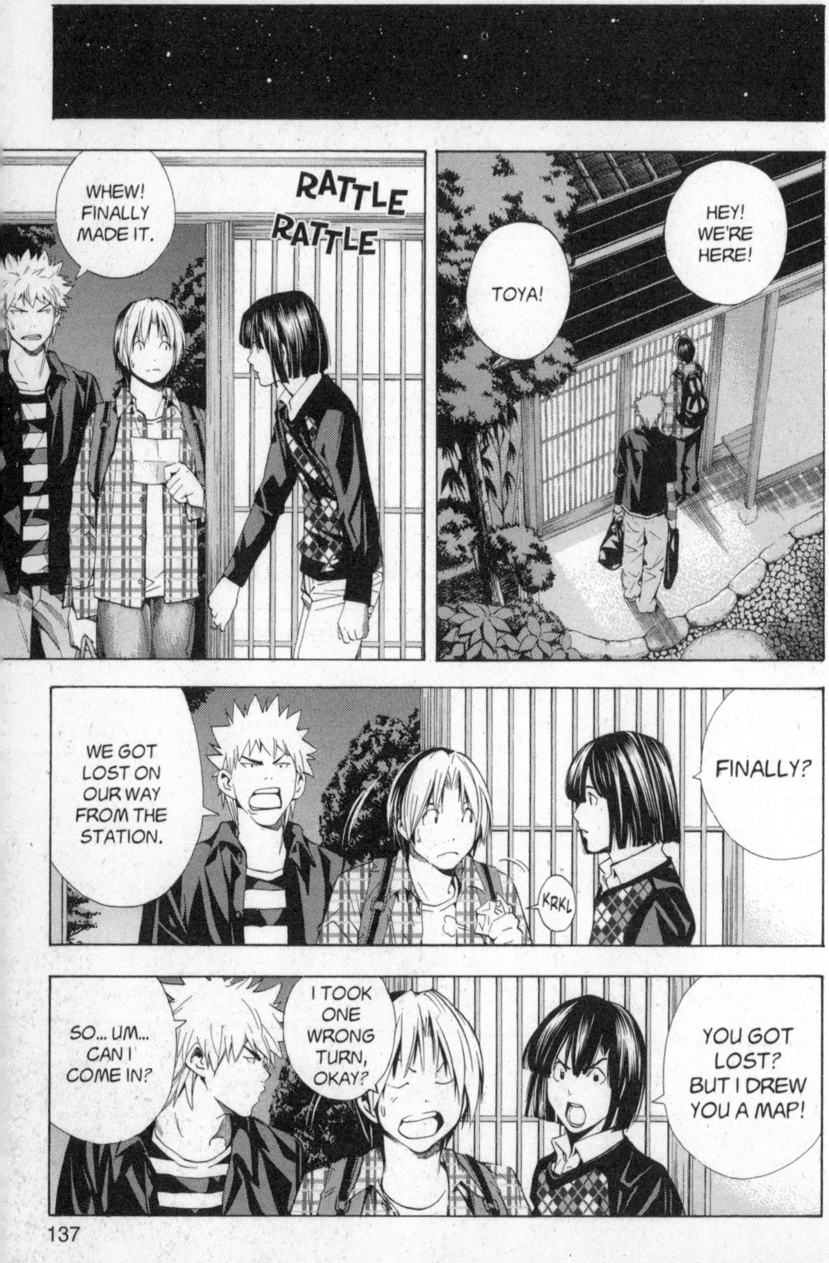
HEY! WE'RE HERE!
TOYA!
RATTLE
RATTLE
WHEW! FINALLY MADE IT.
FINALLY?
KRKL
WE GOT LOST ON OUR WAY FROM THE STATION.
YOU GOT LOST? BUT I DREW YOU A MAP!
I TOOK ONE WRONG TURN, OKAY?
SO... UM... CAN I COME IN?

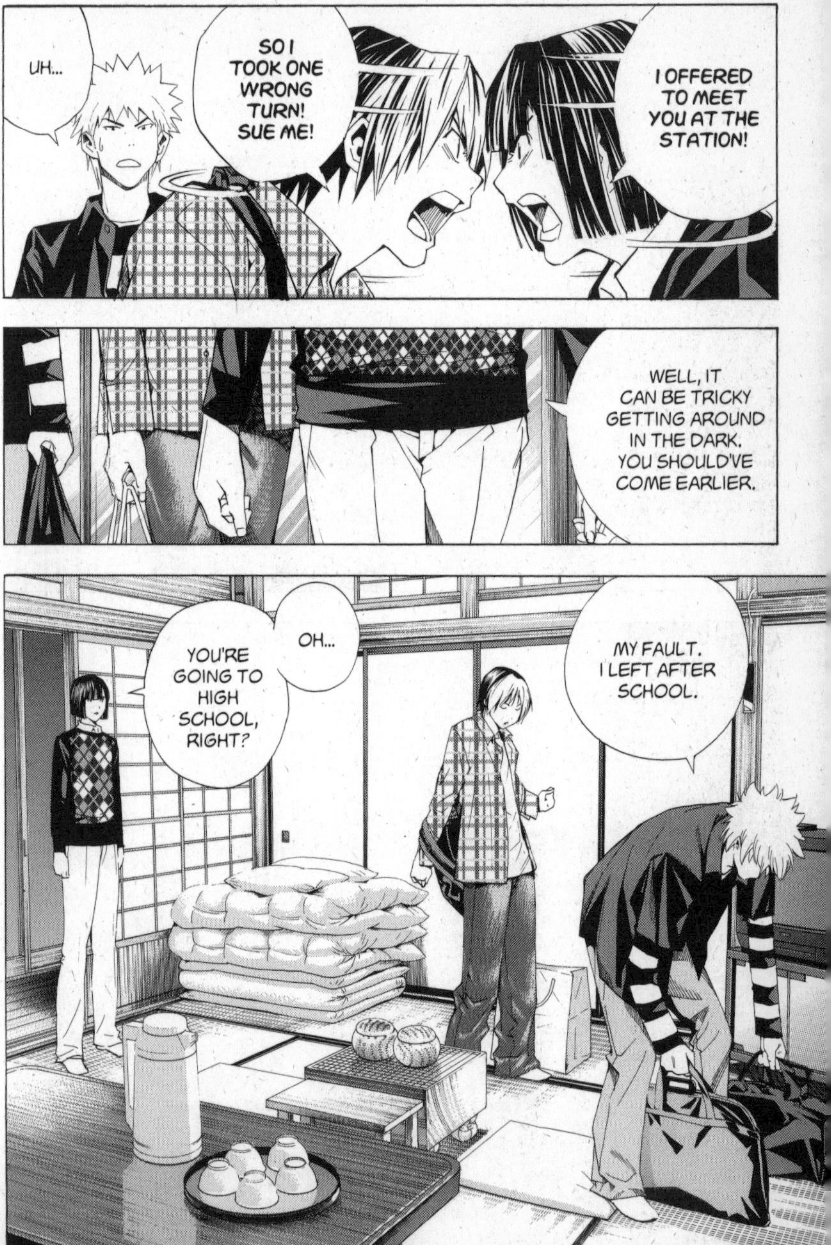
I OFFERED TO MEET YOU AT THE STATION!
SO I TOOK ONE WRONG TURN! SUE ME!
UH...
WELL, IT CAN BE TRICKY GETTING AROUND IN THE DARK. YOU SHOULD'VE COME EARLIER.
MY FAULT. I LEFT AFTER SCHOOL.
OH...
YOU'RE GOING TO HIGH SCHOOL, RIGHT?

READ THIS WAY

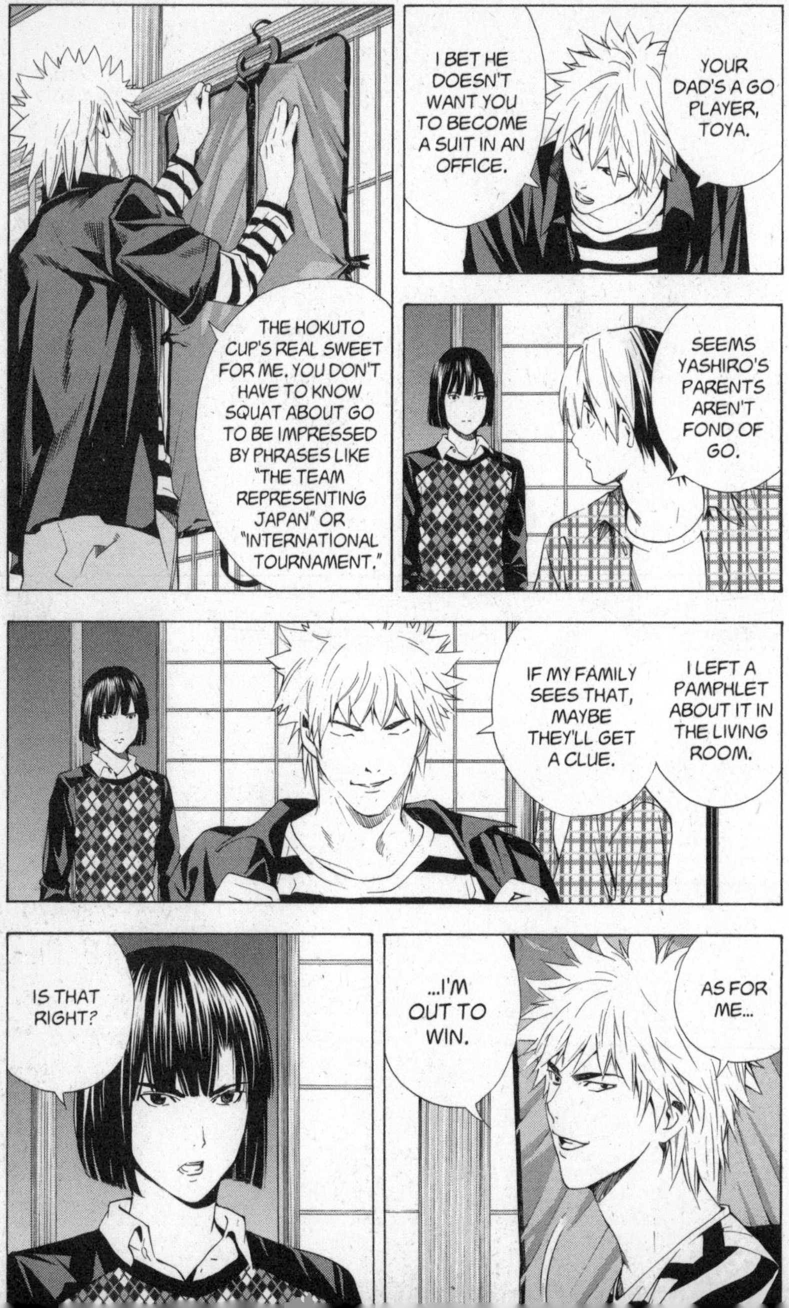

YOUR DAD'S A GO PLAYER, TOYA.
I BET HE DOESN'T WANT YOU TO BECOME A SUIT IN AN OFFICE.
SEEMS YASHIRO'S PARENTS AREN'T FOND OF GO.
THE HOKUTO CUP'S REAL SWEET FOR ME. YOU DON'T HAVE TO KNOW SQUAT ABOUT GO TO BE IMPRESSED BY PHRASES LIKE "THE TEAM REPRESENTING JAPAN" OR "INTERNATIONAL TOURNAMENT."
I LEFT A PAMPHLET ABOUT IT IN THE LIVING ROOM.
IF MY FAMILY SEES THAT, MAYBE THEY'LL GET A CLUE.
AS FOR ME...
...I'M OUT TO WIN.
IS THAT RIGHT?

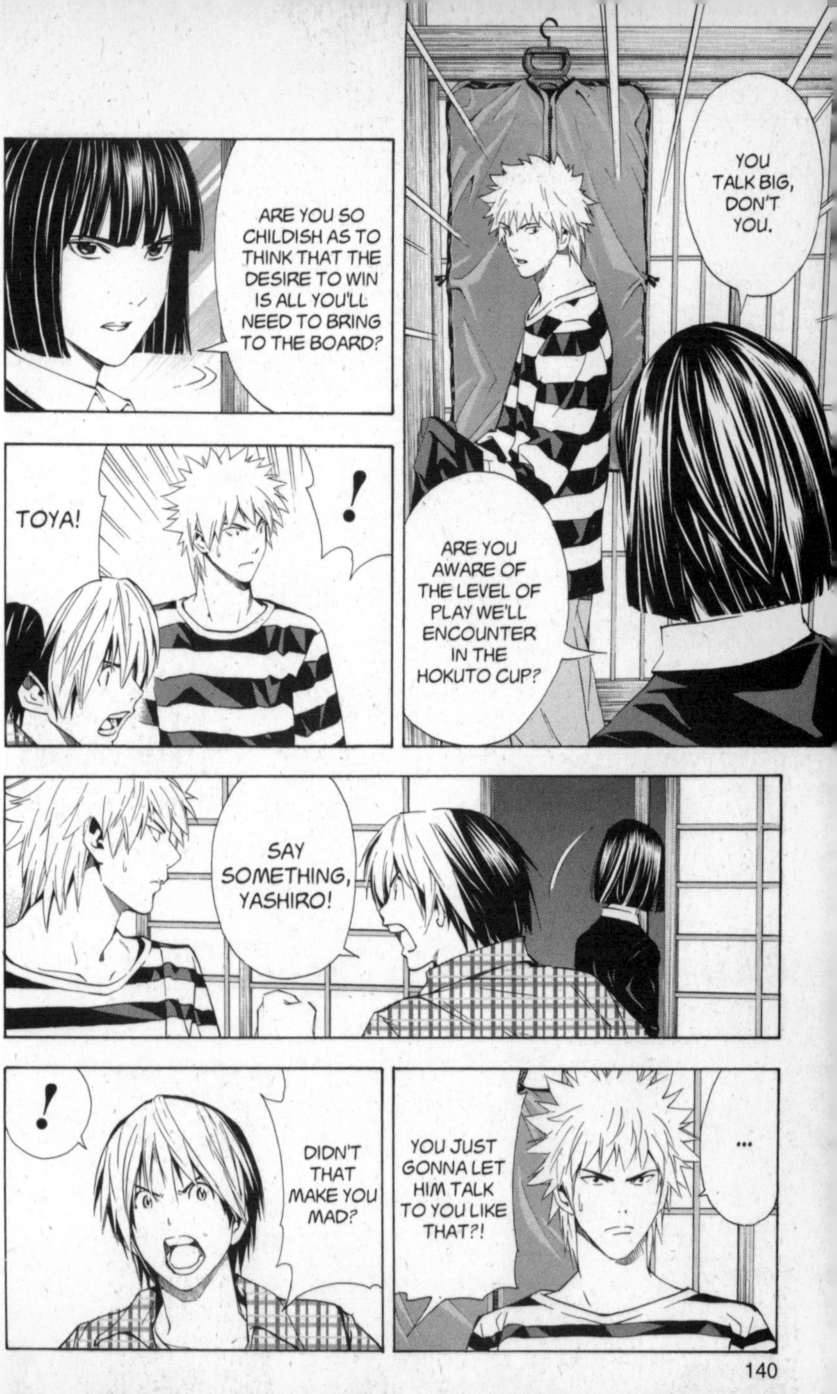

YOU TALK BIG, DON'T YOU.
ARE YOU AWARE OF THE LEVEL OF PLAY WE'LL ENCOUNTER IN THE HOKUTO CUP?
ARE YOU SO CHILDISH AS TO THINK THAT THE DESIRE TO WIN IS ALL YOU'LL NEED TO BRING TO THE BOARD?
!
TOYA!
SAY SOMETHING, YASHIRO!
...
YOU JUST GONNA LET HIM TALK TO YOU LIKE THAT?!
DIDN'T THAT MAKE YOU MAD?
!

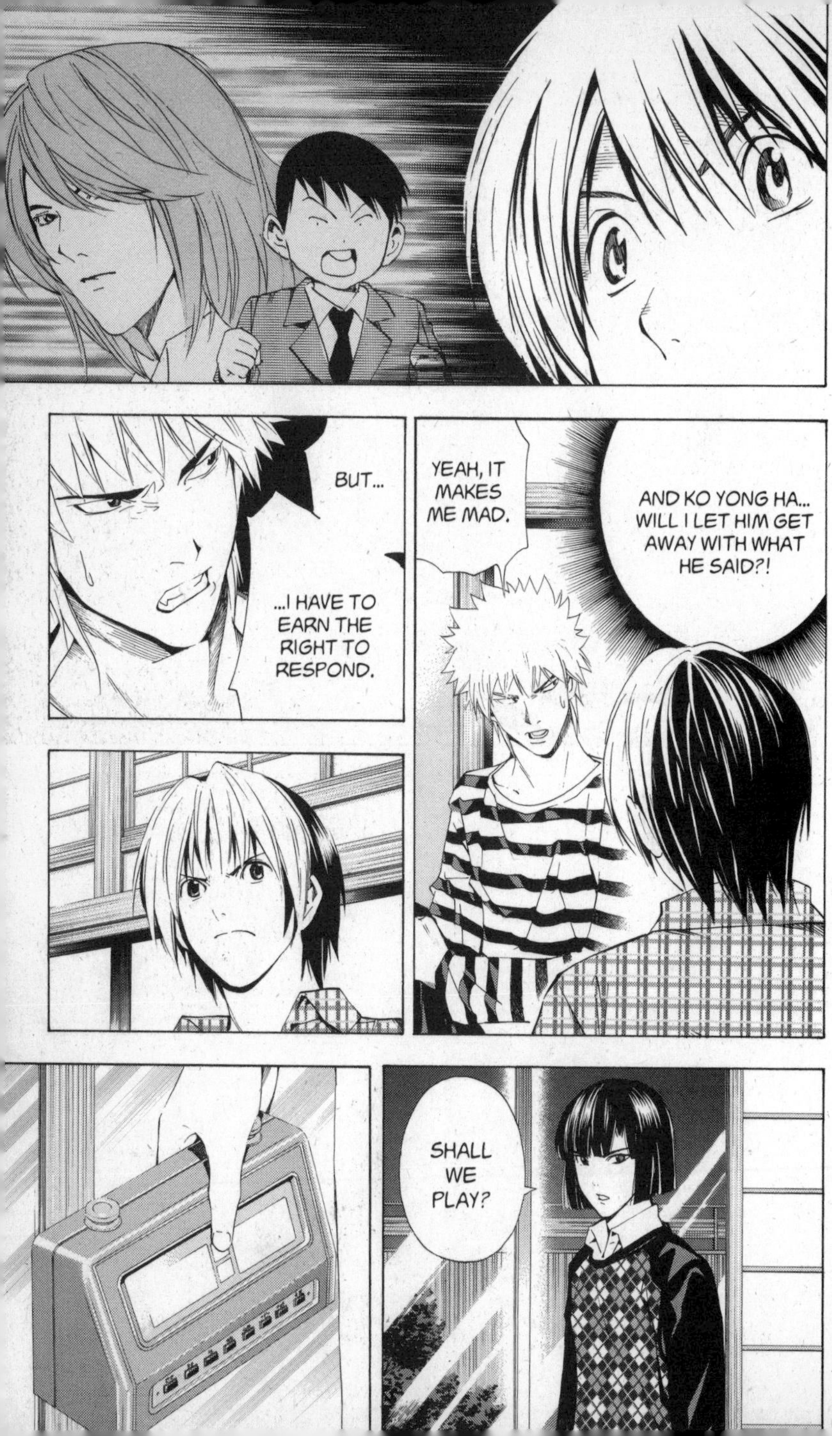
AND KO YONG HA... WILL I LET HIM GET AWAY WITH WHAT HE SAID?!
YEAH, IT MAKES ME MAD.
BUT...
...I HAVE TO EARN THE RIGHT TO RESPOND.
SHALL WE PLAY?

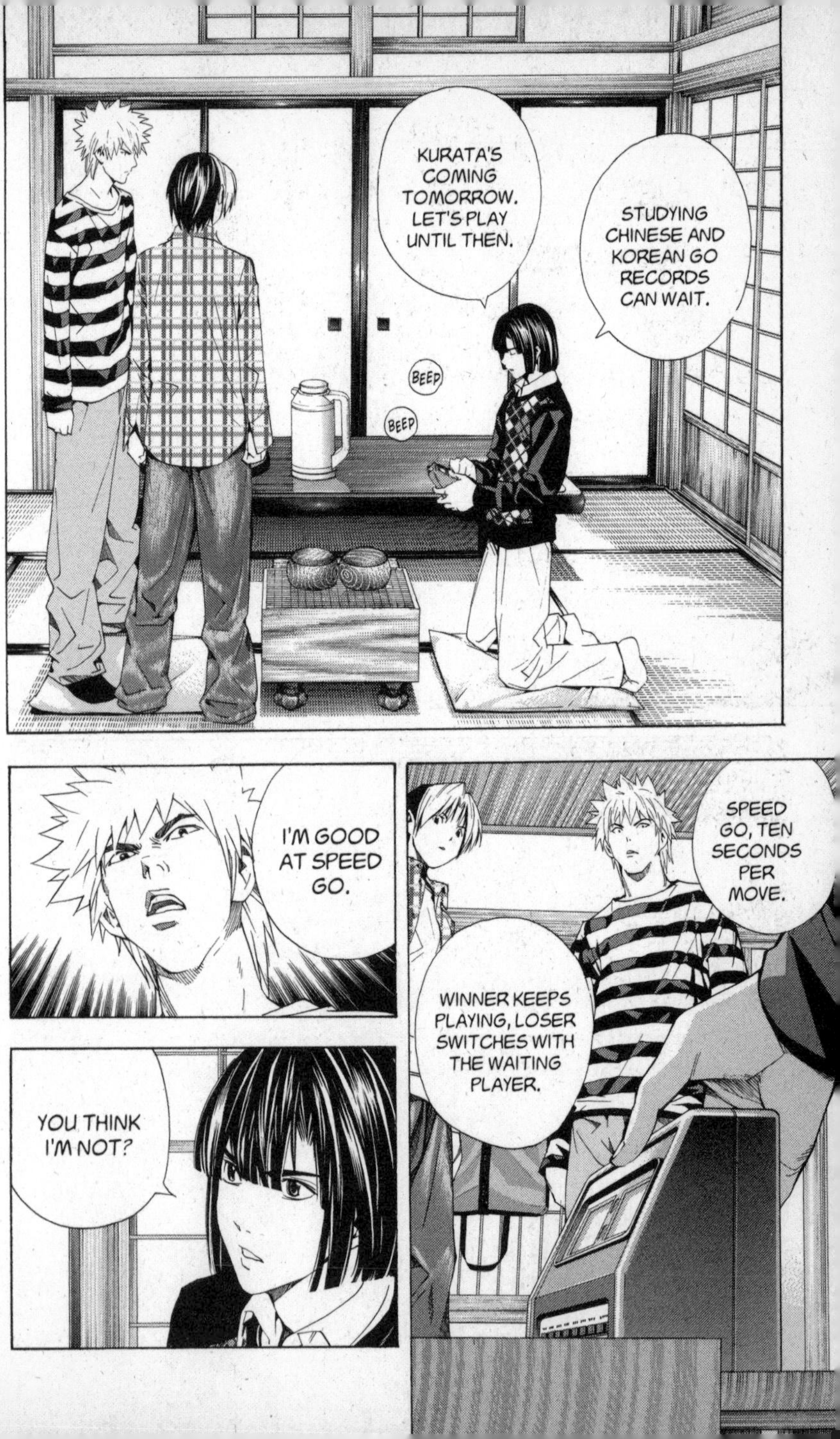
STUDYING CHINESE AND KOREAN GO RECORDS CAN WAIT.
KURATA'S COMING TOMORROW. LET'S PLAY UNTIL THEN.
BEEP
BEEP
SPEED GO, TEN SECONDS PER MOVE.
WINNER KEEPS PLAYING, LOSER SWITCHES WITH THE WAITING PLAYER.
I'M GOOD AT SPEED GO.
YOU THINK I'M NOT?

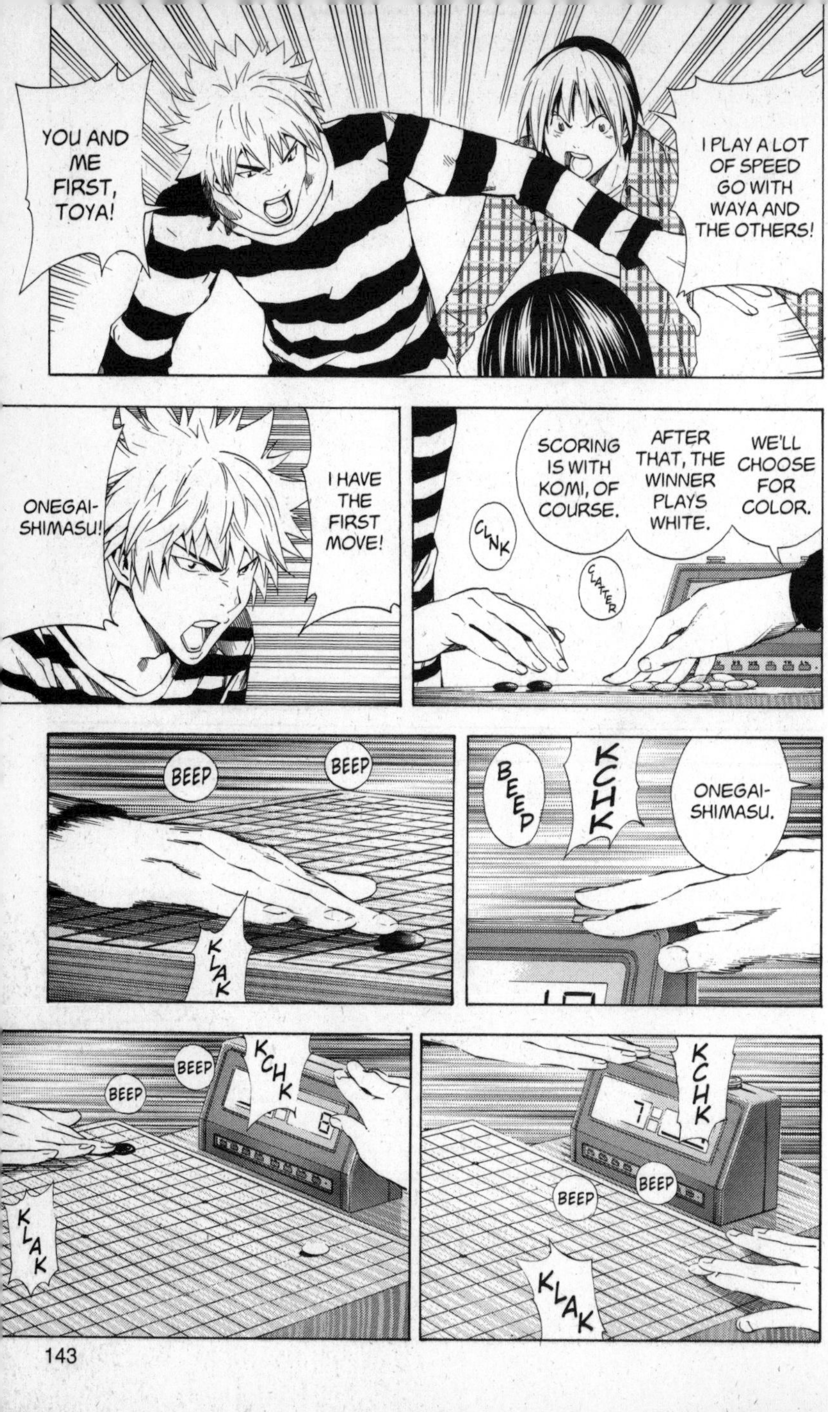
I PLAY A LOT OF SPEED GO WITH WAYA AND THE OTHERS!
YOU AND ME FIRST, TOYA!
WE'LL CHOOSE FOR COLOR.
AFTER THAT, THE WINNER PLAYS WHITE.
SCORING IS WITH KOMI, OF COURSE.
CLATTER
CLNK
I HAVE THE FIRST MOVE!
ONEGAI-SHIMASU!
ONEGAI-SHIMASU.
KCHK
BEEP
BEEP
BEEP
KLAK
KCHK
BEEP
BEEP
KLAK
KCHK
BEEP
BEEP
KLAK

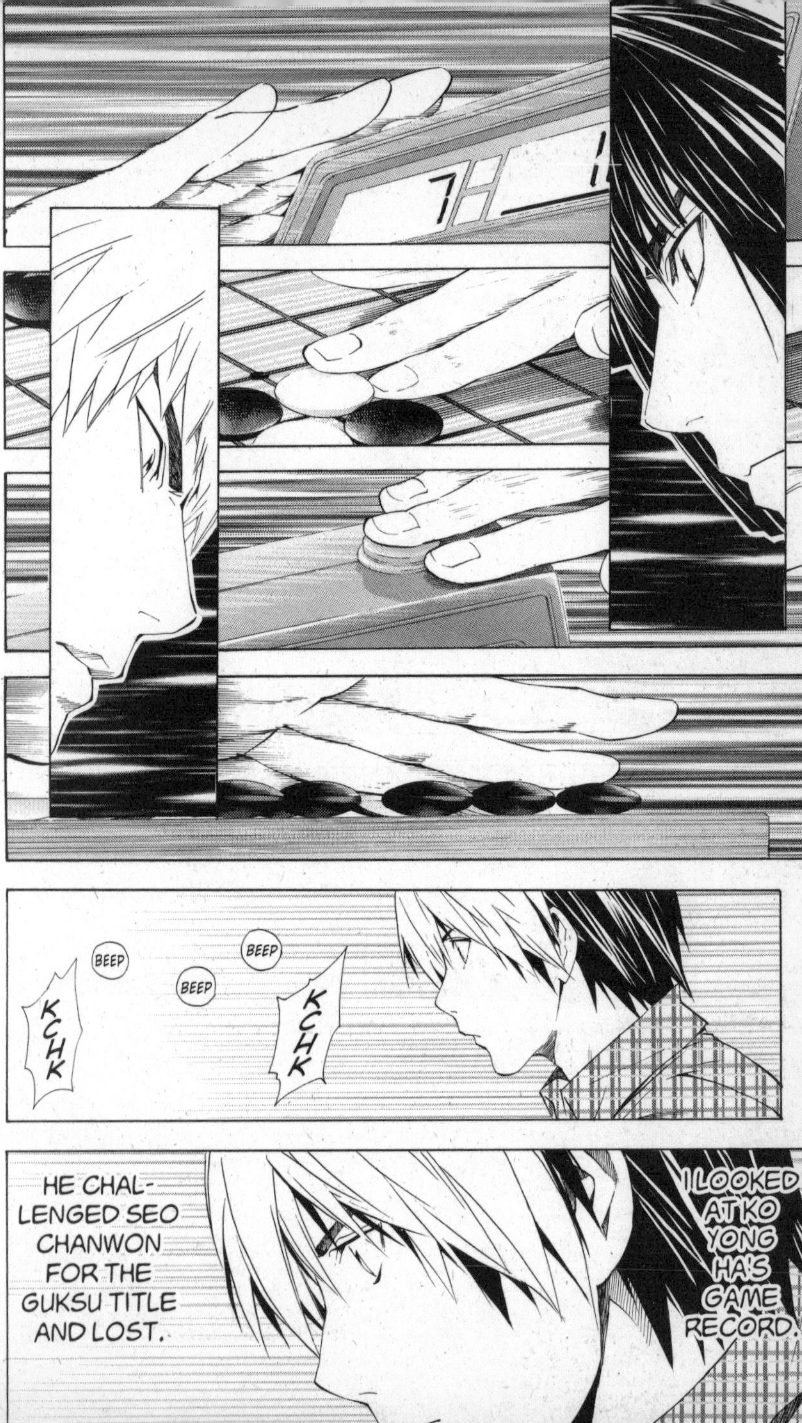
KCHK
BEEP
BEEP
BEEP
KCHK
I LOOKED AT KO YONG HA'S GAME RECORD.
HE CHAL-LENGED SEO CHANWON FOR THE GUKSU TITLE AND LOST.

READ THIS WAY

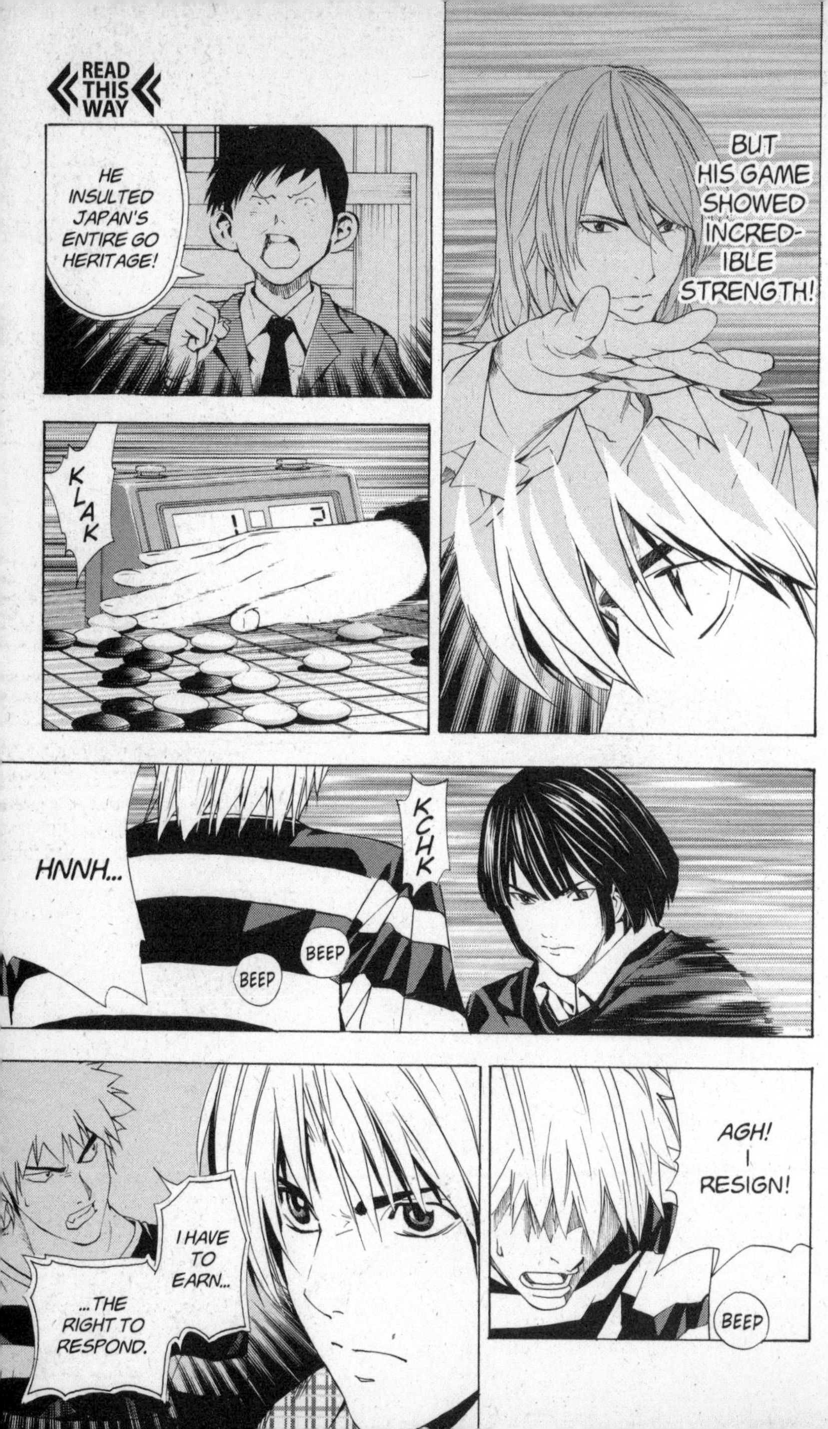
BUT HIS GAME SHOWED INCRED-IBLE STRENGTH!
HE INSULTED JAPAN'S ENTIRE GO HERITAGE!
KLAK
KCHK
HNNH...
BEEP
BEEP
AGH! I RESIGN!
BEEP
I HAVE TO EARN...
...THE RIGHT TO RESPOND.

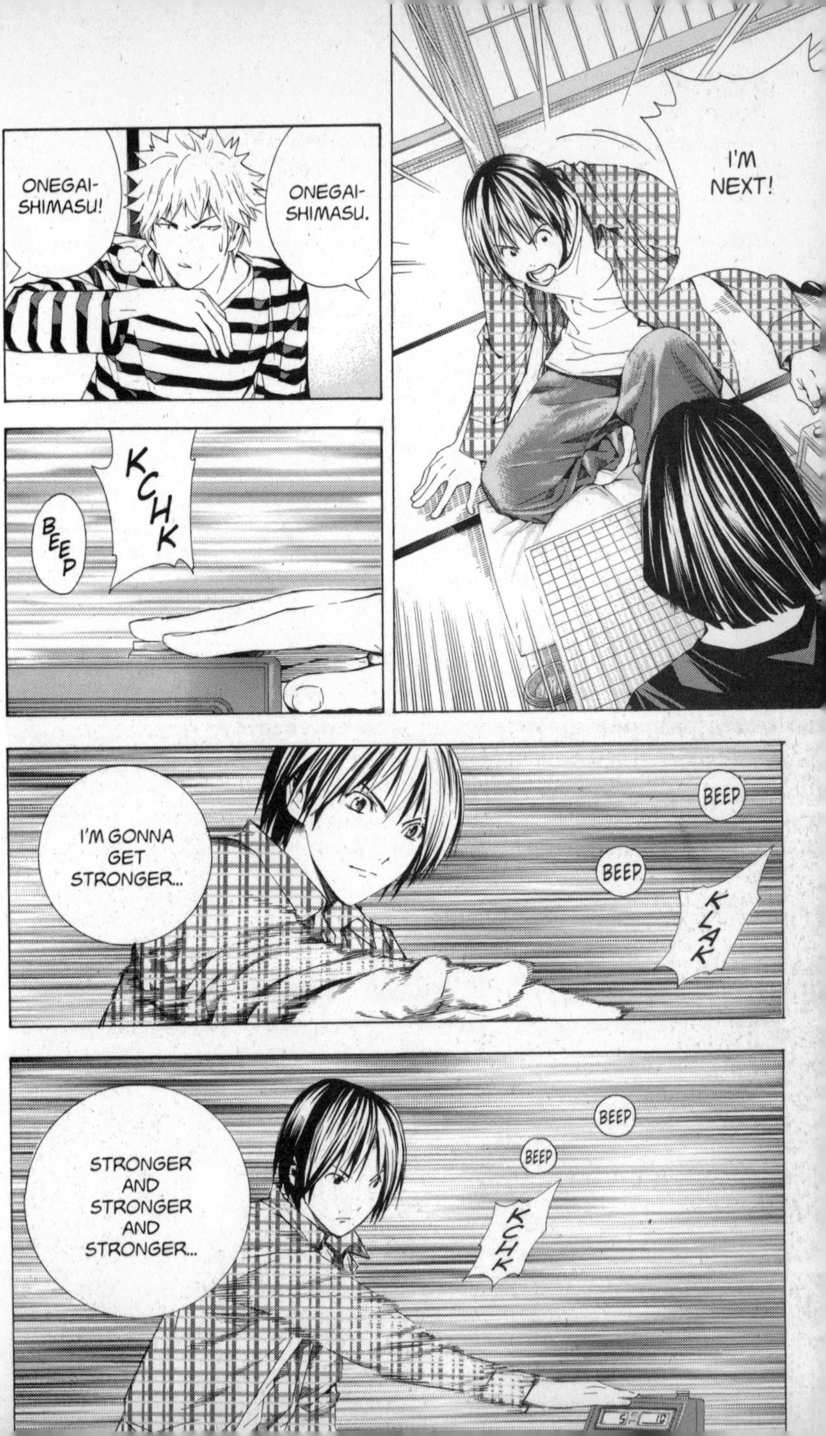
I'M NEXT!
ONEGAI-SHIMASU.
ONEGAI-SHIMASU!
KCHK
BEEP
BEEP
BEEP
KLAK
I'M GONNA GET STRONGER...
BEEP
BEEP
KCHK
STRONGER AND STRONGER AND STRONGER...

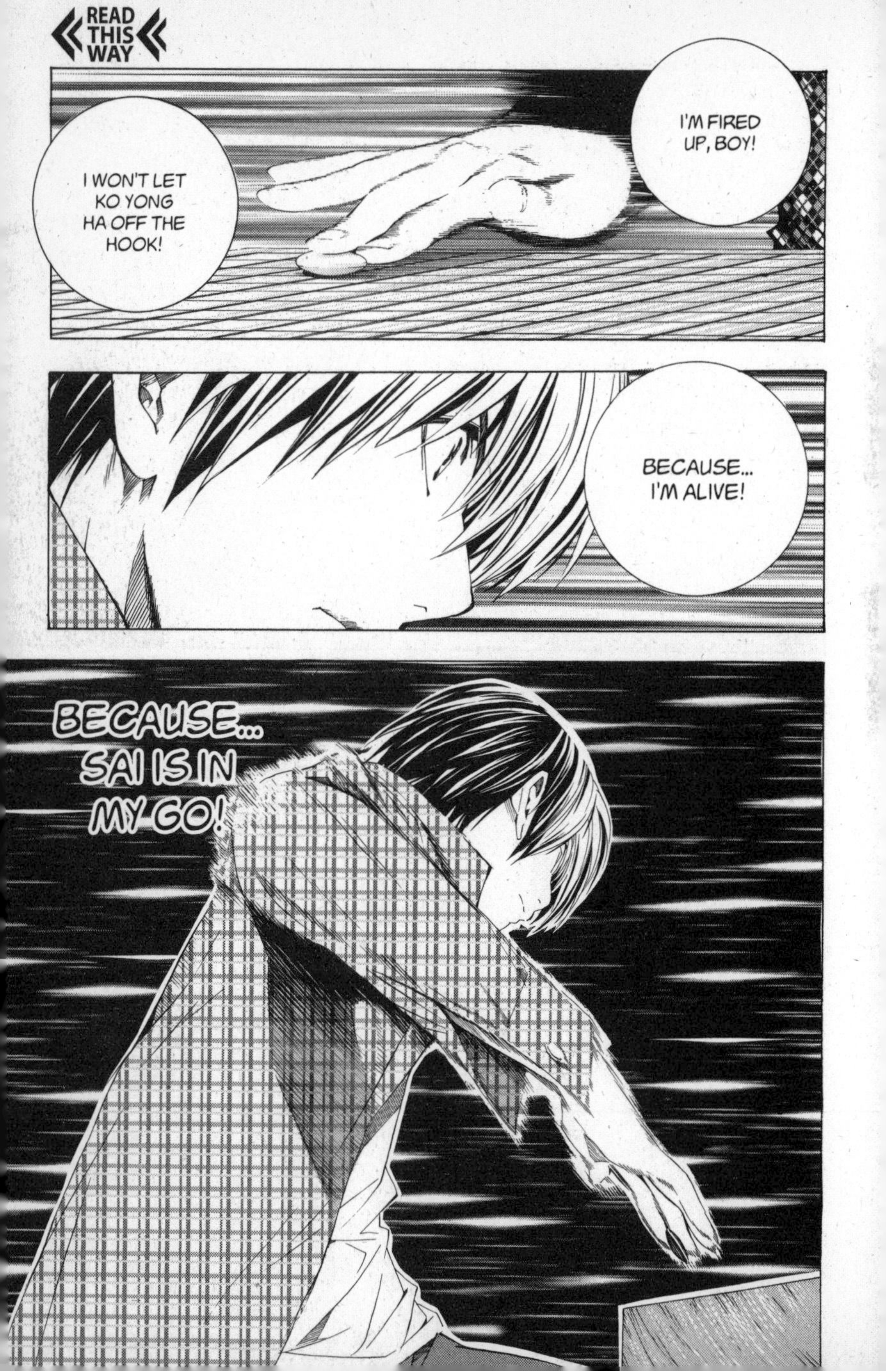
READ THIS WAY
I'M FIRED UP, BOY!
I WON'T LET KO YONG HA OFF THE HOOK!
BECAUSE... I'M ALIVE!
BECAUSE... SAI IS IN MY GO!

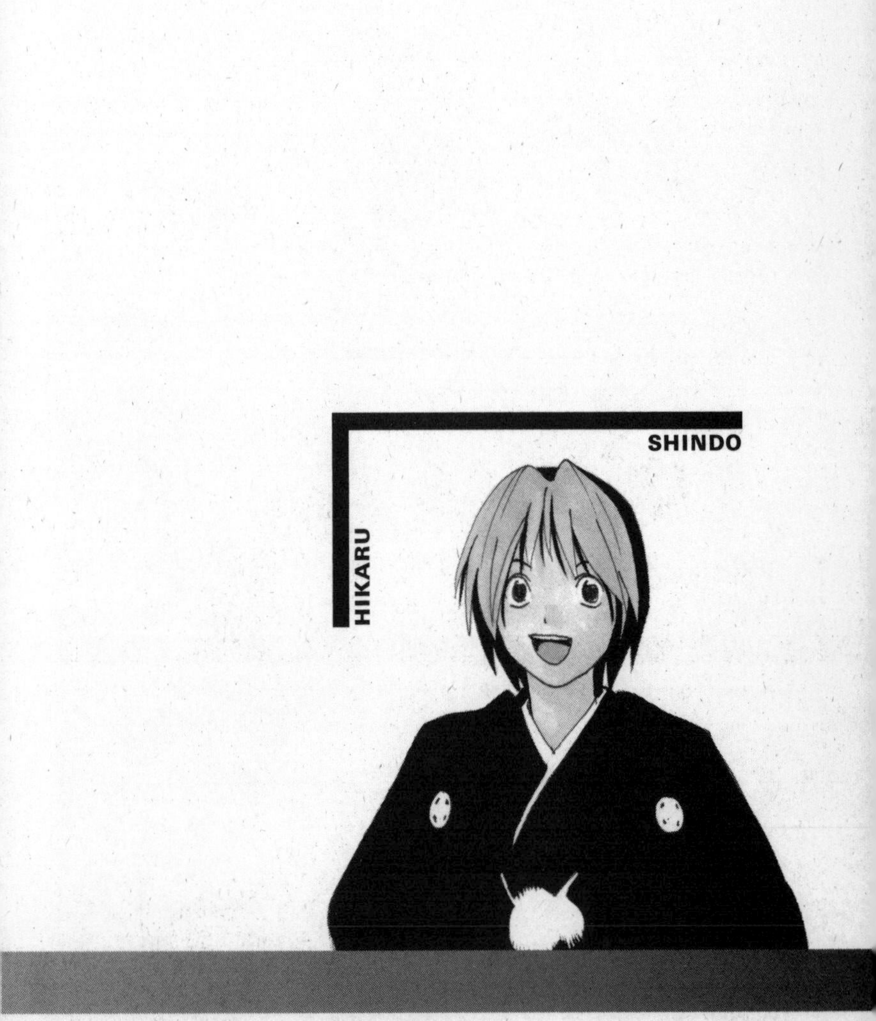
SHINDO
HIKARU

Game 173 "Toya Will Be First"

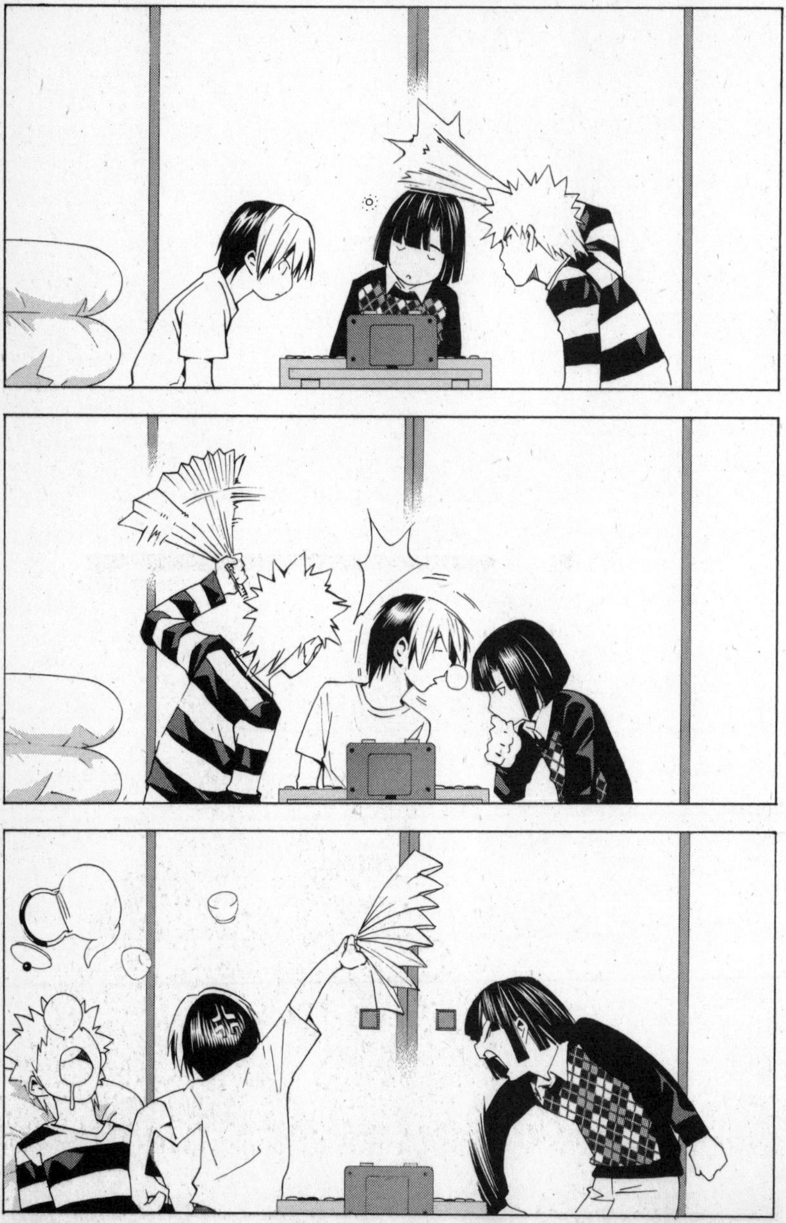

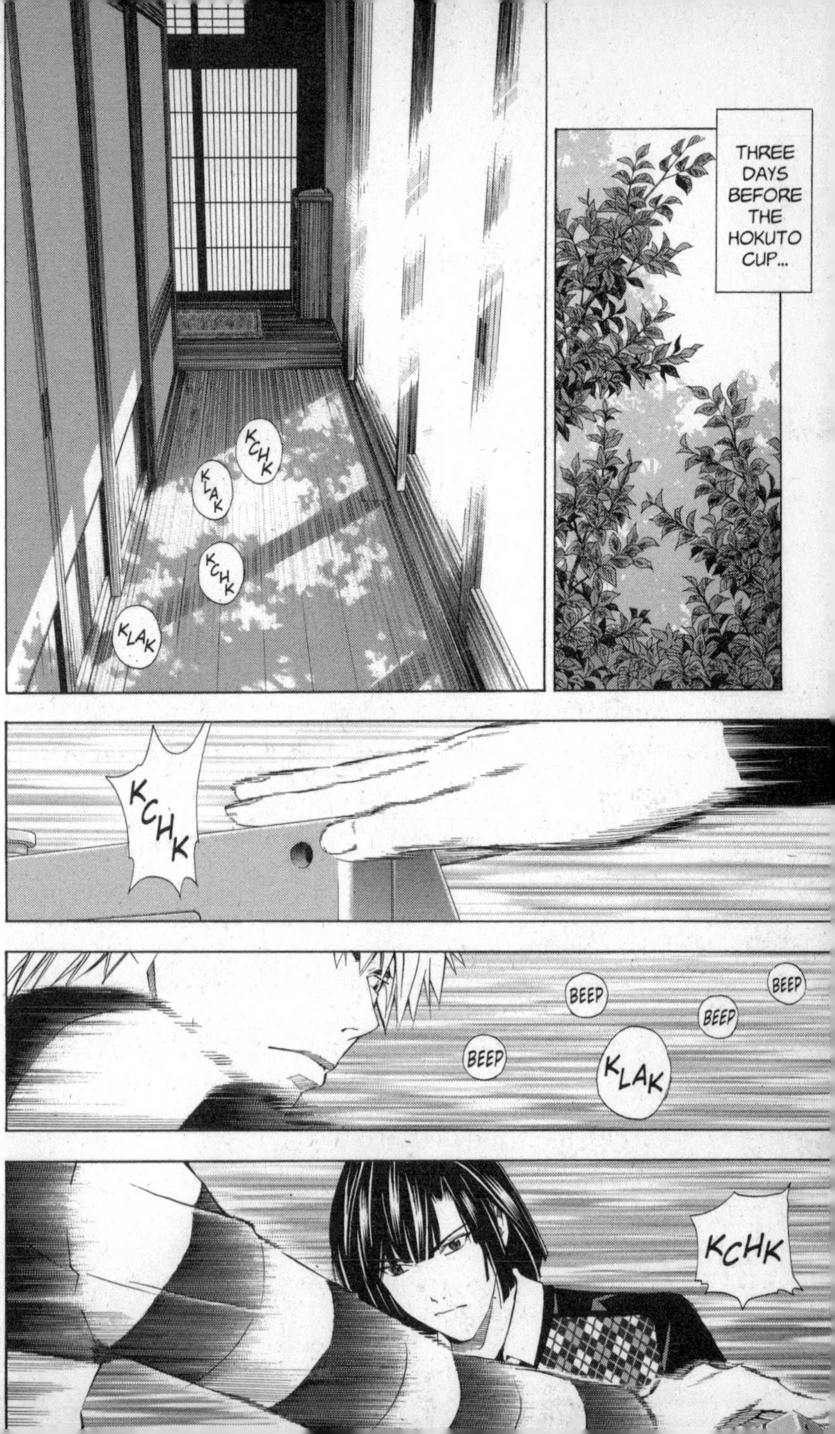
THREE DAYS BEFORE THE HOKUTO CUP...
KCHK
KLAK
KCHK
KLAK
KCHK
BEEP
BEEP
KLAK
BEEP
BEEP
KCHK

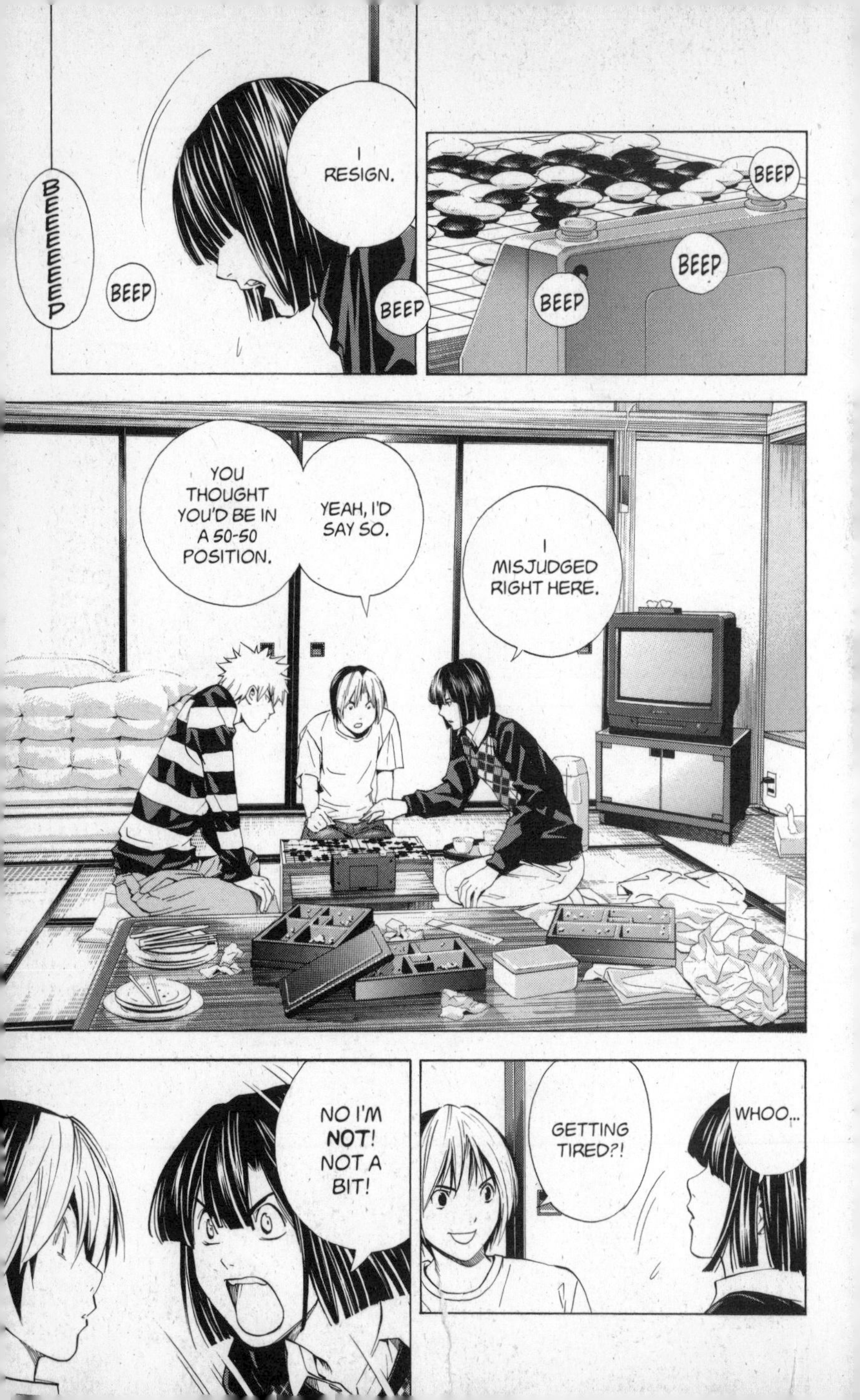
BEEP
BEEP
BEEP
I RESIGN.
BEEP
BEEEEEEP
BEEP
I MISJUDGED RIGHT HERE.
YEAH, I'D SAY SO.
YOU THOUGHT YOU'D BE IN A 50-50 POSITION.
WHOO...
GETTING TIRED?!
NO I'M **NOT**! NOT A BIT!

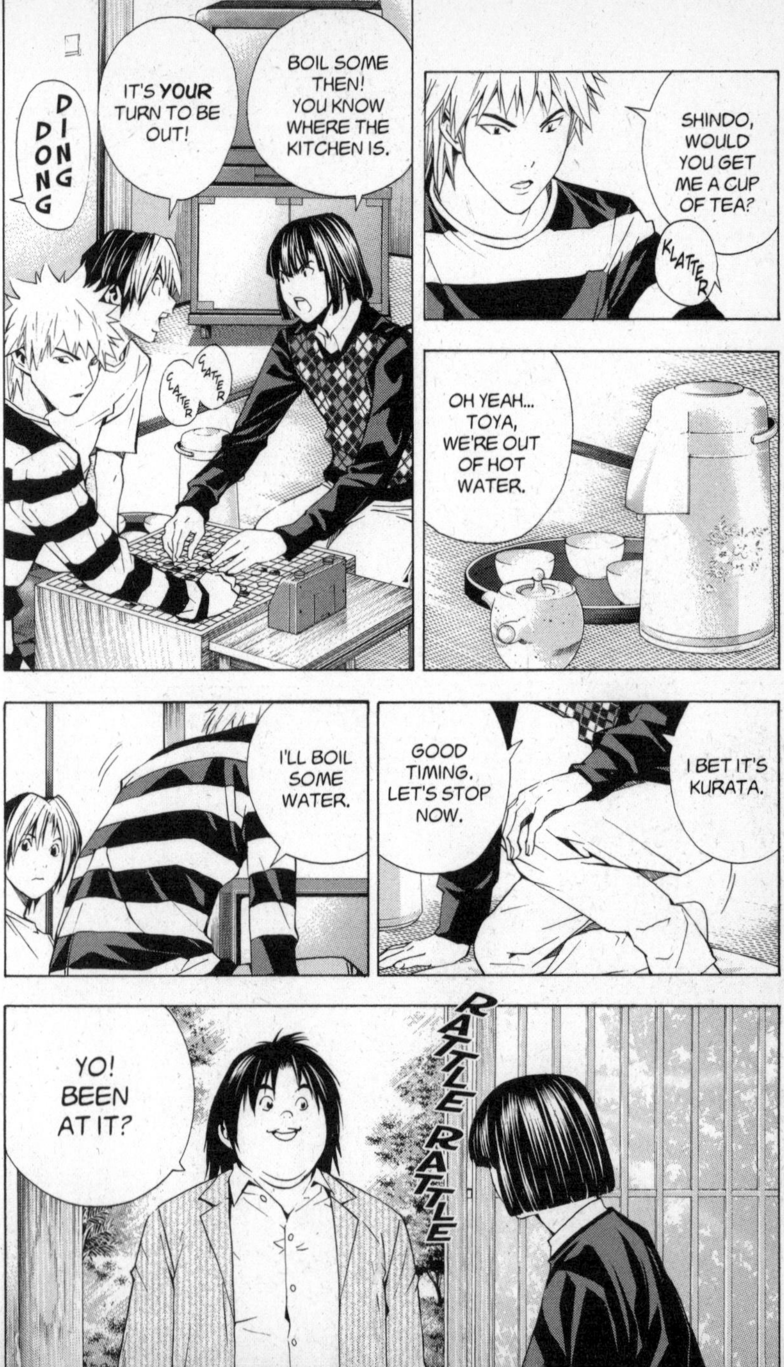
SHINDO, WOULD YOU GET ME A CUP OF TEA?
KLATTER
OH YEAH... TOYA, WE'RE OUT OF HOT WATER.
BOIL SOME THEN! YOU KNOW WHERE THE KITCHEN IS.
IT'S **YOUR** TURN TO BE OUT!
DING DONG
CLATTER CLATTER
I BET IT'S KURATA.
GOOD TIMING. LET'S STOP NOW.
I'LL BOIL SOME WATER.
RATTLE RATTLE
YO! BEEN AT IT?

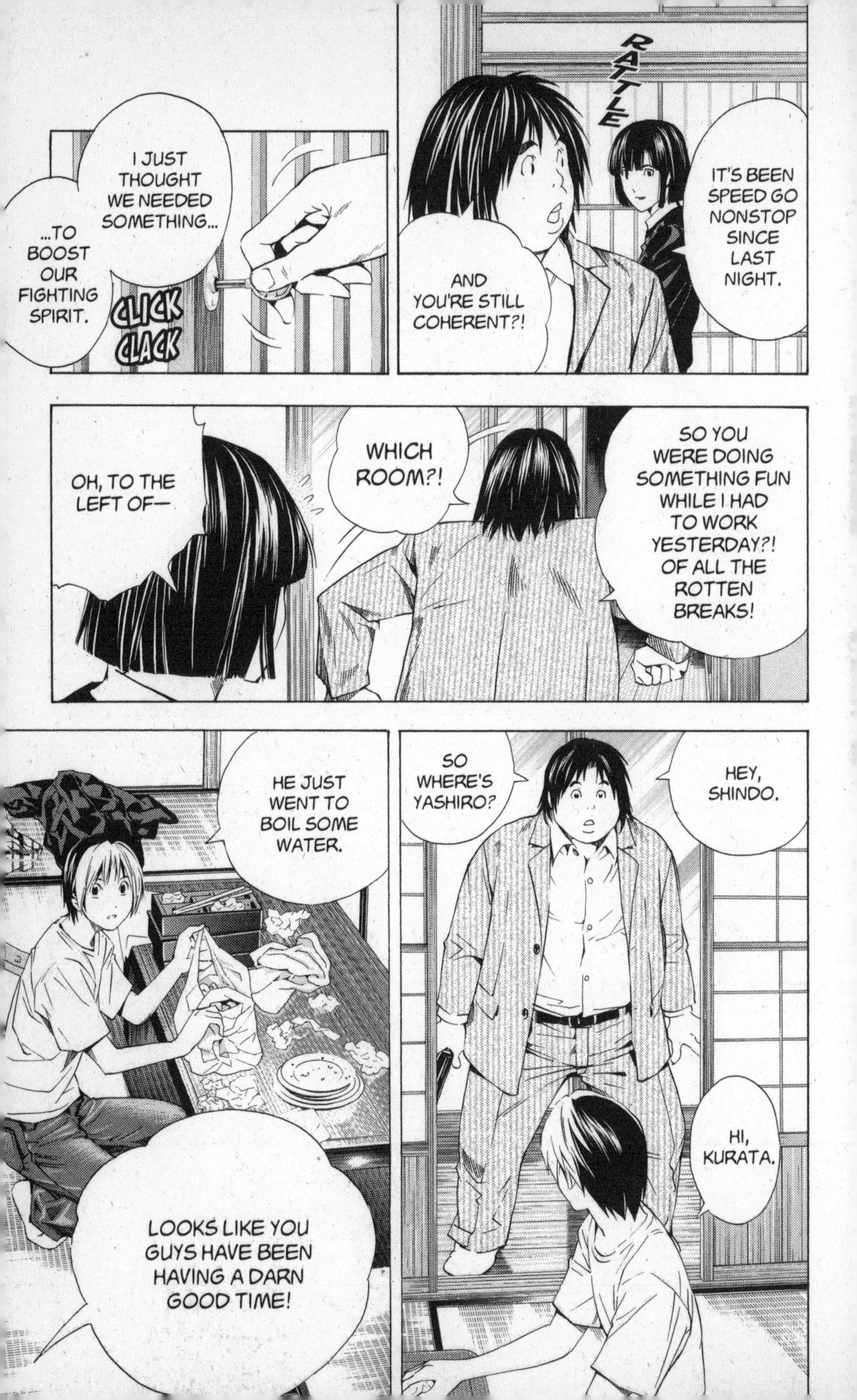
RATTLE
IT'S BEEN SPEED GO NONSTOP SINCE LAST NIGHT.
AND YOU'RE STILL COHERENT?!
I JUST THOUGHT WE NEEDED SOMETHING...
...TO BOOST OUR FIGHTING SPIRIT.
CLICK CLACK
SO YOU WERE DOING SOMETHING FUN WHILE I HAD TO WORK YESTERDAY?! OF ALL THE ROTTEN BREAKS!
WHICH ROOM?!
OH, TO THE LEFT OF—
HEY, SHINDO.
SO WHERE'S YASHIRO?
HI, KURATA.
HE JUST WENT TO BOIL SOME WATER.
LOOKS LIKE YOU GUYS HAVE BEEN HAVING A DARN GOOD TIME!

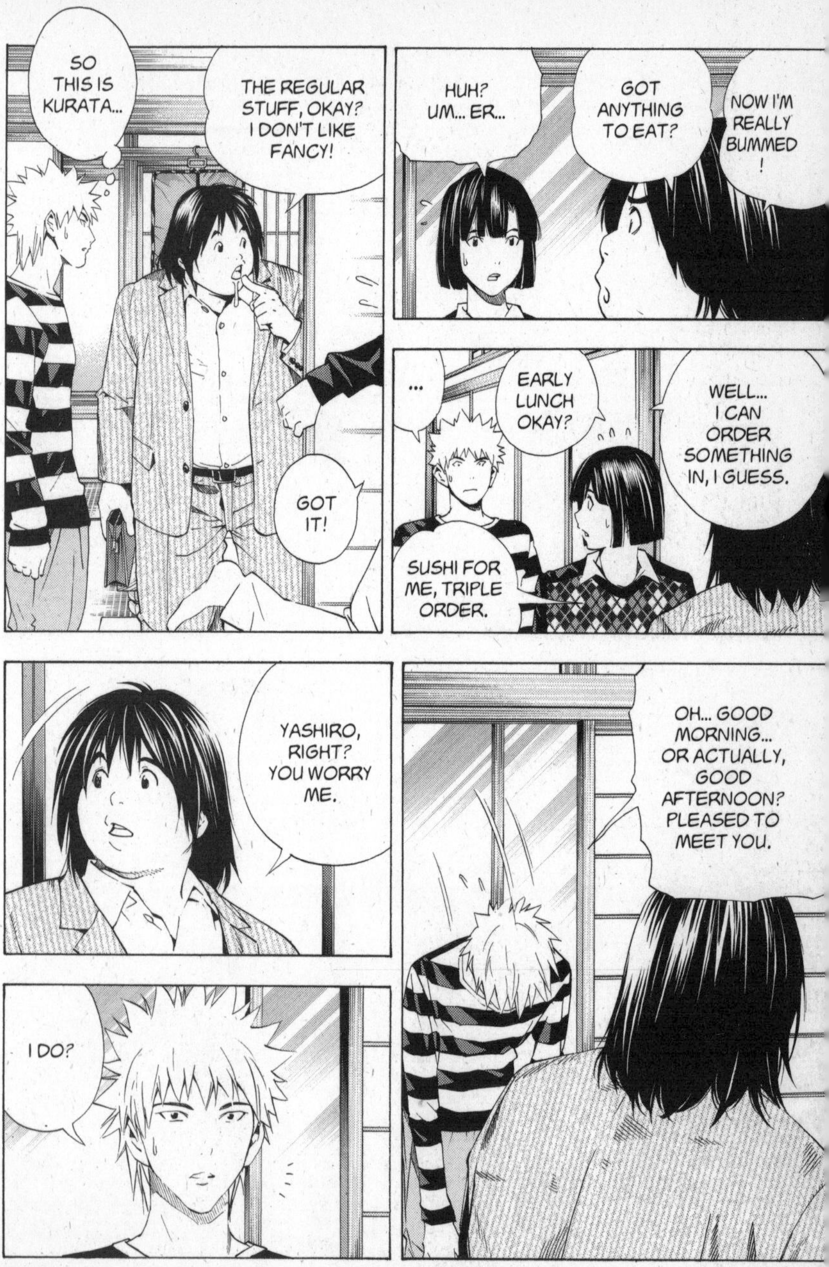
NOW I'M REALLY BUMMED!
GOT ANYTHING TO EAT?
HUH? UM... ER...
WELL... I CAN ORDER SOMETHING IN, I GUESS.
EARLY LUNCH OKAY?
...
SUSHI FOR ME, TRIPLE ORDER.
THE REGULAR STUFF, OKAY? I DON'T LIKE FANCY!
SO THIS IS KURATA...
GOT IT!
OH... GOOD MORNING... OR ACTUALLY, GOOD AFTERNOON? PLEASED TO MEET YOU.
YASHIRO, RIGHT? YOU WORRY ME.
I DO?

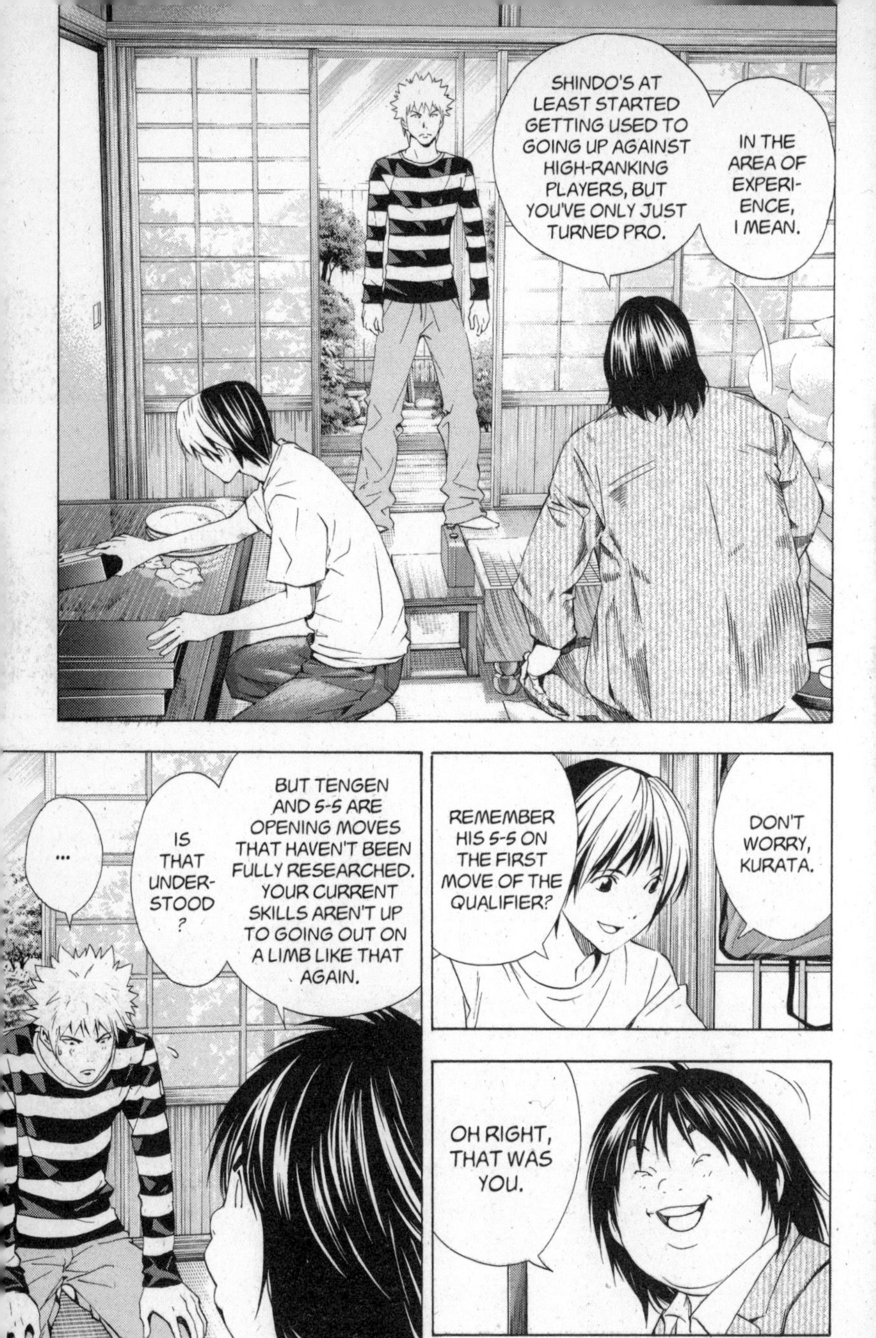
SHINDO'S AT LEAST STARTED GETTING USED TO GOING UP AGAINST HIGH-RANKING PLAYERS, BUT YOU'VE ONLY JUST TURNED PRO.
IN THE AREA OF EXPERI-ENCE, I MEAN.
...
IS THAT UNDER-STOOD ?
BUT TENGEN AND 5-5 ARE OPENING MOVES THAT HAVEN'T BEEN FULLY RESEARCHED. YOUR CURRENT SKILLS AREN'T UP TO GOING OUT ON A LIMB LIKE THAT AGAIN.
REMEMBER HIS 5-5 ON THE FIRST MOVE OF THE QUALIFIER?
DON'T WORRY, KURATA.
OH RIGHT, THAT WAS YOU.

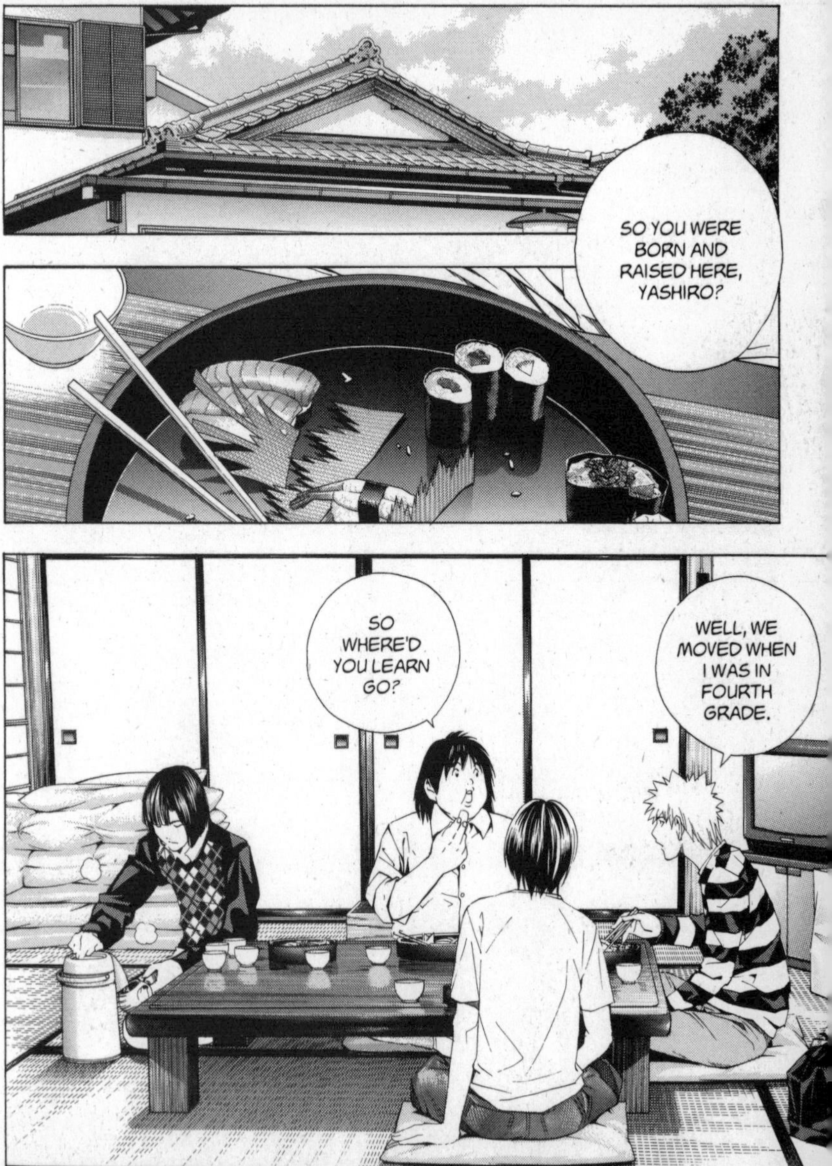
SO YOU WERE BORN AND RAISED HERE, YASHIRO?
WELL, WE MOVED WHEN I WAS IN FOURTH GRADE.
SO WHERE'D YOU LEARN GO?

READ THIS WAY

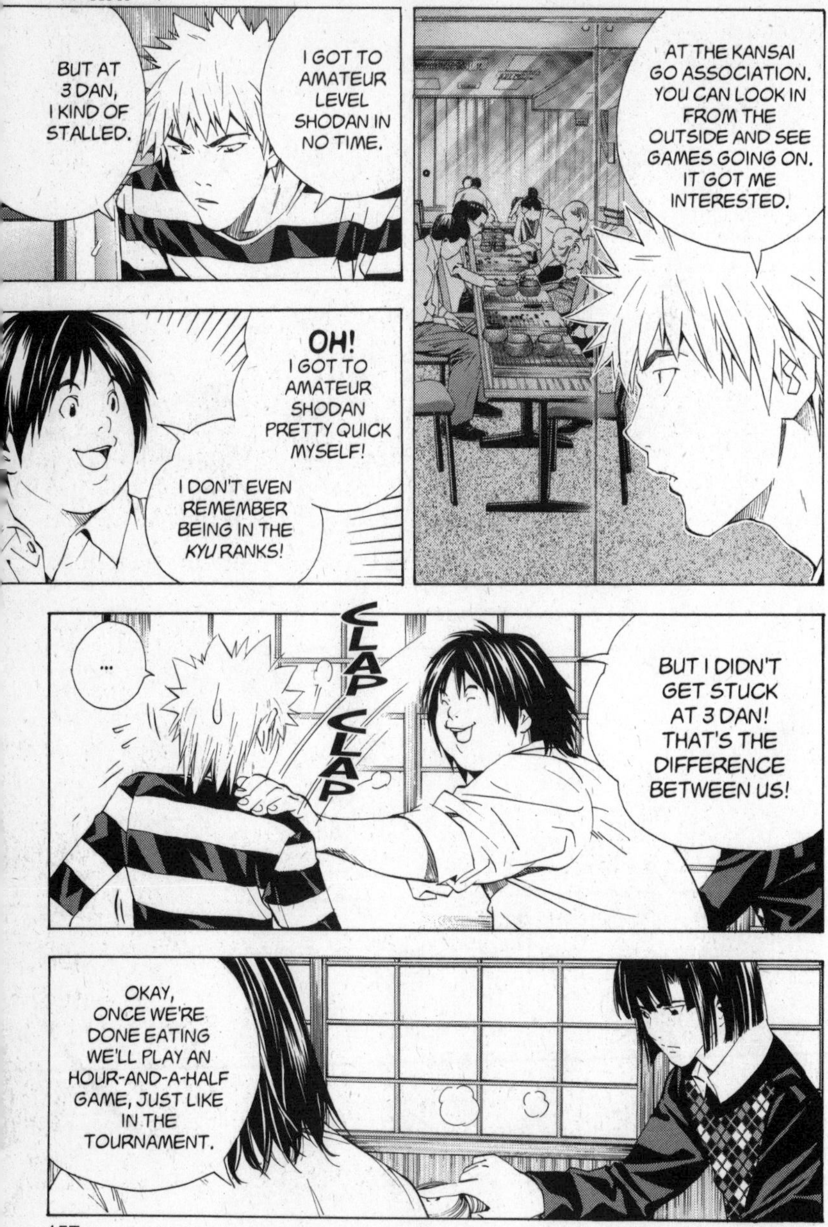
AT THE KANSAI GO ASSOCIATION. YOU CAN LOOK IN FROM THE OUTSIDE AND SEE GAMES GOING ON. IT GOT ME INTERESTED.
I GOT TO AMATEUR LEVEL SHODAN IN NO TIME.
BUT AT 3 DAN, I KIND OF STALLED.
OH! I GOT TO AMATEUR SHODAN PRETTY QUICK MYSELF!
I DON'T EVEN REMEMBER BEING IN THE *KYU* RANKS!
BUT I DIDN'T GET STUCK AT 3 DAN! THAT'S THE DIFFERENCE BETWEEN US!
CLAP CLAP CLAP
...
OKAY, ONCE WE'RE DONE EATING WE'LL PLAY AN HOUR-AND-A-HALF GAME, JUST LIKE IN THE TOURNAMENT.

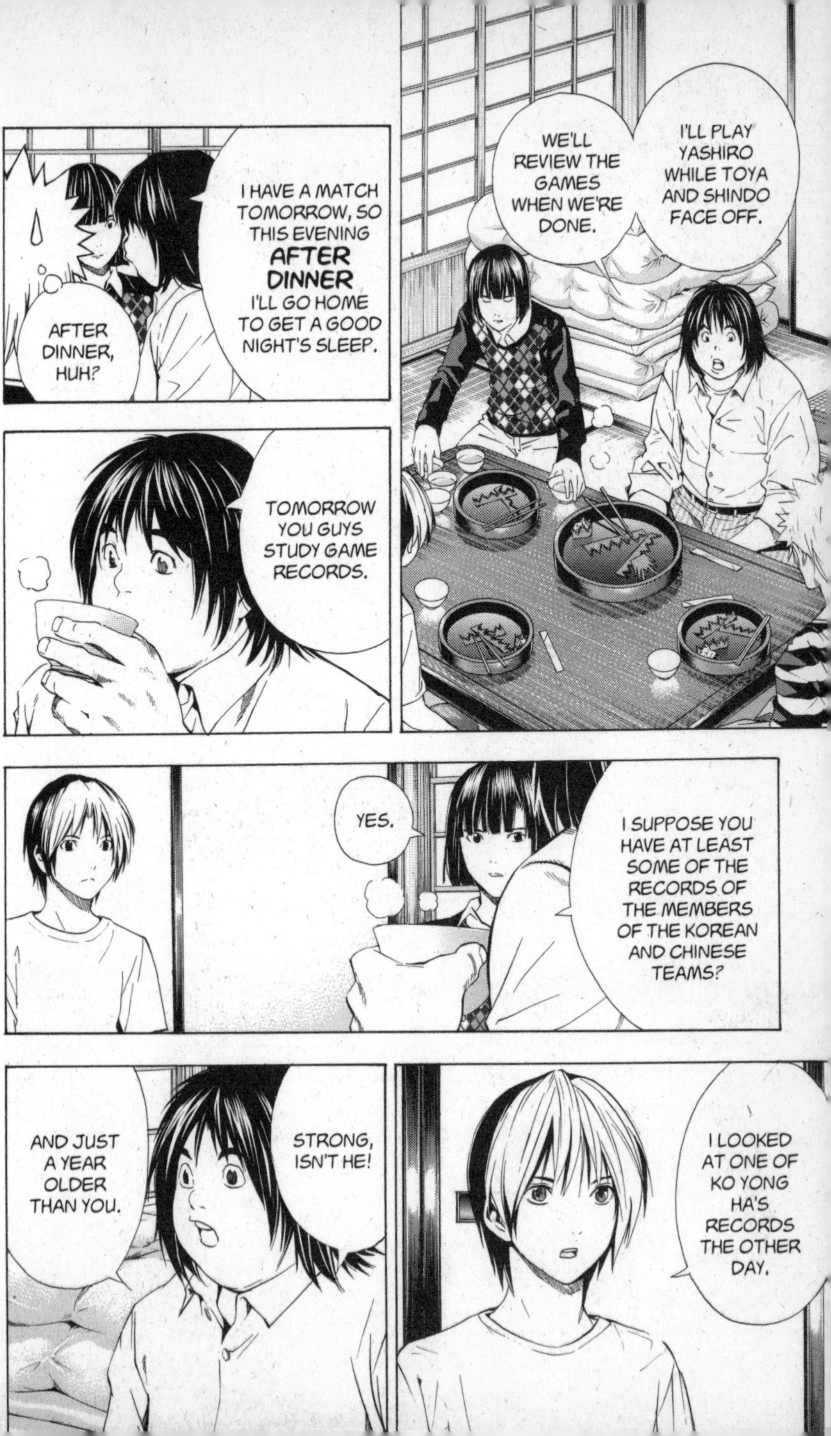
I'LL PLAY YASHIRO WHILE TOYA AND SHINDO FACE OFF.
WE'LL REVIEW THE GAMES WHEN WE'RE DONE.
I HAVE A MATCH TOMORROW, SO THIS EVENING **AFTER DINNER** I'LL GO HOME TO GET A GOOD NIGHT'S SLEEP.
AFTER DINNER, HUH?
TOMORROW YOU GUYS STUDY GAME RECORDS.
I SUPPOSE YOU HAVE AT LEAST SOME OF THE RECORDS OF THE MEMBERS OF THE KOREAN AND CHINESE TEAMS?
YES.
I LOOKED AT ONE OF KO YONG HA'S RECORDS THE OTHER DAY.
STRONG, ISN'T HE!
AND JUST A YEAR OLDER THAN YOU.

READ THIS WAY

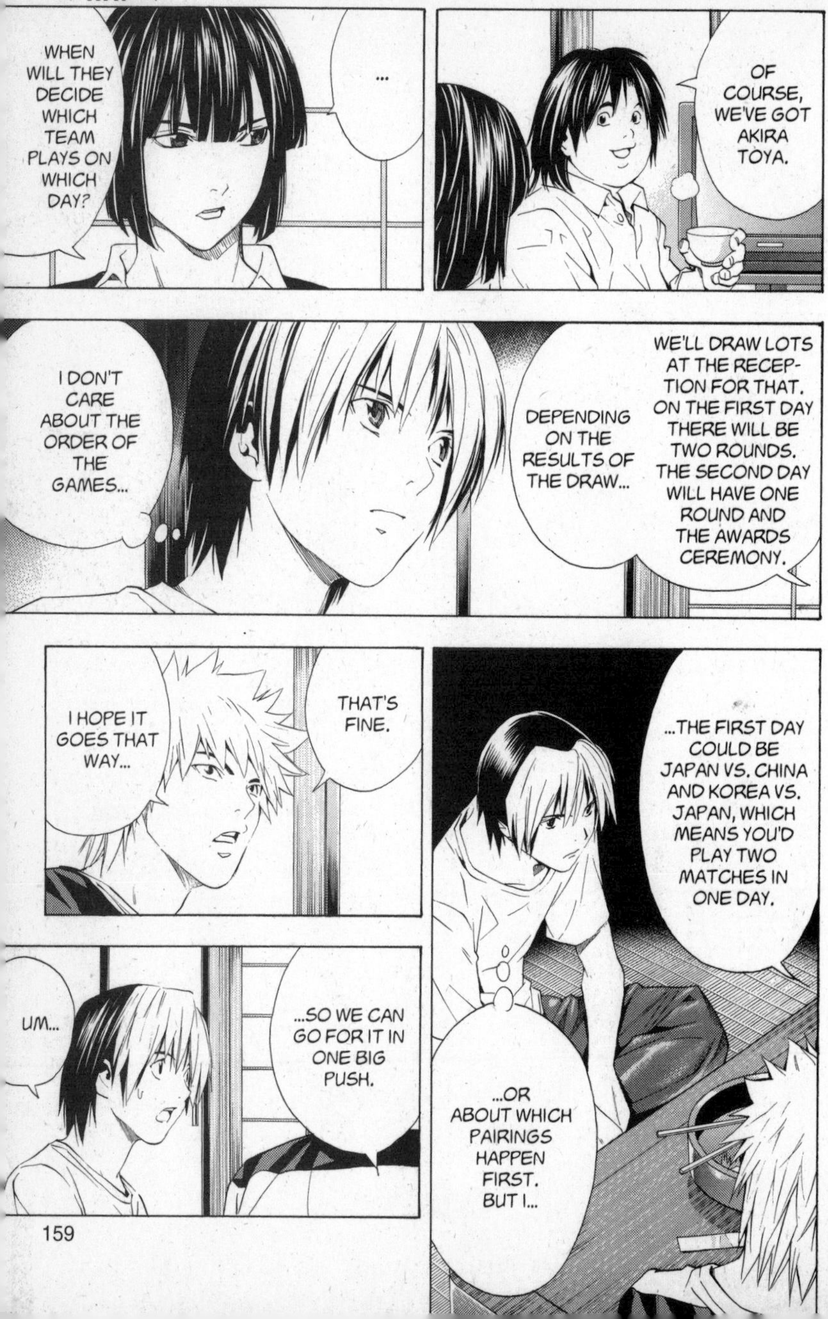
OF COURSE, WE'VE GOT AKIRA TOYA.
...
WHEN WILL THEY DECIDE WHICH TEAM PLAYS ON WHICH DAY?
WE'LL DRAW LOTS AT THE RECEPTION FOR THAT. ON THE FIRST DAY THERE WILL BE TWO ROUNDS. THE SECOND DAY WILL HAVE ONE ROUND AND THE AWARDS CEREMONY.
DEPENDING ON THE RESULTS OF THE DRAW...
I DON'T CARE ABOUT THE ORDER OF THE GAMES...
...THE FIRST DAY COULD BE JAPAN VS. CHINA AND KOREA VS. JAPAN, WHICH MEANS YOU'D PLAY TWO MATCHES IN ONE DAY.
...OR ABOUT WHICH PAIRINGS HAPPEN FIRST. BUT I...
THAT'S FINE.
I HOPE IT GOES THAT WAY...
...SO WE CAN GO FOR IT IN ONE BIG PUSH.
UM...

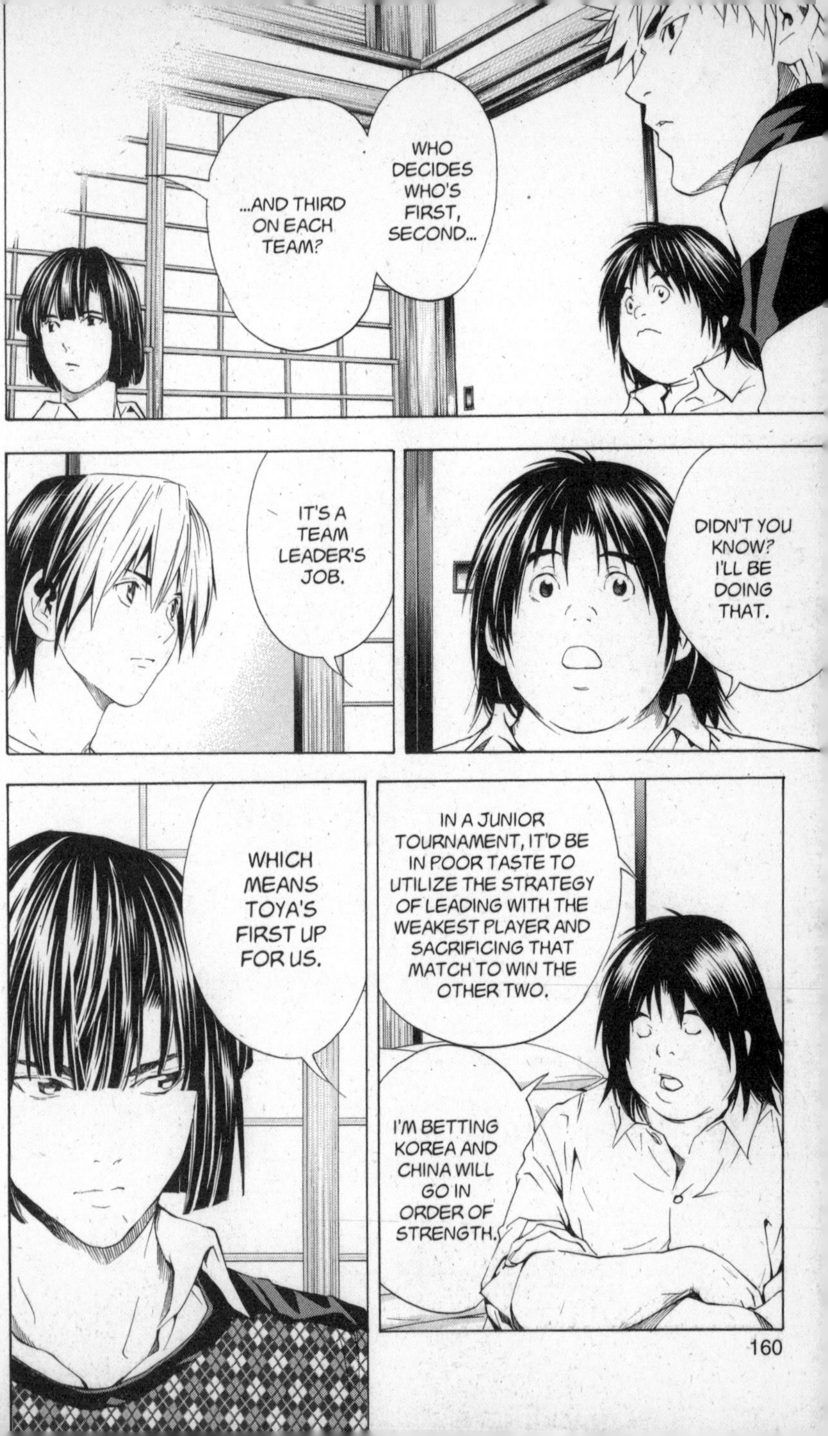
WHO DECIDES WHO'S FIRST, SECOND...
...AND THIRD ON EACH TEAM?
DIDN'T YOU KNOW? I'LL BE DOING THAT.
IT'S A TEAM LEADER'S JOB.
IN A JUNIOR TOURNAMENT, IT'D BE IN POOR TASTE TO UTILIZE THE STRATEGY OF LEADING WITH THE WEAKEST PLAYER AND SACRIFICING THAT MATCH TO WIN THE OTHER TWO.
I'M BETTING KOREA AND CHINA WILL GO IN ORDER OF STRENGTH.
WHICH MEANS TOYA'S FIRST UP FOR US.

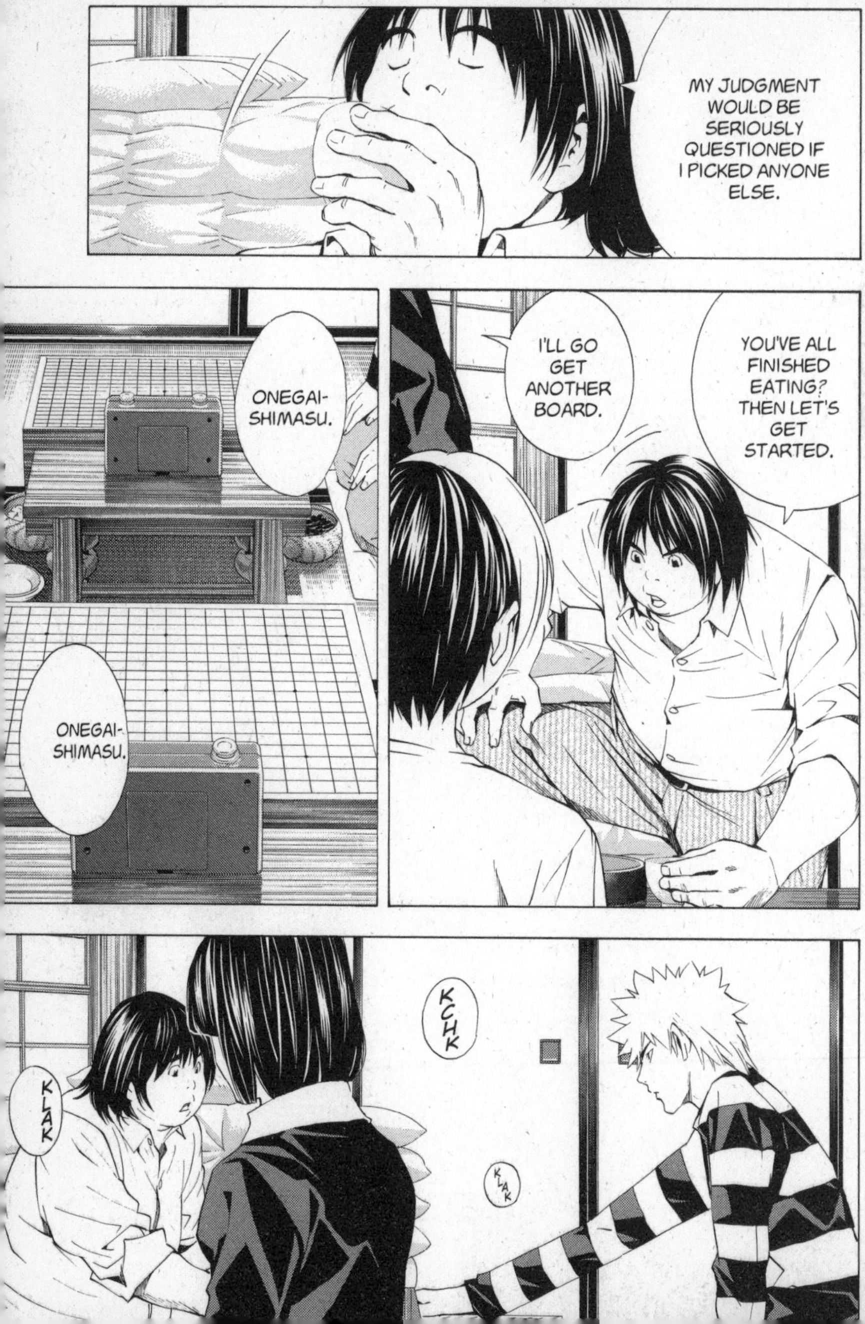
MY JUDGMENT WOULD BE SERIOUSLY QUESTIONED IF I PICKED ANYONE ELSE.
YOU'VE ALL FINISHED EATING? THEN LET'S GET STARTED.
I'LL GO GET ANOTHER BOARD.
ONEGAI-SHIMASU.
ONEGAI-SHIMASU.
KCHK
KLAK
KLAK

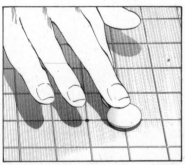

OUR FIRST, SECOND AND THIRD...

READ THIS WAY

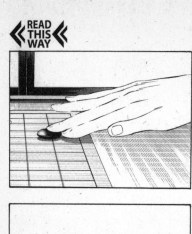

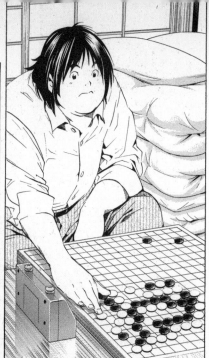

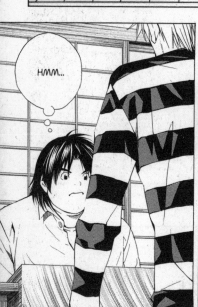

HMM...

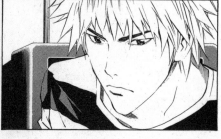

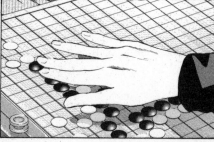

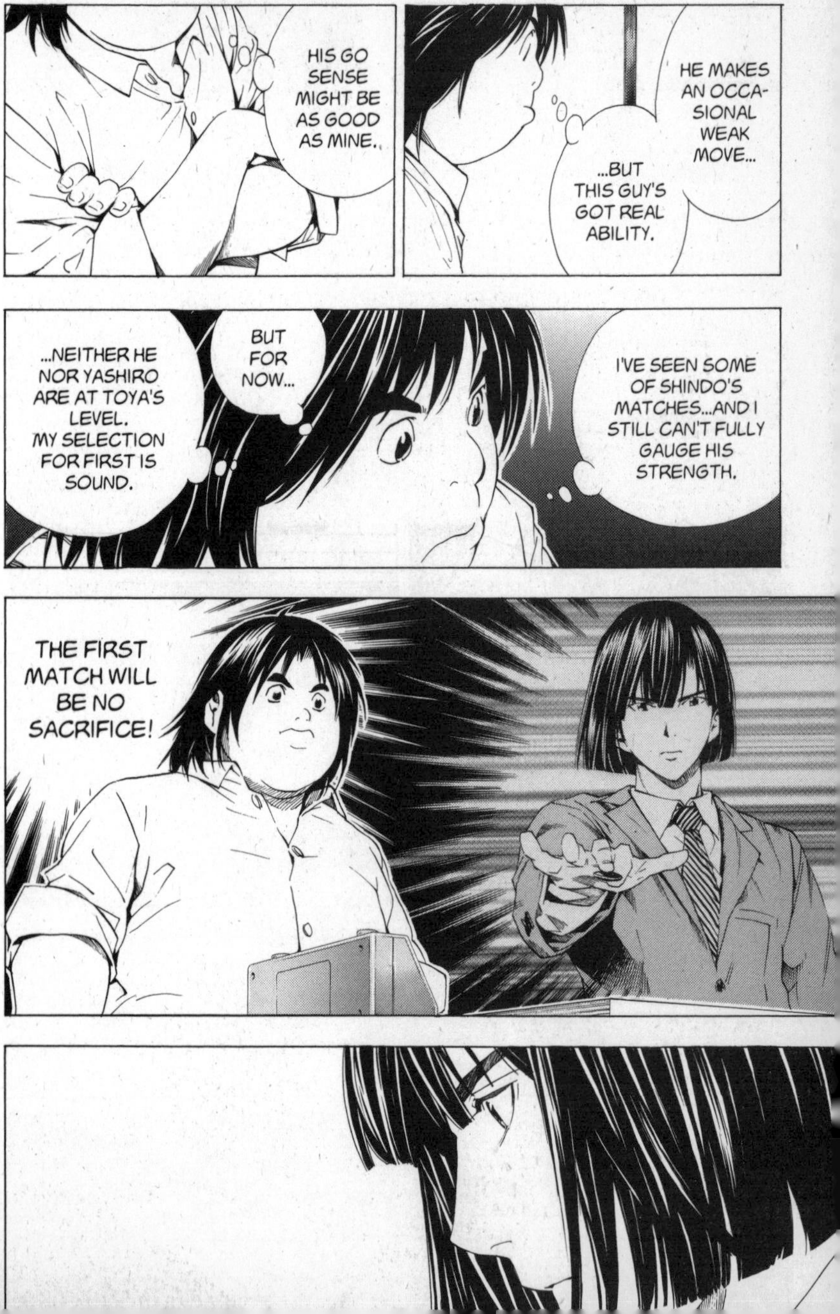
HE MAKES AN OCCA-SIONAL WEAK MOVE...
...BUT THIS GUY'S GOT REAL ABILITY.
HIS GO SENSE MIGHT BE AS GOOD AS MINE.
I'VE SEEN SOME OF SHINDO'S MATCHES...AND I STILL CAN'T FULLY GAUGE HIS STRENGTH.
BUT FOR NOW...
...NEITHER HE NOR YASHIRO ARE AT TOYA'S LEVEL. MY SELECTION FOR FIRST IS SOUND.
THE FIRST MATCH WILL BE NO SACRIFICE!

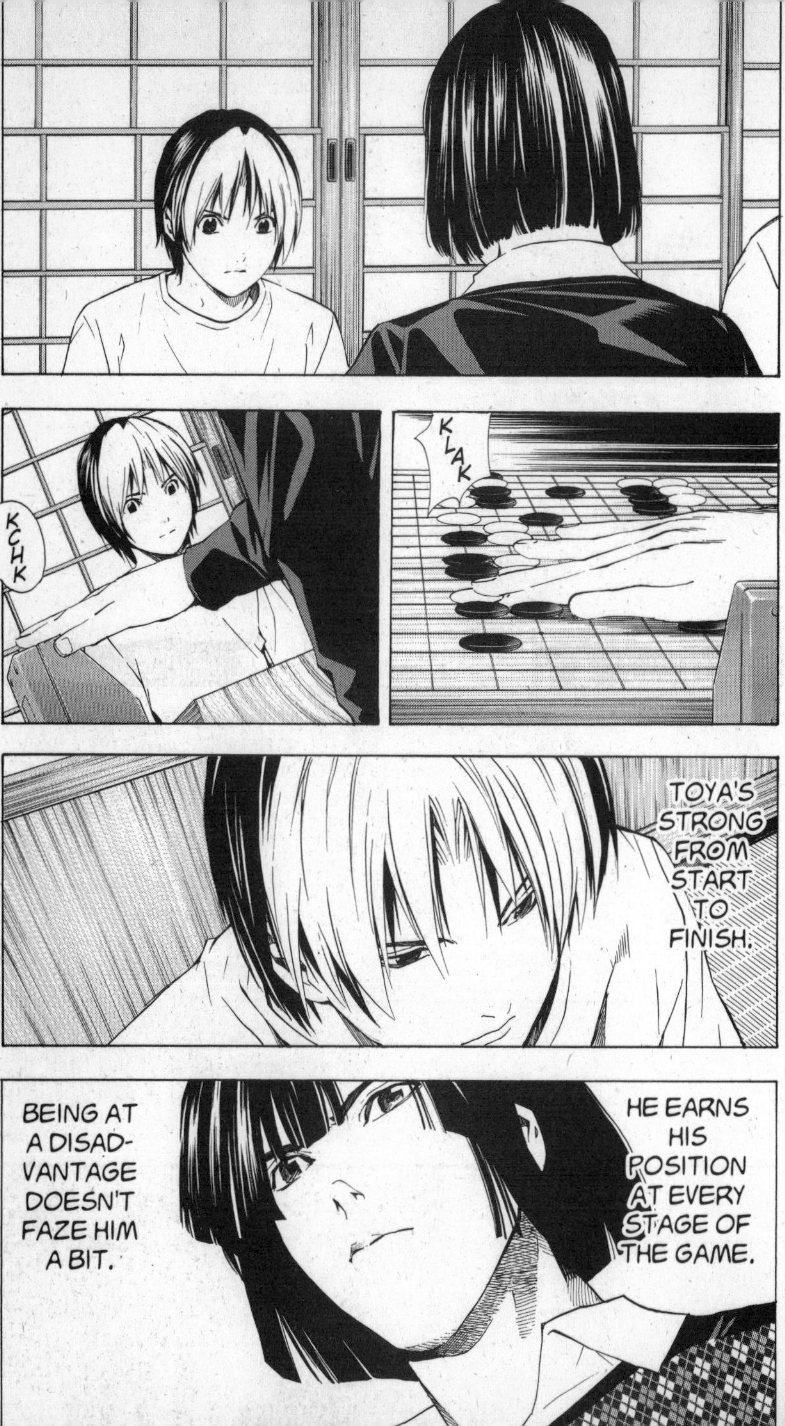
KLAK
KCHK
TOYA'S STRONG FROM START TO FINISH.
HE EARNS HIS POSITION AT EVERY STAGE OF THE GAME.
BEING AT A DISAD-VANTAGE DOESN'T FAZE HIM A BIT.

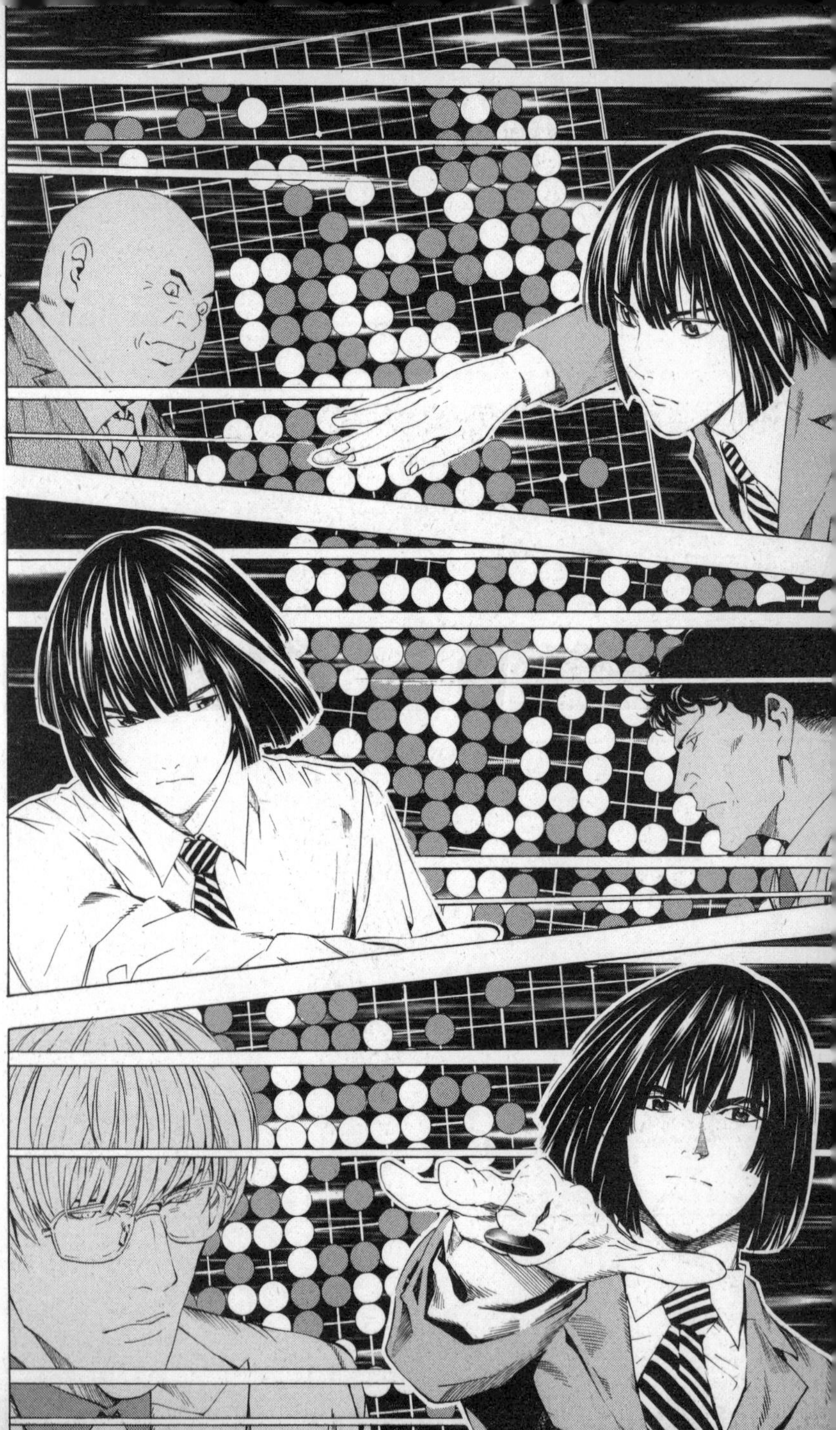

READ THIS WAY

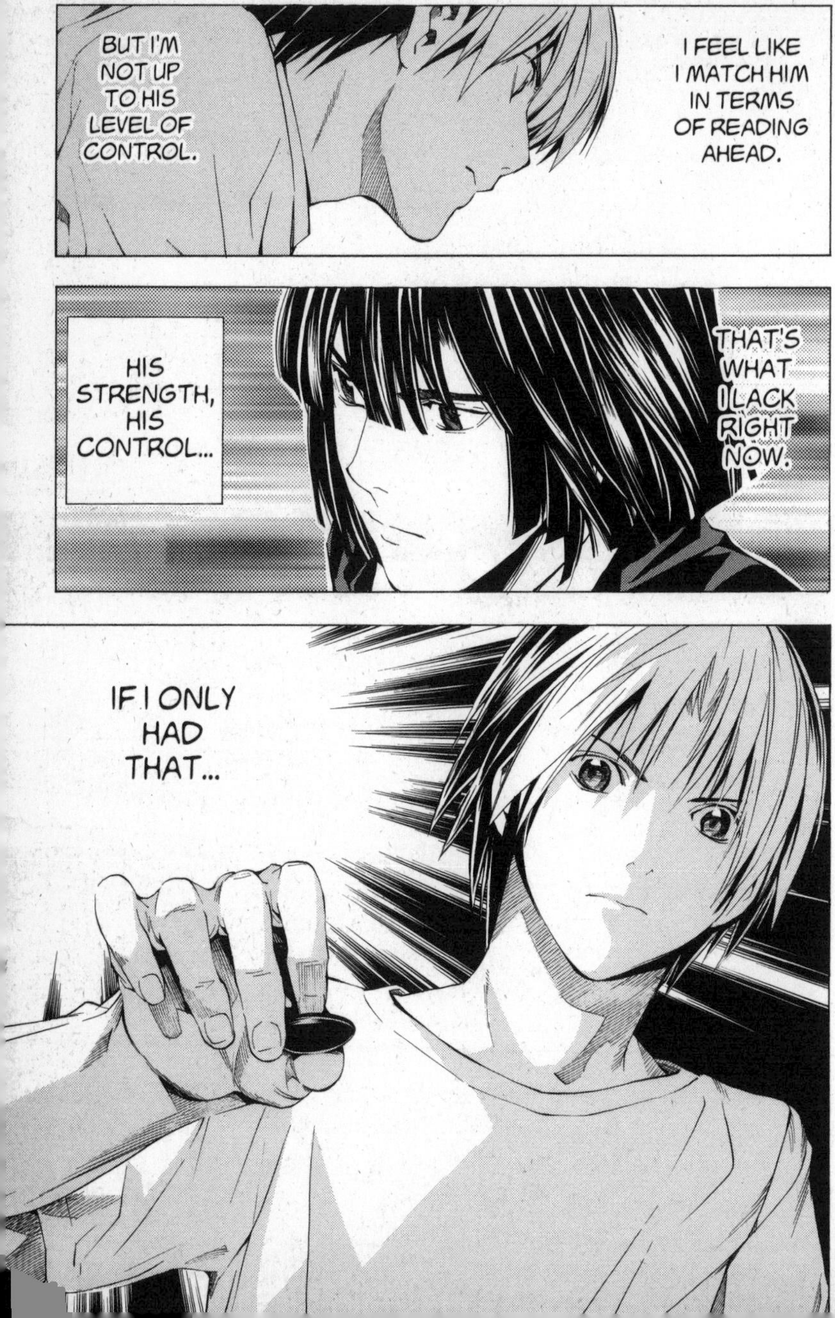
I FEEL LIKE I MATCH HIM IN TERMS OF READING AHEAD.
BUT I'M NOT UP TO HIS LEVEL OF CONTROL.
THAT'S WHAT I LACK RIGHT NOW.
HIS STRENGTH, HIS CONTROL...
IF I ONLY HAD THAT...

A WORD ABOUT HIKARU NO GO

INTONATION

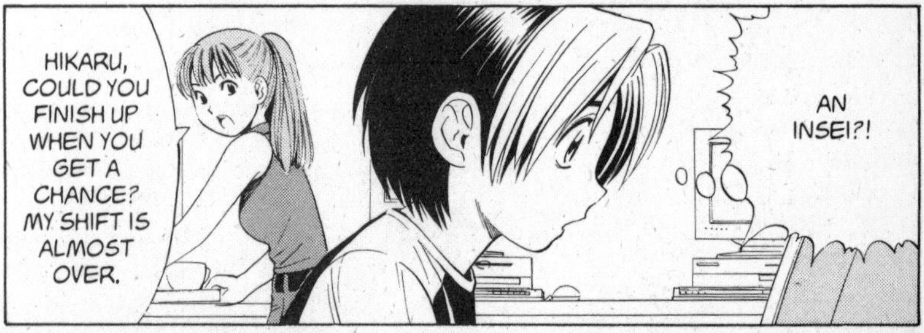
AN INSEI?!
HIKARU, COULD YOU FINISH UP WHEN YOU GET A CHANCE? MY SHIFT IS ALMOST OVER.

"THERE ARE TWO WAYS TO PRONOUNCE *INSEI*. ONE WAY IS FLAT, WITH NO INFLECTION. THE OTHER IS TO ACCENT THE FIRST SYLLABLE. THE FIRST WAY IS USED OFTEN, BUT THE SECOND WAY IS USED TOO." (YUKARI UMEZAWA)

SOME PEOPLE WATCHING THE ANIME MAY HAVE HEARD PHRASES LIKE *TEAI*, *GO WO UTSU*, *SHODAN*, AND SO ON, AND THOUGHT, "HMM... IS THAT REALLY HOW THAT'S PRONOUNCED?"

HON'INBO SHUSAKU IS COMMONLY PRONOUNCED AS YOU HEAR IT IN THE ANIME, BUT FOR MOST OTHER PHRASES THERE IS USUALLY MORE THAN ONE ACCEPTED WAY TO PRONOUNCE IT.

IT ISN'T JUST PRONUNCIATION, BUT KANJI READINGS TOO. 大石 CAN BE READ AS *OOISHI*, OR AS *TAISEKI*.

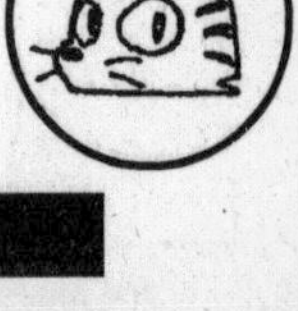

Game 174 "Heading to the Hokuto Cup"

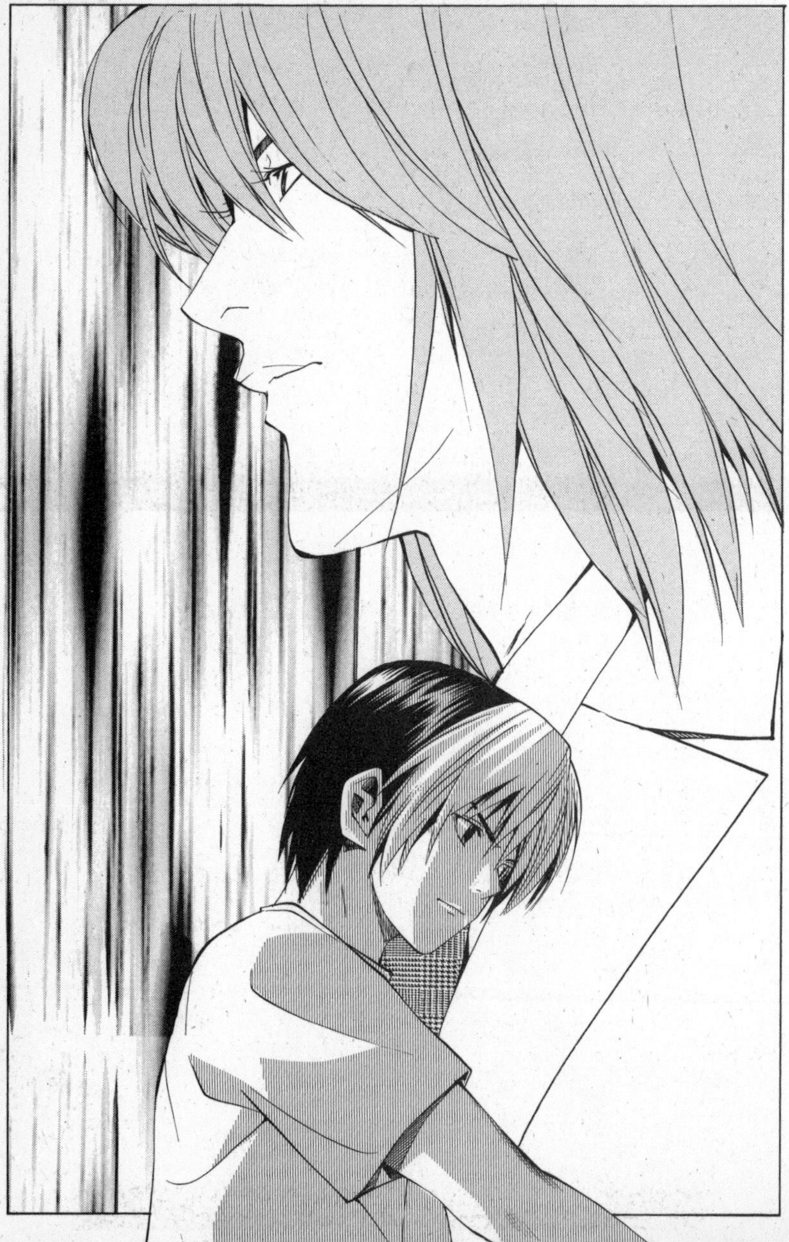

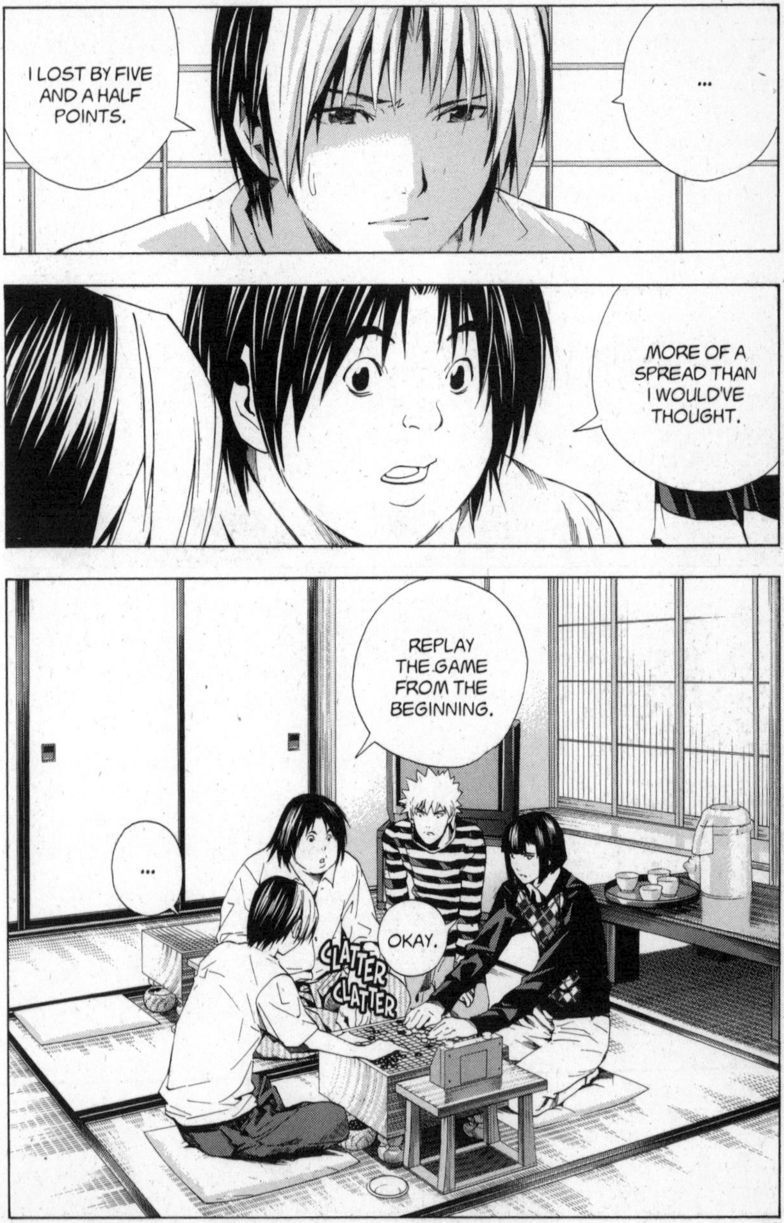
...
I LOST BY FIVE AND A HALF POINTS.
MORE OF A SPREAD THAN I WOULD'VE THOUGHT.
REPLAY THE GAME FROM THE BEGINNING.
...
OKAY.
CLATTER CLATTER

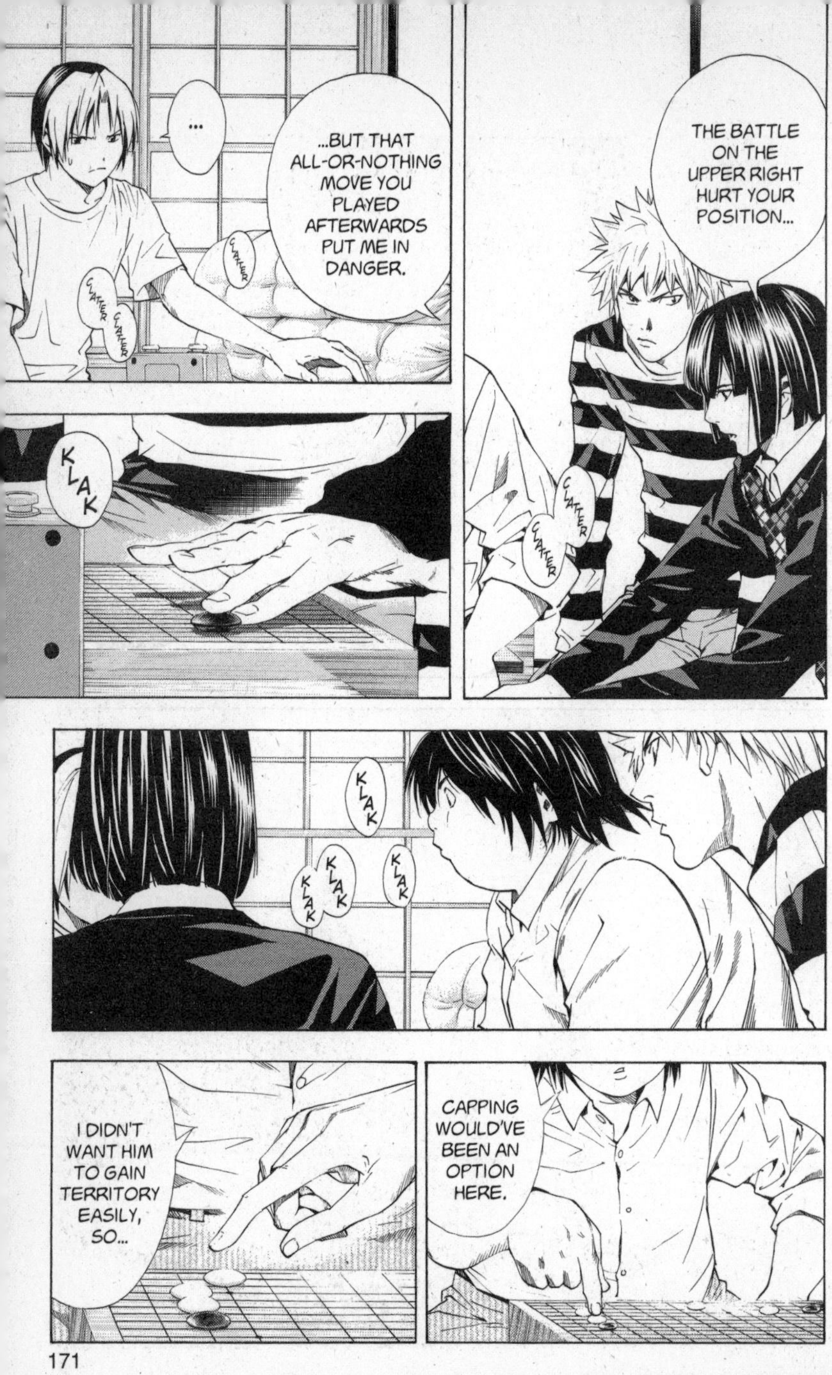
THE BATTLE ON THE UPPER RIGHT HURT YOUR POSITION...
CLATTER
CLATTER
...
...BUT THAT ALL-OR-NOTHING MOVE YOU PLAYED AFTERWARDS PUT ME IN DANGER.
CLATTER
CLATTER
CLATTER
KLAK
KLAK
KLAK
KLAK
KLAK
CAPPING WOULD'VE BEEN AN OPTION HERE.
I DIDN'T WANT HIM TO GAIN TERRITORY EASILY, SO...

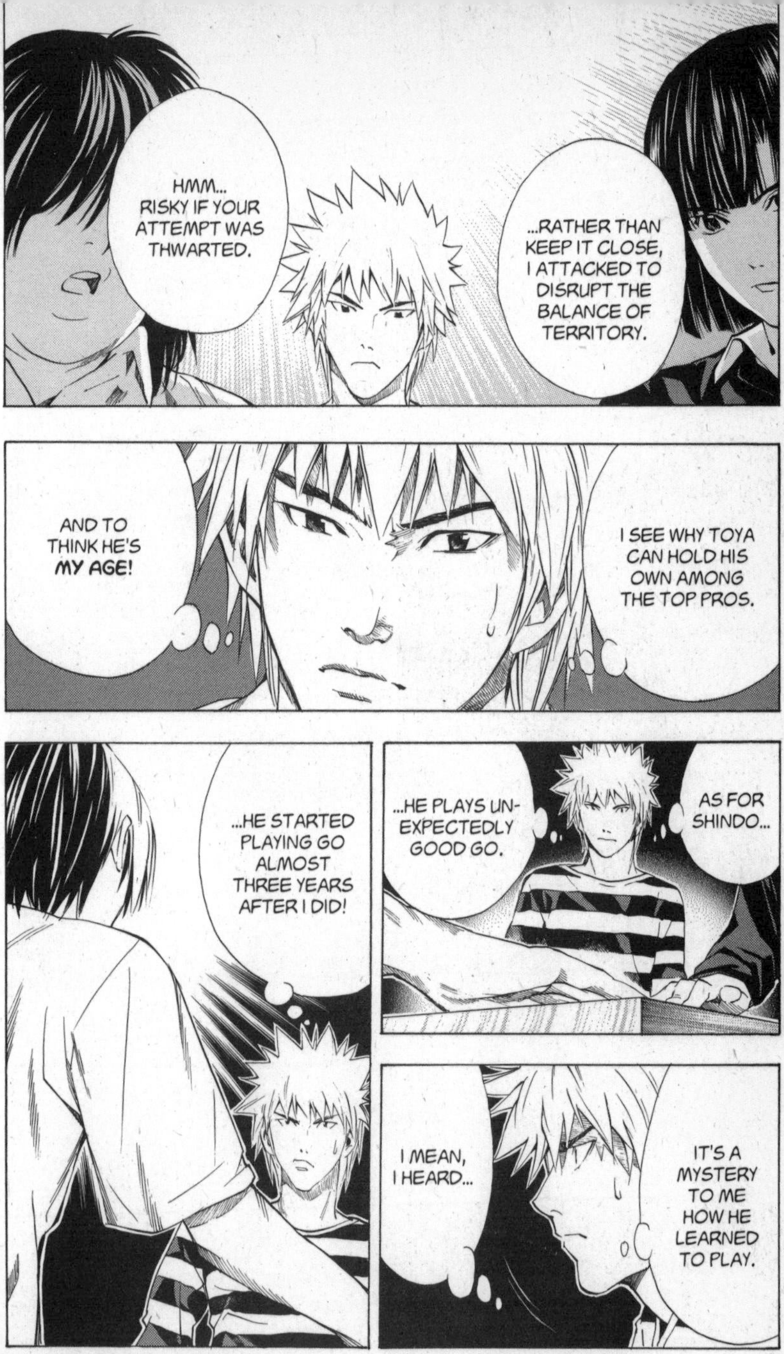
...RATHER THAN KEEP IT CLOSE, I ATTACKED TO DISRUPT THE BALANCE OF TERRITORY.
HMM... RISKY IF YOUR ATTEMPT WAS THWARTED.
I SEE WHY TOYA CAN HOLD HIS OWN AMONG THE TOP PROS.
AND TO THINK HE'S MY AGE!
AS FOR SHINDO...
...HE PLAYS UN-EXPECTEDLY GOOD GO.
IT'S A MYSTERY TO ME HOW HE LEARNED TO PLAY.
I MEAN, I HEARD...
...HE STARTED PLAYING GO ALMOST THREE YEARS AFTER I DID!

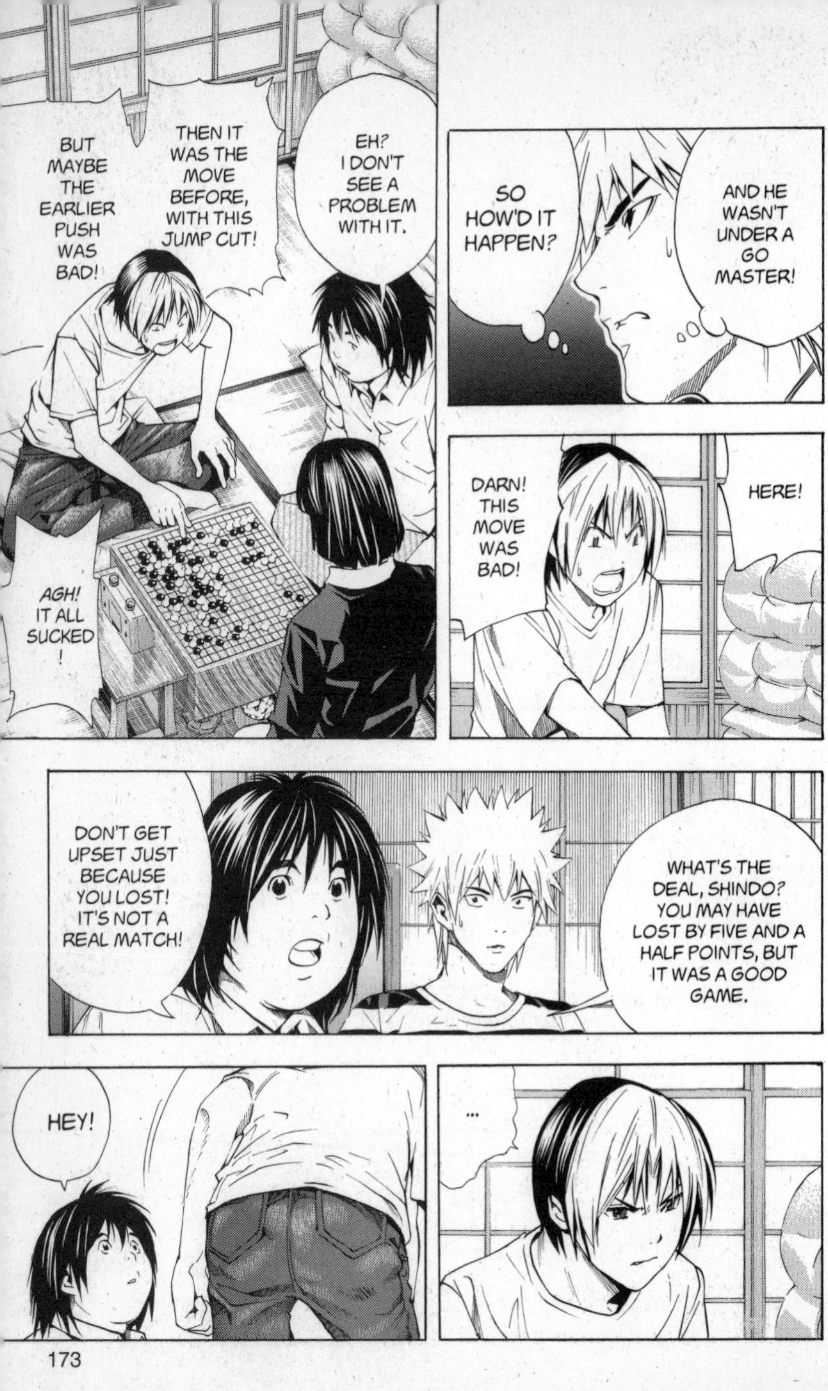
AND HE WASN'T UNDER A GO MASTER!
SO HOW'D IT HAPPEN?
HERE!
DARN! THIS MOVE WAS BAD!
EH? I DON'T SEE A PROBLEM WITH IT.
THEN IT WAS THE MOVE BEFORE, WITH THIS JUMP CUT!
BUT MAYBE THE EARLIER PUSH WAS BAD!
AGH! IT ALL SUCKED!
WHAT'S THE DEAL, SHINDO? YOU MAY HAVE LOST BY FIVE AND A HALF POINTS, BUT IT WAS A GOOD GAME.
DON'T GET UPSET JUST BECAUSE YOU LOST! IT'S NOT A REAL MATCH!
...
HEY!

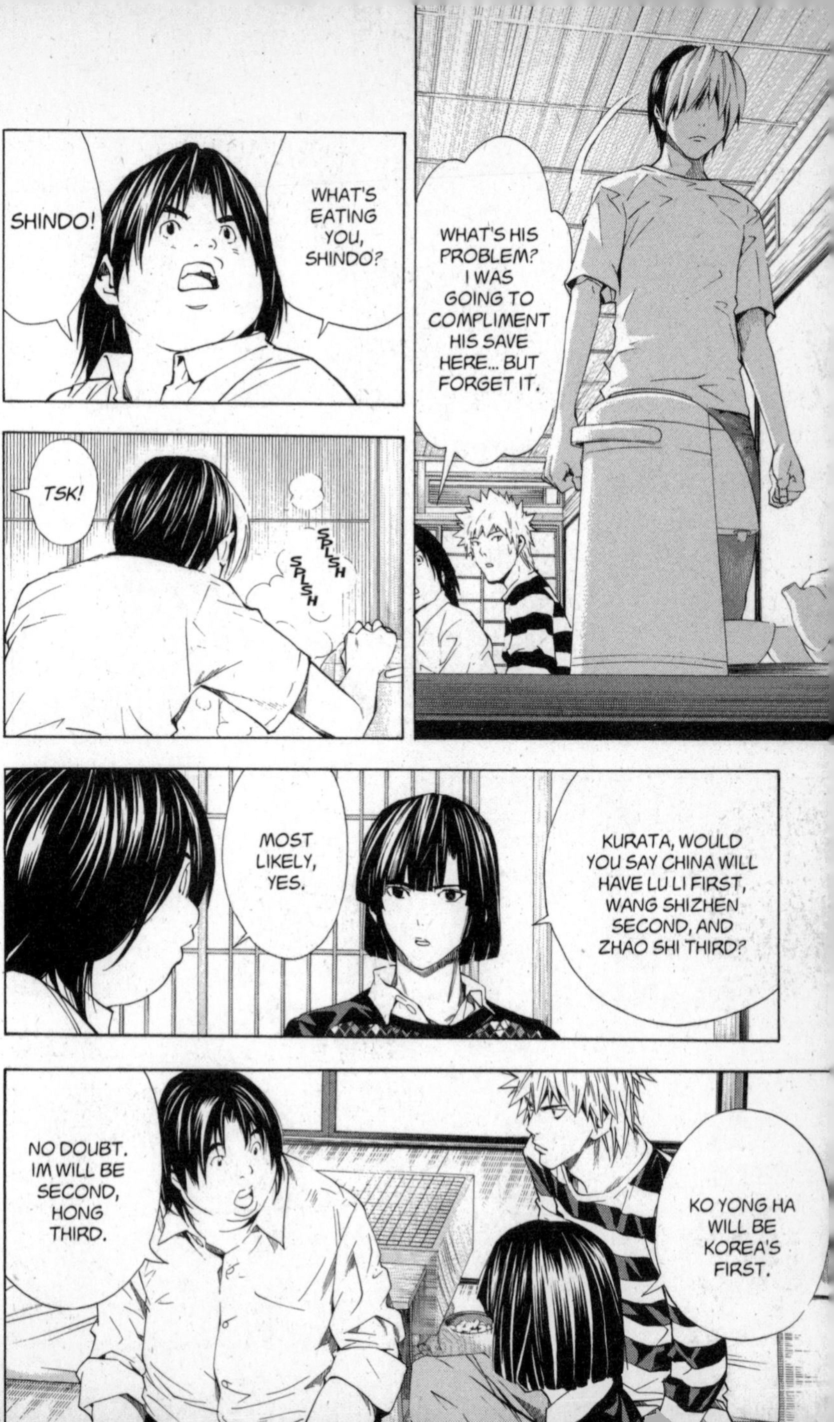
WHAT'S HIS PROBLEM? I WAS GOING TO COMPLIMENT HIS SAVE HERE... BUT FORGET IT.
WHAT'S EATING YOU, SHINDO?
SHINDO!
TSK!
SPLSH SPLSH
KURATA, WOULD YOU SAY CHINA WILL HAVE LU LI FIRST, WANG SHIZHEN SECOND, AND ZHAO SHI THIRD?
MOST LIKELY, YES.
KO YONG HA WILL BE KOREA'S FIRST.
NO DOUBT. IM WILL BE SECOND, HONG THIRD.

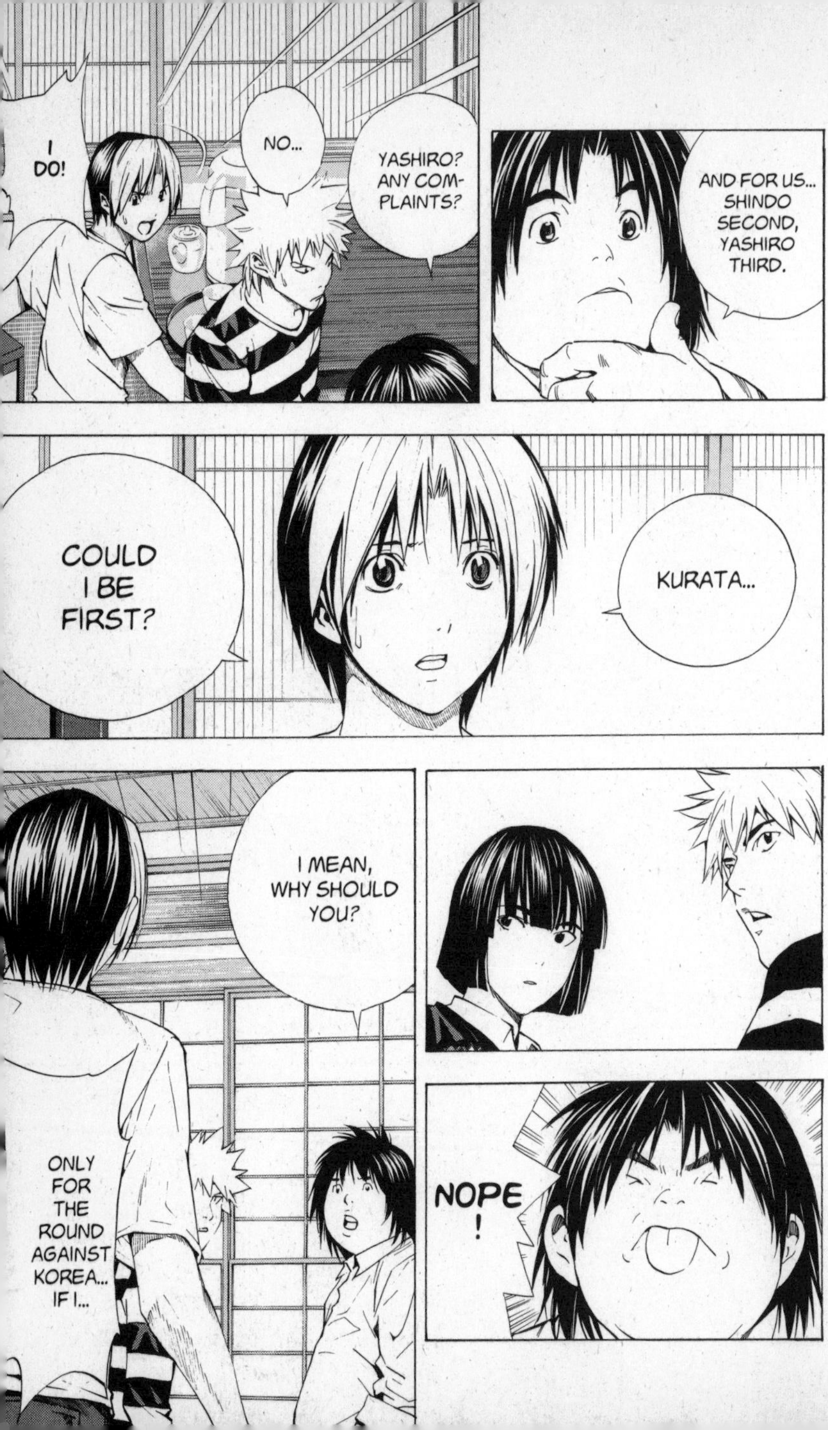
AND FOR US... SHINDO SECOND, YASHIRO THIRD.
YASHIRO? ANY COM-PLAINTS?
NO...
I DO!
KURATA...
COULD I BE FIRST?
NOPE!
I MEAN, WHY SHOULD YOU?
ONLY FOR THE ROUND AGAINST KOREA... IF I...

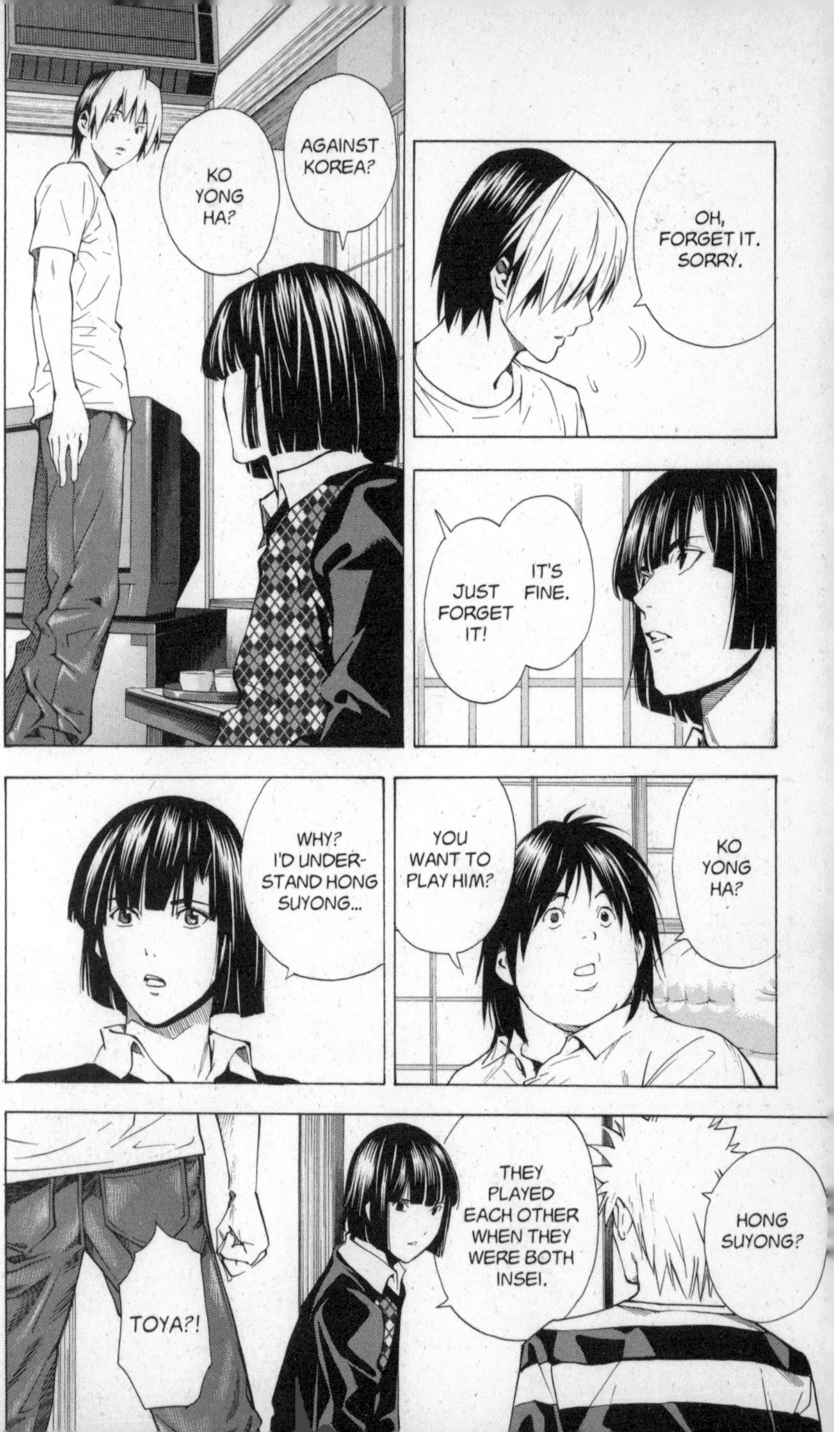
OH, FORGET IT. SORRY.
IT'S FINE.
JUST FORGET IT!
AGAINST KOREA?
KO YONG HA?
KO YONG HA?
YOU WANT TO PLAY HIM?
WHY? I'D UNDERSTAND HONG SUYONG...
HONG SUYONG?
THEY PLAYED EACH OTHER WHEN THEY WERE BOTH INSEI.
TOYA?!

READ THIS WAY

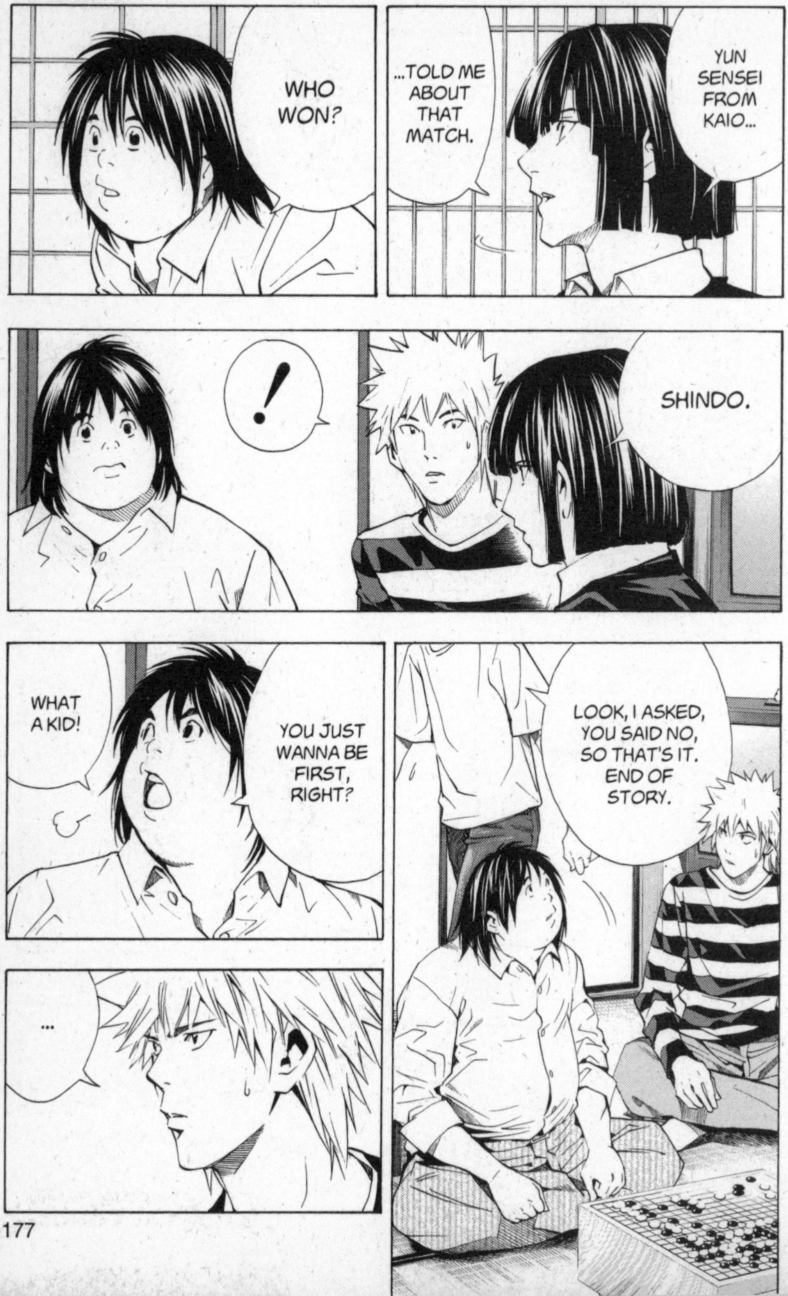
YUN SENSEI FROM KAIO...
...TOLD ME ABOUT THAT MATCH.
WHO WON?
SHINDO.
!
LOOK, I ASKED, YOU SAID NO, SO THAT'S IT. END OF STORY.
YOU JUST WANNA BE FIRST, RIGHT?
WHAT A KID!
...

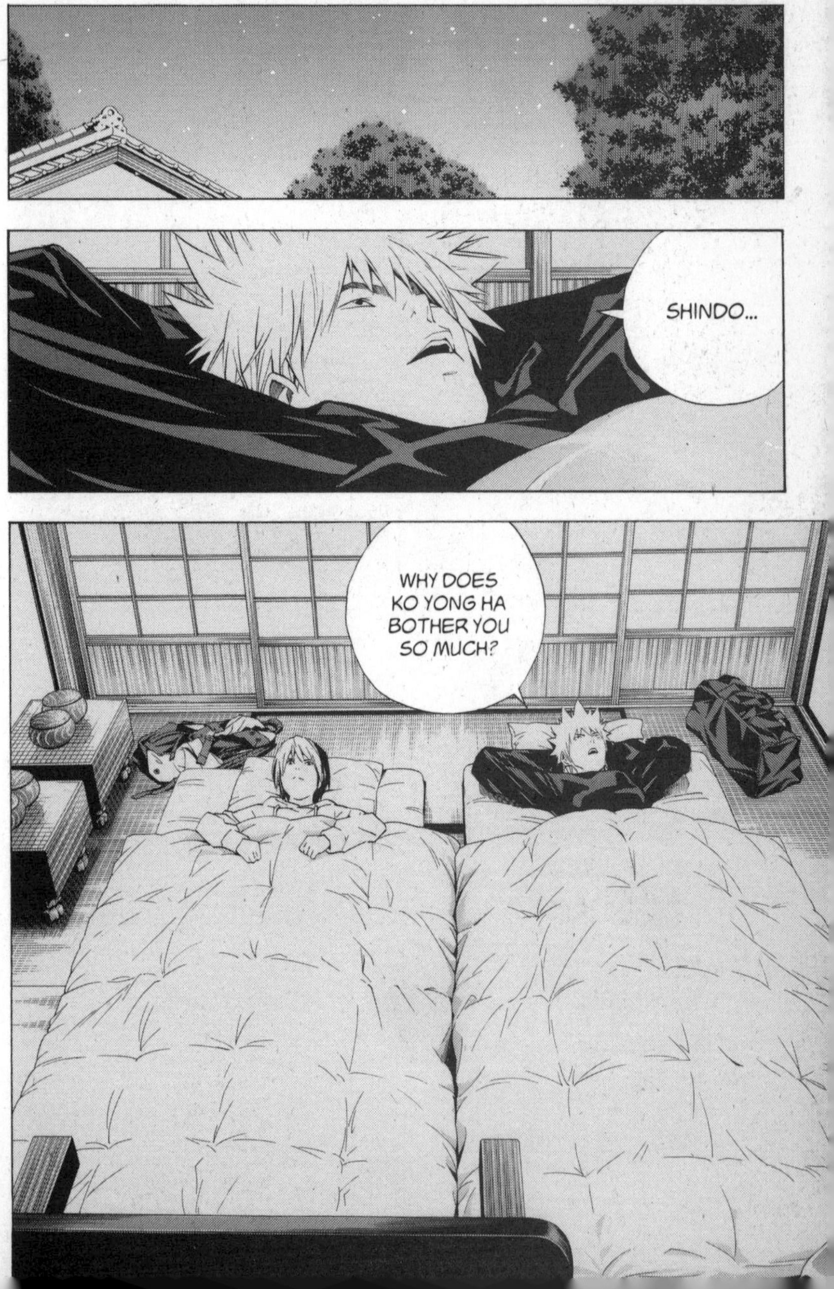
SHINDO...
WHY DOES KO YONG HA BOTHER YOU SO MUCH?

READ THIS WAY

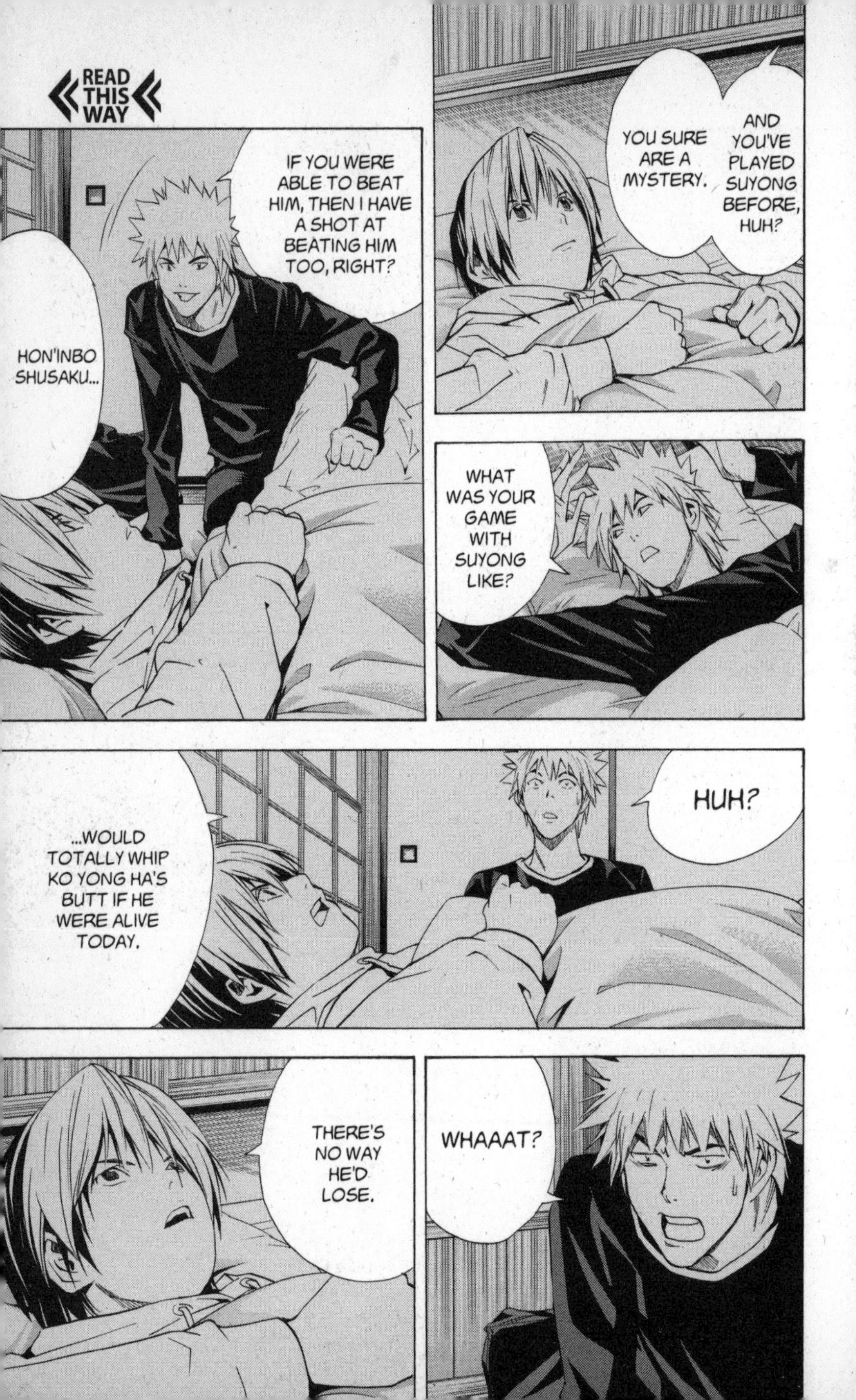
AND YOU'VE PLAYED SUYONG BEFORE, HUH?
YOU SURE ARE A MYSTERY.
WHAT WAS YOUR GAME WITH SUYONG LIKE?
IF YOU WERE ABLE TO BEAT HIM, THEN I HAVE A SHOT AT BEATING HIM TOO, RIGHT?
HON'INBO SHUSAKU...
HUH?
...WOULD TOTALLY WHIP KO YONG HA'S BUTT IF HE WERE ALIVE TODAY.
WHAAAT?
THERE'S NO WAY HE'D LOSE.

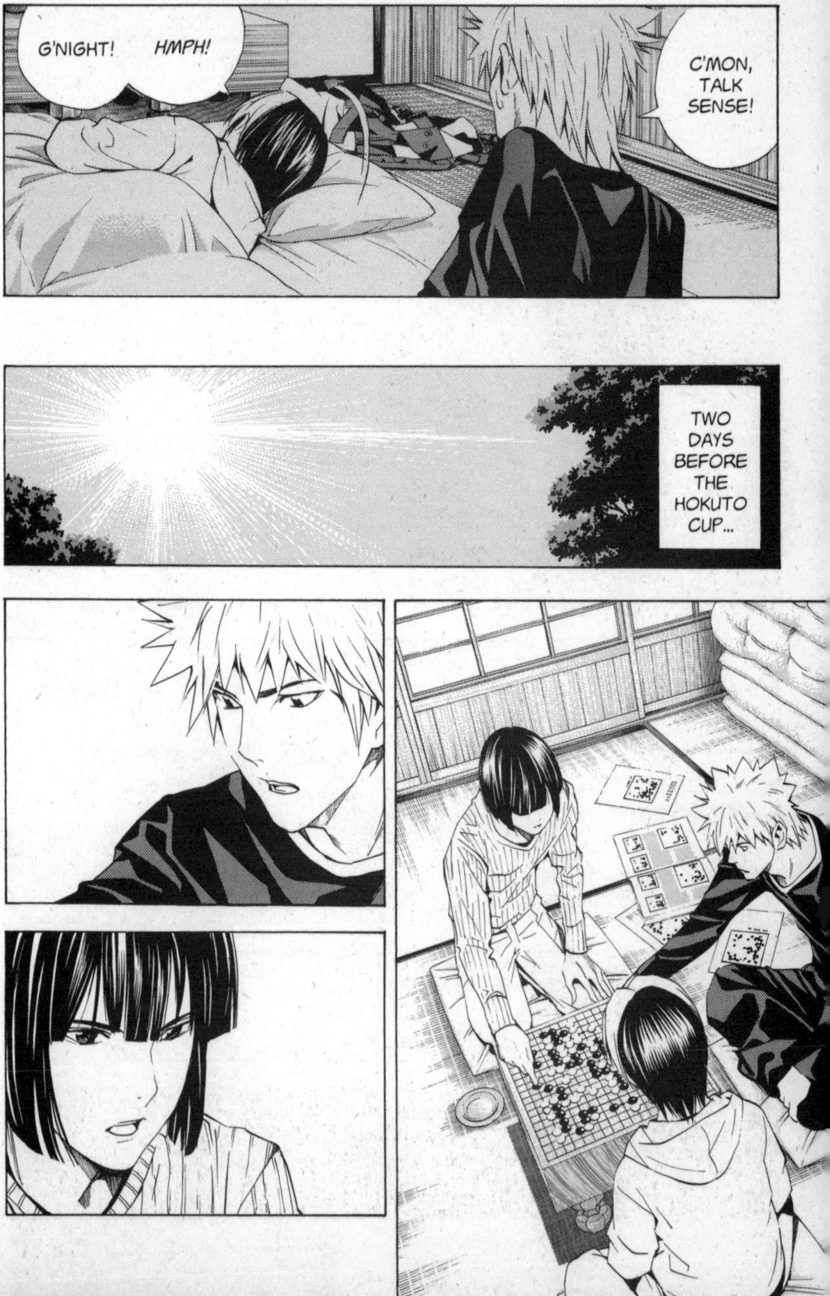
C'MON, TALK SENSE!
G'NIGHT! HMPH!
TWO DAYS BEFORE THE HOKUTO CUP...

READ THIS WAY

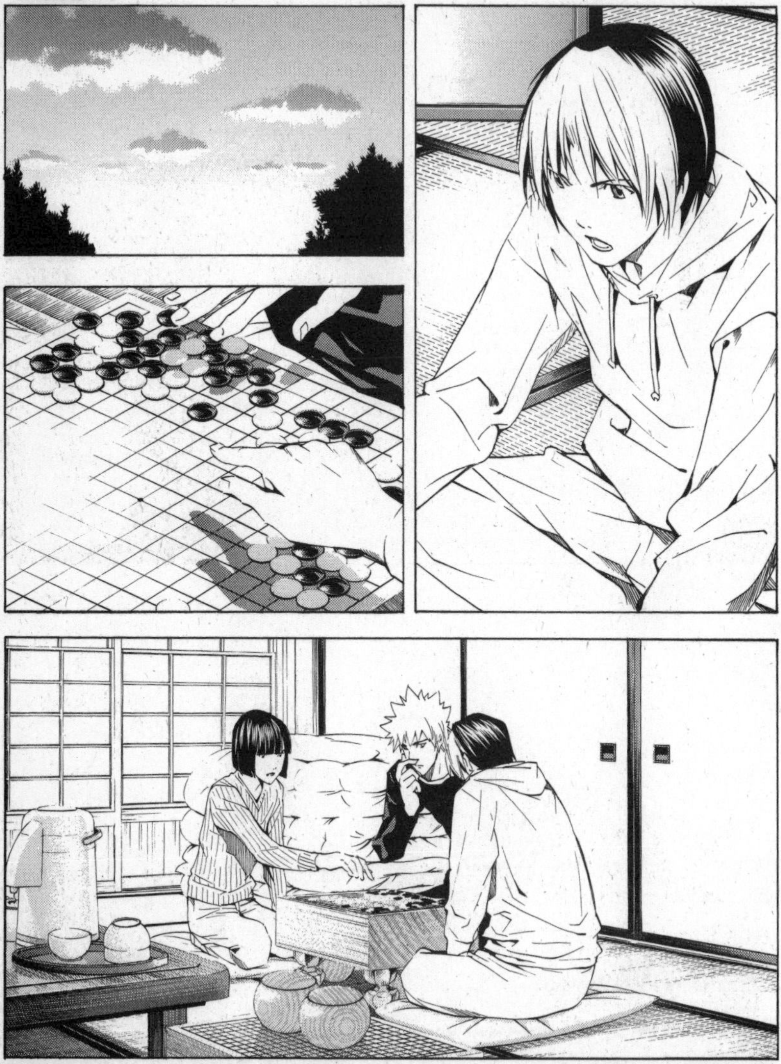

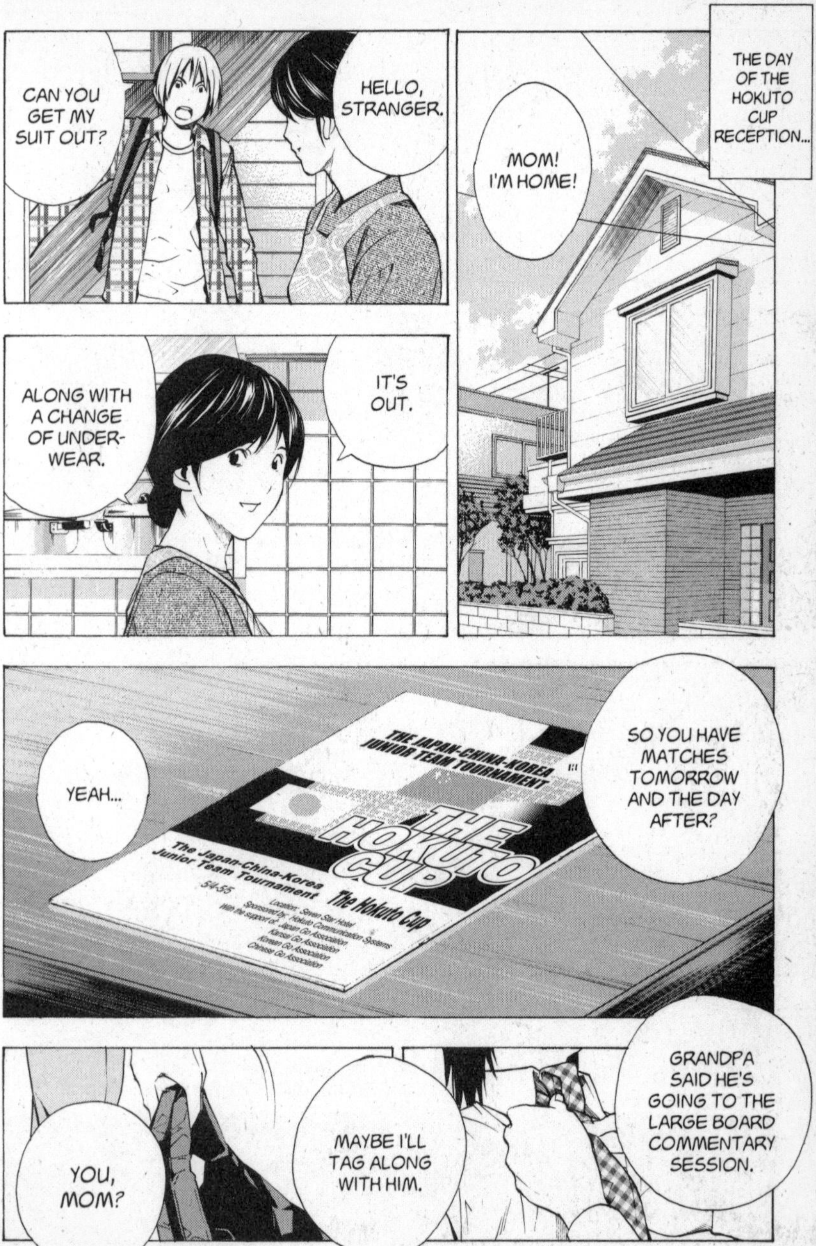
THE DAY OF THE HOKUTO CUP RECEPTION...
MOM! I'M HOME!
HELLO, STRANGER.
CAN YOU GET MY SUIT OUT?
IT'S OUT.
ALONG WITH A CHANGE OF UNDER-WEAR.
SO YOU HAVE MATCHES TOMORROW AND THE DAY AFTER?
YEAH...
THE JAPAN-CHINA-KOREA JUNIOR TEAM TOURNAMENT
THE HOKUTO CUP
The Japan-China-Korea Junior Team Tournament
The Hokuto Cup
Location: Seven Star Hotel
Sponsored by: Hokuto Communication Systems
With the support of: Japan Go Association
Kansai Go Association
Korean Go Association
Chinese Go Association
GRANDPA SAID HE'S GOING TO THE LARGE BOARD COMMENTARY SESSION.
MAYBE I'LL TAG ALONG WITH HIM.
YOU, MOM?

READ THIS WAY

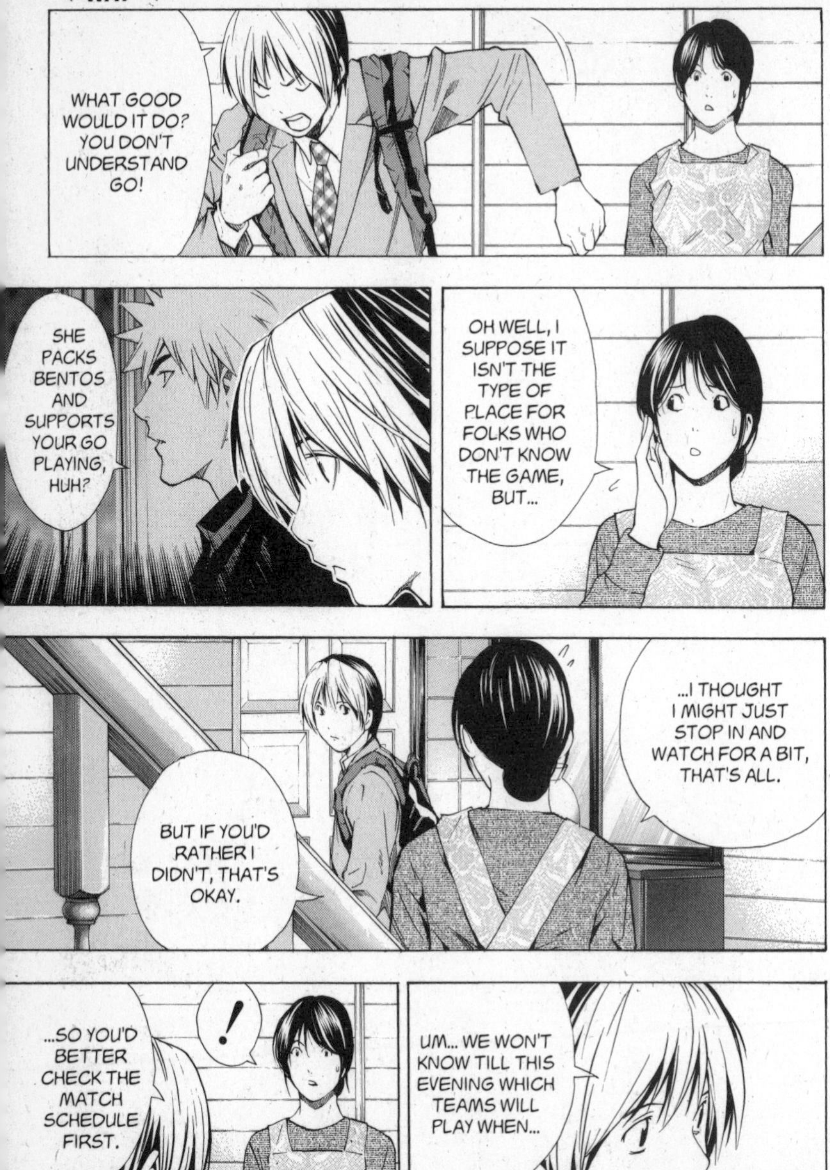
WHAT GOOD WOULD IT DO? YOU DON'T UNDERSTAND GO!
OH WELL, I SUPPOSE IT ISN'T THE TYPE OF PLACE FOR FOLKS WHO DON'T KNOW THE GAME, BUT...
SHE PACKS BENTOS AND SUPPORTS YOUR GO PLAYING, HUH?
...I THOUGHT I MIGHT JUST STOP IN AND WATCH FOR A BIT, THAT'S ALL.
BUT IF YOU'D RATHER I DIDN'T, THAT'S OKAY.
UM... WE WON'T KNOW TILL THIS EVENING WHICH TEAMS WILL PLAY WHEN...
...SO YOU'D BETTER CHECK THE MATCH SCHEDULE FIRST.
!

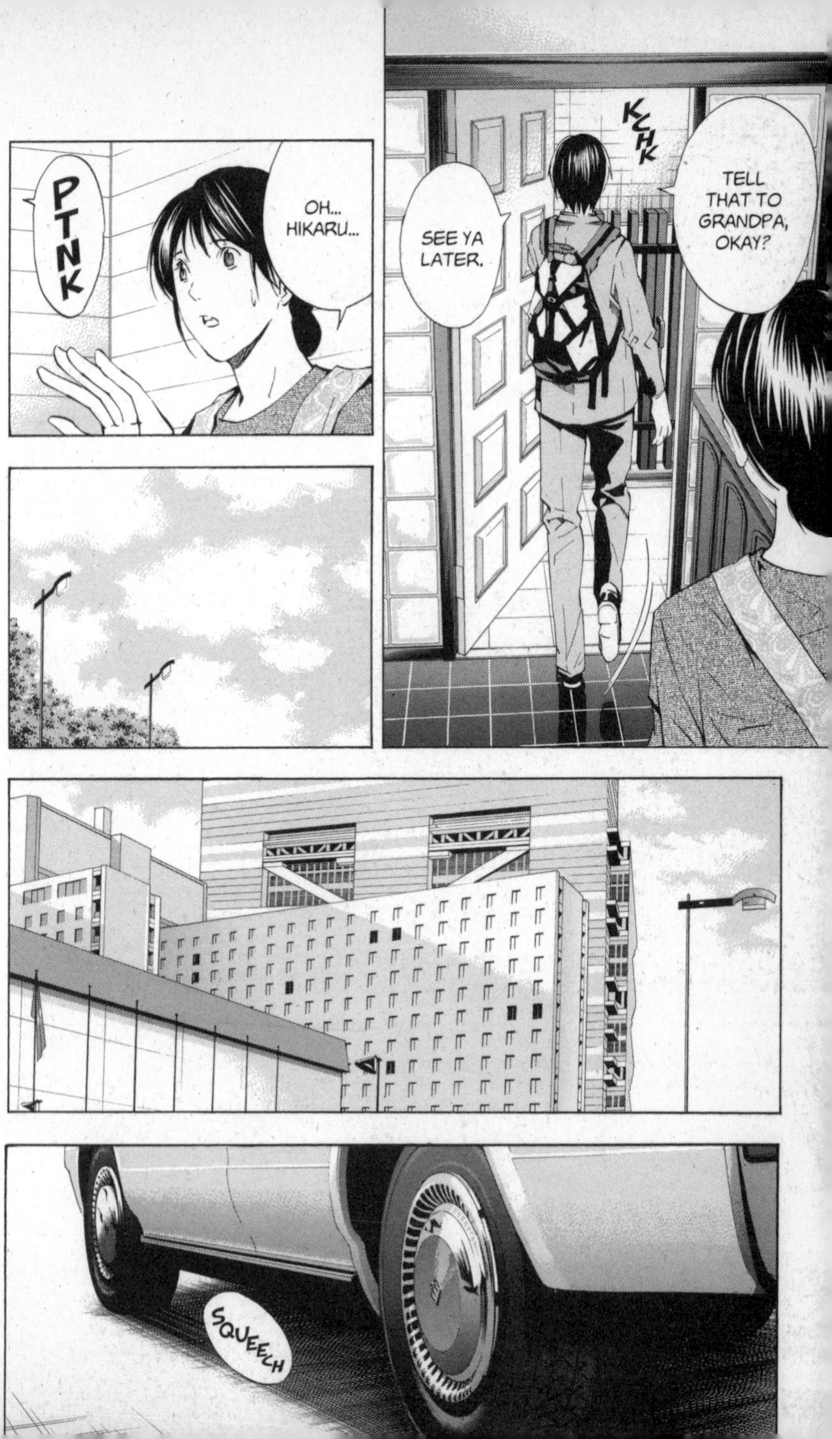
TELL THAT TO GRANDPA, OKAY?
KCHK
SEE YA LATER.
OH... HIKARU...
PTNK
SQUEECH

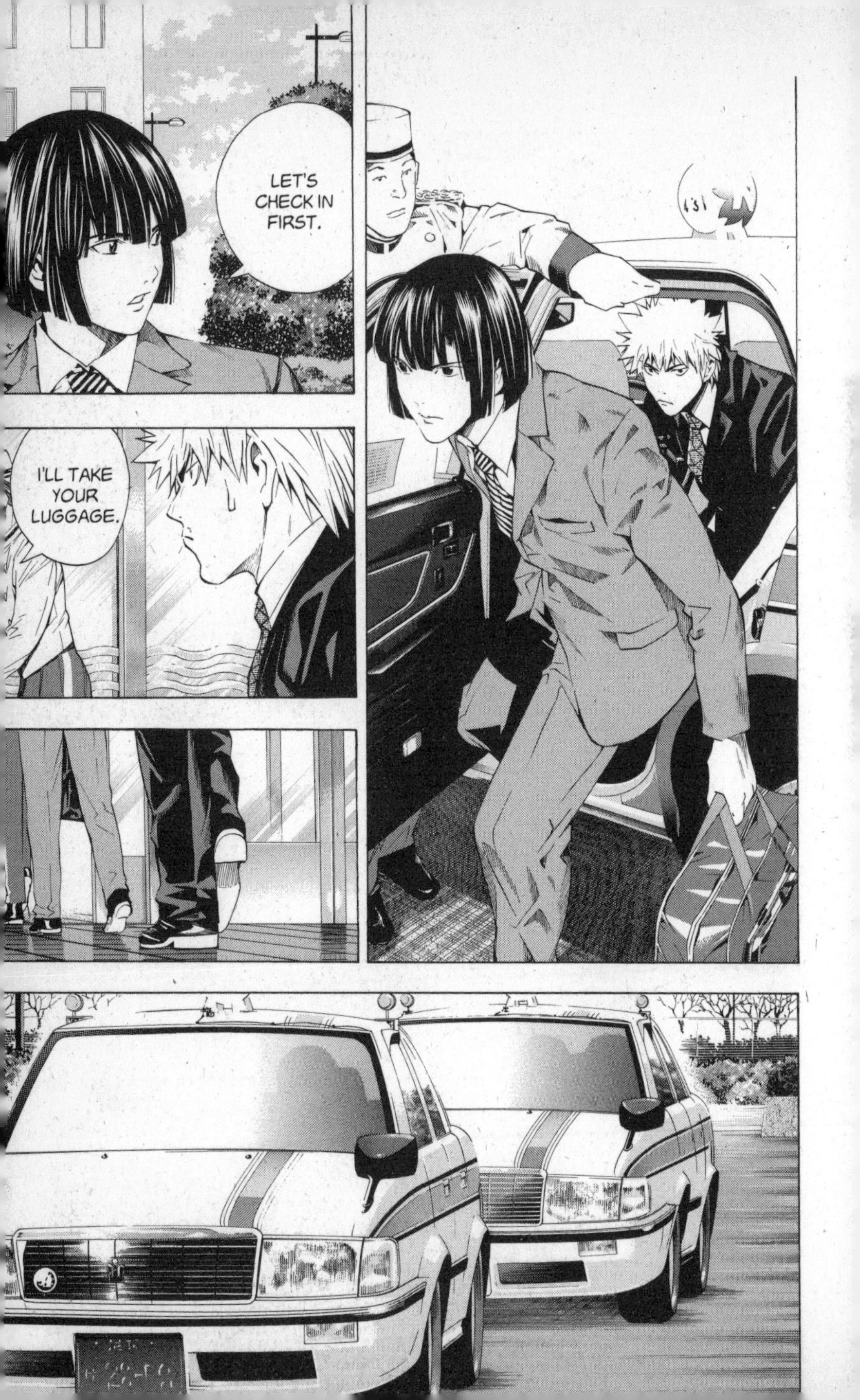
LET'S CHECK IN FIRST.
I'LL TAKE YOUR LUGGAGE.

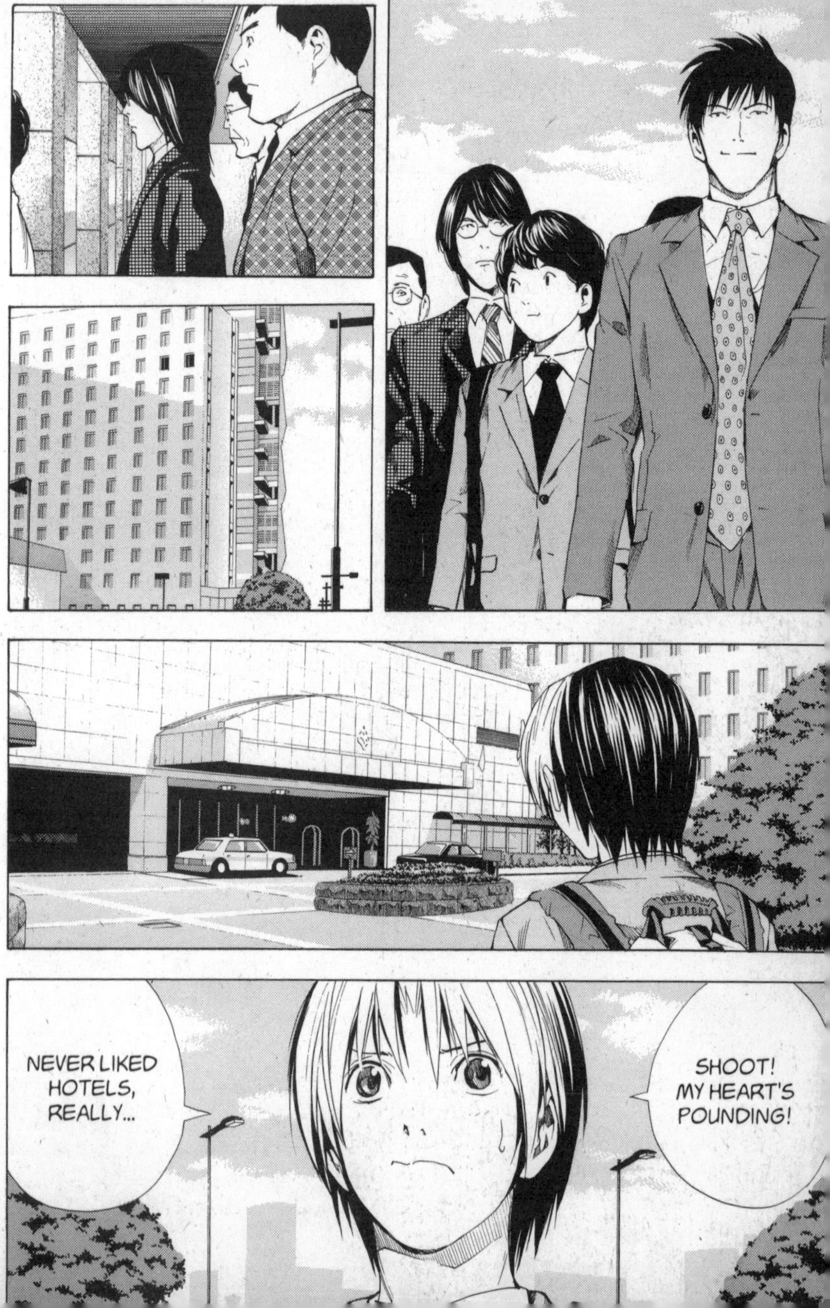
SHOOT! MY HEART'S POUNDING!
NEVER LIKED HOTELS, REALLY...

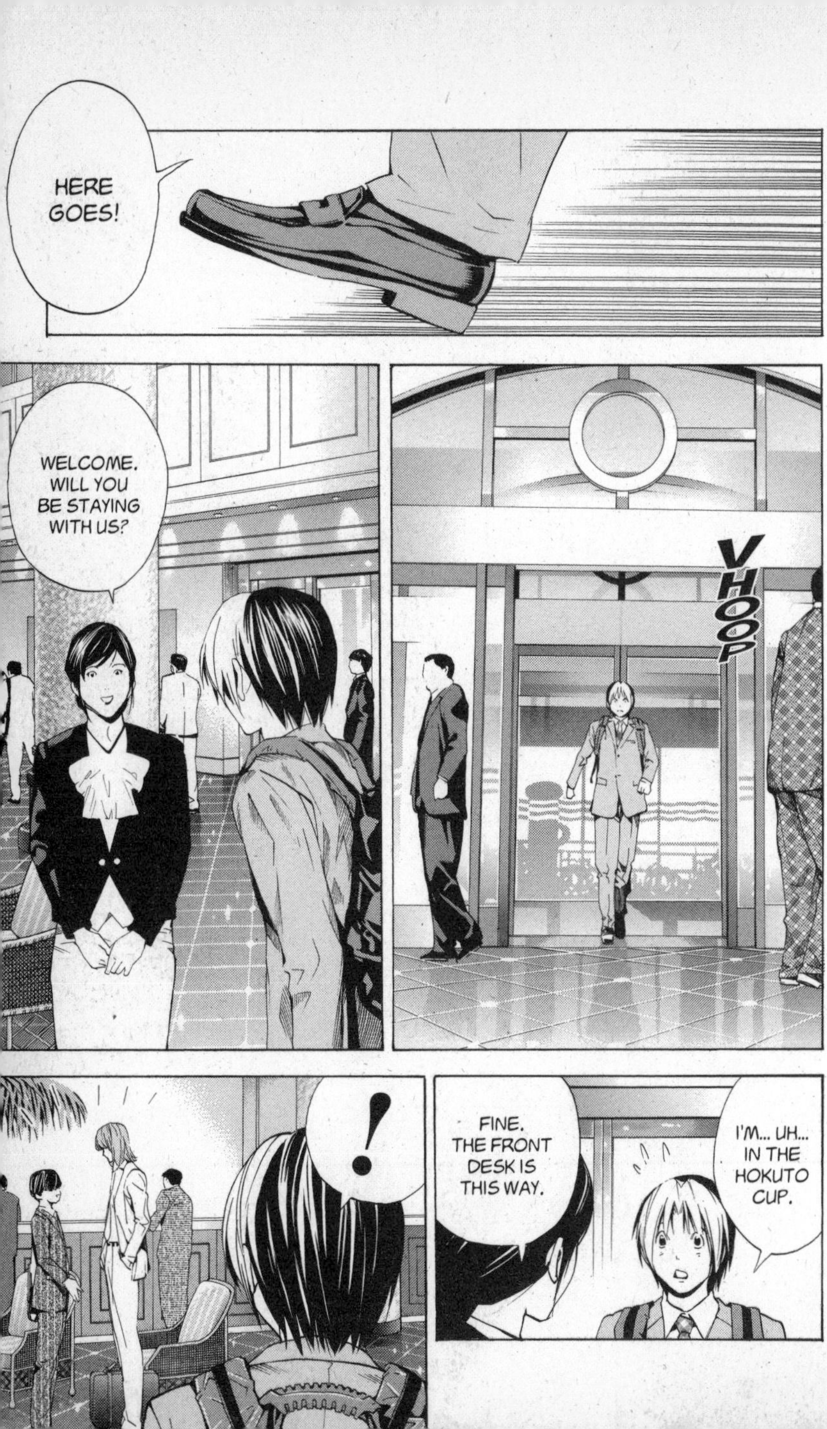
HERE GOES!
VHOOP
WELCOME. WILL YOU BE STAYING WITH US?
I'M... UH... IN THE HOKUTO CUP.
FINE. THE FRONT DESK IS THIS WAY.
!

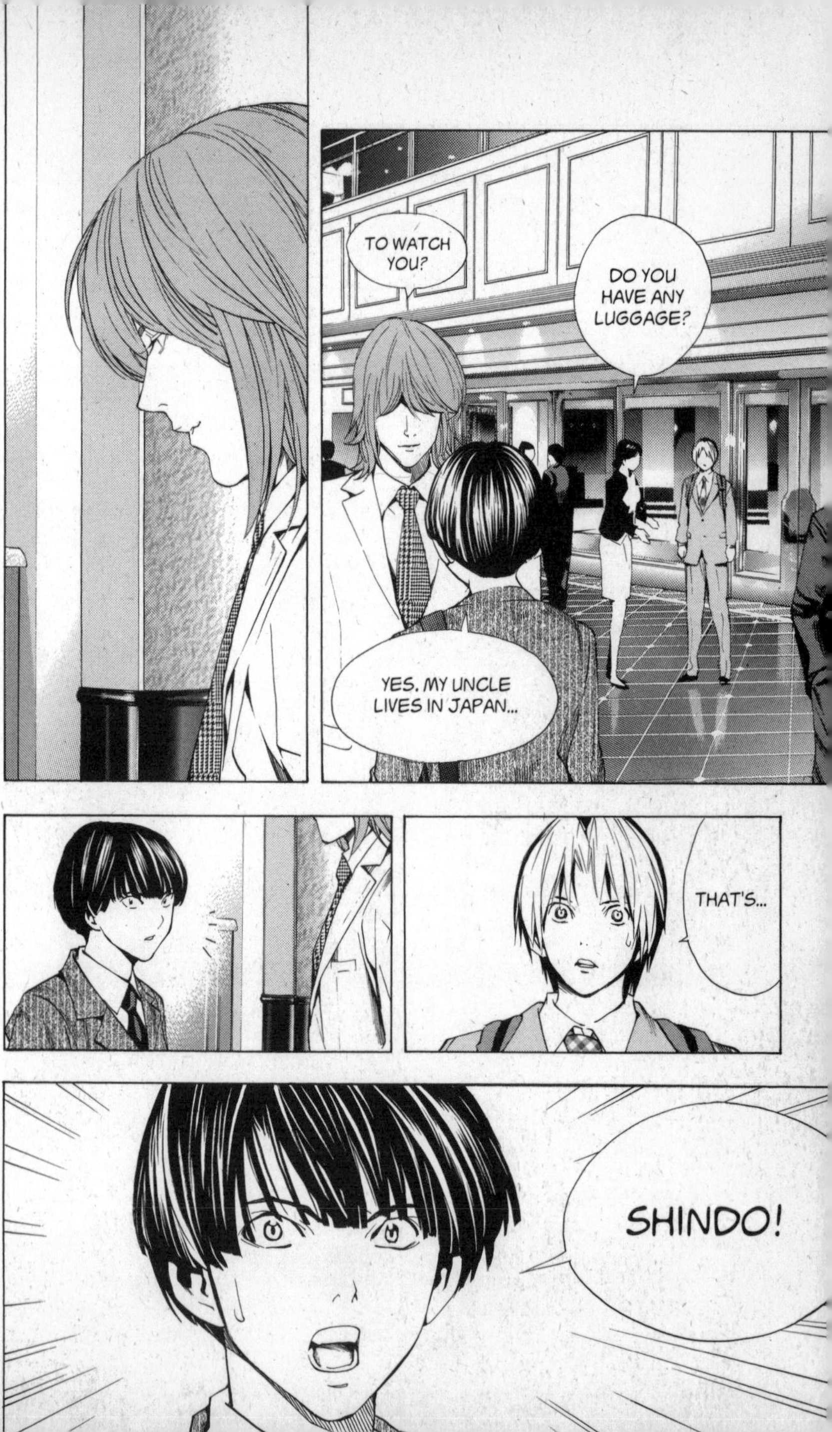
DO YOU HAVE ANY LUGGAGE?
TO WATCH YOU?
YES. MY UNCLE LIVES IN JAPAN...
THAT'S...
SHINDO!

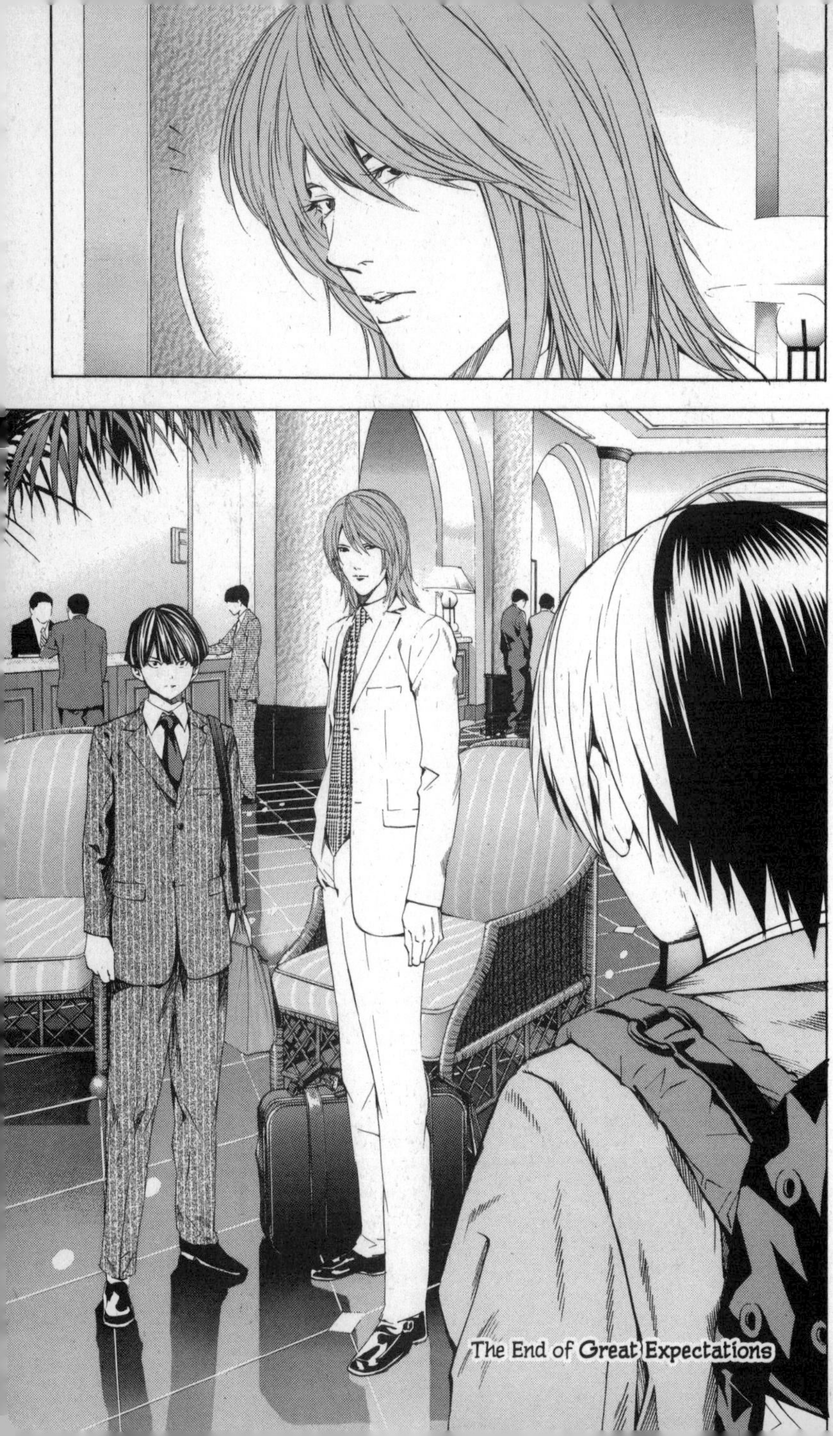
The End of Great Expectations

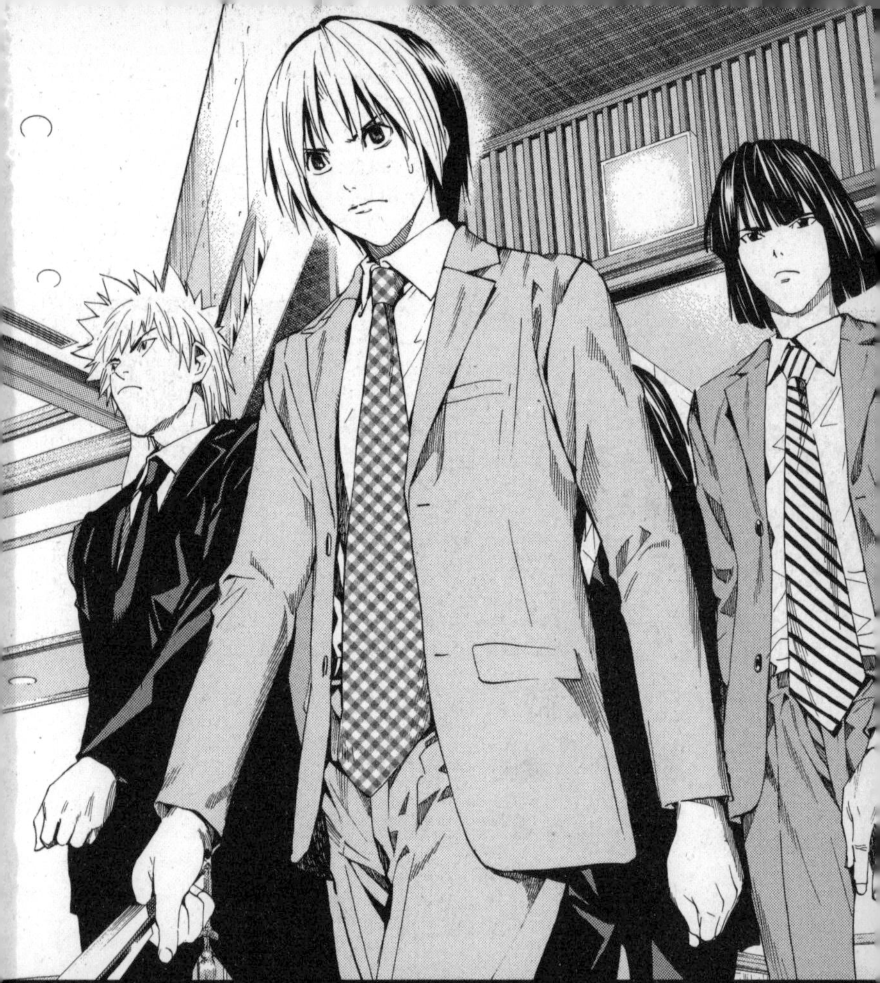

Hikaru is nursing a serious grudge as the Hokuto Cup games get under way. He believes Ko Yong Ha, a member of the Korean team, has insulted Shusaku, one of the greatest Japanese go players of the 19th century. Yong Ha thinks a mistranslation of remarks he made during an interview caused this misunderstanding but decides to let Hikaru think what he will. Does Yong Ha hope Hikaru's misplaced anger will lessen his effectiveness in the tournament?

COMING JANUARY 2011